BURT FRANKLIN: RESEARCH & SOURCE WORKS SERIES 514
Selected Essays in History, Economics, & Social Science 155

THE HISTORY *of* BUSINESS DEPRESSIONS

To one of whom it cannot be
said: "O, ye of little faith!"

THE HISTORY *of* BUSINESS DEPRESSIONS

BY

OTTO C. LIGHTNER

A Vivid Portrayal of Periods of Economic Adversity
from the Beginning of Commerce
to the Present Time

BURT FRANKLIN
NEW YORK

Published by BURT FRANKLIN
235 East 44th St., New York, N.Y. 10017
Originally Published: 1922
Reprinted: 1970
Printed in the U.S.A.

S.B.N. 20619
Library of Congress Card Catalog No.: 71-123511
Burt Franklin: Research and Source Works Series 514
Selected Essays in History, Economics, and Social Science 155

CONTENTS

CONTENTS—CONTINUED

INTRODUCTION

Of our one hundred and thirty years as a nation thirty-three years have been wasted in disastrous and ruinous depression and perhaps an equal number have been marked by over-spending, extravagance and waste of wealth. The remainder have been years of normalcy.

Depressions and trade upheavals have swayed the course of humanity in its struggles equally as much as has war.

The progress of the human race is marked by periods of economic distress when want, poverty, and unemployment set the minds of men to thinking. These were periods when convictions were sharply and vigorously stated and men, by force of extremity, took their complaint to the fountain head. Great changes in government, leading to the emancipation of mankind and to the democracy which exists today were the result of movements that grew out of economic adversity.

Were it not for the demands of commerce we should probably still be in a state of feudalism. When the economic status of the people became debased to such an extent that it became unbearable, they demanded reform and a degree of prosperity, with the alternative of revolt.

When bread is scarce, and his pillow a stone and his family in need, man seeks to find the cause. In times of adversity he studies hard to find a philosophy in life. He ponders dubiously over the promise of the Psalmist, "The Lord is my Shepherd, I shall not want."

Histories relating the glories of nations that have risen to power are classic. They rise to lofty heights; they light the paths of time. But when they come to the gloomy vales of economic decline and depression, where ten pages have been given to glory a line is sufficient to describe the distress that followed and the lessons to be drawn.

Education along this line is of the utmost importance. It should be started with the young business men, or even in

the colleges from whence men go out into the trades and
professions. Depressions affect our well-being and our
money. (And our money is close to our hearts—regrettable
though this admission may be—because we are born with a
degree of selfishness.) But our material prosperity goes
hand in hand with our political and our spiritual advancement and our leaders in education and business have not
given this subject the thought and study it deserves. We
have for our edification an abundance of literature regarding
the intrigues of courtiers, the reigns of kings, the feats of
statesmen and the glory of war heroes, but back of it all, in
this day as in those that are past, some one must foot the
bill. So a study of the economic side is equally important.
Our professional men like to ask fat fees, our officials high
salaries, and our workers big wages, yet little does it ever
occur to them to consider who ultimately assumes the burden. Then, when these periods of depression come on there
arise waves of discontent, bringing disruptions and serious
setbacks in the progress of our lives; all because our economic affairs have not been well regulated. Men stare at
each other helplessly, ignorant of the why and the wherefore, realizing too late that their troubles could have been
largely avoided. It would take a thousand books to point
out what powerful factors these business cycles have been
in determining men's actions, to illustrate how different
things are from what they might have been. Looking back,
every individual can see ambitions thwarted, years of work
gone for naught, the course of life halted or redirected because of the unexpected ebb or flow of the business tide.

After having passed through the second Galveston storm
in 1915, the writer was certain that tropical hurricanes, attended by tidal waves, leaving ruin, desolation and death in
their wake, were the worst things God ever put on earth.
Others of us who lingered in the valley of the shadow in
the dreaded influenza epidemic which swept the world during the great war are ready to believe that plagues are the
worst of earth's calamities. But thousands will agree that

the thing which causes the greatest sum total of suffering is
the series of panics and depressions that sweep over the
world now and again, touching all civilization with a with-
ering hand, leaving loss, misery, ruin and suicide in their
wake. After a struggle of years many find their investments wiped out. Those who have saved and secured a start
along the upward path find stalking them the gaunt spectre
of failure.

An acquaintance had invested judiciously, as investments
go, his charities were many and generous, and he held a respected place in society and industry. The depression of
1920 brought reverses entirely through no fault of his, and
the shock, being unbearable, he preferred to face a gun in
his own hand rather than the future. Another friend of
large means and high standing was carried to an asylum,
his keen intellect and fine ability destroyed forever. Others
fall from the level of comfort to poverty; still others face
worry and misery and want from unemployment. These
cycles not only bring their loss of accumulated wealth, but
a harvest of thwarted human energy as well. They are un-
forgetable periods in the lives of us all.

We are erecting barriers against the storm and establishing posts of warning in its path, and science promises to
eliminate the germs of pestilence. Likewise, then, human
brains and all the resources of mankind must be mustered
to solve the problem of the ever-recurring crises and depressions in our economic life. Some say it cannot be done;
others insist that it can. In my humble opinion, based on
a close study of the question, we shall some day look back
on depressions in the same spirit of tolerant pity that we
now look back upon the famines of the Middle Ages.

The business organism is much more complicated than
the delicate machinery of a watch and is exposed to an infinite variety of perils and accidents. But these are nearly
always preceded by symptoms which do not escape the eye
and ear of the business man whose judgment has been sharp-
ened by scientific study as well as by experience. It has

been said that the past is the only guide by which to judge
the future, and while business may not be so guided by precedent as is diplomacy, yet a great many pitfalls may be
avoided as we travel along the rocky road of industry if we
would but heed the sign posts of preceding events. We
profit from our own mistakes as a rule, so why should we
not profit from the mistakes of our forebears? As a business
man I can testify that I could have made and saved a great
deal more money had I previously the knowledge that the
research entailed in getting together these chapters has
brought me.

It is not only important but necessary these days for a
business man to know when to act. His judgment must be
keen in knowing when his opportunity presents itself and be
quick to take advantage of that opportunity. Likewise, I
believe we must admit, by this time, that it is equally as important to know when *not* to act, when to lay in port until
the storm passes by. In the old sailing days men used to
go out when the skies were clear; now we go when the
barometer and wireless tell us it is safe to go. In business
we have fairly well recognized barometers, if we but heed
them, and our wireless is the signals we get from the pages
of history.

We have a peculiar Anglo-Saxon trait—that of love of
precedent. It is a proverb among us that "history repeats
itself." And it is notable among us that historical incidents have more of a hold upon our minds than any theoretical arguments. No physician worthy of the name will pre-
scribe without some knowledge, great or imperfect, of the
history of his patient's ailment; no worthy lawyer will render an opinion on a client's case until he has a history of
the case. In business, then, if we expect to diagnose and
cure the ailments that have afflicted us periodically since
the beginning of time, we must have before us essentially a
history of what has passed.

Nations will stand up against a foe; fight pestilence;
master famine; overcome fire and earthquake; face catas-

trophe of all kinds with stoic calmness, and then lose their heads entirely in an industrial crisis. Then, if ever, the cowardliness of human nature will assert itself. Why is this? This is a question that there would be many answers to, but most likely it is because of lack of leadership.

Cities of all nations are dotted with statues in memory of heroes who led them in military victories, but few there are erected to the captains of industry who led them out of industrial chaos.

Depression is a disease of the nation, the body politic, and on many occasions in our history the use of stimulants has been required to incite the heart action.

Times of depression tax the resourcefulness of men. They reveal the stuff that is in them. If in times of prosperity they have lived beyond their means and mismanaged their business, or used bad judgment in expanding, they will fail when depression strikes. It is recognized among mercantile agencies that a firm or corporation that can go through a serious depression and maintain its credit is built on a strong foundation. A great injustice lies in the fact that the innocent often suffer for the sins of the guilty. Workers and investors alike suffer unemployment and loss through no fault of theirs.

The present age will be known in history as the age of commerce. We have accomplished much in the arts and sciences. Our inventions are beyond the dreams of former generations, and yet it cannot be said that our commerce is on an entirely scientific basis. Only in recent years have we reached anything like a scientific financial system, and even yet some of the leading countries of the world are backward in this respect. We cannot boast of science in our business until we have overcome the useless uncertainties of business depression. Men still say that trade cycles always have come and always will, but students of the question agree that it is easily possible through proper education to build a fairly even graded road-bed of commerce, cutting down the high spots and bridging the valleys. In this there is a great field for thought and accomplishment.

It is not the object of this work to be an essay or a treatise on panics, crises and depressions. There are a number of works that treat the subject from a theoretical standpoint. It is aimed to give the historical facts and incidents of preceding disturbances and then let the reader theorize for himself. A few chapters are devoted to my own deductions, particularly on recent incidents, arrived at from a close study of the question in practical business life over a period of years.

More space has been given to the business depressions of recent years because of their proximity to our time and their closer relationship to the present existing conditions. In the text credit is given where authors and periodicals are quoted and, as the chapters are classified according to periods, it will be easy to refer to the works of the authorities given in the bibliography. To cover all the details of some of the causes of our crises would, in many instances, make books in themselves, and would be more than any mind could conveniently grasp. I have aimed to portray here only such historical facts and matter as will be useful and informative to the ordinary business man and investor of the present day, and have studiously avoided overburdening it with theory or too large an array of statistical details which are irrelevant to the subject as a whole. The money question, paper currency and bimetalism enter largely into the history of depressions, particularly those of the nineteenth century. This question can be studied by those who desire to do so from various works on the subject, some of which are given in the bibliography. Several books may also be had on the question of unemployment which touch on the subject of depression. The general question of industrial and agricultural economics is also covered by various authors who find occasion to review briefly some of the setbacks suffered from depressions.

CHAPTER I

THE VICISSITUDES OF ANCIENT COMMERCE

The history of ancient countries with the rising and falling tides of their commerce can have little bearing on industry of today. Commerce of the ancient world died out and little is left of its traces to profit the modern world, with the important exception, perhaps, of the old Roman Law. Yet in the precepts of antiquity we may find substance for thought and utility.

In all the struggle of humanity up the steep mountain of progress commercial distress has been one of the greatest obstacles to survive. Thrones of kings have tottered during the numerous periods of poverty and distress which brought with them the spectre of revolution and menaced existing governments. On the other hand, the Ancient Ages have left us stories of their passing glory, peace, contentment and prosperity. Those must have been days of wealth in abundance, "when Greece held the torch of civilization and Rome, the magnificent, was built as the capital of the world empire."

In the 27th and 28th chapters of Ezekiel we are told in glowing language of the prosperity of Tyre and then of its sudden ruin because of its loss of wealth.

The romantic story of the decline of nations and commerce is a history in itself. One country after another has obtained the lead and lost it. Where are the nations of history? Of the six that belonged to the ancient regime only three are of any significance now; of the nine originating in the Middle Ages only three, again, remain. Will our turn come?

Where is Phoenicia, Carthage, Arabia, Babylonia? Where is Chaldea, Etruria, Media, Macedonia? Where is ancient Egypt, Persia, Greece, Rome? Where is the Venice, Holland, Spain, Portugal of the Middle Ages? Where and why?

Theorists have a tendency to attribute the decline of nations in various periods to the commercial spirit. Probably they mean the wrong use of wealth, because business can be as clean and elevating as any other calling if properly conducted. It has been demonstrated, however, that no nation can maintain its greatness or escape decay if it becomes poisoned by frivolity and vice.

In ancient times civilization scarcely touched the wild, barbarous people of Germany, Gaul and Britain, whose inhabitants lived in a state of rude poverty, while in such nations as Arabia, Egypt and Assyria, the people built splendid palaces, developed the arts and lived amidst marvels of luxury. Today conditions are practically reversed, and who would dare say that it was not brought about by the rise and fall of commerce.

Not always did these ancient nations and cities decline through conquests, as is the usual supposition. Some died without the drawing of a sword. As an instance, the State of Venice lost her supremacy through an old-fashioned panic and trade depression brought on by the discovery of a new route to India.

The ignorance and suspicions of men in the early times were the greatest hindrances to the rise of commerce, as they are still in backward portions of the world. In times of depression we still see the outcropping of the distrust of our antecedents of the Stone Age when we become frightened and suspicious, or over-cautious, often delaying the emergence from depression to normalcy.

What became of the mighty commerce of those ancient nations which rose to power and glory we know not. The cycles of trade can be traced back to biblical times, when the Good Book refers to Joseph with his seven fat years and his seven lean years. Demetrius, the silversmith, called on the Ephesians to oppose the Apostle Paul because his teachings were bringing distress to the industries which made shrines for Diana.

Most writers give Greece credit for starting the coinage of money, but according to Genesis (Ch. 17) "Abraham had flocks and herds, and silver and gold, and men-servants and maid-servants, and oxen and asses." And is it not recorded that Abimelech gave to Abraham a thousand pieces of silver, besides cattle and slaves?

The Assyrians, 6000 years B. C., had made quite an advance in civilization. They engaged in trade and commerce and some historians say they had banks similar to those of the present day. Disorganization, and then anarchy, came and the Persians obtained the ascendancy. Ancient Babylon 3000 years B. C. under a Semitic people, supposed to be the original Jewish race, grew to great importance as a commercial nation. The Babylonians are described as "greedy of gain, litigious and almost exclusively absorbed by material concerns."

"It was only when the Europeans found a new path to India across the ocean, and converted the great commerce of the world from a land trade to a sea trade," says Heeren, "that the royal city on the banks of the Tigris and Euphrates began to decline. Then, deprived of its commerce, it fell a victim to the two-fold oppression of anarchy and despotism, and sunk to its original state—a stinking morass, and a barren steppe."

Following Babylon the Phoenicians developed a great commerce about 1500 B. C. Then the Heroic Age of Greece, about 1000 B. C., brought that country to commercial supremacy. Later came the great Roman Empire and domination of the world, and with it the greatest and longest period of peace and prosperity the world has ever known. The Romans were great organizers and skilled administrators. Day says: "They earned all they received by one great contribution, 'pax Romans,' Roman peace, which continued almost unbroken for centuries, and which furnished an opportunity for commercial development before unknown." Then under the Caesars with its corruption came decline in commerce, and the sceptre of Roman authority passed from the western world.

From the scraps that we have been able to sift from the history of China it is apparent that that ancient and interesting people had periods of great trade decline and depression from causes that we are unable now to discover. Otherwise, how could she allow such inventions as printing and the mariner's compass to be forgotten and obliterated, once they had been discovered and used.

In its day ancient Egypt at times basked in the sunshine of luxury, and in periods of depression she put armies of unemployed to work and fed them while they built the pyramids. We know that the history of ancient Egypt was marked by four declines and revivals, and at no time during this period was she conquered, so in those periods, when the records are almost entirely obliterated, there must have been widespread economic distress.

With the rise and decline of commerce the center of civilization shifted from point to point, from Egypt to Phoenicia, from Phoenicia and Carthage to Greece and Rome and then from Constantinople to Italy and Spain, from Spain to Holland, and thence to France and England.

It was the agrarian depression that marked the beginning of the decline of Greece and a similar agrarian depression brought about the establishment of the republic in Rome. "Throughout all the ages those countries in which trade flourished were accounted happy and left glorious history for coming generations to read and follow. While those in which commerce drooped their oblivion was complete and only a phantom shows where they came into history and passed out again."

As to ancient Greece, the poems of Homer sing mostly of her glory and we look to Aristotle for the history of her trade. In the seventh century B. C., under the archons, Greece suffered great distress. The nobles alone were in possession of the government through which they ruled trade and commerce. Great masses of the poor peasants struggled with little hope against the bad economic conditions. Circumstances seemed to have been particularly severe in Attica. The soil of the country was thin and unproductive, unable to support more than a moderate population, and any increase in the number of inhabitants led inevitably to an increase of poverty. The evil might have been met by emigration, but at this date the shipping industry was depressed and the people were too poor to even seek out new homes beyond the sea. There was no capital for the development of trade except the little that could be borrowed at high rates of interest and under the most unfavorable conditions. The laws respecting debtors were very cruel, designed to protect the rich against the poor. The people seemed to have lost their insight into mercantile transactions and there was no knowledge of the cause of the growth of wealth. They were in the same state of mind in those ancient days that we have a tendency to pass through in the depressions of our times. Instead of seeking a way to better conditions through improved trade and greater production, they were cringing with fear, hoarding what little wealth there was and helping to squeeze tighter the grip that held them. A great mass of people that should have been producing wealth became debtors and were placed by law in a very degraded position. At this time Cypselus, a member of the great oligarchical family at Corinth, threw his lot with the masses, and by his energy and insight organized trade and agriculture and led the people out of chaos.

The great depression of 594 B. C., when Solon came forward in a time of public distress and rescued the Athenians from a most serious situation, marks an epoch in the economic history of ancient times. Debt and poverty oppressed the poor citizens, and melancholy, indeed, is the picture which historians draw of the social state of Athens at that time. Among the higher classes there prevailed a spirit of selfish greed whose greatest aim seemed to be to oppress the poor and wring from them their last farthing. So terrible was the depression that Solon perceived great dangers. People were ready to do anything to better their condition, and powerful neighbors were getting ready to take advantage of the situation to attack Athens. Solon by birth belonged to the aristocracy, but his fortunes had thrown him among merchants and there he gained knowledge of the causes, as well as the needed remedies for the distress. Solon averted the impending crisis. "His first measure was the famous Seisachtheia. Every citizen who had been sold into slavery, at home or abroad, was restored to liberty; all debts secured upon the person or landed property of the debtors were cancelled, and for the future no one was allowed to lend money on the security of the debtor's person. Some authorities, as for instance Andretion (Fourth Century B. C.), are of the opinion that the Seisachtheia was no more than a moderation of the rate of interest, but the majority assert that it was a cancelling of all contracts alike, and with this view Solon's words agree." Solon's words are: "In the day of vengeance, dark Earth, mightest mother of the gods of Olympus, will be my surest witness of this, from whom I removed pillars planted in many places, and whom I freed from her bonds. Many citizens, who had been sold into slavery under the law against it, I brought back to Athens, their home; some of them spoke Attic no longer, their speech being changed in their many wanderings. Others who had learned the habits of slaves at home, and trembled before a master, I made to be free men. All this I accomplished by authority, uniting force with justice, and I fulfilled my promise." From this it is clear that by some means debtor-slaves were restored to liberty, and lands burdened with debt were relieved of the incumbrance. At the same time Solon made a change in the coinage, introducing into Attica the standard known as the Euboeic in place of the old Attic or Aeginetan. From the remedies applied by Solon, it is easy to see that the cultivating peasantry of Athens had succumbed before the difficulties of this economic revolution. "Even under the natural economy, which may have existed in the time of Hesiod, the farmer's lot was hard;

but the pressure of the demand of moneyed men rendered it intolerable. Solon's celebrated legislation was intended to relieve the poor citizens, and it was directed against the money-lenders. It cancelled existing debts, and in all probability may have appealed to the common sense of justice. If a large amount had been paid as interest there was no grave injustice in striking off the principal—the money-lenders may have already received 100 per cent. on what they advanced—while it was now made impossible for them to lend on the security of the citizen's person."

It is a mark in history that the law enacted at that time by Solon has been re-enacted almost exactly by different nations on up to modern times in periods of economic depression.

Pericles, in endeavoring to find profitable employment for the people, deliberately turned their energies to unproductive public works. But he took the wrong course. While this public work temporarily relieved the existing depression, it only augmented it in later years. "The magnificent buildings which were reared under his direction absorbed the wealth of the city, without developing any natural resources or trading facilities in return. The treasure was exhausted once for all, and there was no means of replacing it, such as arises with capital employed in industry or trade—it was locked up in forms that are artistically superb, but economically worthless."

Thus the expenditure of enormous wealth in erecting great public buildings of marvelous beauty had the same effect on the economic conditions of the country as the over-building of railroads did in Europe and America in the Nineteenth Century. When money became scarce and economic distress prevailed it was then that kings started on expeditions against their neighbors to gain new wealth by war. This replenished the treasury in case of victory and occupied the minds of the populace. The kings had nothing to do; when poverty reigned the people became unmanageable and their thrones were shaken. Under such conditions there would be trouble anyhow and by going to war there was half a chance.

In ancient Greece bankers were called "table merchants" because they carried on their operations at a table and exercised the functions of money changers or testers. Alexander was not only a conqueror but a traveler and colonizer. He believed in trade, and wherever he ruled the trade of Greece followed.

In one instance, at least, we are possessed of the direct cause of decline and that is the Island of Crete, which for a considerable period had an extensive commerce and thriving cities, but it too fell into decay. No doubt because of commercial corruption, since a proverb for centuries afterward asserted "Cretains were always liars."

When we make a hasty survey of the Roman Empire to find the symptoms of decay there is brought to light as the outstanding feature industrial stagnation and commercial ruin. The year 33 A. D. was full of events in the ancient world. It marked two disturbances as the outgrowth of the mob spirit. The first was in the remote province of Judea, where one Christus was tried before Pontius Pilate, was crucified, dead and buried. The other event was the great Roman panic which shook the empire from end to end. The consternation accompanying the latter died down and it was soon forgotten, but the murmurings of the former swept down the centuries until, bursting into flames, it enveloped the world.

A description of the panic reads like one of our own times : The important firm of Seuthes & Son, of Alexandria, was facing difficulties because of the loss of three richly laden spice ships in a Red Sea storm, followed by a fall in the value of ostrich feathers and ivory. About the same time the great house of Malchus & Co., of Tyre, with branches at Antioch and Ephesus, suddenly became bankrupt as a result of a strike among their Phoenician workmen and the embezzlements of a freedman manager. These failures affected the Roman banking house, Quintus Maximus and Lucius Vibo. A run commenced on their bank and spread to other banking houses that were said to be involved, particularly the Brothers Pittius. The Via Sacra was the Wall Street of Rome, and this thoroughfare was teeming with excited merchants. These two firms looked to other bankers for aid, the same as is done in modern days, but unfortunately at this time an outbreak had occurred among the semi-civilized people of North Gaul, where a great deal of Roman capital had been invested, and a moratorium had been declared by the government on account of the disturbed conditions. Other bankers, fearing the suspended conditions, refused to aid the first two houses and this augmented the crisis.

Money was tight for another reason: agriculture had been on a decline for some years and Tiberius had proclaimed that one-third of every senator's fortune must be invested in lands within the province of Italy in order to recoup their agricultural production.

Publius Spinther, a wealthy nobleman, was at that time obliged to raise money to comply with the order and had called upon his bank, Balbus Ollius, for 30,000,000 sesterces, which he had deposited with them. This firm immediately closed their doors and entered bankruptcy before the praetor. The panic was fast spreading throughout all the province of Rome and the civilized world. News came of the failure of the great Corinthian bank, Leucippus' Sons, followed within a few days by a strong banking house in Carthage. By this time all the surviving banks on the Via Sacra had suspended payment to the depositors. Two banks in Lyons next were obliged to suspend; likewise, another in Byzantium. From all provincial towns creditors ran to bankers and debtors with cries of keen distress only to be met with an answer of failure or bankruptcy.

The legal rate of interest in Rome was then 12 per cent and this rose beyond bounds. The praetor's court was filled with creditors demanding the auctioning of the debtors' property and slaves; valuable villas were sold for trifles, and many men who were reputed to be rich and of large fortune were reduced to pauperism. This condition existed not only in Rome, but throughout the empire.

Gracchus, the praetor, who saw the calamity threatening the very foundation of all the commerce and industry of the empire, dispatched a message to the emperor, Tiberius, in his villa at Capri. The merchants waited breathlessly for four days until the courier returned. The Senate assembled quickly while a vast throng, slaves and millionaires, elbow to elbow, waited in the forum outside for tidings of the emperor's action. The letter was read to the Senate, then to the forum as a breath of relief swept over the waiting multitude.

Tiberius was a wise ruler and solved the problem with his usual good sense. He suspended temporarily the processes of debt and distributed 100,000,000 sesterces from the imperial treasury to the solvent bankers to be loaned to needy debtors without interest for three years. Following this action the panic in Alexandria, Carthage and Corinth quieted.

And so, under conditions very similar to those existing in the Twentieth Century, business of the Roman Empire resumed its normal aspect and the Via Sacra went its normal way, the same as Wall Street has done on many an occasion after a storm has passed. How similar was the business of the world in that year of the crucifixion of Christ to that of the present time!

Rome under Tiberius had probably reached the highest state of civilization that it had known until the dawn of the Nineteenth Century. Some time later its decay set in, resulting from just such panics which were not wisely stopped and allowed to run their course of ruin. Then followed medieval times with its feudalism. The world was centuries getting back to the height of Roman civilization, no doubt because of the disorganized state of its commerce.

The Romans detested labor and trade. Yet they were gluttonous for wealth. They wanted to obtain it, however,

from the labor of slaves and from conquest rather than from
business.

Juvenal wrote, "With us the most reverend majesty is that
of Riches, even though Foul Lucre! Thou dwellest in no tem-
ple, and we have not reared altars to Coin, as we have for
the worship of Peace and Faith, Victory, Virtue and Concord."

The Romans in times of scarcity offered bounties to encourage grain importations so that there would be no distress on the part of the people.   Apparently, they were the
first to use the system of drawing on the reserves of the
past and the credit of the future to alleviate present distress.

As told by Suet: "Once at the time of a great failure of
crops, when it was difficult to provide relief, Augustus ordered expulsion from the city of slaves who were exposed for
sale, of schools of fencing-masters, and all foreign residents,
except physicians and teachers, and, above all, of domestic
slaves, so that at last the supply of corn became cheaper.
The landowners of Rome, in the heigh-day of her insolent
adolescence, had denounced both the commerce and the arts
as the business of slaves or freedmen."

During the palmy days of the Roman Republic, known as
her "Golden Age," the cultivation of the soil and the pur-
suits of industry were regarded as honorable and dignified.
It was then that Cincinnatus left the plow to answer his
country's call.   This age also gave Cato, Scipio and others
of her great statesmen who appreciated the value of commerce and industry to the country.

In times of depression the Romans built the great roads
(to give employment to the people) which spread over the
continent of Europe and India, and the people of modern
civilization still ride over those Roman roads.   The decline
of Rome is an interesting study in economics.   It started
when foreign grain undersold the Italian product and these
barbarians were forced to join the rabble of the cities.
When Rome no longer produced she became pauperized,
because her commerce was nil, trade was degrading, and
when there were no more countries to conquer to bring her

wealth there was nothing but decline ahead. As the years went by great armies of unemployed slaves surged over the land; particularly in the reign of Nero they became threatening and dangerous. All writers agree that had Rome recognized the honor of trade and commerce and established industries, giving employment to the people, she may to this day have been the center of the world's civilization.

The general impression that Rome fell because of sinful indulgence is to some extent erroneous. In studying her economic history it will be found that a decline of her commerce had set in, which undermined her financial stability. This was due to many causes, principally the drain of precious metals to the East, depriving the empire of much needed currency.

Thus when she was called upon to defend the onslaught of the disorganized barbarian invaders which under proper economic conditions would have been no match for her, she fell easy prey to them. It is said that wiser capitalists unable to induce the authorities to take steps to remedy the depression tied their money in a napkin and buried it against the day of abject distress that was sure to come.

An authority says: "If a credit system had been evolved to take the place of metallic currency, Rome might not have been embarrassed by the shortage of metal, but unfortunately nothing of the kind was done. Another cause of bad conditions was the unprofitable investment by the government of much of the capital of the ancient world. A comparatively large share of the surplus wealth of the ancient world flowed to the imperial city in the form of taxes and tribute. Part of this was spent on the army, the navy, the roads, the improvement of harbors, and other public works which increased the prosperity of the empire. A large part of the money, however, was spent on temples, monuments, public baths, and the like, and another portion purchased grain, which was given free to all Roman citizens who wished it. All such investments were very much like burying the capital of the empire, as far as business was concerned. The grain doles were especially bad, as they served to keep thousands of able-bodied men in idleness at the expense of those who were working."

In those times men who held public office were expected to contribute to the maintenance and support of the city. As prosperity declined and maintenance became increasingly difficult the offices became undesirable. Then for once in history the world beheld the spectacle of men fleeing the country rather than hold public office. Woeful, indeed, are times of depression!

So it was not wealth and luxury that destroyed Rome and other great nations, but it was the uncorrected evils which grew up with wealth and unchecked inclinations. Suppose our boom periods were allowed to run in this country un-retarded, who cannot imagine but that it would lead event-ually to national ruin? In that respect depressions are a blessing. Those of our history may have acted as a restrain-ing hand against national disruption.

CHAPTER II

TRADE DECLINES OF THE MIDDLE AGES

The writer on economics is always at a disadvantage. He must necessarily preclude that majestic portrayal of political events by which he might add the flourish of beauty. In my subject, particularly, I am brought to dwell only upon the palls of gloom that hung like darkened clouds over the unfortunate years of history.

A detailed recitation of the commercial difficulties imposed upon the Middle Ages would be of little profit here. Business methods in those days were so absolutely different from those of today that scarcely any lesson could be drawn from them. Undoubtedly the chief causes of their commercial setbacks were famine, plagues and war, which swept intermittently over all countries. The severity and suffering brought on by these times reduced great numbers of poor to willing slaves, retarded civilization and filled the world with beggars.

In this chapter we review ten centuries of time wherein a race of barbarians, whose origin is lost in antiquity, overran the proud sovereignty of ancient civilization, prostituted the fair fields of Rome, and set the world back a thousand years. Only in spots is there a beam of sunlight that comes scintillating through the clouds of these centuries of darkness. In this span of time a short period of economic prosperity was an extreme exception rather than the rule. In writing an economic history of that period one would have to touch only the extremely few high spots in describing the short periods of peace and plenty. The reign of Charlemange in the Eighth Century was one of these. This good king was solicitous for the well-being of his people. He led them out of a long depression, reformed the coinage of money, established commercial enterprises and sought to enrich his kingdom by trade and commerce.

The great plague of 542 A. D. ravaged the Western world. It carried off a third of the population and "was not the least

of the causes of that general decay which is found in the
later years of Justinian's reign.   It swept away tax-payers,
brought commerce to a standstill."

The longest depression on record was when the Hun and
Scythian barbarians overran the western provinces of the
Roman Empire.   The confusion which followed so great a
revolution lasted for several centuries.   The towns were
deserted, the country was left uncultivated and the western
provinces of Europe, which had enjoyed a considerable degree of opulence under the Roman Empire, sank into the
lowest state of poverty and barbarism.   During the continuance of these confusions the chiefs and principal leaders acquired, or usurped to themselves the greater part of the land.

The next longest depression lasted through the hundred
years of religious wars, which kept industrial progress at a
standstill while humanity bled for the sake of a creed.   Mediaeval times passed with little commerce carried on.   The
lack of powerful governments caused the people to organize
into local towns, each making its own trade tariffs and regulations and existing largely to itself.   Trading was crude
and meager until the decay of feudalism and the dawn of
the modern world.   The rise and decline of commerce is
noted in the case of various cities which were centers of the
world's finance and trade in the Middle Ages, such as Venice,
Genoa, Bruges, Antwerp and Amsterdam.

"It was not without justice that the ninth, tenth, and eleventh centuries have been called 'the Dark Ages.'   Literature and art sank back to the level from which Charles the
Great had for a time raised them; history has once more to
be reconstructed from the scantiest materials.   Architecture
was stagnant, save in the single department of casfle-build-
ing—the one development that these centuries produced."
It may be said that there was no such thing as a steady flow
of commerce.   Commercial relations between the tribes of
Central Europe were spasmodic and the domestic trade itself
was constantly interrupted by tribal wars.   It was a period
of intense gloom and depression, and the economic outlook

was blacker than at any time since the descent of the barbarians upon Imperial Rome.

In the Eleventh Century wealth was scarcer in Europe than it had been since the fourth century. Conditions were fered a decline because her wealth had been drained through the purchase of luxuries from the Orient. Conditions were so bad in Western Europe that a scandalous traffic was carried on in supplying the slave market of the Saracens with Christian women. In England it was very common to export lower classes of people to other countries as slaves. All the Western world was in this state of degradation and poverty. The decline of this period affords one of the most interesting studies in the depths to which the human race can fall.

"Not to be killed," says Stendhal, "and to have a good sheepskin coat in winter, was, for many people in the tenth century, the height of felicity."

Describing regions in Italy in the Thirteenth Century, formerly parts of the Roman Empire, Hallam says, "Among the uninhabitable plains travellers were struck with the ruins of innumerable castles and villages. So melancholy and apparently irresistible a decline of culture among the population through physical causes, which seems to have gradually overspread a large portion of Italy, has not been experienced in any other part of Europe."

In these times it was the common religion as well as law that every commodity had a just and equitable price, and for one to charge more than this price incurred the displeasure of God and merited the punishment of man. Mediaeval history is filled with examples of penalties inflicted upon tradesmen, looked down upon in those days, who attempted to raise prices or profiteer. Christians who were fortunate enough to have it were expected to loan money without interest. Interest was sinful and condemned by the Church. In times of money stringency during these centuries pogroms would start against the Jews who were found to have the specie largely corralled. Jews in those days were mostly pawnbrokers, although some took the more dignified name of goldsmiths. They were money lenders and the people borrowed from them. Then, in time of crop failure or distress the Jews would be found to have both money and property. It was during these periods of depression that the Jews were banished from nearly every European country at one time or another. Edward I took all the money away from the Jews and drove every one of them from England.

As politics was in the hands of religion in those centuries, so was commerce, and to persecution and intolerance of religion may be ascribed the decline of a number of great commercial nations. The Crusades were in an extraordinary phenomenon in the economic progress of the world. Population was pressing upon the means of subsistence and a cingle crop failure precipitated the migratory movement among impoverished people whose condition was one of untold misery. It is easily imagined how the minds of these people could be fired by the preachings of religious leaders and the tales of travelers who brought stories of rich spoils awaiting the sword of the conqueror. "There can be little doubt but what some were sincerely animated by a desire to wrest the Holy Land from the Infidels, but undoubtedly the great army of crusaders were homeless itinerants who had nothing to lose and all to gain. These idlers were quickly willing to fight for immediate bread and the promise of future reward. But the movement of these great armies from West to East and back again revived the industries of the nations through which they passed, created new and broadened ideas of the world's affairs, put money into circulation, and started a new system of trade and commerce."

The Crusades had not only a religious aspect, but were a source of great commercial riches for the Venetians, who had risen to commercial supremacy, and as they built the fleets that carried the Crusaders they incidentally took the opportunity to open up new trading posts in the Mohammedan countries, thus profiting at the expense of their fellow Christians. The Crusades brought the East and West together and stimulated business, but after their failure and the return of the Christains to Europe commerce declined rapidly. Oman says that the trade of Constantinople fell off one-third to one-half.

England, Germany and the northern countries of Europe claimed that their trade was injured and depressed because a large portion of their wealth was taken by the Church of Rome. Pope Innocent II called England his inexhaustible fountain of riches. Economic stringency is what brought the revolt against the church.

The Hanseatic League, composed of towns and cities of northern Germany, was the outgrowth of trade conditions. When depression swept over them it set the tradespeople to thinking, and they devised means of forming a league so that trade might be stimulated by trading among themselves. The Hanseatic League became so powerful that in times of business failure its members insisted, and backed up their demands by force, "that they should be paid in full before any other debtors were considered, and they further required that such bankrupt should be banished from the city with his entire family." Through the influence of the Hanseas the city of Bruges became the business center of Europe.

In the Fourteenth Century the financial crisis occurring in England under Edward III was so severe that the king could not pay his personal obligations to his Italian bankers. who then had the upper hand financially after the Jews had been driven out of England through the activity of the Roman Church. Money was so scarce that the Italians were violently attacked. For a time they were expelled from London and nearly ruined.

One of the most peculiar trade depressions in history came about at the time of the Reformation, which changed not only the religion but the commerce of the greater part of northern Europe. In those times fishing was the leading industry, and the Catholic church with its many fast

days had been the best friend to the herring industry, upon
which the Hanseatic League was originally founded. When
the followers of Martin Luther displaced Catholicism the
demand for herrings became almost nil, bringing chaos and
distress in this important industry, affecting all branches
of the trade.

The states of Italy which arose from the ruins of ancient
Rome again made headway. Venice, Genoa and Florence
waxed powerful until reverses came with the closing of the
markets of northern Europe because of religious wars and
tariff barriers. Bankruptcy became frequent and the
woolen manufacturers of Florence, who employed 30,000
men at one time, dropped to 971. The people, thrown out
of employment by disrupted commerce, declined into poverty
and indolence.

In the history of Venice many instances are found of the
rise and fall of trade. A quarrel with Pope Pius II, with the
consequent excommunication, caused the merchants of
Venice to be prosecuted throughout Europe and their merchandise confiscated wherever found. But this did not dim
her prestige for long, and she quickly recovered her trade.
Again when Vasco da Gama discovered the passage to India
by rounding the Cape of Good Hope, returning to Portugal
with a rich cargo, consternation and panic reigned in Venice
and caused her traders many sleepless nights. It sounded
their doom, because the heavy dues exacted by sultans and
rulers, through whose countries the Venetians had to pass
on their way to the Orient, made the cost too great to
compete with the sea-borne commerce of the Portuguese. So
the commerce, and with it the prosperity, of Venice declined, and she gradually passed out as a power in the world.
The Venetians are said to have carried on their trade and
kept their commerce prosperous even amid the vicissitudes
of war. Their great commercial leader, Doge Mocenigo,
on his death bed, with the senators gathered around him,
urged that the commerce of the nation be continued, saying,
"But I beseech you, avoid as you would fire seizing what

belongs to others and engaging in unjust wars, for in such wars God will not support princes."

Depressions were brought about in these times by the policy of prohibiting exports of bullion to other countries. Rulers needed a greater supply of ready money and were eager to listen to the argument of merchants that large exports and small imports created a balance of trade favorable to the nation. When the country found itself with a trade balance against it, instead of taking means to increase their exports to offset their trade balance they brought on great distress by prohibiting exports of bullion to pay such trade balance to other countries. Invariably this further depressed commerce.

At the end of the Middle Ages Holland and Spain were the leading commercial countries of the western world. In the Fifteenth Century we find a depression brought on by conditions similar to those we have today. It was the time of the Guilds. Day, in his "History of Commerce," says: "(1) The privilege of monopoly was abused by limiting entrance to the Guild in various ways, so that production was restricted and prices were raised to the detriment of merchant and consumer. Laborers suffered, also, by the lessened demand for their services. (2) Guilds came into frequent conflict over the question as to which had the right to exercise a particular branch of trade or manufacture: these quarrels were similar to those arising between trade unions at the present time. Manufacturers suffered from the separation of allied trades, and time and money, which ought to have gone into the business, were wasted in long lawsuits. (3) The full members of the guilds, the masters, tried to keep the laborers (apprentices and journeymen) in an inferior position, and granted promotion by favor rather than by merit; laborers lost the incentive to good work and were tempted to idleness and disorder. (4) The masters tried to preserve equality among themselves. Any master who was sufficiently enterprising to attempt to extend his business by introducing improvements or by employing more men was pulled back to the general level. (5) Technical improvements were prevented also by the regulations which were adopted originally to secure good quality of the product, but which hardened into a routine prescribing the details of every process of manufacture. (6) After all the restrictions consumers did not get good quality even when they paid high prices. They could not punish the producers of poor goods by withdrawing their custom, and scamped work, adulteration, and fraud were common."

In the last century of the Middle Ages banking developed into the methods generally used in the present day. About this time the doctrine that it was sinful to take interest lost its force because economic leaders convinced the clergy that money secured through loans could be put to good use and thus encourage legitimate development. In those days bankers were called goldsmiths.

Antwerp was then the leading bourse in the world. There gathered Italian Hanseatics, Portuguese, Spanish, English and German traders dealing in commodities from all over the world. Antwerp being the financial center had loaned money to royal debtors who lost in wars and became insolvent. The panic and depression following brought the decline of Antwerp and the center of the financial world went to London, where it remained for almost five centuries, passing to New York during the recent World War.

That trade cycles involving terrific depression must have swept over the world in the Middle Ages is apparent from the fact that there are lapses in the pages of history in which the records of commerce are entirely submerged and lost. There must have been at times such destitution and disorganization that no accounts were left of what transpired. The thread is often broken, and when the ends are caught again we find civilization moving in a different direction, taking with it the trade supremacy that formerly had been elsewhere.

CHAPTER III

DEPRESSIONS OF MODERN EUROPE

(FROM THE END OF THE MEDIAEVAL PERIOD TO THE NINETEENTH CENTURY)

Passing from the Middle Ages to modern times, we approach the age that witnessed the growing importance of the industrial and commercial classes. In former centuries laborers, no matter of what breeding or state of intelligence, were slaves. Whatever circumstances, whether the fortunes of war or the tides of trade, brought them to the state of labor they automatically became slaves. The close of the mediaeval period found man struggling upward to a state of freedom. Trade and commerce, which had been considered degrading and had been engaged in by the lower elements of mankind, was now becoming dignified, and of growing importance. The old days "when might was right" were giving way to a time when peaceful service to humanity met its just rewards. The world emerged from feudalism because of the demands of commerce for a stronger central government to ward off the evil effects of trade declines and local depressions.

Modern ages begin with the discovery of America by Columbus at the close of the fifteenth century. We then enter the Renaissance, denoting the revival of taste and skill and an awakening of broader intelligence.

Great riches from the new world had encouraged thriftlessness in Spain. As fast as she received cargoes of precious metals she sent them out of the country, importing luxuries instead of teaching her own people to work and produce. It is said that many times before fleets arrived with a new cargo of gold and silver trade was stagnant and depressed because the previous cargo had been quickly spent for imported goods. The wealth of the new world enriched every nation except the one that imported it. The Spanish Inquisition in the 16th century sought to restrict personal initiative and this led to "universal stagnation of the country," affecting alike agriculture and trade. In 1515 the population of Spain was estimated at about twelve million people, but under the disastrous rule of Philip II it declined to less than six million, the cause being attributed to bad economic conditions after the banishment of the Protestants. From the world's richest country she became a bankrupt nation. Gold, instead of proving a permanent blessing to Spain, enriched her more vigorous neighbors to the north.

The year 1548 records a distressing depression in England, attributed to the absorption of the small farms by larger land owners who had turned their farms into pastures for sheep. Gibbon tells of a petition presented to the king in 1536 complaining "of the new use to which land is put, which hath not only been begun by divers gentlemen, but also by divers and many merchant adventurers, cloth-makers, goldsmiths, butchers, tanners, and other artificers, and unreasonable covetous persons which doth encroach daily many farms, more than they can occupy, in tilth of corn—ten, twelve, fourteen, or sixteen farms in one man's hands at once. . . . In time past there hath been in every farm a good house kept, and in some of them three, four, five, or six plows kept and daily occupied to the great comfort and relief of your subjects, poor and rich. But now, by reason of so many farms engrossed in one man's hands which cannot till them, the plows be decayed, and the farmhouses and other dwellings, so that when there was in a town twenty or thirty dwelling-houses they be now decayed, plows and all the people clean gone, and the churches down, and no more parishioners in many parishes.' Sir Thomas More speaks of the increase of pasturage in England, "by which sheep may be said to devour men and to unpeople towns as well as small villages."

Another writer says: "The highways and villages were covered, in consequence, with forlorn and outcast families, now reduced to beggary, who had been the occupiers of comfortable holdings, and thousands of dispossessed tenants made their way to London, clamoring in the midst of their starving children at the doors of the courts of law for redress which they could not obtain."

*The complaints are found voiced in ballads, such as the following:

"The towns go down, the land decays,
Great men maketh now-a-days
A sheep-cote in the church."

In the year 1552 a commission was appointed during the rule of Edward VI to "go over the oft-trodden ground and glean the last spoils which could be gathered from the churches. Vestments, copes, plate, even the coins in the poor-boxes were taken from the churches in the City of London." This was the final resort in extortion of money from a country in the last stages of industrial depression.

All historians refer to the years 1557 and 1562 as years of stagnant business in the world when the financial and commercial credit of all Europe was shaken to its foundations.

A severe financial crisis occurred in 1563, when the famous Fugger family, said to have been worth at one time forty million dollars in our money, failed. This family was the richest family in Germany and financed not only a great deal of the business of South Germany, but loaned to the pope, emperor, and kings of Europe. The bankruptcy of this firm involved widespread disaster, "for as time went on they carried on their business less and less on the money contributed by members, and more and more on their credit. All classes in the community—nobles, burghers, peasants whose savings did not exceed ten florins, even servants— deposited their money at interest with the financiers, and were involved in their fall."

Spain suffered a violent business reaction beginning in 1594, when her population again began to decline on account of large emigration to her colonies. This decrease was significant because it depopulated the cities where her industry

*Quoted by Gibbon.

had been built up, this industry going into the hands of commercial interests of other countries.   Another reason given for the decline was the Inquisition under which a million Meriscoes and thousands of Jews were exiled under ecclesiastical dictation.   The decay of vigor in the Spanish political organization brought with it beggary and vagrancy until it became a national curse.   The depression was so terrific and prolonged that Spain never fully recovered from it. Following the decline of Spain, Portugal rose to great prominence and was a factor in the world's affairs for some years.

The German states experienced a decline in their commerce in the sixteenth century.   It grew out of religious and civil wars and threw their trade in the North to the Baltic States and in the South to Italy.

In the Sixteenth Century arose the mercantile period. Previous to that events moved slowly and depressions were more on the order of trade declines, being gradual and arising many times, though not always, from political causes.

The famous tulip craze centered around the years 1630 to 1635, an incident unique in the annals of commerce.   It is known in history as the "tulip-mania."   "The tulip was a rare flower which had been introduced into western Europe from Turkey and grown in the horticultural collection of Counselor Herwart of Augsburg.   The plants were seen by the collector's neighbors who desired some of their own. The blooms became their pride and others were infected with the desire to possess them.   Before long the single little flower had turned everything topsy-turvy, the public had caught the fever and started speculating in tulips.   All Europe became involved and the flower gradually found its way at first into the gardens of wealthy people and later to all classes.   Holland was the center of the tulip trade, and in that country, as well as most others, it became the requisite of society to possess a collection of tulips.   But the speculative side was probably the most romantic.   The state of the people's mind was such that they wanted excitement and speculation.   We read of a trader of Harlem who gave half his fortune for a single bulb. A book of one thousand pages written on the tulip at the time describes another bulb for which 2,500 florins was paid. The demand for tulips, particularly rare specimens, had increased so that they were quoted daily on the stock exchange of Amsterdam and speculation was rife, not alone in the individual tulips but in the stock of the companies importing the bulbs from Constantinople."

A variety called the "Viceroy" was sold for 2,500 guilders; another, "Semper Augustus," for 4,600 guilders. They were bought and sold even without being in existence, only with reference to the rise and fall of their hypothetical value. An estate in one case had to be sold to meet the deficits of a speculator. The cities of Amsterdam, Harlem, Utrecht, Alkmaer, Leyden, Rotterdam, Woerden, Hoorn, Enkhuisen, Medemblyk, became so speculation-crazed that, by the year 1634, not only every leading merchant, but nearly every citizen, was engaged in the trade.

Selfridge gives the following description of the craze: "Stock jobbers made the most of the mania. Few kept their heads and fewer kept aloof from the mania. At first—and it was at this immediate period that the disease reached its virulent form—everyone had infinite confidence in the values and the speculators gained. The market broadened, and, as is so often prayed for nowadays by Capel Court and Wall Street, the public came in. Everyone seemed to be making profits from tulips, and no one dreamed that prices could fall. People of all grades converted their property into cash and invested in the flowers. Houses and lands were offered for sale at ruinous rates or assigned in payment of purchases made at the tulip market. Foreigners became smitten with the frenzy, and money from abroad poured into Holland. As a result living became more expensive and altered, and in a short space of time almost all conditions of life had to be readjusted because this mania for tulips had turned all the people's heads. The fever of speculation was superseded by an equally intense fever of

pessimism.   The whole country was involved, and it became
imperative that something be done to prevent general bankruptcy.   Public meetings were held everywhere.   The Government was appealed to.   But even governments fail in the
impossible, as well as in matters which require only fair
judgment and unselfishness.   The Government did the usual
thing.   They discussed the matter for three months and
then concluded they could not solve the problems, and thus
the whole matter rested.   Those who had tulips must lose,
and lose they did, and this applied to nearly everyone.   Holland suffered fearfully.   Her people, many of them at least,
had to begin the accumulation of savings or of fortunes all
over again, and for years the commerce of the nation languished."

The mania resulted in calamity when the public finally became aware of the gigantic folly of the whole thing.   The
sharper speculators repudiated their contracts which had
been made for future delivery and the bottom fell out of the
tulip market.   Many who had counted themselves rich in
tulips found themselves in poverty so far as money was concerned.   In one town alone during these three years there
was invested in hypothetical tulips more than 10,000,000
guilders.   London and Paris had followed Amsterdam in the
craze but with a lesser frenzy.   Their losses were great but
were individual instead of universal.

In 1640 Charles I upon ascending the throne of England
found an empty treasury and proceeded to seize the bullion
deposited by the merchants in the Tower of London, then
used for the safekeeping of money.   This act created great
public distress.

In 1662 Sir William Petty, discussing land rents, said:
"The medium of seven years, or rather of so many years as
makes up the cycle, within which Dearths and Plenties make
their revolution, doth give the ordinary rent of the Land in
Corn."

When Colbert became minister of finance in France in
1661, he found business languishing and the country im-

poverished.   England, Holland and Spain filled the country
with their goods and were enriched by her trade.   He saw
that his first duty was to get France out of the depression, so
he proceeded to increase production at home by stopping
largely the importation of foreign manufactures and prohibiting the exportation of gold and silver coin.   Under his administration France began to prosper.

In 1672 Charles II of England found his coffers bare and
his credit exhausted.   He gave a violent shock to business
by a proclamation "refusing payment out of the exchequer
of money advanced, and sequestrating £1,328,526 to his own
use.   The money, although lent by the goldsmiths to the
king, was the property of some 10,000 depositors and its loss
spread ruin and suffering throughout London."   The same
year, when the French army advanced on Utrecht, a run
started on the Bank of Amsterdam, then the largest in the
world, but the bank met all demands and weathered the
storm.

The business depression which shook Holland in 1791
resulted in the failure of the Bank of Amsterdam after
an enviable career of 182 years, and marked the decline
of that nation's supremacy in commerce.   Holland was the
center of stock-jobbing and speculation in the seventeenth
century, and naturally she felt reactions from disturbances
at a distance.   It was the chief aim of Napoleon to shake
the economic structure of his enemies, particularly England,
and he used every means to break the Bank of England.   It
would be useless to go into details regarding the various
business setbacks due to war and invasion, because that
would entail a recital of political history rather than the
subject we have at hand.

In the Seventeenth Century some economists actually
thought that people should be allowed to die in the street.
This was in the days of the English "Poor Laws" enacted to
alleviate pauperism, and which some claimed accelerated it.
In those days vagrancy did not imply distress, but prosperity.   The vagrant laborer was one of high skill who made

good wages, but was constantly wandering in search of
still higher wages.

In the early centuries of modern times trade was severely
depressed from time to time by religious disturbances.
"During the reign of Henry VIII, the property of the Catholic Church was confiscated, which, in connection with the
enclosures, threw large numbers of people out of employment and created great distress among the laboring classes.
The monasteries held large tracts of land, gave support and
employment to multitudes of people, and at the same time
were the only bodies who looked after the poor, and assumed
the burden of distributing public charities. The confiscation of the property of the guilds was another act of Henry
VIII which dealt a severe blow to the industrial masses.
The lands confiscated were handed over to a set of court fa-
vorites and retainers."

"Again (in France), in 1685, Louis XIV revoked the Edict
of Nantes and opened a war of persecution against the Protestants. It is estimated that five hundred thousand Protestants fled and sought refuge in Germany and other
Protestant countries. This was one of the severest blows
ever inflicted upon the industries of France, as the Hugue-
nots were largely artisans and manufacturers who were
placing France among the manufacturing nations of the
world, and laying a foundation for that industrial career
which has always contributed so greatly to the wealth and
prosperity of a country. It is estimated that England received about fifty thousand of these people. Charles I and
James II issued edicts which permitted them to become nat-
uralized citizens of England. Those coming from Nor-
mandy and Brittany settled largely in the suburbs of London, others in Coventry, Sandwich, Southampton, Winchel-
sea, Dover and Wadsworth. They engaged in making silk,
linen, paper, clocks, glass, locks, surgical instruments, and
many other articles requiring a high order of skill and
artistic taste."

In 1696 the goldsmiths organized a run on the bank of England which was competing with them and strongly threatening to put them out of business. In that year business was in a terrible condition. Coinage had become so debased that a law had been enacted requiring recoinage, and during this period business languished miserably.

The first instance of what we today call "runs" on banks was when the Dutch fleet entered the Thames. When their guns were heard consternation reigned in London. Everyone who had any money had deposited it with the goldsmiths, the bankers of those times. This money was known to have been lent to the government, which at the moment seemed to offer no security; "each man then hastened to his banker in the hopes of being in time to save some remnants of his fortune."

Describing conditions in France in 1689 La Bruyere wrote, "Certain savage-looking beings, male and female, are seen in the country, black, livid and sunburnt, and belonging to the soil which they dig and grub with invincible stubbornness. They seem capable of articulation, and, when they stand erect, they display human lineaments. They are, in fact, men. They retire at night into their dens where they live on black bread, water and roots. They spare other human beings the trouble of sowing, ploughing and harvesting, and thus should not be in want of the bread they have planted." During the years following people died in herds from actual poverty. Taine estimated that by 1715, in twenty-five years, one-third of the population, six million people, had died of starvation.

At the end of the Seventeenth Century the Darien scheme was inaugurated by William Patterson, a Scotchman, who raised a large sum of money to colonize the Isthmus of Darien, now called the Isthmus of Panama, and its failure had the most serious effect on Scotland, impoverishing that country for the time. It brought also a period of financial disturbances in England, which disheartened the business people of that country. Patterson claimed that his business was wrecked and the panic brought on by his commercial enemies who were jealous and envious of his company. This has a familiar sound today. It was during this period that the Bank of England first functioned to allay the distress of depression. In those days there were long periods of prosperity the same as now, and they all ended in a crash. There were no oil wells then to take the money of the gullible, but it is recorded that one company was formed in England for the purpose of importing jackasses from Spain in order to breed a more hardy mule in England, one writer remarking "as if there were not enough jackasses in London already."

The various depressions that affected European countries in the Eighteenth Century were more or less of a local character, mostly confined to one particular country because commercial operations were not linked by international banking credit and cable connections as at present. The nearest approach to a general crisis came in 1720 when all Europe was struck with the speculative mania, as evidenced by the South Sea Bubble in England and the Mississippi Bubble in France. This year marked the most famous financial crash in the history of the world. It was a double-barreled explosion. The first, in England, by the bursting of the South Sea Bubble and the second, in France, by the pricking of the Mississippi Bubble. In England more than two hundred other companies, formed along similar lines, followed in the wake of the South Sea Bubble. The company had undertaken the preposterous promise of paying the national debt through a monopoly of the whale fisheries and certain trading privileges in India. For a while it prospered, but in 1719 its capital was raised to 12,-000,000 pounds and turned into a speculative enterprise. On the strength of its concessions it sold stock to the people, making the most extravagant and exaggerated promises.

According to Andreadea money was invested in schemes that "stamped the minds of those who entertained them with what may be truly termed a commercial lunacy." One

project was for the discovery of perpetual motion, another
for building of hospitals for illegitimate children, another
for making silver out of lead, another to make salt water
fresh, and, finally, the most remarkable of all was a project
to found a company "for carrying on an undertaking of
great advantage, which shall in due time be revealed."
This promoter secured 2,000 guineas in a single morning
and made off with it.

The bursting of the bubble caused an extraordinary industrial upheaval. The speculation approached insanity.
Speculation at that time was on more nearly a gambling
basis than even at present. The buyer of these stocks
simply bet that there were bigger fools than he, and very
little trading was done except on the arbitrary basis that
the shares should pay dividends to justify the rise in prices.

In promoting the South Sea Company the promoters
employed the same strategy that the modern stock hawker
employs. They promised gold, which they claimed to be on
their land, and made various other wild statements. Their
shares were first sold at a small price, then suddenly the
price was raised and raised again. People who profited went
wild with speculative fever, and when the stock had come to
several hundred times its original price promoters hastily
sold out and the scheme collapsed. Some writers claim the
plan of the South Sea Company was feasible and would have
made good if the speculative spirit had not entered into it,
but it was more profitable to sell stock than to earn dividends. It was calculated that the value of all stock issued
in the mushroom companies was 500,000,000 pounds sterling.
The South Sea Company itself started the panic by launch-
ing a campaign to put its competitors out of business, in-
stituting legal proceedings against all companies that they
claimed were illegally issuing stock. In slaying its rivals
the company struck a blow at itself which pulled them all
down together. A cry of rage arose against the Government, it being blamed for having fostered the South Sea
scheme. Old families were ruined and new ones enriched.

The principal damage was done by the business depression
which followed, together with attempted readjustments of
the financial system.   The Bank of England itself would
have been ruined had its own proposals been accepted in an
endeavor to save the South Sea Company.

During the run on the Bank of England ruin was staved
off by payments in light sixpences and shillings and by engaging men to fill up the line, draw money and redeposit it
at another window.   This slowed up the run until a holiday
permitted legal closing, after which the alarm subsided.   In
an investigation that followed in the House of Commons, it
was found that the Chancellor of the Exchequer and several
members of Parliament were involved, and these latter were
expelled from the House.   The government did much to alleviate the existing distress, and unanimously passed a resolution to the effect that "nothing could tend more to the establishment of public credit than to prevent the infamous
practice of stock-jobbing."   Following this speculation and
the failure of the South Sea Bubble, Sir John Barnard spon-
sored an act in Parliament against stock-jobbing and speculation.   This is the first effort on record to curb the evil of
speculation.   For a century and a half the old building that
housed the South Sea Company on Threadneedle Street,
London, known as "the Bubble," stood as a melancholy land-
mark of what has been termed "the Folly of the Ages."
Robert Walpole became first Lord of the Treasury in 1721
and his wise statesmanship averted national disaster.   He
settled the South Sea affairs, made treaties of peace with
other European countries, extended the colonization scheme,
and a period of quiet and prosperity followed.

With the South Sea Bubble in England and the Mississippi Company in France, coming at the same time, Europe
experienced a surfeit of speculative disaster.   The Mississippi Bubble was similar in plan to its English neighbor, also
uniting with its commercial projects an attempt to finance
the government.   A Scotchman, John Law, was the promoter.   The Company of the West, known as the Mississippi

Company, was organized in 1720 to develop the resources of French holdings in Louisiana and Canada.

The ambitious schemes of Louis XIV had burdened France and were such an incubus on the industry of the country that the entire revenue was needed to meet the interest. Law offered to "accept at par all the government securities then afloat, although their market value was but 50 per cent. As an equivalent the bank was to be declared a state bank, and its notes were to pass as current money. Shares in the state bank were secured upon the produce of the gold mines in Louisiana, the direction of which was to be controlled by a Mississippi company. Although gold had not as yet been found in that region—and its geological structure proves that gold never will be found there—shares in the company were eagerly sought. Money poured into the bank treasury, and Law was enabled to declare a dividend of 40 per cent. A dividend of 100 per cent was as easy as that of 5 per cent when paid in a paper currency, the amount of which was limited only by the means of printing. Government proclamations of the most mischievous as well as absurd character were issued, in order to meet the difficulties of the moment."

*"Extravagant ideas were formed of the possibilities of Law's system, and the roads to Paris were blocked by people hurrying there to speculate in shares. Two of the ablest scholars in France deplored the madness at one interview, and at the next found themselves bidding against each other. Coachmen, cooks, and waiters became millionaires by lucky speculation; tradespeople in the street where the exchange was established made fortunes by letting out their stalls and chairs. The price of stock rose until it frightened even the promoter of the system, who interfered in the hope of checking speculation, but who found soon that he was unable to check either the rise or the fall of the stock."

The shares of the Mississippi Company advanced to thirty-six times their normal par value. Legitimate business enterprises suffered by the community gamble in these stocks.

*Day's "History of Commerce."

The crash which quickly followed was especially serious, as the whole currency consisted now of discredited notes issued by the company. Ruin was widespread, and credit received a blow which made the promotion of legitimate enterprises difficult for a long time thereafter.

The investors became so desperate that the decree of October 5, 1720, forbade speculative operators on the public streets of Paris, and the speculators were driven into obscure corners of the city. Despair spread throughout the kingdom. A few were made rich, but thousands were impoverished. Insurrection was imminent, and with great difficulty prevented. The result of an investigation instituted by the Regent proved that nothing but worthless paper remained to represent deposits of 2,000,000,000 livres. Law left the country to escape the wrath of his victims. The experience of the French people in this fiat money enterprise, although it entailed great suffering and hardship on those who were victimized, served to furnish the world a lesson in high finance that has never been forgotten. Law's system was not so bad, perhaps, if he had been allowed to work it out in an orderly way. Many features of our Federal Reserve System are the same as embodied in Law's original plan. That Law believed in the scheme he promoted is more than probable. He died destitute at Venice. Nor was the Regent enriched. The political consequences of this disaster were as detrimental to France as were the commercial results.

In our time we refer to "Black Friday" as of the year 1869, but the original "Black Friday" came to pass the 6th day of December, 1745, when a panic spread through England based on a rumor of French invasion. A run started to withdraw specie from the Bank of England. The confusion was so great that all the business houses closed. But the merchants met and agreed to accept bank notes, passing a resolution urging all citizens and merchants to adopt the notes. This declaration was signed in the course of a single day by 1,140 merchants and fundholders.

England experienced another crisis in 1763 which spread
to the Continent. The Seven Years War had given rise to
much speculation and when peace came the day of reckoning
was at hand. This brought with it the ruin of merchants
and speculators as well. The failure of a firm of brokers in
Amsterdam carried with it eighteen important Dutch houses
and many merchants in Hamburg. The shock was so great
that for some time business was transacted for cash only.

In 1772 another commercial crisis passed over England,
starting when a member of the banking firm of Heale defaulted, causing the ruin of creditor merchants. The number of failures that year reached 525, the greatest since the
memorable year 1720. Writers of the period say it was a
return of the South Sea year, the losses reaching £10,000,-
000. During the depression which followed a series of vigorous measures were put into effect to alleviate dangers of
the kind in the future. During this crisis the mismanagement of the affairs of the East India Company was an important factor in the depression. Adam Smith, in "The
Wealth of Nations," describes the conditions thus: "Their
debts, instead of being reduced, were augmented by an ar-
rear to the treasury in the payment of the £400,000, by another to the custom house for duties unpaid, by a large debt
to the bank for money borrowed, and by a fourth for bills
drawn upon them from India, and wantonly accepted, to
the amount of upwards of £1,200,000. The distress which
these accumulated claims brought upon them obliged them
not only to reduce all at once their dividend to 6 per cent, but
to throw themselves upon the mercy of the government, and
to supplicate, first, a release from the further payment of
the stipulated four hundred thousand pounds a year; and,
secondly, a loan of fourteen hundred thousand, to save them
from immediate bankruptcy."

Another alarming crisis occurred in 1783, following the
treaty of peace with the American States. That year, following the surrender of Cornwallis to General Washington
and the British fleet to the Admiral of France, British con-

sols fell to 63¼, the lowest on record. The coming of peace had brought about a wide extension of international trade. New markets were developed very rapidly and extravagant transactions were indulged in. All of this produced a strain on the gold reserves and finances of the country and the crisis followed.

A very brief review of the conditions which prevailed in France immediately preceding, and which culminated in the French Revolution in 1789, will serve to show how difficult industrial progress had been. "All the privileges, property and political rights had become vested in the clergy, the nobles and the king. They enjoyed immunities, favors, pensions and preferments, while the mass of the population bore the burden of taxation. The privileged classes numbered about 270,000 persons, 140,000 nobles, 130,000 clergy. There were 25,000 to 30,000 noble families, 3,000 monks, 2,500 monasteries, 37,000 nuns, 1,500 convents, and 60,000 curates and vicars in the churches and chapels." The privileged classes owned one-half of the kingdom.

Taine's description of the economic condition of the people is vividly drawn:" Examine administrative correspondence for the last thirty years preceding the Revolution. Countless statements reveal excessive suffering, even when not terminating in fury. Life to a man of the lower class, to an artisan, or workman, subsisting on the labor of his own hands, is evidently precarious,—he obtains simply enough to keep him from starvation and he does not always get that. Here, in four districts, 'the inhabitants live only on buckwheat,' and for five years, the apple crop having failed, they drink only water. There, in a country of vineyards, 'the vine-dressers each year are reduced, for the most part, to begging their bread during the dull season.' . . . In a remote canton the peasants cut the grain still green and dry it in the oven, because they are too hungry to wait."

"Many farms remain uncultivated, and, what is worse, many are deserted. According to the best observers, 'one-quarter of the soil is absolutely lying waste. . . . Hundreds and hundreds of arpents of heath and moor form extensive deserts.' . . . This is not sterility but decadence.

The regime invented by Louis XIV has produced its effect; the soil for a century past is reverting back to a wild state. . . . In the second place, cultivation, when it does take place, is carried on according to mediaeval modes."

"Peasants and laborers were compelled to work on roads and bridges without pay. The small farmer was under the absolute control of the nobles and subjected to the most arbitrary exactions and species of robbery. He must grind his corn at the lord's mill and press his grapes at the lord's wine press, and pay whatever sum was exacted. Louis engaged in corrupt schemes of impoverishing the people and filling the public treasury. The shipment of grain was prohibited from one province into another, while he lowered the price and bought up the surplus, and when the scarcity thus brought about enhanced prices he sold at a profit. He laid tribute on the business and industrial classes by granting licenses and selling to individuals the sole right to engage in a particular calling or trade. Class hatred became intense and a spirit of unrest and jealousy pervaded the whole nation. The nobles looked upon the trading, industrial and laboring classes with contempt. The king treated them 'only as a sponge to be squeezed.' "

This was the condition under which 26,000,000 people existed in 1789 and was the scene of economic depression that brought on the terrible and bloody French Revolution.

In 1795 England experienced another severe depression. The country passed quickly from abundance to scarcity, scarcity to famine, and famine to bankruptcy. The Bank of England suspended cash payments. The disorders in business were severe. The harvest in 1792 was very bad, as were most of the harvests between 1789 and 1802, the price of corn had risen 13s, and in addition to the agricultural distress, a serious economic crisis occurred.

The year 1797 marked a period of crisis in Ireland which coincided with the fall in exchange unfavorable to Ireland and an increase in issues of the Bank of Ireland. These events bring us to the nineteenth century.

CHAPTER IV.

FOREIGN DEPRESSIONS FROM THE BEGINNING OF THE 19TH CENTURY TO THE PRESENT TIME

The beginning of the Nineteenth Century found Europe warring and in need of the products of the new republic that had sprung up across the seas, giving America an opportunity to gain a foothold among nations without interference and to wax prosperous economically at the expense of the Old World.

The economic situation in France in 1805 was extremely bad and the victory of Austerlitz was all that saved the financial structure of the Empire. It is said that the financial crisis absorbed the thoughts of Napoleon on the battlefield as much as the fighting itself.

"The liquidation which followed the crisis of 1805 caused coin to pile up in the Bank of France to such an extent that the bank was obliged to invest a part in the obligations of the receivers generally and to reduce interest to 2 and 3 per cent. Commerce began to expand again after 1808, and the discounts of the Bank of France reached in that year 142,000,000 francs and in 1810, 187,000,000 francs."

The business depression of 1808 affected all the western world. Following trouble in North America it spread to English institutions in Lancashire. That country held American investments to a large extent. From there it spread over England, Ireland and on to the Continent. When the trouble started in America, London houses attempted to help conditions here because it would not do to let their American creditors fail. But they were soon forced to turn their attention to the home situation, and it was several years before matters had worked themselves out and conditions returned to normal. At the height of French power, from 1806 to 1815, under the Berlin decree of Napoleon prices on commodities rose very high in England and there was a tendency to unprecedented speculation. While the French decree did not shut off English commerce, there was fear that it would have this effect.

Some writers claim that the depression following the Napoleonic Wars started in 1815, but from the best authorities it is found there was an over-lap of several years of good times, due to the large amount of inflated money still in circulation. This lasted until about 1819. Alison is authority for the statement that: "Yet the years from 1815 to 1819, though checkered with suffering from these causes, and from two bad harvests in 1816 and 1818, were upon the whole prosperous." The depression came on at its worst in 1819 when, with a comparatively small amount of gold on hand, specie payment was resumed under the gold standard, and this not only caused a sudden and great contraction in the volume of currency, but it reduced everything from inflated and fictitious valuations to a gold basis. The country banks of England increased under the stimulus of speculation from 270 in 1797 to 600 in 1808, and 721 in 1810. The Bank of England, in the meantime, increased its discounts from £9,100,000 in 1804 to £16,400,000 in 1809 and £21,400,000 in 1810. The circulation of the Bank of England rose from £16,400,000 in 1801 to £24,200,000 in 1810, but the increase was trifling up to 1809, and was the consequence rather than the cause of the great increase in prices due to speculation.

The quick recovery of France from the most terrible industrial depressions usually connected with her wars has been indeed a marvel. After Waterloo she was obliged to issue 500,000,000 francs, resulting in a disastrous fall of her securities and values in general. "The metallic reserve of the Bank of France fell from 117,000,000 francs on July 1, 1818, to 37,000,000 francs on October 29th. The bank shortened the term of commercial discounts to forty-five days, and in 1819 was flooded again with idle capital."

America began to feel the effects of the Napoleonic Wars about 1818, and this lasted through 1819 and 1820, but France felt the effects previous to this time, although the disturbance reached its height in Europe in 1820. The long stretch covering the Napoleonic Wars in Europe helped the United States to get on her feet economically, while England was having her own troubles. The Bank of England suspended cash payment on its own notes when the war broke out and it was not for twenty years, or until 1819, that it was again resumed. During all that time England was on a paper credit basis, and yet she carried on some of the greatest wars and commercial projects of her history.

Let us compare existing conditions of 1920-21 with those following the Napoleonic wars, a little over one hundred years ago. Osgood's description of that period follows:

"The Battle of Waterloo, in 1815, brought peace to England, and with it a great business depression which plunged thousands of people into misery. With her great navy England had been able to give her merchant ships better protection on the seas than any other nation, and so her goods had little competition from her European rivals in many markets. Now that peace was declared, France and Holland were selling their wares in competition with the English. The English factories had made up more stuff than they could sell under peace conditions, and they were obliged partially to close down; but at the very time when they were discharging their workers, soldiers and sailors were coming home by the thousand, looking for employment. For every job there were two applicants. Wages fell with a crash. The farmers were in much the same predicament as the manufacturers; they had brought more land than ever before under cultivation just at the time that the factory people in England had less money than ever to buy. One farmer competed with another for what business there was, and prices fell. Those who had bought or rented land at war prices found that they could not make the interest on their investment or pay their rent; those who had mortgaged their land were sold out. Much of the land that was reclaimed had to be allowed to return to its wild state. At the same time farmers who held their land were driven to farming in a more careful way than ever before. To produce with the least possible expense means efficiency in farming, and this the hard times taught to those who survived the depression.

"The effect of the Napoleonic wars on the industrial and commercial life of the German States and Prussia was most ruinous. Lying between France, Austria and the Russian frontier, they became the battle-ground during this great struggle for the contending hosts of Napoleon, Russia and Austria. Through the continental policy of Napoleon their markets were open to the competition of French goods, while they were compelled to pay tribute to the support of French armies and subjected to the most oppressive and burdensome taxation."

In the early part of the Nineteenth Century it was said that Switzerland was the barometer which indicated the state of business in Europe. Switzerland was a neutral, never at war, although affected by the wars which raged around her. Because of her position conditions within her borders reflected the general commercial atmosphere of Europe as a whole.

"Lyons was the chief manufacturing city in France, being the centre of the silk trade, and possessing a valuable traffic with England, America, Germany, Belgium, Russia, Turkey, and Spain. The operatives suffered from the vicissitudes peculiar to their trade, and held the reputation of being turbulent and disaffected in times of depression, when they have frequently risen against the authorities."

Recovering from this stagnation, a boom started, lasting several years, until, following this period of intense speculation and wide inflation, the inevitable crash came, leading to the depression of 1825. "In October, 1824, the coin and bullion at the Bank of England amounted to eleven and three-quarter millions; in August it barely reached three and three-quarter millions sterling. These figures tell their own tale. At the beginning of December several banks failed, panic reigned, the Bank of England was almost drained of its gold. The story is told that the credit of the country was saved only by the accidental discovery at the last moment of a box containing one-pound notes to the amount of upwards of half a million sterling; but although such a box was undoubtedly so discovered, the tide of the panic had, it seems, been stemmed by that time. The Bank of England, by the wise freedom with which it discounted bills and paid out money, exhausted the terror of the public."

Previous to the crisis of 1825 money could be borrowed from English banks at 2 per cent. At that time there was a proverb current in the financial world that "John Bull can stand many things but he cannot stand 2 per cent." When the price of money remains at a low level for any considerable period people will turn to risky investments if no good ones offer themselves, and a crisis is the necessary result of such experiments. This low rate of interest is what brought about the crisis of this year, particularly encouraging speculation in South American enterprises. This began following the South American Revolution, which threw off the yoke of Spain and left several countries open to free trade with England. Some writers estimate that 150,000,000 pounds were invested in Latin America, and when it was evident that they would not begin to pay the collapse came. The Bank of England realized its mistake at the last minute and raised its discount rate to 5 per cent. But the bank reserves continued to decline until December 31st, 1825, when they reached only 1,260,895 pounds, which led to unheard of confusion. The scarcity of coin was such that business was almost at a standstill. Sixty financial companies went down. The London bank failed. General distress inincreased by the failure of thirty-six country banks and numerous important commercial firms throughout Great Britain. The stringency in gold was due to "the immense loans contracted by the governments of Europe and Latin America and the fever of speculation in domestic and foreign companies, which drained England of her specie. Besides, considerable financing was necessary to establish the new States in Europe that had been carved out of the French Empire. All of this seriously lowered the stock of gold in London. It was estimated that £150,000,000 of British money, including that invested in government loans, had been sunk in Mexico and South America alone. Domestic activities were marked by extensive building of canals and turnpikes. Besides, there were six hundred and twenty-four domestic stock companies organized in the two years preceding, with a nominal capital of £372,173,100. Demands for so much capital caused a sharp increase in the value of money and the prices of commodities, and manufacturers were forced to borrow money at the increased rates to carry on their ordinary operations. The reserves of the Bank of England became depleted with the large loans; foreign exchange turned against her; rates of interest went higher, and business broke under the load. From June 11, 1838, to June, 1839, there were 306 failures in London, and 781 in the provinces.

The condition of woolen manufacturers in England in 1826 was described by an English manufacturer who wrote to his brother in America: "If you were in this country you would scarcely hear the sound of a woolen-shuttle in all the neighborhood; and, take all Saddleworth through, you will not find one shuttle out of forty going. It is indeed one of the greatest convulsions the mercantile world has ever known, and, since the date of the South Sea trouble, probably has not had a parellel."

From 1836 to 1839 depression again stalked through Europe. England experienced a crisis in 1836, which may have been the forerunner of our trouble of 1837. On top of her own difficulties England was particularly affected by our panic because of her large investments in this country. In that year France felt the flurry less, and the Bank of France was able to lend aid to the Bank of England, as well as to the United States and to Belgium. The Bank of Belgium suspended in 1838. A series of reverses occurred in Holland in the years 1837 and 1838. Numerous mercantile failures took place and a brief panic ensued.

The European troubles started in November, 1836, with the failure of two banks, one in Ireland and one in Manchester. "Three large business houses known as the three W's,—Wilkes, Wilde, and Wiggin,—which had closest relations in the granting of credit to America, were in particular affected. Since the imports of the United States to this time largely exceeded the exports the balance was met not by settlements in specie, but by the sale of American securities of one sort or another and by the securing of credits abroad." The distress continued in England until 1839. It was so severe that revolutionary propaganda was spread broadcast and the "Condition of England" was seriously discussed in the Cabinet.

A vivid description, typical of old time panics, is given by writers of the time. We have witnessed them in our country, but our children, perhaps, never will. John Francis wrote: "Consternation reigned paramount, and almost every third man was a defaulter. All foreign securities were without a price; the bankers refused to advance money; the brokers' cheques were at first doubted and then rejected. With a desperation which will never be forgotten, the jobbers closed their books, refused to transact any business, and waited the result in almost abject despair."

From 1845 to 1847 England had what is called her Railroad Panic. Fifty-two new railroad companies were chartered in England in the first four months of 1845. In addition a large number had already started building. So fierce was the mania for buying railroad stock that disaster was early predicted. The London Times said: "We can not add fifty millions of money to railway enterprises without the most ruinous, universal, and desperate confusion." To the newspaper efforts were added repeated warnings by leading financiers. Finally came a general uncovering of big frauds. The London City Press said: "Never since the days of the old South Sea Bubble has wild speculation run so rampantly mad."

A large number of the new railway schemes had to be abandoned, and many persons possessed of property and estates found themselves involved in sudden and unforeseen disaster.

At the same time there was great speculation in grain and cotton. In 1847 business on the whole European continent suffered severe reaction because of heavy railroad building which was reflected in this country by a temporary crisis and depression.

The severe depression occasioned in Ireland by the potato crop failure in 1847 paralleled famines of the darkest ages of the human race. Peasants literally died of hunger in large numbers. In some districts it became impossible to provide coffins. The population decreased from eight to six million in two years. More than 700,000 migrated to the United States.

France experienced another severe depression between 1835 and 1840, the period when the failure of the Bank of France to meet expanding commercial needs being most keenly felt. Louis Philippe owes his fall in 1848 to the financial crisis and business depression which preceded it. There had been a long series of business failures, and the economic situation was so strained that the people became desperate. In 1848 and again in 1871 the Bank of France suspended payments, but its notes did not depreciate seriously.

The panic which started in the United States in 1857 spread over the entire commercial world. The news of the failure of the Ohio Life and Trust Company caused intense alarm in England for the £80,000,000 of English money which was believed to be invested in American securities. A group of speculators added to the alarm in London by forming a combination to 'bear' the market, by finding flaws in securities and working through the press to excite general distrust and depress prices." Runs started on banks all over England and the Bank of England itself was about to suspend when "a letter reached the bank on November 12th authorizing them to issue notes in excess of the legal limit, provided they maintained the rate of discount at 10 per cent." Public excitement was suddenly calmed, but the demand for discounts continued heavy for more than a fortnight.

The English iron and textile industries were especially affected. Factories were closed, blast furnaces extinguished, and the greatest distress prevailed amongst the working classes.

The pressure on the money markets of Europe was severe and prolonged, and those with investments in America were obliged to absorb their losses. Great prosperity in America during the ten years preceding 1857, referred to as the "Golden Age," had attracted millions of dollars of European capital. Europe had over-loaned and we had over-spent. There was a crash due in both countries. So heavy were the American investments that money again became scarce, but the cry had gone up against sending so much money to America. It seemed that everybody had investments in the New World. English banks holding American securities closed their doors one after another. As was customary in England, the crisis was followed by an inquiry. English people want to know the why and wherefore of their losses. The discussion brought out the old, old story of speculation and the entire lack of discretion on the part of public, banks and business.

Simultaneously with the development of the American panic of 1857 mutiny broke out in India. With this came the news of the failure of the Western Bank of Scotland. During this crisis the discount rate of the Bank of England reached 10 per cent. Seventy members of the London Stock Exchange failed. Officials of the Bank of England afterward said that there was more commercial distress caused by the panic of 1857 than by that of 1847.

An important step was taken by the Bank of England, following the panic of 1857, for the protection of its gold reserve. This consisted in raising the rate of interest rapidly by degrees of one per cent at a time, instead of fractions of one per cent, in order to curtail the export of gold. Other countries on the Continent suffered in the crisis, though less acutely than England, France and America, because of the smaller scope of their commercial affairs.

France experienced her troubles also. The Credit Mobilier had paid 10 per cent in 1853; 13 per cent in 1854; 47 per cent in 1855; 24 per cent in 1856; and then the crash came. Paris and other cities felt the same stagnation in trade, the discharge of workmen, and the glut of commodities, as existed in England and the United States. The same phenomena existed in Germany, Austria, Belgium and Scandinavia in smaller degree. Hamburg, which was closely connected with American trade, felt it most. It spread to India, China, Australia and South America. But once more Europe recovered as usual, and prospered for a few years, until the cotton industry was almost ruined by the effects of the Civil War in America. A "cotton famine" occurred in Lancashire, when 800,000 wage-earners were deprived of their livelihood.

The cotton famine of 1861 marks another epoch in the commercial history of the world. It was one of the most terrible depressions on record. Scherer in his book, "Cotton as a World Power," gives a graphic account: "English cotton manufacture had grown to such enormous proportions as to support one-fifth of the entire population, with an annual pay-roll of $55,000,000. Over a thousand million pounds of cotton were consumed every year, producing for exportation 2,800,000,000 yards of cloth and nearly 200,-000,000 pounds of twist and yarn. There were 2,650 factories, of which 2,195 were localized in Lancashire County and on the borders of its two southern neighbors, these factories containing over 30,000,000 spindles and 350,000 looms run by 300,000 horsepower, and employing nearly half a million operatives, of whom 56 per cent were females. Before the close of the year 1862, 485,454 of the inhabitants of Lancashire were recipients of organized charity."

"The cause of this swift and appalling catastrophe is not far to seek. A vast population in a limited area was dependent for its daily bread on the cotton industry. During the year 1860 America furnished 84 per cent of the entire European supply of cotton, and during 1862 only 7 per cent, while the increased imports from India had not yet had time to alleviate the situation even measurably, and the demand for cotton in the northern states had meanwhile become so intense that Liverpool actually re-exported 52,000 bales to the United States in 1862, so that the net receipts from America were less than 1,000 bales a week, as against 78,000 bales in 1860."

The London Times on December 7, 1861, said: "Christmas comes this year on a country bright with sun and frost, but on a people oppressed with a national loss and threatened with a formidable war. Already closed mills and short time have given some part of our population an earnest of what they may hereafter expect; already speculation is more careful than it has been for many years, and the somber appearance of our churches and chapels last Sunday portends a bad season next spring."

The same paper said a fortnight later: "There should have arrived by this time at the southern ports of America, for shipment to England, from 500,000 to 1,000,000 bales of last year's cotton crop. By the latest estimate it was calculated that not 1,000 bales had been sent down, and it was known indeed that small stocks of cotton remaining over from the preceding year's crop had been removed from the ports to the interior of the country."

During the first half of 1862 only 11,500 bales reached England from America, less than a hundredth of the quantity for the same period of the year preceding. Half of the Lancashire spindles were idle, and the prices had jumped to thirteen pence a pound. In August it went up to twenty pence, and in the following month to a half crown.

A midsummer issue of the Saturday Review gives a vivid picture of the crisis at its height: "The cotton famine is altogether the saddest thing that has befallen this country for many a year. There have been gloomy times enough before this. We have seen Ireland perishing from actual starvation, and England half ruined from commercial distress. War and rebellion have taken their turn among the troubles from which a great nation can scarcely expect to be long free. But in the worst of our calamities there has seldom been so pitiable a sight as the manufacturing districts present at this moment."

Continuing, Scherer says: "By the close of that awful year the resources of organized charity for the relief of Lancashire pauperism had been exhausted, and alms were trickling in from Australia, Canada, India, and even China. Nearly a quarter million operatives were entirely out of work, while only 121,129 were working full time, and, as already noted, 485,454 people were receiving alms, comprising 24.1 per cent of the entire population affected."

Richard Cobden wrote from Lancashire in November to a friend in Staffordshire: "Few people can realize the appalling state of things in this neighborhood. Imagine that the iron, stone and coal were suddenly withheld from Staffordshire, and it gives you but an imperfect idea of what Lancashire, with its much larger population, is suffering from the want of cotton; it reverses the condition of the richest country in the kingdom, and makes it the poorest. A capitalist with 20,000 pounds invested in buildings and machinery may be almost on a par with his operatives in destitution, if he be deprived of the raw material which alone makes this capital productive. Unhappily, the winter is upon us to aggravate the sufferings of the working people."

The London Times of December 31st said: "The memory of the year which ends this day will hereafter be chiefly associated with the American war and its consequences at home. No crisis in modern times has been so anxiously watched, nor has any European war or revolution so seriously threatened the interests of England."

This was the final climax of the famine. George McHenry was too late in 1863 with his book on "The Cotton Trade," addressed to the people of England in behalf of the Confederacy, and as an apology for slavery. The machinery of the mills had been adjusted to Surat or Indian cotton, of which 1,179 bales came in during the year, together with increased supplies from Egypt, Turkey and Brazil. In 1864 the supplies from India proved sufficient to meet the demand, and the weekly number of applicants for alms was reduced to 135,000. Surat cotton was very unpopular, however, being short, harsh, brittle, and one-third less than normal wages were paid; so that many of the operatives preferred to be treated as paupers. Hammond cites reports that "the word Surat" became an odious epithet in Lancashire, so that a firm of brewers brought a libel suit to recover damages for having been maligned as "Surat brewers," and John Bright used to tell a story of a church-going operative who once interrupted his pastor's prayer for increased cotton supplies with the fervent ejaculation, "Amen, O Lord! but not Shoorat!"

In 1865 the famine ended, having cost the British cotton trade in the neighborhood of $350,000,000, not including about $20,000,000 expended by the public in alms. Many mill owners, says Ellison, regained a part of their losses, but a large number lost nearly everything they were worth, while many were reduced to bankruptcy.

John Bright, always an active friend of the Union, was astute enough to write to Sumner, during the height of famine: "This country is passing through a wonderful crisis, but our people will be kept alive by the contributions of the country. I see that some one in the States has proposed to send something to our aid. If a few cargoes of flour should come, say 50,000 barrels, as a gift from persons in your northern states to the Lancashire working men, it would have a prodigious effect in your favor here." Three relief ships accordingly came out from New York to Liverpool, laden with bread, meat, and flour, a gift which, coming as it did from "those involved in the real agony of war to those for whom that war had occasioned distress, passing though sharp, was neither unnoticed nor barren of results."

France also suffered in the cotton famine, consuming as she did 240,000,000 pounds annually, which was two-thirds as much as America itself consumed. All their cotton came from America and when it was shut off 300,000 people in one district alone were made absolutely destitute, subsisting, according to one writer, "by roaming at night from house to house, and demanding, rather than asking, alms." At Rouin, out of 50,000 operatives 30,000 were laid off, and in the surrounding country only one-fifth of the hand weavers had work.

Conditions were so bad in France that Louis Napoleon, who then had an army in Mexico under Maximilian, attempted to induce England and Russia to join him in intervening in the American war on the side of the South. In America the cotton famine was only slightly felt. New England mills, of course, curtailed, but the manufacture of war munitions took the place of cotton manufacturing in giving employment and stimulating business.

It will be seen that for three decades Europe had experienced a panic regularly every ten years, beginning 1837, then 1847 and 1857. Is it possible that her people were superstitious enough to believe that another would inevitably come in 1867 and thus, by their fear and preparation for it, cause the stringency and depression of 1866? It is reasonable to suppose that people would be getting ready a year ahead. There is no direct evidence that this is a fact, but there were a number of articles going the rounds of the press in those days on the subject of the recurrence of panics and depressions every ten years. It came a year ahead of time, in 1866, when the financial structure of Great Britain was shaken by failures of important brokerage houses, although trade itself was little affected.

The crisis of 1866 was precipitated by the failure of Overand & Guerney Company. Again it was the result of overspeculation. The announcement of failure was followed by what is referred to as the second "Black Friday" of English history. The Overand & Gurney Company had

liabilities of £19,000,000, and, with the exception of the
Barings, was the largest brokerage house in England. Up
to this time this was the largest single failure in commercial
history. A number of other banks and joint stock companies failed, carrying with them numerous investors. For
some months after the panic English credit fell into entire
disrepute on the Continent and a circular from the Foreign
Office containing an accurate explanation of the distinction
between scarcity of money and insolvency, appeared only
to aggravate the prevailing suspicion.

The disclosure revealed the irregularity and unsoundness
of the affairs of a large portion of the English business
world, and it was some years before confidence was fully
restored. Duguid described it as the financial crisis of the
century. Describing the second "Black Friday" of May 11,
1866, Andreadea says: "The prevailing excitement is in-
describable; Lombard Street was impassable, it seemed
that demands for accommodation must increase to an extraordinary extent, and doubt was thrown upon the position
of the most respected houses. On this day alone the Bank of
England made advances to the value of nearly four millions,
and its reserve, which had been 5,727,000 pounds in the
morning, was reduced to about three millions."

English and French cotton manufacturers were again
upset by the crisis of that year. During the Civil War
blockade, when these countries were unable to get sufficient
cotton, prices had practically trebled. Under the stimulus
of demand India, Egypt, China and Brazil began growing
cotton. These crops reached Europe at a time when the
released crop of America had thrown large quantities on
the market and a crash in price caused great disorganization in the cotton trade, which was reflected in all other
industries.

Various nations of Europe have at times attempted to
start industries which were not adapted to their people or
their conditions, and as cycles of depression came along
these industries were wiped out. England attempted to

establish a silk industry, but trade depression wiped it out
and the factories for cotton spinning and weaving in Holland have never really thrived in competition with England and have always been influenced adversely by every
depression in trade. At the time of the separation Belgium
tried to make herself industrially independent of Holland,
but the trade depression which followed wiped out these
weaker industries. In depressions the rule of the survival
of the fittest seems invariable. Holland survived the
monetary crisis of 1866, when confidence was lost throughout Europe and interest rates were 8 per cent in Amsterdam; when shipbuilding was brought to a standstill, and
colonial trade collapsed.

The panic of 1873 swept over all Europe, America and
the entire world, although its effect was felt worse on the
Continent than in England. Some writers describe it as
"the most widespread and representative of all crises."
Brazil, the Argentine Republic and Peru, all experienced the
distress, as well as the countries of the Orient. For several decades the nations of the world had been becoming
closely linked together by commerce and trade so that they
were all affected by European financial troubles at times.
Another writer says: "The crisis of 1873 was perhaps the
first world-wide depression affecting all branches of trade,
even in the most distant countries like Australia and South
America." The money panic was felt from New York to
Moscow, affecting trade, commerce and agriculture in all
the intervening countries. It is supposed that the panic
started in Germany as a result of over-speculation following the payment of enormous indemnity by the French to
their conquerors. Prices were inflated on every European
bourse, and when the crash came the fall in securities
on the Berlin market alone was estimated at 131,138,000
thalers.

The German government feared the results of over-speculation and instructed the Bank of Prussia to refuse the paper
of new joint stock companies. The speculators transferred

their operations to Vienna and in the first quarter of 1873 $140,000,000 of so-called securities, but with little real security behind them, were issued at the Austrian capital. In reality, the crash in Vienna was the first signal of approaching disaster. The Bank of Austria was permitted to lend largely on such securities in order to keep the speculators from failure, but on May 27th, the day before the opening of the International Exposition, seventy failures occurred, and on the next day one hundred and ten, involving establishments of the first importance. "The bourse was closed, the government suspended the limit upon the note issues of the bank, loans were made by the treasury, and a syndicate of bankers was formed to make advances on sound securities. A general panic was thus prevented, but credit was so far impaired that it was not until 1875 that business in Austria resumed its wonted activity." France, having been forced to liquidate in 1870, after the Prussian War, felt only the ripples of the crisis which were wafted back from the storm in other countries.

England passed through another short depression in 1875, when a number of large concerns failed, including several in South America and India, but the Bank of England got behind the situation and after a brief shakeup business resumed its normal course.

The disturbance of 1882 in Europe started in France by the failure of the Union Generale, a banking institution founded in 1878 as an adjunct and backed by the Roman Catholic Church, being devised to aid her members as against the Jews and the Unbelievers, who, through a series of political upturns, had secured control of the finances of France. M. Eugene Bontoux, its promoter, was in a class with Law, only not so conscientious. The story of the Union Generale is a book in itself, and Zola wrote his novel, "L'Argent," based on its history. "In this institution was concentrated the money of the Church, its institutions, the hierachy, and its followers. At first it succeeded in beating the Jews, causing one of the French Rothchilds to com-

mit suicide, but gambling in its stock became widespread
and the crash came in 1882, affecting all of France and
spreading to neighboring countries. France had so fully
recovered from the Franco-Prussian War that stock-jobbing
and other forms of reckless speculation flourished in Paris.
Investment companies and various schemes had sprung up
like mushrooms in the speculative atmosphere of the preceding years, and those which were upon too grand a scale
for any but the great financiers and the rich had their
imitators among the adventurers of the street, who accepted
gratefully in installments the petty savings of the poor."
The panic started in Paris and Lyons in January, 1882, with
the collapse of the Union Generale, followed by a fall in all
classes of securities. The sum of £924,000 was withdrawn
from the Bank of England for France on January 30th, and
£2,000,000 was drawn out during the week. The resultant
liquidation was attended by much loss and the uncovering
of many corrupt financial practices.

Great Britain experienced a long period of depression
beginning about 1875, gradually growing worse until in
1885 a commission was appointed to investigate the causes
and means for business recovery. This commission took
evidence during a portion of the years 1885 and 1886.
"Questions were submitted to the Chambers of Commerce,
principal business men's associations and labor organizations, calling for answers upon the conditions of trade, industries and wages, during a period of twenty years, between 1864 and 1884." Various causes were given for the
depression, but as usual the commission reported a
multiplicity of suggestions after the natural course had
brought about some relief. The commission reported that
wages had held up and the incomes of business and professional men had actually increased, although profits had been
smaller, land rents lower. The causes were given as over-
production and keen competition, together with changing
conditions throughout the world, particularly as to relations between capital and labor.

The year 1890 marked the famous Baring failure in England, which started in Argentine. In Great Britain, during the seven years preceding the disturbance, the trade and industrial situation, although differing in detail, was practically identical with developments in the United States during the same period. The name of Baring had been closely connected with the financial world, and held in high esteem for more than one hundred years. At one time they were the fiscal agents for the United States Government in England. They were a strong house and represented some of the largest financial interests in foreign countries. As far back as 1819 the Duc de Richelieu had said: "There are six great powers in Europe—England, France, Russia, Austria, Prussia and Baring Brothers." And it was later on the loss of these foreign investments that the firm was wrecked. It was their Argentine investments which got them in the quicksands.

On account of the prosperous conditions in England a considerable percentage of the population, including even laboring classes, had been able to accumulate savings which they were eager to place in some remunerative investment. The successful conversion of the national debt of Great Britain during the year 1888 had produced a considerable decline in the rate of interest and had stimulated the appetite of the public for new investments. The firm of Baring Brothers underwrote Argentine public loans and disposed of them to the British public. Thirteen Argentine provinces during the period 1886-90 floated securities in London to the extent of £38,700,000, the National Government negotiated loans amounting to almost £25,000,000, and Argentine municipalities floated about £5,000,000 of their bonds in London. British investors also placed between forty and sixty million pounds sterling in Argentine railroad projects, besides an equal amount in miscellaneous investments. During the distress a total of 765 firms went into liquidation in Great Britain. The country, however, was saved from a panic. There had been no real panic since 1866, when by the banking act of that year the Bank of England was enabled to assure the public that all solvent business would be able to secure loans to carry it through periods of distress.

Money had been poured into the Argentine Republic from all Europe for the development of her resources until the natives might have well though their credit abroad was without limit. A boom began in 1866 which "carried up the price of lands, which a few years before could be had almost for the taking, to $50,000 per league, while suburban lots bounded upward from a few cents to several dollars per square metre. Extravagance and luxury ruled among the governing classes, and the banks which were opened in 1887 under the Guaranteed Banking Law advanced money without security by the hundreds of thousands to men of prominence and by the thousands to their humble followers."

Germany was also involved in the Argentine crisis, a total of over $88,000,000 worth of Argentine securities having been floated in Germany. It was this period of heavy investments and establishing branches of German banks in Argentine that was later reflected in the World War when German interests succeeded in keeping the moral influence of Argentine on the side of Germany. Germany recovered from the Argentine crisis very quickly, the rate of discount at the Reichsbank reaching only 5½ per cent.

France was scarcely affected by the catastrophe. It was many years before conditions in the Argentine Republic returned to normal and her business recovered its balance.

The first shock of the crisis of 1893 was felt in Australia, where great headway had been made and people were fast piling up wealth, based mostly, however, on highly inflated valuations. The United States was next, and from here the shock was communicated to Berlin and Vienna. Italy was also affected by the prevailing distrust and France saw her importations shrink from 4,767,867,000 francs ($920,000,-000) in 1891 to 3,936,720,000 francs ($760,000,000) in 1893. Even Turkey suffered in the widespread depression because of the fall in prices and lessened demand for her

products. In no country, however, was depression felt
as badly as in the United States.

The collapse of business in Australia in 1893 was one of
the most severe ever recorded in any country. Large sums
of capital had been poured into that country from Europe
and the natives made the mistake of thinking it was a part
of the accumulation of their own wealth. This year, when
the time came to pay interest, difficulties were faced. The
Australian banks were plunged deeply into land loans which
could not quickly earn returns, and as Europe was no longer
willing to send new money to take the place of the interest
withdrawn, serious stringency was created. The signal of
the actual crash came on January 29th, when the Federal
Bank of Melbourne failed. The other banks attempted to
create the impression that this failure was due anyhow and
simply cleared the atmosphere and left the others still
stronger, but withdrawal of deposits began against all banks
and one after another stopped payment, among them the
English and Australian Bank, with 91 branches, and the
London Charter Bank with 58 branches. Altogether fourteen large institutions failed with aggregate deposits of
£85,000,000.

England again felt derangement in business in 1895,
following the inflation of the Boer War. The war had
drained Britain, and her consols declined to such an extent
that the Government was sorely puzzled. The depression
was not lengthy, however, and in two years business had recovered its stride. The German industrial crisis of 1901
probably was confined to that country. Our crisis of 1903
followed this industrial upheaval in Germany and the one in
England in 1902.

Turkey has been very backward in modern business,
although she has experienced periods of prosperity and
depression along with other countries. Turkey's people are
very suspicious and distrustful, and do not like paper money.
In 1894 some counterfeit bank notes were found in circulation and a rush was made on the Imperial Ottoman Bank

to redeem the notes, a total of $1,000,000 being presented within a week.

In 1907 the Imperial Bank of Germany was put to a severe test, not merely as a reflex of the crisis of the United States, but of the pressure from excessive demands at home, due to expansion and speculation. The commerce of Austria was particularly affected in this crisis. In 1907 the Bank of Spain was the only institution in Europe that did not raise its discount rate. That year the Bank of France sent part of its gold to London to counteract the effects of the American crisis.

Japan led the recent depression when her financial panic broke in May, 1920. This spread to one country after another until the whole civilized world was in the throes of depression with the possible exception of defeated Germany.

Europe felt the depression about as much as did the United States. Great Britain had more men out of employment in proportion to population. The stagnation was felt throughout the world, the Orient and South America being particularly affected, and Scandinavia and Denmark suffered seriously. France was less affected than any other country in Europe. Germany stimulated an artificial prosperity which may finally end in utter collapse. In Holland most trading companies suffered heavy losses, and only by the most conservative administration kept their capital intact. The Dutch banks were generally wise enough to keep ample reserves from their years of enormous profits to tide over the period and no important failures were reported. Denmark's trade was severely depressed because of German competition. Other Scandinavian countries suffered from the same conditions. The shipping of the North European countries was badly affected. The unemployment in these countries took on a serious aspect, presenting a problem of grave proportions, the paper, textile, glass and shoe industries of the Scandinavian countries being particularly affected by German competition. A very notable change began in 1921, when England took the first steps to gain

control of its war-time currency notes. The minimum of
£368,200,000 outstanding in December, 1920, had been reduced to £316,000,000, or nearly 15 per cent during the
year. The paper money issues of the Bank of France, which
in November, 1920, were 39,600,000,000 francs, had been
reduced 2,500,000,000 francs within ten months. Considering how gradual the process of currency contraction has
been in the past, this certainly was a remarkable achievement.

The financial chaos was so widespread that cancellation
of international debts was seriously discussed in all countries. Along this line Alexander D. Noyes, financial editor
of the New York Times, recently said: "England was
declared to be on the road to ruin half a dozen times during
the century of costly wars which ended with the Battle of
Wataerloo. . . . France was declared 'economically
ruined' three times within two centuries. She had not only
been depleted of men and treasure by the disastrous cam-
paigns of Louis XIV., of Napoleon, and of the Franco-Prussian war, but on all three occasions she lost, like Germany,
great portions of her national domain. France paid so-
called impossible indemnities. History after 1720 and 1815
and 1871 is an open book."

CHAPTER V

DEPRESSIONS OF THE COLONIAL PERIOD

Religious persecution has probably been played up too much by historians as influencing the colonization of America. It was economic distress prevailing in Europe and the efforts of men to get a living, more than any other one thing, that caused immigrants to come to America. This country offered a great attraction to the industrious settler, who was assured an independent existence owing to the great quantity of free land to be had practically for the asking. Capital was not required to finance agriculture as is the case today, for the reason that the pioneer with little or no money could set itself up and earn a living from the very beginning.

In the earliest times, since there was no paper money, credit was not easily inflated. Gold and silver were fairly scarce, so that very little business was done in money transaction, and fortunate was the colonist who could get hold of enough specie to buy necessary tools brought over from Europe. Barter was resorted to and certain staple commodities were declared by law to be legal tender in payment of debts. Furthermore, a jail sentence was imposed upon debtors so that the borrower measured well his prospects for payment before going in debt.

The first money of the early colonies was wampum, the currency the Indians used, but it was found inadequate for the growing needs. While wampum money was nothing but white and black beads made from shells, yet it had a definite value the same as gold or silver money have. It was not fiat money, as is generally supposed, because it was redeemable among the Indians in beaver skins and these had a definite, stable value in Europe. The decline of the beaver trade brought wampum money into disrepute.

When it ceased to be exchangeable in large sums for an article of international trade the basis of its value was gone.

While in these pioneer times there were periods of keen distress, there were no long continued and widespread depressions such as we began to experience later, because there was little speculation and over-production. Overproduction was impossible when the producer lived next door to the consumer and knew his wants. Even the manufacturer, who was the country shoemaker and village blacksmith, knew exactly how many pairs of shoes the townspeople would want and how many plows the farmers would need.

There must have been at least a financial stringency in the year 1649 when a student at Harvard, later president of the college, "settled his bill with 'an old cow,' and the accounts of the construction of the first college building include the entry, 'Received, a goat 30s. plantation of Watertown, which died.' " As the population of the colonies grew wider business relations became necessary, and with it came a demand for capital with which to develop the latent resources of the country. This agitation brought the Pine Tree Shilling, which was designed to take the place of the Spanish coins in circulation and to serve in the place of "country pay," which was simply an exchange of farm commodities, the price of which was set by the town judge or in similar manner. The coinage of Pine Tree Shillings was started in 1652, but this coin soon depreciated in value and their minting was stopped by order of the Crown in 1684.

At various times the colonies were depressed by acts of the English government, which gave trade and industry severe setbacks. In 1651 it was enacted that the colonies should export only to England such products as they had to sell and that they should send them only in English built ships. "In 1697 the exportation of wool yarn, or woolen manufactures, to any place whatever was prohibited. In 1719 the House of Commons condemned all American manufactures as tending to independence. In 1732 the exportation of hats was forbidden; and in 1750 rolling mills, iron furnaces, and forges were declared nuisances to be suppressed by the colonial governors."

According to Hinsdale: "The finest pine trees in the forests were marked with the 'broad arrow,' denoting that they had been selected as masts for the King's ships, and that they must not be cut by the lumbermen. Even Lord Chatham said that in a probable contingency he would not allow the colonists to make a hobnail." The year 1666 was a year of greatly depressed trade which was so bad that the colonies of Maryland, Virginia and Carolina made a treaty under which they all agreed to stop planting tobacco for one year in order to raise the price.

The first general depression which swept through the colonies as a whole, so far as records show, was in 1669. "The glorious revolution' of that year did not bring the results that the people had wished, although a new charter had been won, but the friction between colonial and home government almost immediately became greater than ever, because many of the most pressing needs of the colonists were ignored, and the Americans felt obliged to help themselves. The business situation in the colonies was worse than it had been for a long time. Indian troubles at home and wars in Europe interfered with commerce and the help they should have had from England did not come. Moreover, the West Indies, with which the colonies had so much to do, were far from prosperous. The people of the Massachusetts Bay Colony were the first to devise a scheme to remedy the money troubles; they believed that if these could be helped, the commercial situation could not fail to improve. The immediate cause of the legislation was the scarcity of money and the necessity of meeting the expenses of the wars with the Indians. An issue of paper money was authorized, the first on the Western Continent, as a means of relief.

"In 1683 an extraordinary series of occurrences grew out of the low prices of tobacco. Many people signed petitions for a cessation of planting for one year for the purpose of increasing the price. As the request was not granted, they banded themselves together and went through the country destroying tobacco plants wherever found."

Another big depression occurred in 1690. Massachusetts issued paper money to put out an expedition against Quebec. Bills of credit were issued to the amount of $40,000, which sum was used mainly to pay the soldiers. The movement was frustrated and this money also depreciated in value until it was brought up to par by the governor of the colony making it legal tender for taxes. New York and Pennsylvania soon followed in issuing paper currency. Later Rhode Island, Connecticut and New Hampshire resorted to this expedient and finally the southern colonies. By 1750 the paper money of Massachusetts had depreciated to one-half of its face value in silver. The country was flooded with issues of twelve distinct colonies, resulting in hopeless confusion. General business depression followed. There were few banks then, and those that did exist were private in character and under no governmental regulation or control whatever. A pamphleteer of 1690 said, "Silver in New England is like the water of a swift running river—always coming and as fast going away."

In 1710 trade was adversely affected in the Province of Virginia, and there was much hardship on account of the confusion of coins in circulation. Such heavy discounts were exacted that "the General Assembly fixed the value of the coins of Peru, Mexico, Portugal, Flanders and other countries, and made the penalty for refusal to take them a loss of the debt. It was even necessary to enact a similar law to save the copper coins of the mother country from ruinous discount."

In 1714 John Colman, a merchant of Boston, proposed a scheme for the establishment of a bank as a "remedy for the existing embarrassment of trade." All colonies issued paper money, and they all suffered from the results.

In 1722 a notable industrial depression swept the colony of Pennsylvania. There was little currency and great discouragement. The people had no money with which to buy, shops were deserted and many people were leaving Philadelphia. The farmers' crops were reduced to the lowest value. "All the European goods imported, as well as the bread and flour or country produce, were bought up and engrossed at a low price by a cabal of only four or five rich men, who retailed them again on credit at what rate they pleased, taking advantage of the people's necessities and circumstances. By this means they soon got the whole country into their debt, exacting bonds of everybody at 8 per cent."

The year 1740 is another one of marked depression. That was the year of the legislation in England against the colonies issuing paper money. The depreciation was so great that every department of business and industry was affected. (That year sterling exchange in Massachusetts was quoted at 550).

Pelathiah Webster, a merchant of Philadelphia, writing about conditions which existed in 1741, said: "We have suffered more from this than from every other cause of calamity; it has killed more men, pervaded and corrupted the choicest interests of our country more, and done more injustice than even the arms and artifices of our enemies."

A pamphlet of 1743 speaks of the bills of credit in New England issued on loan "to themselves, Members of the Legislature, and to other Borrowers, their Friends, at easy and fallacious Lays, to be repaid at very long Periods; and by their provincial Laws made a Tender in all Contracts, Trade and Business, whereby Currencies, various and illegal, have been introduced which from their continued and depreciated nature in the Course of many years have much oppressed Widows and Orphans and all other Creditors."

In 1748 New England again sent an expedition against Louisburg, a fortress on the Island of Cape Breton. The expedition was successful, but again too much paper money was issued and depression followed when it depreciated ten to one. This was the last paper money issued until the Revolution, as Parliament had already voted to enforce the "Bubble Act" in the colonies, which prohibited the issuance of paper money. Despite their experience, the colonies liked paper money. It was demanded in all colonies and all made the error of issuing too great an abundance. Naturally, this led to depressions when periodical house-cleaning of finances came around. Much of the paper was never redeemed, being a total loss to the holders. All through our history we have had a peculiarity that stands out among all the nations of the world in that paper money was always popular with us. The denial of the right to make paper money was not the least of the grievances which led to the Revolution. One of the first things the Continental Congress did was to authorize an issue of paper money. Long before Cornwallis surrendered to Washington at Yorktown "continental paper money had depreciated to the value of 75 to 1, and during the formation of the Union fell to 1000 to 1 and then expired, but the people, satisfied with gaining their freedom, suffered the result without a murmur."

The years preceding the Revolution found no organized activities in our banking or industrial system. An economic depression prevailed during the decade prior to the Revolution. This was due to the fact that the colonies depended largely on foreign trade for their prosperity, which was adversely affected by the enforcement of the unpopular English measures and from the colonies' retaliatory policy of non-importation. The depression of this period was accentuated by the "Sugar Act," which practically destroyed the lucrative business of rum distilling in New England, together with other branches of the trade connected with it. Dissatisfaction over existing conditions lurked in every corner, and a large element of the people inflamed by "hard-times" agitators, ranged in a body on the side of the Revolution. This depression set in in 1764 and lasted through to the outbreak of the Revolution. It had more to do with the Revolution than has ever been recorded in history.

The Colonists had outlived the barter days of their early history. They demanded a medium of money exchange outside of the English specie, distribution of which was controlled from the other side of the water. There is no doubt but that the English government aided in bringing about the depressed economic conditions because of the spirit of revolt that was growing in America. England naturally did not want the Colonies to build up a monetary system of their own. It might later be used to finance a revolution; therefore the decree against the issue of colonial paper money. Students of economic history agree that the plan on which this paper money was issued was financially sound in principle, which fact cemented some of the more conservative element with the radicals. When the war broke out the Colonists had been through a long period of depression. They had no accumulation of wealth to fall back on and no system of money of their own with which to finance the conflict. The Continental Congress was only an emergency body with little authority and no compelling power, yet at the beginning of hostilities this congress authorized the first issue of paper money to an amount equivalent to two million pounds. A total of $241,552,780 of this paper money was issued. As the amount was so enormous for those times, and greatly in excess of the actual needs of the people, the different states failed to support their credit and the bills began early and rapidly to depreciate. The Continental paper dollar fell to the value of two or three cents in silver, and at that time an expression synonymous of utter worthlessness, "Not worth a continental" was started—an expression that we still hear to this day.

Thus did our colonial ancestors experience these cycles of business in their repeating monotony, the same as we of the Twentieth Century.

CHAPTER VI

CRISES, PANICS AND DEPRESSIONS DEFINED

In our national history there has been twenty-one major business depressions. In addition, there have been nu-erous local disturbances or temporary setbacks that might be classed as minor depressions. Those described in this book, however, are the ones which carried business below the normal line as shown by official statistics. Various writers, sometimes for a particluar end, have ascribed certain depressions to certain years, but the unfailing truth of statistics does not bear them out. Some claim that we had business depressions in such years as 1867, 1882 and 1900, but the most authoritative statistics show them to be normal years.

Our eagerness to make progress, and our constantly increasing population, make it sometimes appear that we are having depression when in reality statistics show that we are only standing still. When we are passing through normal times we do not seem to know it; our mind wants to tell us that we are in one state or another, either boom or depression. When times are not actually booming, we think they are depressed. Such is the American spirit.

We probably have the most severe depressions in this country because of our inane desire to make money rapidly, or in the language of the street, "to get rich quick." Therefore we take long chances, emboldened by examples which we see on every hand. We live in the only country in the world where a person can make a million over night, so to speak. A large element of our business people believe that liberality pays and that we can make money by spending money. A foreigner who visited us said we are a great people because "we spend more accidentally than we do on purpose." Our individualism leads to recklessness. Then when some untoward incident happens the bubble bursts and we are called to account by the natural order. It can be seen, however, that we are getting over our individualism to some extent. Our government is becoming more paternal, and we lean more and more on our neighbor and co-operate more extensively with our competitor. The gambling element in our business is being routed to some extent. We demand greater stability in business, and with this movement we are eliminating many panics and making depressions less violent and destructive. The ambition of the average American is in the direction of money. Money brings him power. A generation back the spectacular American would risk his last dollar on the chance to win big stakes, and when he failed he carried many others with him. In recent years there have been some changes in this procedure because the rest of us do not care to be pulled down by the gambler, and his tactics are being disclosed and discounted.

The best definition of what we call a commercial cycle is given by Lord Overstone: "A state of quiescence; improvement; growing confidence; prosperity; excitement; overtrading; convulsions; pressure; stagnation; distress; ending again in quiescence."

The progress of the world and the advancement of civilization has gone forward in rising and receding waves. The world has been afflicted with economic convulsions at periods the same as it has been with war and pestilence. The phenomenon of national or world depression may be likened to the "blues" which come over most individuals. The great writer, Defoe, in 1728 said: "The prosperity of a nation rises and falls just as trade is supported or decayed."

A panic is a sudden outbreak or fit of hysteria in financial circles. It is a frantic effort to get hold of money either by withdrawing deposits or selling securities for fear of loss.

A crisis is a brief period of acute strain and may be either financial or commercial; financially, because of a stringency in the money market and commercially, because of uncertainty from various underlying causes.

A depression is a state of lowered vitality of more or less lengthy duration in financial or commercial circles or both. Usually depression is brought about as a result of panic or crisis, although that rule is not invariable. A panic breaks suddenly, although it may have been smouldering for a long while, only waiting for a match to touch it off. A crisis is the peak of a multiplicity of troubles which have come to a head. If a crisis is not promptly and properly met, it will break out in panic, but with the proper application it will pass off without affecting the industrial structure to any great extent. Crises occur, as a rule, at the height of periods of great activity and speculation. They usually mark the close of such periods and the coming of depressions.

The literal definition of the word "depression" is: state of dullness or inactivity; a protracted season when business falls below normal. A depression is a decrease in the rate of production in wealth, both by lack of power to buy by one class and unwillingness to buy by another class.

Sometimes we recover from depression quicker when it is accompanied by a panic, because when the financial structure is threatened all the resources available to the Government are thrown into the breach and the currency is placed where it will do the most good and bring quicker relief. Where no panic accompanies depression it is often allowed to wear itself out, which is a long and painful process. Business depressions are not necessarily the outgrowth of panics or money stringency, although with few exceptions they have followed that phenomenon. In the short depression of 1914, as a recent instance, there was neither panic nor money stringency, but purely an uncertainty which prevailed on account of the outbreak of the European war. A crisis often marks the culmination or turning point from expansion to liquidation and accompanying depression. It is the result of the use or abuse of capital leading to exhaustion of funds. Webster describes crisis in this manner: "The point of time when it is decided whether any affair or course of action must go on or be modified or terminate; a state in which a decisive change one way or the other is impending; specifically, a time of difficulty, danger and suspense in commerce or finance."

An essayist on the subject says: "Unless new resources are placed in the breach crisis will lead to panic. In 1907 the United States Treasury was too late in coming to the rescue of the New York banks, which caused a panic. The crisis of that year occurred several months before the panic broke in October."

A crisis is something we will always have, but with proper legal and economic safeguards provided, the danger can be avoided through the same process as the signal system on a railroad. We should have reached a station now where we can safeguard against panics by being prepared for such crises as unlooked for conditions might bring about. While there can be crises without panic, there can be neither crises nor panics without depression, either local or general.

Panics do not necessarily bring general depression. We have had many panics that have passed away without affecting more than the financial centers, and these only temporarily. Some of them never got on the first page of the newspapers. As to whether or not a panic will lead to depression depends upon whether its force has broken the credit structure. If the prosperity phase of the cycle has not run its course, and inflation has not reached its height, a panic will have little effect on business in general. If, however, it happens at a time when inflation and speculation have run rampant, and the elasticity of credit has reached its limit, then depression will result because there are no resources at hand to stem the evil effects.

The depressions of 1837, 1857, 1869, 1873, 1893 and 1907 started with panics. Such depressions as 1809, 1819, 1847, 1914, 1920 were not accompanied by panics, although they set in following crises.

From medical science we learn that anything that stimu-
ulates the heart will bring an indirect reaction. The same
may be said of our economic life.

Bagehot expresses it well: "At intervals . . . the
blind capital of a country is particularly large and craving;
it seeks for some one to devour it, and there is 'plethora;'
it finds some one, and there is 'speculation'; it is devoured,
and there is panic."

Panics, crises and depressions are often interlocked. Back
of the entire structure of business, however, is money, and
some details of money panics and crises here are given when
they are directly responsible for the depression of the
period.   Only those panics directly bearing on trade depressions are recorded here.   England has had no panic
since 1866, although she has had a number of severe and protracted industrial depressions. Not even the Baring failure
of 1890 caused a panic.

Men writing of their day unanimously say that the people
were in much better condition to withstand the shock of the
depression about which they wrote than were those of previous times.   This shows that as the decades go by we have
at least made some progress in softening the blow, spreading the periods of frequency and preparing resources to
withstand the strain.   Depressions run their course in all
countries. France particularly suffered from depressions
at the end of the Eighteenth and beginning of the Nineteenth Centuries. Had we not declared our independence
when we did, it is doubtful whether we would have received
any help from France. After her war with England, which
was raging during our revolutionary period, France's
finances were in such a condition as a result of a terrific
depression that it is a practical certainty she would have
been unable to render us any help whatever.

All writers agree that the most severe depressions occur
in countries whose business is highly developed, and this is
obviously true because there is more money in circulation,
more commodities and securities changing hands and, there-

fore, more possibility for wide fluctuation. In the older countries, such as France, Germany and Italy, depressions have been less violent than in America, which was new and on a more speculative basis. For one hundred and fifty years previous to 1844 England experienced the most desperate panics. Her money then was placed on a sound basis and the government practically took control of the Bank of England. They have not suspended specie payment since that time.

In the world-wide depression of 1920 Japan was the only important country that experienced an actual old-fashioned panic. This was no doubt because of the fact that her finan‧ cial system lacked a sound basis and her inflation was so extraordinary that a panic was inevitable when the turn came. A country in a state of rapid development is more exposed to fluctuations than an older country whose values have become stabilized over a long period of years.

Consular reports, as filed with the Department of Commerce in Washington, reveal business depressions in every country at different times, or at the same time. Business depressions usually follow the accumulation of idle capital in the banks in the form of deposits, the swelling of the cash reserves, and the reduction of commercial loans.

Newton believed that the voluntary actions of men en masse are subject to the Law of Action and Reaction. Says a contemporary: "We look upon a mob as the last thing which would work in accordance with scientific law, but psychologists tell us that the mob is one of the best illustrations of Newton's Law of Action and Reaction."

There is more in that than one would credit on first thought. ✓Men's minds follow the spirit of the times, but what creates that spirit often requires deep study to ascertain. We know that we have the phenomena of political uprisings, racial upheavals, the rise and passing of social fads or fashions. These pass away and oftentimes look foolish to us afterward. The phenomenon of the business cycle affects our minds in the same way. When a spirit of prosperity prevails, people's minds run in that direction and they are entirely over-sanguine. Then the tide turns, they lose confidence, and all people talk about is disaster. We saw a perfect example of this in 1920. There was no panic, no untoward incident, but a variety of small local conditions that started men talking hard times. Early in 1920 the highest peak had been reached; buyers were determined that they would not pay the exorbitant prices asked. It therefore was to their interest to talk hard times and predict depression so as to bear the market. This may not have been a major cause of the depression, but it all had its psychological effect and spread rapidly, and actual conditions followed the thoughts that were in the minds of the people.

Waves have come over the United States that historians now look back upon and find almost inexplicable. They simply must be attributed to a state of mind, a mania that existed at the time. Admittedly, if we have these periodical social phenomena, there may be something to the claim that we can have economic phenomena as a result of a peculiar state of mind. We can readily see where theorists have some foundation to stand on when they point out that nature is in itself a succession of waves. The tides of the ocean have never been explained; epidemics appear and reappear; religions take hold of people and die out. Who can explain the Salem witchcraft, if it was not purely a craze that temporarily affected the minds of the people? How can we account for the waves of resentment that swept our country in its early years, at one time against the Quakers, again against the Baptists, still later the Anti-Masonic outbreaks, the "Know-Nothings," the Ku-Klux Klan, or Anti-Catholic movements? Such phemomena have swept through our history from time to time; they could not be explained at the time and have never been explained since. But business and financial panics are not altogether the result of fear or a state of mind. There are deep underlying conditions which must be met by real action.

It has been a practice since the days of the Mississippi Bubble to legislate against business depression, and from time to time legislation has helped. Hard times will almost invariably turn a poltical party out of power. Statesmen have repeatedly promised on the stump relief from distress, and after getting into office have taken the stand that economic conditions could not be changed by legislation.

In times past economists have gone to a great deal of trouble in writing books and articles on the causes of depression, and many were quite sure that they had found the seat of all the trouble. Today, causes they attributed are entirely removed and yet we still have depressions. A century and a quarter ago Adam Smith insisted that the production and importation and exportation of corn was the one controlling barometer of business. He said, "the money price of corn regulates that of all other home-made commodities."

In my opinion, Ricardo, himself a successful business man, wrote far better on economic questions than Adam Smith, whose admittedly classic works are the bible of theoretical economists.

History indicates that we have a general depression on an average of every nine or ten years, some more severe than others. Sandwiched in between, about every five years, there has been a minor depression or temporary setback. Statistics prove that business has never remained below normal for more than three years, and, on an average, only a year and a half. While production is shown not to remain below normal for more than this average, it may remain at normal for three or four years, after which time great upward strides are made and a boom usually sets in.

Our panics have usually occurred in the Fall of the year when finances are ordinarily strained on account of crop-moving demands. The crises of 1837, 1847, 1857, 1873, 1890 and 1907 all occurred in the Fall. The minor crises nearly all occurred in the Spring, breaking out in March and May. It stands to reason that there is no accurate regularity as to the time of arrival of depressions, because if that were true safeguards could be taken that would to some extent eliminate depressions.

One of the most interesting stories bearing on this subject is that told by a Chicago real estate man, which gives the history of a quarter acre of land in the heart of Chicago. The story tells of its original value at $20.00 in 1830, when Chicago had a couple of hundred people, and how it rose and declined through the vicissitudes of boom and panic, each succeeding wave of good times carrying it higher and making it more valuable, reaching a value of $1,250,000 in the nineties and probably two or three times that today.

One early European writer referred to *America as a backward country*, giving his opinion that backward countries which produce raw material largely for export felt depressions far more than manufacturing countries. He said: "The specialization impressed upon a backward country by commerce with advanced industrial countries, confining it to growing cotton or wheat or sheep or wine, exaggerates the irregularity imposed by nature upon its productivity, by making it subservient to the fluctuating demands of distant and wholly incalculable markets."

There is no one outstanding cause of depressions, unless it be speculation, and all crises can hardly be laid to the door of this evil. We have had depressions caused by war, currency inflation, political changes, and many other causes. One panic, that of 1857, was caused largely by too much gold. This will probably be a revelation to the average citizen, because in our day we have heard so much of lack of money as a cause of depressions. The discovery of gold in California in 1848 flooded the country with great quantities of gold until it became cheap. This gold reached the East in such abundance that it brought about a development far beyond the needs of the country at the time. These new enterprises, together with needless numbers of new banks, could not pay dividends, with the result that confidence was undermined and panic ensued. However, this is the only depression on record caused by too much gold. In practically all of the others the question of too little gold entered, unless an exception might be made in the depression of 1920, when we had so much gold that the exchange rate was decidedly against us, causing us great loss of foreign trade. Periods of abundant gold have their handicaps the same as periods of lack of gold have theirs.

In classifying our depressions five can be attributed to financial panics, and these are the worst in our history. These were in 1819, 1837, 1857, 1893 and 1907. They brought the most far-reaching effects because confidence in the financial system itself was shaken. When people lose confidence in the value of the currency that is handed them in payment for labor or commodities, it takes a long time to recover. In each of these periods a new system of money had to be adopted and the old financial system reorganized.

Herbert Hoover recently said there had been fourteen depressions since the Civil War. No doubt, included in that number were some minor crises that were largely confined to Manhattan Island. The old idea that Wall Street is a barometer of the business of the country has long been exploded and, to a large extent, its manipulations have but little effect on the balance of the country.

The history of our nation has not been the steady triumphal march so often depicted, but an irregular growth interspersed with periods of depression in length equal to those of prosperity.

CHAPTER VII.

THE DEPRESSION OF 1785-89

Following the Revolutionary War, the country went through an experience similar to that following the late World War. For the three years 1782, 1783 and 1784, following peace, conditions were fairly prosperous because of the reaction from the strain, the jubilant feeling of victory, and as a result of war demands and the comparatively abundant specie left in the country by the British and French armies. But this was not to last long. The brief period of over-trading led to the depression of 1785 to 1789. The specie quickly left the country for payment of imported goods, and industry and commerce were hampered by the absence of a good monetary system.

They also suffered severely from the falling prices and the loss of the markets that were now more than adequately supplied, as regards many articles, by importations from Europe, mainly from England. Not only did peace in England and other European countries affect our exports adversely, but what wealth we had was soon spent in supplying our urgent needs from those countries.

American merchants had become embarrassed and were unable to pay for the goods they had bought on credit. The position of both producers and traders in the United States was made much worse by the closing of the British West Indies to American shipping. In 1785 the panic came. The monetary situation was deplorable, not only because the coin had been exported to pay for imported goods, but also from the fact that the Confederation had no authority to coin money and to establish a uniform system of currency.

Politically and economically that was the gravest crisis in American history. Both the government and the people were bankrupt. There was no money to pay the ministers to foreign countries, and they actually had to beg the foreign governments for funds. It was made a part of their duties as envoys to solicit loans without security for their government and, incidently, for their own expenses.

Franklin attempted to borrow from France and got only insignificant sums. France was having her own economic troubles that year, which were brought to a climax by bad crops and the scarcity of metallic money.

A petition addressed to Congress by the tradesmen and manufacturers of the town of Baltimore represented the sentiment of the manufacturing sections of the country:

"Since the close of the late war, and the completion of the Revolution, they have observed with serious regret the manufacturing and the trading interest of the country rapidly declining, and the attempts of the State Legislatures to remedy the evil failing of their object; that, in the present melancholy state of our country, the number of poor increasing for the want of employment, foreign debts accumulating, houses and lands depreciating in value, and trade and manufactures languishing and expiring, they look up to the Supreme Legislature of the United States as the guardian of the whole empire, and from their united wisdom and patriotism, and ardent love of their country, expect to derive that aid and assistance which alone can dissipate their just apprehensions, and animate them with hopes of success in future, by imposing on all foreign articles which can be made in America such duties as will give a just and decided preference to their labors; discountenancing that trade which tends so materially to injure them and impoverish their country; measures which, in their consequences, may also contribute to the discharge of the national debt and the due support of the Government."

John Jay wrote: "Our commerce was then (before the Revolution) confined to Great Britain. We were obliged to carry our commodities to her market and, consequently, sell them at her price; we were compelled to purchase foreign commodities at her stores and on her terms, and were forbidden to establish any manufactures incompatible with her view of gain. In future the whole world will be open to us, and we shall be at liberty to purchase from those who will sell on the best terms and to sell to those who will give us the best prices."

No country is prosperous with trade balances so largely against her, and it is little wonder that American business suffered at this period with a heavy trade balance against her. During this period, known as the Industrial Revolution in England, that country had come into possession of many marvelous inventions which gave her an advantage over our manufacturers in producing cheaply.

It was during this period of depression that the first effort was made on behalf of the distressed "Infant Industries" to secure a protective tariff against foreign competition. The second act passed by Congress under the new constitution on July 4, 1789, opens with the preamble, "Whereas, it is necessary for the support of the government, for the discharge of the debts of the United States, and for the encouragement and protection of manufacturers that duties be laid on goods and wares and merchandise imported locally." Thus was the beginning of protection for the express purpose of "encouragement and protection of manufacturers."

The country was flooded with foreign goods, largely from England. The industrial isolation during the war, as well as the demand for material for sustaining the army and navy, gave a decided stimulus to the struggling manufacturers of the colonies. Many iron works and other manufacturers were called into existence, and in some cases were given encouragement by a system of bonuses. Upon the resumption of imports these industries suffered immediate and disastrous setbacks. Many were not firmly established and were forced out of existence. In 1784 the imports from England amounted to £3,679,000 and in 1785 to £2,308,000. These goods largely took the place of those manufactured in the states during the war. To make matters worse, the exports fell off proportionately to a large extent, as against an average of £1,045,000 dur-

ing the ten-year period before the war they dropped to
£749,000 in 1784 and to £894,000 in 1785.

Following the war, starting in 1781, in spite of previous
disastrous experience, seven of the states again plunged
into the issuing of paper money. This money, of course,
depreciated in value to almost nothing, and, in fact, this
depreciation helped the already depressed conditions, and
the resentment was such that when the Constitution was
adopted, the emission of bills of credit as legal tender by the
states was forbidden and an end was put to the issue of
government paper money for seventy years. The loss of
the West India trade amounted to £1,537,664. This was
caused by an Act of Parliament which excluded American
vessels from the West Indian trade, by admitting only
British built and manned vessels. The economic prosperity
of the states depended largely upon our trade with the
West Indies, and its loss was a third important factor in the
depression of that period. Such were the stagnant conditions of business in the states at that time that it is little
wonder that predictions were freely made in England that
the new government would never survive. The Revolution
was primarily a struggle for commerce, and tactics of Great
Britain through trade and navigation laws largely destroyed
our foreign commerce for some years after independence
was won.

In 1787 a Philadelphia man came into possession of two
carding and spinning machines which were supposed to
save the labor of one hundred and twenty men a day. These
machines were purchased by an agent of a British manufacturer and shipped back to Liverpool, the object being to
nip American manufacturing in the bud.

Bolles says: "The hostility to American manufacturing
was manifested in another way during the same period.
Experiments were then rife for introducing the cotton-plant
into the country. Whether the English manufacturer at
that early day foresaw the adaptation of the plant to the
climate and soil, we do not know, but, with the vain hope of

destroying its cultivation, and preventing its manufacture, a considerable quantity of cotton-seed was purchased and burned in Virginia by a British agent. The same spirit continued for years, and was exhibited in many unexpected and exasperating ways to the American manufacturer."

"It is notorious," says Niles, "that immediately after the close of the Revolutionary War great sums of money were expended to destroy our flocks of sheep and ruin our rising manufacturers. They bought up and immediately slaughtered great numbers of that useful animal, and spared no expense to send 'home' the few artisans who had struggled hither, with their machines and implements of trade."

The depreciated Continental currency augmented the demoralization of business. The immense profits that were anticipated from Independence were far from realized. The non-intercourse with foreign countries during the war had involved merchants and shipbuilders in financial embarrassment. Independence placed us outside the British Navigation Act and deprived us of the commercial advantages hitherto accorded American vessels in British ports, so that, in addition to our depreciated currency and lack of a definite financial foundation, we were faced with the problem of building anew our foreign trade.

European manufacturers accumulated stocks which they were ready to dispose of at 25 per cent below London prices in order to regain their American trade. "Ships filled with sail duck and linen from Holland and Russia, muslins and silks from India and China, thronged our ports and found eager buyers among the wealthy Americans who had been deprived of these luxuries during the war. Such a trade balance of $18,397,335 worth of imports against $3,746,725 worth of exports was bound to bring depression because the difference had to be made good in gold and silver, which could not be spared."

The feature of the depression of this period, with its attendant economic chaos, was the emigration of people from the seaboard over the mountains into the Central West, where a cheap living and a new start in life were possible.

That the laborer should take advantage of this situation to better his lot in a new country was only natural. This is in direct contrast to the depressions of the later part of the Nineteenth Century, when the reverse was the rule: the new settlers of the newer parts of the West finding no market for their products and the mortgages threatening foreclosure returned to their old homes in the East, where they were among friends and relatives. The migration westward had a beneficial effect in aiding depressed conditions, by bringing about a scarcity of skilled labor and other wage earners. Those remaining began to receive increased pay. This condition was confined almost entirely to the North. The agriculturists of both the North and the South were able to produce or secure the necessities of life, the standard of living being low. There were few of extreme wealth and few in extreme poverty.

The payment of bounties was one of the means adopted in different states to aid industry and trade to recover from the depression. "New York gave liberal bounties on hemp; New Jersey gave similar assistance to wool, flax and hemp; Maryland encouraged salt production, and Georgia assisted the producers of hemp, flax and wheat."

Fiske describes conditions in his Critical Periods of American History: "The War of Secession (Revolution) was a terrible ordeal to pass through, but when one tries to picture what might have happened in this fair land without the work of the Federal Convention the imagination stands aghast. Certainly it cannot be too strongly insisted that the winning of the Revolutionary War did not establish the liberties of the American people; it merely cleared the path for their establishment."

The depression of the period was a large element in the ratification of the Constitution. There was a strong paper money partly in all of the states who feared that if the states were federated they would not be permitted to issue paper money. In reading the history of debates in the different states on the question of ratification, it is noted that the principal point at issue was the best means to relieve the existing distress. New York ratified because she feared economic pressue from New Jersey and Connecticut. Delaware was the first to ratify because she had a big trade with Philadelphia. But it was still a serious question whether the Union would ever be perfected because of the attitude of Virginia, which finally ratified by a very narrow vote. There was a strong movement in Virginia to withdraw from the Confederation and join Spain through an alliance, as shown in a letter from Wilkinson to Governor Miro, of Louisiana: "I can give you the solemn assurance that I found all the men belonging to the first class of society in the district, with the exception of Colonel Marshall, our surveyor, and Colonel Muter, one of our judges, decidedly in favor of separation from the United States and of alliance with Spain."

New Hampshire demurred from ratification for some time on the paper money issue, as shown from the following extract:

"There are perhaps (if it could be impartially known), three-quarters at least, and more likely seven-eights of the people so fractious and discontented as to wish paper money on loan may be made by government to give a spring to commerce and agriculture . . . extreme disorders require extreme medicines as their remedies. Paper money, or even leather buttons, when stamped by authority and funded with realities, will answer for internal commerce as well as silver and gold."

New Hampshire furnished quite a number of men for Shay's Rebellion.

Further borrowing at home or abroad was almost impossible; requisitions were of slight avail; domestic creditors were thoroughly alarmed. Furthermore, the depression lasted much longer than was expected. The hopes of the new states were very slow in being realized. It was the economic stress of the times that prompted Alexander Hamilton to start gathering statistics for his memorable report on manufactures. Had it not been for the genius of

Hamilton the commercial future of our country would have been dark indeed. Hamilton took hold and established a reasonably sound financial system which gained the confidence of the business communities, and industry was helped to regain its feet. It required ten years to get our industries on any kind of a stable basis and start a general upward trend.

Before the war the fishing industry had given employment to the largest number of people, but it was virtually destroyed, and the people who had formerly depended upon it for their livelihood were reduced to destitution and misery.

"For a time the coastwise trade prospered, but before long, in common with the other branches of trade, it experienced a severe depression. Credit everywhere was impaired, there was little money, and the various states, jealous and fearful of the commercial prosperity of one another, began to erect barriers that crippled the commerce of all. New York attempted to break up the trade of Connecticut and New Jersey by imposing heavy fees on every vessel entering from those states. Delaware and New Jersey tried to attract to their ports the foreign trade of Pennsylvania and New York by a system of legislation offering lower import duties and more favorable trade regulations. When Massachusetts and Rhode Island placed almost prohibitive duties on imports carried in British ships, Connecticut admitted such imports free, hoping to obtain a monopoly of domestic trade in British products. Several of the states imposed heavy duties on goods from all other states with the two-fold object of encouraging domestic production and of conserving the supply of coin."

In those days even the mails were of little aid to business, the postal service not having been organized on a practical basis. There were very few concerns doing a national business. Each state was a political parcel to itself, and economically so to a great degree. We can imagine the extent of intercommunication when a decade after the Constitution was adopted and the permanent government established, in the year 1801, the gross receipts from the post-office were only $32,000. "Nearly all the clothing was made in the family, as was the cloth from which it was cut. The leather was tanned and the grist ground at a near-by tannery and mill, but the boots and shoes were made by father during the long evenings of autumn." This was the business situation in those days outside of the cities which had a shipbuilding and carying trade. The general poverty, therefore, was felt and described as a general scarcity of money.

A writer of the day said: "Many are willing to buy and pay fair prices, but they have no money; they cannot borrow it, although they have large stocks of goods to hypothecate."

While there was plenty of specie immediately after the war, prices were abnormally high, which of itself indicated a scant supply and accompanying poverty. Outside of land wealth the colonists had been largely drained, and toward the end of the war, and perhaps two years after, we had more specie wealth than anything else. John Marshall, describing the situation at that time, said:

"The discontent and uneasiness, arising in a great measure from embarrassments in which a considerable number of individuals were involved, continued to become more extensive. At length two great parties were formed in every state which were distinctly marked, and which pursued distinct objects with systematic arrangement. The one struggled with unabated zeal for the exact observance of public and private engagements. The other party marked out for itself a more indulgent course; viewing with extreme tenderness the case of the debtor, their efforts were unceasingly directed for his relief. They were uniformly in favor of retarding the administration of justice; of affording facilities for the payment of debts; or of suspending their collection and remitting of taxes."

Mass meetings were held, radical speeches were made, and complaint was general. There was particularly an under-current of agitation against the extortion of lawyers, who profited from suits against debtors, pauperizing many for their own gain. It was charged that salaries of public officials in Boston and the State of Massachusetts were unreasonably high, and that taxes due in 1786 in that state were estimated to amount to nearly a third of the income of the people.

All this had its culmination in the outbreak of Shay's Rebellion, which involved a total estimated at 12,000 to 15,000 men recruited from Massachusetts, largely, and augmented by men from Rhode Island, Connecticut and New Hampshire. This nondescript army was composed of the ignorant in their respective communities, who imagined their condition might be bettered by fighting, although they knew not how. It could not be said that taxes fell heavily upon these men because they were generally not property owners, but men who felt the pinch of poverty and entertained the idea that their new liberties meant license. The Massachusetts Gazette in 1787 published the following letter from New York City: "This morning the Governor, the Attorney General, Adjutant, etc., set out for Albany to take measures to quell any insurrection that may happen in that quarter. The Legislature of this State are decided in preventing any adherents from joining the Shays, but there are a great proportion of people who are ripe for confusion and war. This is because they are so embarrassed in their affairs that they believe no disturbances can make them worse."

No doubt they complained most against the extravagance of officials. The rebellion was soon put down, however, and before long had passed into history. The depression gradually cleared away. The nation grew and prospered to such an extent that the children of those who took part in Shay's Rebellion became some of the wealthiest families in New England.

Under conditions existing at that time there could be nothing else but depression. There was no legal money and no central government. Trade of every kind was awaiting the adoption of the Federal Constitution, which went into operation in 1789. The Constitution gave the Federal Government the exclusive right to coin money, and as soon as the Government began to function the First Bank of United States was chartered in 1791, under a charter granted by Congress. Business then began to take on a better aspect.

CHAPTER VIII.

THE DEPRESSION OF 1808-09.

The new republic of the United States of America had become well established when the depression of 1808-09 came on. Washington and Adams had both served as President and retired, and Jefferson was at the head of the government. This depression followed a period of great prosperity. In 1793 war broke out between France and England and involved all the nations of Europe. For over twenty years the best energies were devoted to destruction and warfare. This was America's day. While England was sweeping French merchantmen off the seas American shipbuilding showed an enormous expansion. France, who was hard pressed, bitterly resented the fact that America would not enter the war as her ally, claiming that we had agreed to make common cause against Great Britain in return for the help she had rendered us twenty years previous. Against the generally accepted view, this nation did at one time enter into a foreign alliance. This was with France, made in 1778, but in the year 1798 Congress abrogated this treaty and never since then have we entered into any alliance whatsoever with any foreign power. It was in this period that America practically was master of the seas so far as merchant carying trade was concerned. There was a large and steady demand for our agricultural products among the belligerent countries. Our foreign trade increased fourfold in a decade. It was a situation very similar to that which existed during the recent World War. America captured the trade in the western hemisphere of most of the countries at war, and by the time the struggle was over American shipping tonnage exceeded that of any other nation except England. The temporary check in 1802 during a short peace in Europe gave our commerce a slight setback, but at the outbreak of hostilities, in 1803, commerce expanded until in 1807 it amounted to $138,500,000 in imports and $108,300,000 in exports. Pitkin says, "the increase in American tonnage during this period has no comparison in commercial annals of the world."

The depression that followed set in in 1808 and lasted through 1809, starting as the result of various Orders in Council and Napoleon's decrees which were directed against the neutral trade, largely American. Our shipping felt the full force of the British blockade and the retaliatory measures taken by the French. About sixteen hundred American vessels and $60,000,000 worth of property were captured by France, England and other privateers. Jefferson recommended to Congress that an embargo be placed on American shipping or, as he expressed it, "immediate inhibition of departure of our shipping to ports outside of the United States." This had a far-reaching effect on the business of the country. The announcement of the embargo came almost without notice and caused a violent shock to business, which was paralyzed for a period. In a single year our exports fell from $108,300,000 to $22,400,000, far greater proportionately and much more abruptly than any cessation of business known in our history. Quoting from an article written shortly after this period, "in the large shipping towns business of every kind fell off and soon utterly ceased. Rope walks were deserted, sail makers were idle, shipwrights and draymen had scarcely anything to do. Pitch and tar, hemp and flour, bacon, salt fish, flax seed became drugs upon the shippers' hands, but the greatest sufferers of all were the sailors." It was estimated at the time that 30,000 seamen, an enormous army of people at that time, were thrown out of employment, and that in all 100,000 men were out of work for a year. The $50,000,000 of capital invested in American shipping brought in no revenue.

In the year 1809 customs fell from $16,300,000 to $7,200,-000 and the Secretary of the Treasury, Mr. Gallatin, was forced for the first time to confront a deficit of $1,300,000.

Prices of foreign commodities doubled, while prices of domestic goods fell below cost of production. Lumbermen and fishermen were reduced to beggary, and farmers unable to dispose of their produce offered their lands for sale. In New York the depression caused one hundred and twenty bankruptcies and threw twelve hundred debtors into prison. Farmers, who had been buying land on credit, and who had planted great crops in expectation of foreign demand, soon began to feel the effects, and many of them, together with merchants depending upon them, were forced into failure and bankruptcy. This depression was brought on entirely because of stoppage of trade with the outside world. Local conditions entered very little into it.

When our ships were idle British merchants were capturing the West Indian and South American trade. Gibbins in his "Economic and Industrial Progress of the Century" tells that more Manchester goods were shipped to South America in a few weeks than in twenty years preceding, and the quantity of English exports that poured into the city of Rio de Janeiro was so great that warehouses could not be provided sufficient to contain them. While the Continental edicts which brought on the embargo were the primary cause of the depression and caused great resentment in this country against Great Britain who enforced them—eventually leading to war with that country—yet it is generally overlooked that France originated the blockading policy.

In those days debt was a crime and the jails were full of debtors. New York was described as a graveyard, so dead was its commerce, and while New York and New England were the greatest sufferers, the South and West felt the effects disastrously. The depression ended when Jefferson yielded to pressure and the embargo was repealed in 1809, after which American commerce quickly responded and our tonnage engaged in foreign trade the following year reached 981,000 tons. Those were the days known as our heyday of shipbuilding. We built fine wooden ships, an art that later passed out of existence and was not resurrected until the late war, when several hundred wooden ships were built.

The period of this depression makes what might be termed the turn from industrial dependence of the United States and the starting of manufacturing and commercialism largely as it exists today. It was at this time that we first began to realize that we were really a nation. What business we had, previously had been carried on much the same as during colonial days. The shipping depression turned the attention of both capital and labor to the development of our own country. Henceforth, we looked less and less across the waters to the eastward for our material prosperity, but rather we faced to the west, where a great empire lay ready for development after Jefferson had purchased Louisiana. In many respects the depression was a blessing in disguise. We now started to develop our own resources and get rich by trading among ourselves. We are the only nation in the history of the world that has ever been able to do this. Countries like China and Russia which, in previous centuries, largely traded among themselves became impoverished.

Mr. Gallatin, Secretary of the Treasury, in 1809, estimated the annual product of American manufacture at $120,000,000 and strongly approved of the policy of overcoming the existing depression by developing our own resources and our own markets.

Unsound banking existed in New England up to this period the same as in other sections of the country, but following the crisis the Massachusetts Legislature adopted stringent measures to correct the system and thenceforth New England banks have been the healthiest and soundest in the country in every period of trouble. They even passed through the crisis of 1814 without suspension. After a breathing spell industries again started up, and 1809 saw sixty-two new cotton mills with 31,000 spindles erected in New England and building steadily continued until the end of the European War.

CHAPTER IX

DEPRESSION OF 1814

The year 1814 records a financial flurry which might be termed a short panic. However, it was of brief duration because the war with England was on and the entire resources of the nation were of necessity thrown behind the situation. The shock was caused by the capture of Washington by the British on August 24th, 1814. So severely was it felt in financial circles that practically all the banks except those in New England were forced to suspend specie payments and the country was again put on a paper money basis. All the old evils of the Continental period began to appear— over-issue, depreciation and inequality of value. The notes of the New York banks were 10 per cent below par, those of Washington and Baltimore 22 per cent, while in the West some of them fell to as low as 50 per cent. The people were compelled to use this depreciated and fluctuating currency because there was no other to take its place. It was this crisis that led to re-establishment of the Second Bank of the United States, the First Bank of the United States having been dissolved in 1811, at which time $7,-000,000 in specie—an enormous sum for those times—was returned to Europe, this amount having been held by Europeans in the stock of the First Bank.

The military events of the war were mostly disastrous and humiliating to the United States. The outcome can be said to have been no better than a draw. It was at this time that the importance of American manufactures was forced upon the attention of the nation. Munitions of war, clothing, and articles of living had to be provided. Speculation and extortion were practiced to a large extent, high prices as usual bringing temporary prosperity, checked only by the uncertainty caused by the events of 1814.

New England had at this time "cornered" the available supply of specie. In 1814 there were $7,000,000 in specie lying in the Boston banks, while the states south and west of New England were practically stripped of metallic money. To make up for the deficiency in a circulating medium, the banks resorted to the expedient of issuing large sums of paper money. During 1814 the unfavorable turn in the fortunes of war and a sharp attack on all paper issues by the disgruntled Boston banking interests caused a great depreciation in this credit currency and the nation suffered from the ensuing panic.

The New England banks were the only institutions in the country that did not suspend specie payment. When three wagon loads of specie had been collected in New York and had started on their way to New England to balance accounts, the shipment was seized by the collector of the port at New York on the pretext that it was the intention of the New England banks to send the money to Canada.

As an instance of how bad the money situation was, the Government failed to redeem Treasury notes and actually paid some of the soldiers in bank notes which were not receivable for taxes. The War Department could not pay a bill for $3,500, and the Secretary of the Treasury went begging for smaller sums. Yet business flourished. Manufacturers increased their output to supply the needs of the war and the people patriotically took state bank notes, many of which were caught in the jams of later panics and were never redeemed.

The following table of our imports and exports will show the effects of the year 1814 on industry:

Year	Domestic Exports	Total Imports
1811	$45,294,000	$ 53,400,000
1812	30,032,000	77,030,000
1813	25,008,000	22,005,000
1814	6,782,000	12,965,000
1815	45,974,000	113,041,000
1816	64,782,000	147,103,000
1817	68,313,000	99,250,000

The demand for goods and the general inflation brought on by the war and stoppage of imports increased the number of banks from eighty-eight to two hundred and eight. During the panic of this year ninety banks suspended.

The close of the war brought a period of fairly good times with its consequent evils of speculation and reckless banking. The fact that good times followed peace in 1815 is another instance that belies the claim that depression invariably follows war.

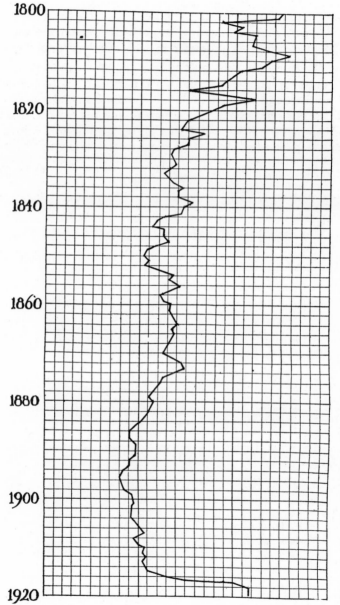

Average price levels 1800 to 1920, showing that prices were higher in 1815 than at any period in our history, and lower in the depression of 1893.

From figures by Jevons & Sauerbeck—Recalculated by Layton.

CHAPTER X.

THE DEPRESSION OF 1818-19

In the first few years following the signing of peace which ended the War of 1812, business experienced a remarkable revival. Credit money issues to prosecute the war made currency free and easy. The total volume of exports and imports in 1816 amounted to ten times that in 1814, but this prosperity was short lived, and 1919 saw a lamentable decline.

The poor and inadequate banking system in vogue at the time was a major cause of the depression. In addition may be mentioned the speculation in western lands, the over-rapid commercial expansion and the unstable position of the manufacturing industries which had grown abnormally during the embargo, and after the war were left exposed to foreign competition. At the same time the State banks contracted their note circulation of $100,000,000 in 1817 to $45,000,000 in 1819 and thus reduced the credit facilities at the very time they were most in demand. Specie payments were again generally suspended, prices fell disastrously, and failures occurred in every part of the country.

This depression set in during the year 1818. The worst conditions existed, however, in 1819, and this is commonly known as the crisis of 1819. It continued during the whole of 1820. Our three years of prosperity following the war made us eager buyers with our inflated money. Furthermore, it had taken Great Britain that long to realize that America was becoming independent of her manufactures, and when realization came British manufacturers, eager to regain control of their lost markets in this country, began sending in ship loads of merchandise which they offered on most liberal terms. These goods began arriving during the height of our prosperity, and as money was readily available they were snatched up at low prices. But the people finally paid the bill with compound interest when our own industry began to feel the pinch. American woolen mills closed down, many of them being ruined.

In spite of the suspension of specie payment in 1814 the country had prospered because of the large amount of paper money put into circulation during the war, which was readily accepted after its close. During the prosperity preceding this depression the prices of commodities rose higher than ever before or since in American history.*

Europe, as well as America, suffered commercial reverses in this year. Our finances were probably somewhat strained as a reflection of the severe crisis that was sweeping over Europe following the Napoleonic wars.

The causes of the panic only indirectly resulted from the war. A period of three years of great prosperity followed the War of 1812, which ended in 1815. With the coming of peace came renewed activity in shipping. In 1816 our imports reached the high mark of $147,000,000. Surplus stocks of European goods fairly flooded the country. American merchants liked the situation because the consumers were buying, but the manufacturers gradually began to feel the strain of competition and again set up a cry for stronger protection. Short crops abroad, together with other favorable conditions, created such a market for our own agricultural products that we could for a time readily absorb the large imports, but as soon as the demand for our staples was supplied disorder resulted. The prevailing prosperity and accompanying high prices blinded the people to the dangers ahead. Currency had again become inflated.

In 1818 the report became widespread that the banks were in a critical condition. An attempt had been made to resume specie payment, but this had failed, being successful only in spots or for a limited time. In preparation for this the banks had restricted their loans, limiting credits to busi-

*See Chart Page 108.

ness and agriculture. The following year business felt the full effects of depression. In 1819 steps were taken to compel banks to pay specie or forfeit their charters. Many banks seeing this was impossible suspended, bringing the first widespread panic in our history.

The first national bank which Hamilton had organized had failed of re-charter ten years previous, and to take its place hundreds of so-called joint stock companies secured charters and proceeded to issue bank notes with no adequate provisiòn for redemption. The banks of Massachusetts and New York, which sections had learned their lessons in the evils of over-inflation, were restricted as to the issues and assets, but in the South and West, where an abundance of money was needed to develop their resources, the people hankered for cheap money and plenty of it, and the state authorities and bankers sympathized with the movement. Our circulating medium had increased to $100,000,000, when it became so apparent that trouble was ahead that business men began to petition for a national bank of issue in order to provide a sounder currency.

The Second National Bank was accordingly chartered with $35,000,000 capital. The notes issued by this bank proved a welcome addition to the currency and were taken in many parts of the country where local issues were thoroughly discredited. But the national bank had assumed too much of a load in undertaking to force the state banks to a specie basis, particularly in view of the mismanagement in its own affairs, as charged by some historians. Of the $7,000,000 specie required in the charter, but $2,000,000 was actually contributed, and of the $21,000,000 bond subscriptions but $9,000,000 was made good in government bonds, the personal notes of subscribers being accepted in lieu of the stipulated payment.

Unwarranted accommodations and speculation brought the institution to the verge of bankruptcy in 1818, when the Baltimore branch failed for $3,000,000. An investigation of its affairs was ordered by Congress and a vigorous reform

prescribed. The original management was obliged to re-
sign. Langdon Cheves, of Charleston, was elected president,
and under his conservative administration the national
bank retrieved its financial standing. But a reform administration could not avert the business crisis which years
of speculation and wild-cat banking had engendered. The
sudden contraction of credit, following upon a period of
reckless financing, jeopardized banks and business enterprises everywhere outside of New England. These curtailments were ordered in March, 1819. The bank at that
time was in a truly deplorable condition. Vast sums of
specie had been imported at large expense to maintain
specie payments, but nearly all was gone. On the 21st of
April there was only $126,745.28 and the bank owed to the
city banks of Philadelphia $79,125.99. In April, 1819, the
circulation of the Second Bank of the United States was less
than half that of the year previous, April, 1818. The failures of the State banks began in 1818, the year after the
Second United States Bank came into existence. In the
year preceding, June 26, 1819, according to later authorities,
$800,000 in specie was drawn from banks in Ohio—an
enormous amount for those times. The financial stringency
was such that everyone was in debt and payment was almost
impossible.

In 1819 state banks, following the national bank, contracted their circulation as shown by the following figures:

```
On November 1, 1816 to_____$4,756,000
On November 1, 1817 to_____ 3,782,000
On November 1, 1818 to_____ 3,011,000
On November 1, 1819 to_____ 1,318,000
```

It was during this period that savings banks got their
first impetus. During periods of business adversity people
were thrown out of employment, and improvidence during
prosperity brought consequent suffering and even pauperism in times of depression. Agitation started among the
working people and the poorer classes to provide savings
against these gloomy days. Thus was the great savings
bank system of today founded.

Not only the banks, but business men of all classes had been mortgaging the future beyond warrant. Manufacturers, encouraged by the prospect of adequate protection, enlarged their plants and doubled their output. Land companies invested borrowed money in property that could not be sold at a profit, and farmers mortgaged their lands for the funds with which to make improvements. Large sums were sunk in canals and post roads that could not pay dividends on the investment, much less make good the obligations incurred. Confidence in the resources of the country and its ultimate prosperity led men to anticipate industrial development by a generation and to risk too much upon the immediate future.

The contraction of the currency and the refusal of the National Bank to discount any but well-secured paper, called a sudden halt in this mad career of speculation. Hundreds of business enterprises were prostrated and thousands of apparently prosperous men were ruined. The closing of factories threw workmen out of employment, and the streets of Philadelphia, Baltimore, New York, Pittsburg, and many lesser manufacturing and commercial centers, were thronged with destitute men and women seeking work. Prices fell, and the value of real estate shrank to one-third the level of the speculative period.

During this time speculation was so wild that no one failed on account of a smaller sum than $100,000. A drawing-room that had cost $40,000, and a bankrupt's wine-cellar estimated to have cost $7,000, were cited as instances of the general prodigality.

Congress appreciating the condition, immediately set about to ascertain the effects of the panic, and a Senatorial Committee of Inquiry, appointed for the purpose, declared that the panic imposed ruinous losses upon landed property, which had fallen from a quarter to even a half of its value. In consequence forced sales, bankruptcies, scarcity of money, and a stoppage of work occurred. House rents fell from $1,200 to $450. On the 13th of December, 1819, a committee of the House of Representatives reported that "the panic extended from the greatest to the smallest capitalists."

Lands and agricultural products fell to one-half the prices which were readily obtainable ten years previous. In the Mississippi Valley the speculative demand for money had been even greater than in the East. Virgin soil and limitless possibilities in the way of development created a reckless system of financing that brooked no restraint. Silver sufficient to serve as the medium of exchange came into the country through the New Orleans trade with the West Indies and Mexico, but the demand for capital with which to develop the country could only be met by credit agencies. In 1817-18 forty banks of issue had been chartered in Kentucky, and Tennessee and Ohio hastened to adopt the same alluring expedient. The banks issued money without stint and loaned to speculators on easy terms. Prices rose, and though the silver went over the mountains to New York and Philadelphia, the Mississippi Valley seemed in the heyday of prosperity. Then when the National Bank presented an accumulation of notes for redemption, the state banks, unable to meet their obligations, were forced to suspend specie payment, and the boom collapsed. To mitigate the general distress the state legislatures passed relief laws, staying proceedings against debtors.

Knox's "History of Banking" quotes a Connecticut paper of that period, which comments on the distress as follows:

> "Why is the community so much embarrassed?
> Because banks lend money that they have not go to lend.
> And because people spend money they have not got to spend.
>   REMEDY
> Own the money before you lend it!
> Earn the money before you spend it!"

Nile's Register, which is unquestionably the best authority for details on our early economic history, prints a letter from a United States Bank director to a friend in England vividly portraying conditions of the period:

"Our difficulties in commerce continue without abatement. Men in business are like patients in the last stage of consumption, hoping for a favorable change but growing worse every day. You have some regular and profitable trade (in England), we have none. It is all scamper and haphazard. A long continuance of distresses in the commercial world has had a bad effect on the morality of the country. The vast number of failures takes away the odium. Men fail in parties for convenience, and the barriers of honesty are broken down by a perpetual legislation suited to the convenience of insolvent debtors . . . The farmer is become as poor as a rat; the labor on the farm costs him more than the produce is worth. He cannot pay the storekeeper and the storekeeper cannot pay the merchant."

Various State legislatures undertook to pass laws to strengthen the banking system, particularly in New York and Ohio, where stringent banking laws were enacted. In those days communication was slow, there being no railroads or telegraphs and the panic spread gradually from East to West. It did not reach Tennessee until 1820, at which time the State authorized the Bank of Tennessee to issue bills to relieve the distress. Some states at this time passed replevin laws which gave debtors as long as two years within which to reclaim their property from their creditors. Kentucky undertook to meet the situation by establishing the Bank of the Commonwealth, authorized to issue notes on the basis of the State revenues and to lend the same to needy persons on land security. But the remedy was worse than the disease. In a short time the notes of the bank were worth 50 cents on the dollar. The farmers lost their land and left the State by hundreds and thousands, and business men were put to every expedient to provide money for cash payments.

A Scotch traveler described the situation as follows: "In this western country there is a great diversity of paper money. Small bills are in circulation of a half, a fourth, an eighth, and even the sixteenth of a dollar. There small rags are not current at a great distance from the places of their nativity. A considerable portion of the little specie to be seen is of what is called cut money—dollars cut into two, four, eight or sixteen pieces. This practice prevents much money from being received in banks, or sent out of the country in the character of coin, and would be highly commendable were it not for the frauds committed by those who clip the pieces in reserving a part of the metal for themselves . . ."

Again, writing of Cincinnati: "There is here much trouble with paper money. The notes current in one part are either refused or taken at a large discount in another. Banks that were creditable a few days ago have refused to redeem their paper in specie, or in notes of the United States Bank . . . The creation of this vast host of fabricators and vendors of base money must form a memorable epoch in the history of the country. These craftsmen have greatly increased the money capital of the nation and have, in a corresponding degree, enchanced the nominal value of property and labor. By lending and otherwise emitting their engravings, they have contrived to mortgage and buy much of the property of their neighbors, and to appropriate to themselves the labor of less moneyed citizens. Proceeding in this manner, they cannot retain specie enough to redeem their bills, admitting the gratuitous assumption that they were once possessed of it. They seem to have calculated that the whole of their paper would not return on them in one day. Small quantities, however, of it have, on various occasions, been sufficient to cause them to suspend specie payments. The money in circulation is puzzling to traders, and more particularly to strangers, for besides the multiplicity of banks, and the diversity of supposed value, fluctuations are so frequent, and so great, that no man who holds it in his possession can be safe for a day. The merchant, when asked the price of an article, instead of making a direct answer, usually puts the question, 'What sort of money have you got?' Supposing that a number of bills are shown, and one or more are accepted of, it is not till then that the price of the goods is declared, and an additional price is uniformly laid on to compensate for the supposed defect in the quality of the money."*

The Legislature of the State of Pennsylvania appointed

---

*As told in "Flint"'s Letters from America."

a committee to inquire into the causes and extent of the
distress. It brought in a report in substance as follows:

†1. Ruinous sacrifices of landed property at sheriff's
sales.

2. Forced sales of merchandise, household goods,
farming stock and utensils, at prices far below the cost of
production.

3. Numerous bankruptcies and pecuniary embarrassments of every description.

4. A general scarcity of money throughout the country
which renders it almost impossible for the husbandman, o'
other owner of real estate, to borrow at a usurious interest.

5 and 7. A general suspension of labor, and a universal
suspension of all large manufacturing operations.

6. An almost entire cessation of the usual circulation
of commodities, and a consequent stagnation of business, as
are absolutely required by the season.

8 and 9. Usurious extortions, and the overflowing of
prisons with insolvent debtors, most of whom are confined
for trifling sums.

10 and 11. Numerous law suits, and vexatious losses
arising from the depreciation and fluctuation in the
value of bank-notes, the impositions of brokers and the
frauds of counterfeiters.

12. A general inability in the community to meet with
punctuality the payment of debts, even for family expenses, which is experienced as well by those who are
wealthy in property as by those who have hitherto relied
upon their current receipts to discharge their current engagements.

During the four years between 1817 and 1821 the holders
of property in the United States were supposed to have
suffered a depreciation of nearly eight hundred million
dollars. General bankruptcy spread its darkness over the
land; many of the wealthiest families were reduced to poverty; laborers suffered for want of bread; improvements
of all sorts were abandoned, and a scene of the most intense national distress ensued.

As the tide of internal commerce had risen, there had
been a general expansion of business. A depression had to
come for several reasons: first, as a reflection of European

---

†As told in Raguet's "Currency and Banking."

troubles; second, a stoppage of overproduction; and third, to get money on a better basis.

Spanish dollars were bringing 7 per cent premium in New York, and it was apparent that there was an untold amount of bank notes issued that could not possibly be redeemed.

From the close of the war in 1815 to 1818 there was a perfect mania for chartering state banks and gambling in their stocks was a marked feature of the day. Says Niles: "Wherever there is a church, a blacksmith's shop and a tavern seems a proper site for one of them!"

It is little wonder that with all of this the Bank of the United States was forced to contract its loans because of mismanagement, causing the president to flee from the wreck. As one writer put it, "The bank was saved and the people were ruined."

Business suffered immensely, and it was a rare case where a business firm was not embarrassed. In the county of Morris, New Jersey, there were about forty manufacturing concerns at the close of the war. Of these, all save four or five were either abandoned or sold during the next eight years. The few textile industries that had survived the competition with England after the war were ruined, the iron industries of Pittsburg and Cincinnati, some of which had not been disturbed by the importations because of the protection afforded by high freight rates and the increased duties of 1818, were compelled to close down on account of the heavy fall in prices and the general depression. Prices of all kinds fell, cotton goods going down from 25 cents to 19 cents a yard.

The West felt the distress with extreme severity. There was no specie and the notes of the newer banks in that section were practically worthless. Farmers and business people alike had mortgaged their lands and other assets, and as they could not pay a great deal of it fell into the hands of the banks, particularly the Bank of the United States. At the end of the difficulties it was found that "the bank owned a large part of Cincinnati; hotels, coffee houses, warehouses, stores, stables, iron foundries, residences, vacant lots, besides over 50,000 acres of good farm land in Ohio and Kentucky." In those days redemption of bills rested with the agents of the individual banks, many times these agents using the utmost skill and resourcefulness to keep the bills from being presented for payment.

Niles, writing of that day, said that "he had more than $100 in small notes of the Bank of the United States and could not pay the postage of a few letters."

Throughout the country failures were continuous through 1819 and 1820. In Georgia the State Legislature passed an act suspending the law allowing 25 per cent damages on the failure of a state bank to redeem its notes in specie. The month of August, 1819, found 20,000 persons seeking employment in Philadelphia, and a similar condition of affairs in the other great cities of the North.

The provision market of the western farmers was greatly injured, and manufacturer, farmer, planter, and merchant all succumbed before the general catastrophe. "Before long prices fell so low that from the eastern seaports to Cincinnati, Pittsburg, and Nashville in the West, men were thrown out of work by the closing of factories. Cotton, woolen, silk, flax, iron, lead, tin, brass, and copper manufactures, glass and earthernware, haberdashery, hats, and other English goods were sold at low prices in auction sales; cheap India cottons came in large bulks; silks, cotton goods, wine, and brandy came from southern Europe and France; woolen, linen, iron, lead, and glass manufactures, spirits, cheese, and paints from northern Europe; sugar, rum, and molasses from the West Indies."

The depression lasted until 1821, very little headway being made until then.

In order to draw a clear picture, it is fitting to close this chapter with a recital of conditions in the country as reported by the Committee on Ways and Means in Congress:

"From the extraordinary depression of commerce, within the last three years, the stagnation of our navigation, the depreciation in the value of our exports, the corresponding depreciation in the value of property of every description, and the serious embarrassments under which every branch of industry now labors, economy and retrenchment in the expenditures of every citizen are imperiously required."

And a little later a report by the House Committee on Manufactures:

"It is not a matter of very great consolation to know that, at the end of thirty years of its operation, this government finds its debt increased $20,000,000, and its revenue inadequate to its expenditure; the national domain impaired, and $20,000,000 dollars drawn from the people by internal taxation, $341,000,000 by impost, yet the public treasury dependent on loans; in profound peace, and without national calamity; the country embarrassed with debts, and real estate under rapid depreciation; the markets of agriculture, the pursuits of manufacture, diminished and declining; commerce struggling, not to retain the carrying of the produce of other nations, but our own. There is no national interest which is in a healthful, thriving condition: the nation at large is not so; the operations of the government and individuals alike labor under difficulties which are felt by all."

CHAPTER XI

THE DEPRESSION OF 1825

Most authorities attribute our troubles in 1825 entirely to the European reverses of that year, during which England experienced one of her greatest catastrophes. American obligations were called in, and the banking houses of New York and Philadelphia became seriously embarrassed. The English cotton factories curtailed production and the price of cotton fell. The New Orleans banks, accustomed to lend freely on cotton securities, were the first to break down. Many of the cotton factors failed and the Cotton Exchange was prostrated. The general business of the country felt the shock only slightly and it passed over without any serious consequences. But the stringency of that year would probably have resulted in a condition as bad as in 1819 had it not been for the able management of Nicholas Biddle who guided the affairs of the Bank of the United States at the time. The bank rendered splendid service in getting business back on its feet. Mr. Biddle at that time said that the crisis of 1825 was the most severe that England had ever experienced, superinduced as it was by the wild American speculation in cotton and mines. Cotton cloth fell from eighteen to thirteen cents per yard; and out of four thousand weavers employed in Philadelphia in 1825 not more than one thousand remained. The reaction of liquidation had spent its force by 1826 and money was again abundant.

At that time commercial crises of the most tremendous proportions were running through not only England, but other parts of Europe; it failed, however, to spread seriously to the United States. A small boom had set in and stock companies started their usual wild-catting. As an instance, three millions were subscribed to the "New Jersey Protec-

tion Company" in one day.   But in July, when the decline
on the London market was reported, the want of hard
money forced itself into notice.   Exchange on England rose
from 5 per cent to 10 per cent; the discount on New Orleans
notes from 3 per cent to 50 per cent, and on the 4th of
December it had fallen back to 4 per cent.   The depression
was short-lived because inflation had not run its full course
nor reached undue proportions.

It was the widespread interest in the financial and business situation at this period that caused the newspapers to
start their financial pages.   These consisted mostly of reports of conditions furnished by a brokerage house and this
practice continued up until recent years.

WEATHER BAROMETER OF OUR BUSINESS HISTORY

Year	Conditions	Year	Conditions	Year	Conditions
1781	Fair.	1829	Fair.	1877	Fair.
1782	Fair	1830	Fair.	1878	Storm.
1783	Fair.	1831	Fair.	1879	Clearing.
1784	Partly Cloudy.	1832	Fair.	1880	Fair.
1785	Cloudy.	1833	Partly Cloudy.	1881	Fair.
1786	Storm.	1834	Fair.	1882	Fair.
1787	Stormy.	1835	Fair.	1883	Partly Cloudy.
1788	Bad.	1836	Threatening.	1884	Storm.
1789	Extremely Bad.	1837	Hurricane.	1885	Fair.
1790	Clearing.	1838	Stormy.	1886	Fair.
1791	Clear.	1839	Continued Storm.	1887	Fair.
1792	Fair.	1840	Clearing.	1888	Fair.
1793	Fair.	1841	Fair	1889	Threatening.
1794	Fair.	1842	Fair.	1890	Storm.
1795	Fair.	1843	Fair.	1891	Fair.
1796	Fair.	1844	Fair.	1892	Fair.
1797	Threatening.	1845	Fair.	1893	Storm.
1798	Squall.	1846	Fair.	1894	Stormy.
1799	Clearing.	1847	Storm.	1895	Continued
1800	Fair.	1848	Storm.		Stormy.
1801	Fair.	1849	Fair.	1896	Clearing.
1802	Fair.	1850	Fair.	1897	Fair.
1803	Squall.	1851	Squall.	1898	Fair.
1804	Fair.	1852	Fair.	1899	Fair.
1805	Fair.	1853	Fair.	1900	Fair.
1806	Fair.	1854	Fair.	1901	Fair.
1807	Fair.	1855	Fair.	1902	Fair.
1808	Stormy.	1856	Fair.	1903	Squall.
1809	Stormy.	1857	Tornado.	1904	Fair.
1810	Clearing.	1858	Clearing.	1905	Fair.
1811	Fair.	1859	Fair.	1906	Fair.
1812	Fair.	1860	Storm.	1907	Cyclone.
1813	Fair.	1861	Stormy	1908	Clearing.
1814	Storm.	1862	Fair.	1909	Fair.
1815	Fair.	1863	Fair.	1910	Fair.
1816	Fair.	1864	Fair.	1911	Fair.
1817	Fair.	1865	Fair.	1912	Fair.
1818	Threatening.	1866	Fair.	1913	Partly Cloudy.
1819	Hurricane.	1867	Fair.	1914	Storm.
1820	Gale.	1868	Threatening.	1915	Partly Cloudy.
1821	Clearing.	1869	Black Friday.	1916	Fair.
1822	Fair.	1870	Fair.	1917	Fair.
1823	Fair.	1871	Fair.	1918	Fair.
1824	Fair.	1872	Fair.	1919	Fair.
1825	Storm.	1873	Cyclone.	1920	Partly Cloudy.
1826	Fair.	1874	High Winds.	1921	Stormy.
1827	Fair.	1875	Clearing.	1922	Stormy.
1828	Squall.	1876	Fair.		

CHAPTER XII.

THE DEPRESSION OF 1837-39

Let us compare conditions in this country after passing through the depression of 1819 with those that existed in 1836, after a period of sixteen years of prosperity and the accumulation of wealth, marred only by minor stoppages in 1825 and 1828. The following is taken from the report of Secretary of the Treasury Rush, under President Jackson:

"The receipts of the existing year is greater by nearly two millions of dollars than had been foreseen, with a prospect of income for the next scarcely less abundant, the receipts of the last four years presenting a large and gratifying excess over those of the four years preceding; the foreign commerce of the country in a state of solid prosperity, from the improved condition of its leading departments of industry at home, and consequent increase in the exportation of its products; the increase of its tonnage (that foundation of naval strength, as well as commercial riches) keeping pace with the increase of commerce; the public debt annually and rapidly decreasing under the application of surplus funds; the public revenue preserved at an equal value in every part of the Union, through the power of transfers promptly made by the Bank of the United States, without expense or risk to the nation; and the currency maintained in a healthful state by the same institution. Such is the great outline of the financial and commercial condition of the country, a condition of the result of good laws faithfully administered, and of the aggregate industry of an enterprising free people."

Foreign capital became available in great quantities for loans to the American people after the recovery from the crisis of 1825 in England, and specie imports kept up with an excess of imports of goods. As evidence of the heavy loans which Europe was making to us, imports in seven years amounted to $140,700,000. The agricultural and industrial output in 1836 totaled $2,600,000,000, an increase of three-fold in fifteen years, a record that had never before been approached since civilization began.

But a crisis was fast approaching when President Van Buren took office. It was already being felt in New York, and a committee rushed to Washington to ask him to rescind the specie circular. Van Buren, however, refused, holding that his election denoted the approval of Jackson's hard money policy by the people.

While a crash was unavoidable sooner or later, because of the instability of the banking system and the heavy obligations incurred for speculative purposes, most writers attribute the starting of the trouble to Jackson's specie circular requiring that only gold and silver and notes redeemable in gold and silver be used in payment for public lands. The crisis was precipitated in the western states, where there were many "wild cat" banks that had issued irredeemable paper currency. The last of the national debt had been paid in 1835, and the Federal Government had started a system of distributing surplus funds to the several states. It is claimed that had the United States Bank been rechartered this panic could have been avoided. How much stronger the financial structure would have been under the United States Bank is only to be surmised. There were other influences, however, which added to the growing difficulties, and any one of them might have had as much to do with the final outbreak as the other one. Crop failures in 1835 to 1837 left the farmers without ability to meet their obligations in the western states where the trouble started. The panic and bank failures in England the preceding year, 1836, were also factors. The prosperity of the preceding years had stimulated large importations of European goods, leaving a big trade balance in Europe's favor which necessitated the sending out of specie, leaving the banks of this country with means insufficient to meet the needs in a crisis. While it is true Europe's trade balance was largely reinvested in our securities, interest payments in themselves were large and necessitated exports of specie.

A connection is here again shown between the economic affairs of this country and Europe in the failure of important business houses in England at the end of 1836, which caused a lessening in the demand for cotton, thus involving the South. This of itself should not have caused the panic if there had not been the accompanying speculation. In fact, not until recent years have our commercial relations with the outside world been such as to necessarily cause a depression by reason of one existing in another country. Even now such an authority as Forbes claims that we can be economically independent of Europe and the outside world if our own commerce is well and properly regulated.

As an instance of the wave of extravagance that preceded this depression the figures of the public debt of the states may be cited. At the beginning of the decade, 1830, the debt was $26,470,417, which mounted to $170,000,000 in 1838, a year after the depression had set in. Practically all of this enormous expenditure had gone into public improvements, such as roads, canals and railroads—most of them enterprises that were premature and unnecessary. Many were extravagantly, if not corruptly managed, millions of dollars being sunk in useless undertakings. When the debts so easily contracted began to press, several of the states repudiated their indebtedness, notable among them Mississippi, Louisiana, Maryland, Pennsylvania, Indiana, Illinois and Michigan. Some of these afterward paid in part or in whole.

Previous to the crisis of 1837 money was cheap and easy. The high credit then enjoyed by the American states, which had been greatly enhanced by the payment of the national debt, enabled them to borrow enormous sums abroad, especially in England, where capital had been accumulating, at comparatively moderate rates of interest.

When the depression came on public works already built

by the states were sold to private interests in many cases, and this period marked the last widespread effort on the part of individual states to appropriate money for state-owned improvements and utilities. The people resenting the suffering caused by the depression eagerly voted into many state constitutions prohibition of the use of state funds or credit for specified internal improvements. Up to that time railroads had been built or largely helped by the use of public funds. These now passed into the hands of private individuals and corporations.

The panic began on May 10th, when the banks of New York City decided to suspend specie payments. Within two months the catastrophe had spread to all the financial and industrial centers of the country. Another period of reckless speculation had come to a sudden close. The discredited bank notes depreciated in value and prices shrank to a hard money level. Factories and workshops, organized on a boom basis, closed in anticipation of a falling market. Thousands of operatives were discharged, and the cities were crowded with the unemployed. All classes curtailed expenditure, the demand for goods being thus further reduced. Imports exceeded exports during the speculative period of 1830 to '37, leaving a staggering trade balance against us amounting to $140,000,000. Failure of the New York banks dragged down many business houses within a few months. The public, unable to withdraw deposits, grew desperate, and the militia was called in to protect the terrified financiers. The panic spread next to Philadelphia, whose banks were in solvent condition but were unable to stem the onrushing tide of frenzy. When the panic had swept the country 618 banks had failed within the year. New England felt the shock less than any other section. Although the general government was free from debt, there was no money for current expenses and Congress was called in extra session and voted ten million dollars in Treasury notes to meet the emergency.

Although the act passed Congress, President Jackson vetoed it. The easterners accused him of being friendly with "wild cat" bankers of the West, where he hailed from, being a Tennessean. The western bankers wanted to defeat the national bank because they claimed it restricted development of the newer states. As there was no government paper issue, and not sufficient gold and silver to supply the needs, a stringency existed. This breach was filled by notes issued by state banks. New banks sprung up in every state until they had increased in number from 329 to 788 in the period of eight years preceding the crisis of 1837. During the same interval the volume of the currency was trebled and bank loans were extended at an even more rapid rate.

When the Second Bank of the United States failed to recharter there was no means of checking speculation. The state banks went wild and expansion proceeded beyond reason. Jackson's enemies said the panic was due to the placing of public funds in the state banks, but that could hardly be taken seriously, because deposits were only $41,-500,000 at the time. It is obvious that that would not have been a large factor in a healthy money market, and a still smaller factor in a period of inflation. It was not the placing of public funds in the state banks, but the over-issue of state bank notes, that caused the trouble. There is hardly a connection between the two. Had the counsel of President Biddle been heeded as early as 1833 the panic of 1837 might have been avoided.

During the debate on the Second National Bank question in 1832 Senator Clayton, of Delaware, prophesied the panic of 1837 in these words: "In less than four years the pecuniary distress, the commercial embarrassments, consequent upon the destruction of the United States Bank, must exceed anything which has ever been known in our history. Overtrading and speculation on false capital in every part of the country; that rapid fluctuation in the standard of value for money, which, like the unseen pestilence, withers

all the efforts of industry, while the sufferer is in utter
ignorance of the cause of his destruction; bankruptcies and
ruin, at the anticipation of which the heart sickens, must
follow in the long train of evils which are assuredly before us."

Moore in his "Industrial History of the American People" blames President Jackson in these words: "Jackson, our
greatest financial blunderer, killed the idea and brought
the Nation to the panic of 1837 with his ill-timed attempts
to stop a movement that he himself had started."

Thomas H. Benton, who was in the Senate at the time,
says in his "Thirty Years' View" that the panic was manufactured by interests connected with the Second National
Bank, who sought to bring on a crisis in order to embarrass
President Jackson.

"For this purpose loans and accommodations were to
cease at the mother bank and all its branches, and in all the
local banks over which the national bank had control; and
at the same time that discounts were stopped, curtailments
were made; and all business men called on for the payment
of all they owed, at the same time all the usual sources of
supply were stopped. This pressure was made to fall upon
the business community, especially upon large establishments
employing a great many operatives so as to throw as many
laboring people as possible out of employment.   At the same
time politicians engaged in making panic had what amounts
they pleased, an instance of a loan of $100,000 to a single
one of these agitators being detected; and a loan of $1,100,-
000 to a broker, employed in making distress, and in relieving it in favored cases at a usury of two and a half per
centum per month. In this manner the business community
was oppressed, and in all parts of the Union at the same
time.

"The first step in this policy was to get up distress meetings—a thing easily done—and then to have these meetings properly officered and conducted.   Men who had voted
for Jackson, but now renounced him, were procured for
president, vice-presidents, secretaries, and orators; distress
orations were delivered; and, after sufficient exercise in
that way, a memorial and a set of resolves, prepared for the

occasion, were presented and adopted. After adoption, the old way of sending by mail was discarded, and a deputation selected to proceed to Washington and make delivery of their lugubrious document. These memorials generally came in duplicate, to be presented in both Houses at once, by a Senator from the State and the representative from the district. Yet, Van Buren, who was supported by Jackson, was elected overwhelmingly, and the country beheld 'the gratifying spectacle of a full and overflowing treasury, instead of the empty one which had been predicted; and left to Congress the grateful occupation of further reducing taxes, instead of the odius task of borrowing money, as had been so loudly anticipated for six months past."'

Jackson's antagonism to the Second Bank of the United States had caused large amounts of treasury revenues to be deposited in state banks. The national debt had been paid and this brought on a great period of expansion and the organization of all these new banks which went wild in a general inflation of the circulation. The circulating notes of all banks exclusive of the Bank of the United States rose in seven years prior to 1837 from $61,000,000 to $149,-000,000. The Bank of the United States after failing to recharter had become the United States Bank of Pennsylvania, having been chartered by that State, and it claimed to have kept its resources and organization intact. But this bank failed with the rest of them. As an example of how the public confidence was undermined by the terrible crash, it may be said that the banks of Philadelphia made three attempts to resume payment on their notes from 1837 to 1841, and each attempt resulted in failure. The banks of New York and New England were the first to resume, having imported quantities of specie from abroad. It was seven years before the banks resumed a state of regularity. During this period "they reduced their circulation from $149,000,000 in 1837 to $58,000,000 in 1843, which is $3,-000,000 below the amount at which it stood thirteen years before."

In the three years from 1834 to 1837 one hundred and

ninety-four new banks were organized in the United States. This includes only those that were recorded with the Secretary of the Treasury at Washington, and the number does not include a great many institutions known as "wild-cat" banks. It was a peculiarity that while Jackson was influenced by his western friends, yet he issued a specie circular which he must have known would have brought destruction to the West, since it was sure to cause a run for specie upon the western banks, which had little or none. That Jackson was honest there is little doubt. Apparently he wanted a larger distribution of money so as to develop the West and South, but he wanted the money to be sound. No doubt Jackson saw the way things were going, that the country was threatened with a panic, and while he precipitated it, he probably foresaw that it might have been worse had it been allowed to continue.

It was during the distress of this period that the Free Banking Law was agitated and put into effect in several states, the story of which is a history in itself. In general, these laws granted the privilege to associations and individuals to issue paper money unrestrained, and the practice was carried on for years in the various states, always adding to business troubles as they revolved in their cycles. During the period of specie payment suspension in 1837, ending with the resumption in 1842, the state banks held specie amounting on an average to 31.7 per cent of their circulation and 18 per cent of their circulation in deposits. This period practically swept the Michigan banks out of existence. By the end of 1839 only two chartered banks and four free banks were doing business in the state. Forty-two were in the hands of receivers and many others had gone out of business.

Frequent investigations were made as to causes of the panic. The Ohio Legislature by a resolution required the auditor of the state to submit to the banks twenty different questions inquiring into the causes which led them to suspend specie payment. One banker replied, "The causes which led to the suspension of specie payments by the Ohio banks, in May last, were so notorious at the time the suspension took place that we did suppose they were known to everyone. But it seems to be otherwise." The great slump of business activity brought about a serious decline in the government revenues, and as a result, the tariff duties which had been gradually lowered was raised to a level of 20 per cent, which was the highest tariff the country had experienced up to that time.

It is no wonder that there was inflation in that period. There was everything to bring inflation. Things never looked so rosy. In 1835 it was estimated that the receipts of the treasury would be $20,000,000; actual receipts proved to be $35,000,000. Suppose such a condition existed today. Would it not start a great boom in business? In 1836 the national government started distributing its surplus to the various states. Each quarter an installment of $9,367,214 was sent out, a total of over $37,000,000 a year. Think of such a condition existing today. The confidence it would instill in the public mind. Suppose we were out of debt, our taxes low, a great surplus of money to be distributed, we would probably lose our heads the same as our ancestors did in those days.

The increase in sales of public lands had been fairly steady and healthful up to 1834, when the sales were 4,659,218 acres and the amount received was $6,099,981. The next year witnessed the sale of 12,364,478 acres and receipts of $15,999,804, and 1836 witnessed sales of 20,-074,870 acres and receipts of $25,167,833. That these sales were speculative in character is indicated by the steady decline in receipts after 1837, until they fell in 1842 to only $1,417,972. With the rapid sales of its lands the Government was soon able to pay off the public debt, and had still a surplus of $50,000,000 in the treasury. But the Federal Treasury was bankrupt when the sale of public lands dropped to one-twenty-fifth its former figures. Many of the individual states, particularly the newer ones, were in the most straightened circumstances.

Previous years had been flush times in Alabama as a writer of that State's history portrays: "So complete was the intoxication of the people with the paper money craze that the General Assembly on January 9, 1836, passed an act abolishing direct taxation in the State and setting aside $100,000 of the bank money to defray the expenses of the State government. The crisis of 1837 led to an investigation of the discounts and it was found that over $6,000,000 were worthless. Confidence in the paper money, 'supported by the faith and credit and wealth of the State,' to use the favorite phrase of the champions of government paper money, suddenly collapsed and with it the whole structure of business and credit in Alabama."

The old adage, "It's an ill wind that blows nobody good," obtains in the matter of depressions as well as other things. The canals built during the high tide years enabled produce of the Central West to reach the Atlantic seaboard, and the agricultural exports of the State of Ohio, for instance, grew rapidly without recession during the panic from an equivalent of 544,000 bushels of wheat in 1835 to 3,800,000 in 1840.

Banking figures again show the havoc wrought. In the beginning of the depression in 1837 the 788 national banks were capitalized for $290,800,000, with a circulation of $149,200,000 and loans of $525,100,000. Five years later, at the end of the depression, shows 691 banks, a capital of $228,900,000, a circulation of only $58,600,000, and loans reduced to $254,500,000. Over-expansion of course rendered its due share with its accompanied extension of undue credit for speculative purposes.

Altogether about 900 banks failed during the years 1837 and 1838. It was at this time that legislation was invoked prohibiting loans by commercial banks on real estate mortgages, the attitude being taken that short time paper and quicker assets should be the only basis for loans. It is only recently that this law has been changed, and during the eighty years that it was in existence the resources of the country more and more got into the hands of speculative interests instead of actual developers of the country.

According to Dewey, "the value of real estate in New York had in six months depreciated more than $40,000,000; in two months there had been more than 250 failures; there had been a decline of $20,000,000 in the value of the stocks of railroads and canals which centered in New York; the value of merchandise in warehouses had fallen 30 per cent; and within a few weeks 20,000 persons had been discharged by their employers."

New Orleans and New York, particularly, had experienced building booms. More than fifteen hundred houses were erected in New York City between January 1 and September 1, 1836. The depression years, from 1837 to 1839, produced, according to some supposedly accurate reports of 1841, 33,000 failures, involving a loss of $440,000,000.

"Bicknall's Counterfeit Detector and Bank-Note List of January 1, 1839, contained the names of fifty-four banks that had failed at different times; of twenty fictitious banks, the pretended notes of which were in circulation; of forty-three other banks, for the notes of which there was no sale; of two hundred and fifty-four banks, the notes of which had been counterfeited or altered; and enumerated thirteen hundred and ninety-five descriptions of counterfeited or altered notes then supposed to be in circulation, of denominations from one dollar to five hundred."

This depression reduced our foreign trade from $300,-000,000 at its highest figure in 1836 to $125,000,000 in 1837.

Some writers of that time said the panic was due to the great New York fire in 1835 which destroyed $18,000,000 worth of property and burned 528 houses. This conflagration could have had very little effect on the depression, however, and at the time the Nation was proud that she could undergo such a conflagration without ill effect and boasted of her strength.

An article written by a New York newspaper man at
that time read: "The South and Southwest were the first
to give way. The cotton interest was prostrated. Inflation had stimulated production and inflated in turn manufacturers of England." Reaction was bound to set in, and
when it came at this time bankers and merchants who had
made large advances on cotton became panic-stricken.

New York and Philadelphia papers of March 27 and 28,
1837, after receiving the news of the cotton break at New
Orleans, predicted that the flurry would be over within a
few days and belittled the incident, seeking to calm the
people. The New York Herald finally came out with the
true situation and was followed on April 6 by the New York
Transcript, which said: "It is estimated that the Southern
merchants do not pay five cents on the dollar what they owe
in New York."

The following excerpts were taken from New York papers
of that day:

"May 4: John Fleming, president of Merchants Bank,
fell dead from excessive anxiety with regard to the affairs
of the bank. A run set in on all banks."

"May 5: Merchants failed by whole blocks. The American said, "It is vain to disguise that the whole frame of
society is out of joint.""

"May 6: The failures are worse. U. S. Bank Stock, for
first time in twenty years, fell below par. Not a stock in
the market brought par."

"May 8: Steady drain on banks. Failures too numerous
to chronicle. No bank stock at par."

"May 9: Furious run on all banks. Depositors and bill
holders mingling in one indiscriminate mass, all desperate
to get their money."

"May 10: All banks suspended. Chaos, bewilderment,
despondency and lamentation were the order of the day.
Three hundred firms failed in New York."

In February 1837 flour reached $12 a barrel. Men de-
prived of work and in a distressed condition started riots.
The rumor was current that dealers had combined and the
unemployed men were incensed. Several commission houses
were broken into, and when the police and mayor inter-

fered they were man-handled. The riots were finally stopped by the promise of the merchants to give flour to the poor.

A newspaper of that period gave as one of the causes of the crisis, "General neglect of the homelier and manlier occupations, particularly farming and excessive fondness of the meaner callings, such as store-keeping, banking and speculation."

The newspaper paragraphers wrote humorous poetry and printed jokes. Apparently, thousands of ruined men had nothing left but a sense of humor. They made fun of different commodities that were passed for money. The New York Commercial Advertiser said, "The egg currency is better and more convenient than that of some countries we *wot* of—Texas, for instance, where they pay in cows for large sums and throw in the calves for change."

As usual, immediately after a crisis, politics entered into the ascribed causes; the Whigs blamed Jackson and the ·Democrats. The New York American said, "When the cause of our calamities is traced mainly to misgovernment, we hear it said, 'Oh, for God's sake, do not make this a political matter.' Not make it a political matter? Why, it is from politics—base, vile, mercenary, personal politics— that the evil is what it is."

From March 1st to April 18th one hundred and sixty-eight business firms failed in New York City alone. There was considerable agitation against the banks. A town meeting is recorded as being held in Philadelphia, at which resolutions severely condemning the banks were passed. An anti-bank convention was held at Harrisburg on July 4, 1837, which issued an address to the people of the State, in which all the troubles of the time were attributed to "an unchecked and uncontrolled banking system."

The distresses of the day are set forth as follows:

"If we turn to the streets of our cities it (the financial distress) is proclaimed in language not to be mistaken. If we traverse our canals and railroads we find the 'panic' prophecy fulfilled; they are indeed a barren waste and bear the indelible marks of premature desertion and decay."

That the banks themselves saw trouble ahead is evident from articles by financial writers appearing in the Philadelphia papers at the time, in which great pains were taken to reassure the public. Between the lines can be noted the subtle signs of impending danger. A peculiar incident of the time was noted when the Philadelphia banks suspended specie payment. The New York newspapers criticised them, one remarking that it was "characteristic of Philadelphia to yield to a money crisis." Philadelphia papers countered by charging New York banks with draining Philadelphia of her specie through various devices which compelled the banks of that city to suspend. Shortly after the New York banks in turn suspended with the single exception of the Chemical Bank.

After a breathing spell the country looked back upon the wreckage and took stock. No wonder a debacle resulted from such a mess of financiering. The currency of the country consisted of a small amount of gold and silver; a large amount of state chartered bank notes, convertible; a far larger amount of bank notes inconvertible; notes of private non-specie paying banks; unauthorized notes of companies and associations, and a conglomeration of post notes, deposit notes, checks, states scrip and bills of exchange; all circulated for money. Imagine a currency such as this today. Who could not see trouble ahead? Some historians say we had two crises, one in 1837 and the other in 1839. But they were both one and the same, there being a continual state of crisis from 1837 through 1839.

"Banks were started for the sole purpose of foisting worthless notes upon a confiding public," wrote John J. Knox, former Comptroller of Currency. "Losses from the failures of these 'wild-cat' banks and business concerns have never been calculated."

With the previous experience with the national banks and on top of it the experience with the state banks, the confidence of the public was shaken almost beyond recovery. It is little wonder that the people were ready to listen to the agitation against banks of any kind. Cleveland says: "From the ruins of their own fortunes the people looked out on bankrupt cities, bankrupt towns, bankrupt counties, bankrupt states."

In Europe not only England was affected, but the bank of Belgium suspended payment. Numerous failures occurred in commercial circles of that country and in France. In Holland finances were so burdened that it became necessary to declare the colonies legal mortgage for the state debt.

With such severity did this catastrophe shake the financial foundation of the country that the people almost lost confidence in the Government itself. Greater disorder and chaos could not be described. It was by far the most terrific financial panic in the history of our country and proportionately more far reaching. It lasted fully three years, and 1840 saw only a start toward a return to normal. It has been said we are a people of extremes, that we are either miserly or extravagant, and there is good ground for this assertion, as is proven by our economic history. In 1837 we reached the lowest ebb of activities in our industrial life, yet coming out of this period we enjoyed the greatest activity and most abundant prosperity that we had ever known; the rapid building of railroads, the opening up of the West, the increase of immigration, the expansion of our agricultural output to supply the ever increasing population of Europe, the discovery of gold and lowered taxation—all these followed close upon the heels of this period of deepest depression.

CHAPTER XIII

THE DEPRESSION OF 1847-48

The depression of this period was short and not so thorough and widespread in its ill-effects. The occurrence is seldom mentioned in current histories of our economic and political life. Probably it would have been of greater concern had not the discovery of gold in California restored confidence and enthusiasm in the minds of the people. In fact, the twenty year interval between the crisis of 1837 and that of 1857, with this short exception, witnessed the most remarkable industrial advancement yet achieved in the United States. Writers universally refer to it as the "Golden Age" of our history. The depression was probably a reflection, to some extent, of what was known as the "Universal Revolution" which swept Europe. It was a year of severe depression in Germany, causing an uprising among the peasants. Likewise in Austria the finances were in a precarious state, due to revolutions in Vienna and Hungary. There the export of coin was forbidden by decree and the forced circulation of paper notes was ordered. The same year great financial confusion existed in Italy on account of the insurrection which broke out in many parts of the nation. France also was involved in uprisings of the people, as were the various smaller nationalities of Europe.

These developments found us in a position where capital was so locked up in internal improvements as to prove largely useless. The year 1847 was backward; the Mexican War was on and an air of uncertainty pervaded, but conditions in this country were fundamentally sound. Furthermore, we were helped by crop failures in Great Britain and France. They became so desperate that they were driven to pour their gold and silver into the lap of the United

States for the purchase of her bounteous harvests. The end
of the year saw prosperity returning. The depression extended over the last nine months of 1847 and the first nine
months of 1848, altogether a period of a year and a half.
Embarrassments were slight and brief; discounts, never-
theless, fell from $344,000,000 to $332,000,000. The store
of bullion, in spite of the surplus and the favorable balance
produced by the export of grain to Europe, fell from $49,-
000,000 to $35,000,000. Toward the end of the year 1848
the forward movement recommenced.

The Mexican War ended favorably and immigration from
Ireland on account of the potato famine was large. The
influx of these newcomers stimulated activity and was a
factor in ending one of the shortest depressions in our history.

CHAPTER XIV

THE DEPRESSION OF 1857

A financial crisis in this year burst into a panic. It was occasioned by speculation, over-expansion and injudicious bank credits. A violent depression followed, and while its ravages were intense, yet the country quickly recovered and the following year returned almost to normal. The census of 1860 showed practically no traces of it. Some writers claim that the panic of this year was the result of reduction of the tariff, including the placing of many articles on the free list. Others attribute other factors as equally or more important. It is true that there had been an enormous addition to the circulating medium of the country in the form of both gold and bank notes, and speculation both in lands and industrial enterprises was rampant.

"In no other period has this or any other country made such remarkable strides in the accumulation of wealth as during the Golden Age. During the period of 1850 to 1857 President Buchanan calculated the production of gold in the United States at $400,000,000, and while this was unprecedented, had it not proportionately increased prices it would have served as a stimulant to business unheard of in history. The previous year, 1856, 3,642 miles of railway had been constructed. At that time America had seven-ninths of the railroad trackage of the world. Development was far beyond the needs of the time. People apparently invested purely in their imagination of the future. The number of banks had increased rapidly, having practically doubled in the ten years from 1847 to 1857. In 1847 the number was 715. In 1857 there were 1,416. The discounts increased in like proportion and rose from $310,382,945 to $684,456,887. The circulation increased from $105,519,766 to $214,778,822."

In his inaugural address in March of that year President Buchanan said: "No nation has ever before been embarrassed from too large a surplus in the Treasury."

In 1856 reports, presumably from government sources and published broadcast, said that "the year 1856 had given results of which the past had afforded no example. Enormous advance had been made; the cultivation of new territory, the produce of harvests, the extension of factories, the exploitation of mines, the exports and imports, the carrying trade, shipbuilding, the railway returns, the spread and improvement of cities."

Business firms in the West began to fail in the summer when bills on eastern points went to ten to fifteen per cent premium, but eastern banks were the first to succumb, probably because of the drain on them from the West.

The panic broke suddenly with the failure of the Ohio Life Insurance Company, whose home office was in Cincinnati, but having an important branch in New York. It occurred in August, when business men were away; first, a few small business failures, then a large bank, and in a week trade of every kind was demoralized and money went to 25 per cent. Bankruptcies among business houses were the rule rather than the exception. By October the panic had spread to the entire country and runs were being made on banks in every large city. Large city banks refused to receive the notes of country banks, which not only caused great inconvenience, but the value of notes depreciated and business suffered through the confusion brought about.

The failure of the Ohio Life Insurance Company created greater havoc in New York than it did in its home state, although it is said that at one time its failure threatened the existence of the State Bank of Ohio. When the Government recalled its deposits from the state banks, the only one to respond with payment in specie was the State Bank of Indiana, which sent gold to Washington in a stage coach.

Warehouses were flooded, with no buyers, and money

was up to sixty to one hundred per cent. Industry suffered as badly as finance. Mill after mill closed, the strongest running only part time. Factories that a few months before had been running double shift to fill the demand, closed down entirely and prices fell, wiping out all profit and even to 20 per cent below production cost.

Great quantities of goods from Europe which had been purchased on credit and brought in under the low tariff were being held for higher prices. Under such conditions the panic was bound to affect Europe as well as this country. In England houses connected with American firms began to fall one after another, and soon panic was as widespread there as in the United States. Only the suspension of the Bank Act of 1844, on November 12th, saved the financial structure of Great Britain. An Englishman writing at the time said: "The chief blame should be laid to the wild go-ahead spirit of the Yankee."

This depression marked the turn in the ways of commerce of the nation, particularly in the financial centers. The old and conservative element had fallen in the general upheaval and younger men took hold of the reins of business for the first time. Previous to this, gray hairs were considered essential in business, and no man under fifty years was considered sufficiently experienced to handle heavy financial responsibilities, but the panic removed the obstructions to the younger men who arose and filled the places of the old conservative leaders.

Up to this period financial depressions were the signal for new western movements. Steady streams of settlers descended on the western plains when hard times existed in the East. The history of western migration shows that wave after wave rolled out upon the great plains as depression followed depression in the cycles of trade.

The panic affected every section of the country, the East as badly as the West. Thirty-seven banks failed in the State of Maine alone. It was a great day for "wild-cat" banks.

State banking laws were very loose, some throwing out practically no safeguards whatever. The story is told that in the State of Michigan a bank commissioner was watched carefully so that specie could be transported from one bank he had visited to the one he was next to visit. The same boxes and bags of gold and silver went from bank to bank where some official was ready to swear that the owner-ship was vested in the present possessor. At times it is said the bags of gold and silver passed the commissioner on the road, sometimes overtaking him at night and again "arriving too late, it was handed in at the back door of the banking house while an examination was in progress. The bank of Sandstone, for instance, never had any specie, and although its liabilities exceeded $38,000, it had no assets of any kind at the time when it was reported upon. The Exchange Bank of Shiawassee had in its safe but seven coppers and a very small amount of paper, while it had bills in circulation to the amount of $22,267. The Jackson County Bank was discovered by the commissioners to have many large and well-filled boxes, but on being opened and examined it was found that while the top was covered with silver dollars there was nothing below but nails and glass."

State bank notes in circulation at the time were indeed of very flimsy value. They were not "legal tender." The person to whom they were offered in payment of a debt was not obliged to accept them. Had the government real-ized that in time these state bank bills would do great mis-chief, these banks would not have been allowed such a privi-lege. For the time being, the bank bills were convenient, and "the government winked at the practice of issuing them. If one was obliged to take bills that he knew nothing about, he got rid of them as soon as he could, and in ac-cordance with the workings of Gresham's law, when a man found bills in circulation at a great distance from the bank of issue, he felt fairly sure that something was wrong, and paid them out promptly. Such a condition of things was due largely to an absence of any good system of state supervision of banks." Even in the most normal times, when no immediate danger threatened, such money was bound to be doubted by the public. Banks were too often managed by unscrupulous men, who were interested primarily in the speculative side of banking.

Bank management had been conservative and wise in the ten years, 1843-1853, notably in the eastern cities. Few new banks were established, loans were extended with caution, and the issue of notes was kept within reasonable limits. The $100,000,000 worth of gold sent to the mints from California mines furnished a sufficient specie basis for bank currency. Credit agencies kept pace with the normal business development of the country. But in 1853 a speculative mania took possession of the financial world.

In view of the insecure condition of the banks of New York during the years leading up to the panic, it would seem that almost anyone would have known that something was bound to crack. This condition is shown by the following table:

BANKS OF NEW YORK

Year	Metallic Reserve	Deposits	Discounts Advances	Prop. of Met. Res. to Dep.
1854	$15,000,000	$ 58,000,000	$ 80,000,000	26%
1855	9,900,000	85,000,000	101,000,000	11%
1856	10,000,000	100,000,000	112,000,000	10%
1857	7,000,000	99,000,000	122,000,000	7%

The collateral deposited by the banks represented $2,-500,000 in 1856, on which credit of $2,000,000 in notes was granted. In 1857 the same collateral did not exceed $560,-000, estimated value, on which a credit of $383,000 in paper was granted. In his message President Buchanan ascribed the crisis to the vicious system of the fiduciary circulation, and to the extravagant credits granted by the banks, although he was aware that Congress had no power to curb these excesses.

In the Pacific States, where gold was used as money and was very plentiful, the panic of 1857 was scarcely felt, although the San Francisco banks experienced a local panic in 1855, due to over-expansion, during which the well known houses of Page, Bacon & Co., and Wells, Fargo & Co. suspended temporarily.

One feature of the panic of 1857, and the depression that followed it, duplicated the experience of 1837, and that was the almost universal prevalence of what were called "shinplasters." They were practically "I. O. U's" given as change by anyone who had received a bank-note or check for more than the amount due him in payment for anything. In New York the notes of solvent New York banks were never refused in payment, while those of banks elsewhere were tabooed; but in making change no specie was given, the banks having suspended specie payments. So, unless the exact amount was tendered, shinplasters were given for the balance.

"The city was flooded with these personal evidences of debt for small amounts, issued by storekeepers, hotels, restaurants, saloons, barbers, and the rest of mankind, and many of these were passed from hand to hand till they became too dirty and dilapidated to be handled. They were the worst kind of filthy lucre, and understood to be redeemable only on a return to cash payments by the banks. But, of course, many of them never were redeemed. They ranged in amount from one cent to several dollars, and this sort of script was more or less extensively issued from Maine to Texas."

Previous to the outbreak of the panic a terrible strike occurred on the Baltimore & Ohio Railroad. Trains were molested and many fights occurred. The militia was called out and a desperate battle ensued, in which many were killed and wounded. Men were warned in newspapers to keep out of New York City for the winter, to stay where they were known and struggle through as all work shops were closed or over-supplied with hands.

In those days there were a number of publications which apparently prospered by publishing lists of counterfeit, altered and spurious bank notes. Apparently, all kinds of illegal notes were in circulation, including money on imaginary banks, and the public no doubt had to beware of what paper money it accepted. In the year 1858 Nichols' Bank Note Reporter carried 5,400 separate descriptions of false money. Other publications of this time were Thompson's Reporter and Monroe's Descriptive List of Genuine Bank Notes.

That year witnessed an inexplicable manifestation of religious revival in New York. A Dutch Reformed minister, Rev. Lamphire, conceived the idea that an hour of prayer would bring consolation to afflicted business men. He was astonished at the results. Several churches in the financial district were opened and finally a theatre was hired, and for some months all of these were crowded to their capacity by business men who sought consolation for their loss. Even the firemen and policemen held their prayer-meetings.

While admittedly the depression was due to underlying causes, such as speculation and over-expansion of credit, together with the unprecedented high prices occasioned by the enormous output of gold from California and Australia, it is generally accepted that a single incident pricked the bubble, as usual. The story goes that the Ohio Life Insurance Company had $5,000,000 tied up in railroad loans and their New York agent defaulted, causing the failure of the company with large liabilities. One institution after another followed suit, as did many of the eastern railroads. In 1857 there were almost 5,000 failures.

CHAPTER XV

THE DEPRESSION OF 1860-61

The country had made rapid recovery from the panic of 1857 and business had recovered its stride. Grain crops were good, cotton production unparalleled, and diminished imports had brought considerable gold into the country. When the attitude of the South began to be taken seriously, northern creditors curtailed their business with southern debtors and a period of expectancy was abroad in the land. The economic status of the country at the time was described thus:

"The cotton crop in 1860 reached 4,675,770 bales, nearly a million bales more than in any previous year, great gains had been made in the crops of wheat, corn, and other cereals; the production of anthracite coal in Pennsylvania was nearly 800,000 tons greater than in any preceding year; the output of pig iron was 913,000 tons, or 130,000 more than the average of the six preceding years; exports, including the precious metals, had reached the highest point then known, $400,000,000 (of which $316,000,000 was domestic merchandise), or $43,000,000 more than in any other previous year. The consuming powers of the people had never been so high, as was proved in particular by the unprecedented demand for sugar and tea; there was but little pauperism, and wealth on the whole was evenly distributed; 179,000 immigrants landed in 1860, or 58,000 in excess of the preceding year. The tonnage of American shipping was greater than ever before or since, and two-thirds of our imports and exports were carried in vessels having an American register."

Toward the end of 1860 business began to feel the depression keenly on account of the uncertainty attending the presidential election. The country was torn by the slavery question and the South threatened rebellion. Probably the election of that year had greater effect on business

than any other election in our history. When the election
of Lincoln was announced business stood breathlessly
awaiting developments. The southern banks suspended
specie payments on December 12, 1860. While conditions
in the North were bad, they were probably worse in the
South.

It was in this crisis that the plan of combining reserves
was first put into effect. The secession movement had
become so alarming that industry was paralyzed, and the
fifty banks of New York set about to save themselves from
the impending disaster. It was necessary to satisfy depositors of the solvency of the banks so as to prevent withdrawals and hoarding of specie, thus bringing suspension
of the banks themselves. Credit had been expanded in
order to relieve the depression of 1857 and reserves were
low, but leaders felt that they were sufficient to tide over
the crisis if they were all pooled. It was very difficult at
the time to secure concert of action because the banks were
more or less jealous and suspicious of each other. Necessity
forced the issue and finally, on November 21, 1860, clearing house certificates were issued for the first time, amounting to $10,000,000 all to be redeemed by February 1, 1861.
All the banks entered the agreement except the Chemical
Bank, which was noted for years as one of small capital and
remarkably large deposits. This institution felt secure
by itself and proved to be so. The arrangement met with
good response by the public, and the anticipated panic
passed over with only an inconsiderable loss in specie. The
Boston banks considered the same plan but failed to put it
into effect, although their banks eventually weathered the
storm with the help of New York institutions. Business
depression, however, continued until after the outbreak of
the Civil War. When South Carolina seceded December 20,
1860, wild confusion ensued, in spite of the general belief
that the trouble would be of short duration.

Bankers and financiers the country over perceived the

gravity of the situation. They feared that the nation's trade would collapse and the whole framework of our political and financial system would be in danger. "Not only was the domestic situation dismal, but sombre clouds floated over from Europe, where unfriendly nations were awaiting a favorable opportunity to cut up the American Continent as it had been a hundred years before." Under these circumstances it is manifest that the economic situation was extremely dark and business practically paralyzed. At the announcement of the bombardment of Fort Sumter business came to a standstill; stocks went down to almost nothing; money was unobtainable; and distrust everywhere prevailed.

The general opinion was that there would be more economic trouble than political trouble. Nobody thought there would be a prolonged war. Secretary Seward predicted that it would be over in three months, but economic troubles were comparatively short-lived and political troubles prolonged. On December 30, 1861, following the initial fighting, gold was demonetized and later brought a premium as high as 285 per cent over United States legal tender notes. An issue of $20,000,000 of United States 5 per cent bonds brought subscriptions for only one-fourth of the amount, and some of this was never paid for in full, owing to the severely depressed times.

Lincoln certainly faced extraordinary difficulties. Coming into office under stressful and threatening times, he was faced with an empty treasury. Interest payments on the public debt were about to fall due and there was no money in the vaults even for this. The Secretary of the Treasury under Buchanan, Howell Cobb, resigned with surprising suddenness and left for the South, leaving his department in a deplorable condition. So depleted was the treasury after Lincoln's election that the warrants on the treasury for the pay of members of Congress were turned down for want of funds. John Sherman, chairman

of the Ways and Means Committee, speaking in the House
of Representatives on December 10, 1860, said: "Most of
the members are aware that the government has not been
able to pay for the last week or two our own salaries and
many other demands at New York and other places."

The depression was felt very severely in the West. The
securities of the Illinois banks consisted of southern paper
to the extent of 60 per cent, and when the war threatened
frantic attempts were made to turn these securities into
money. But the South was not in a hurry to pay and the
Illinois banks began to be undermined. The Legislature of
that year took cognizance of the situation and passed a law
requiring that all future securities of the banks of that
State should consist of United States or Illinois stocks and
bonds. Large amounts of southern state bonds had been
pledged by various northern banks to secure their circulation. This shrinkage in the value of the security for the
notes caused further apprehension and it was apparent that
a large portion of the northern banks would fail unless they
were given time to gradually replace these securities with
others. In consideration of the stress of the times, the
various State Legislatures permitted this. In Wisconsin
it was said that at least three-fourths of all the banks would
have failed had the immediate demand been made to replace
these securities.

In 1861 the South proceeded to repudiate its obligations
to the North. A great deal of the money was owed in New
England and deposits fell in Boston from $20,811,889 to
$17,176,778 in two months, and specie reserves fell to $3,-
491,348, far below the limit required by law. The whole
amount of southern indebtedness to the North was estimated by intelligent merchants in New York and Boston
at $2,000,000,000 and a large part of it was lost by the
breaking out of war. The disaster of 1857, which spread
to England, had affected the confidence of the whole world
in American securities, and we soon realized that we could

not look to England for financial help in case of protracted war. It was apparent that this country would have to do its own financing. This suspicion was borne out when the United States War Bonds met a cold reception in England. The Government discouraged the circulation of specie, requesting all banks to keep it in their vaults, and issued legal tender notes which were to be taken for all debts, public or private. These notes circulated freely, as it was considered an unpatriotic act to refuse them, and they soon became plentiful under stress of war. Failures in 1861 amounted to 6,993 in number, with liabilities of $207,210,-000. Wages continued high, while only 89,724 immigrants came into the country.

Conant says: "The legal tender notes, which followed quickly on the heels of the demand notes, changed the standard of value in the United States, drove gold across the ocean or into private hoards, deprived us of foreign help and sympathy, advanced prices from 100 to 200 per cent, and added enormously to the profits of speculators and to the costs of the war to the people of the country. The price of gold advanced steadily from the suspension of specie payments until the summer of 1864, when it touched 285. The wholesale prices of nearly all articles climbed upward with the gold premium and retail prices in many cases advanced still more, increasing the paper cost of every contract for carrying on the war."

CHAPTER XVI

THE DEPRESSION OF 1868-69.

Following the peace in 1865, the North settled down into a period of contentment, breathing a sigh of relief that not only the bloodshed and carnage was over, but that the Union had been saved. There was a feeling of security in the North, and while no excessive prosperity was enjoyed fairly normal conditions prevailed until the latter part of 1868. This, however, included only the North, where the soldiers were given receptions of welcome home and where money put into circulation during the war was still plentiful. In the South, however, the worst form of depression existed. The victorious North made it one of the conditions of the surrender that the debts of the Southern States which had been contracted for the purpose of aiding the rebellion should not be assumed by the nation. As a consequence of the repudiation of these debts and the deplorable conditions resulting from defeat, the South was stricken with poverty.

Its only immediate resource was a surplus of cotton, but this had passed from the hands of the producers to interests, mostly foreign, which had it stored in the ports awaiting the end of the war. In the twelve months following the close of the war the exports of cotton, though less than half the quantity of the years immediately preceding the war, reached the unprecedented money value of $200,000,000. Could this money have been distributed to the planters throughout the South that year great suffering could have been alleviated.

The collapse did not follow immediately after the Civil War because of two chief reasons: first, the fact that the customary payment for military debauch was not exacted immediately but deferred for almost a decade; and the other was because of the high protection that had been

given our industries during the war and which was retained, preventing an influx of foreign goods with the coming of peace and maintaining a price level in keeping with
that of the war period.

One cause of the depression of this year was from the
policy of retiring a certain amount of the greenbacks which
had been placed in circulation during the war. The total
amount had been reduced to $356,000,000, when the con-
traction was felt to such an extent that the public clamor
became general against it. On February 4th, 1868, Congress by law stopped the further retirement of this currency
and even attempted to authorize the issue of greater
amounts, a bill providing for same being vetoed by President Grant.

The woolen goods trade was the first to feel the depression which started with that industry the latter part of
1867, as indicated by decreased demand, no doubt due to
the extremely high prices prevailing.

For several years previous to the crash of 1869 there had
been a stringency in the fall of the year when crops were
moving. On investigation it was found that the practice of
certifying checks and the use of national bank capital
and credit in New York stock speculation was the root of
the trouble. It was estimated that $70,000,000 of capital
and $112,000,000 of credit were used in this way. The
Comptroller, in 1868, referred to this condition and suggested a remedy lest the stringency become so acute that
panic would result. No steps were taken, and the very next
year the situation culminated in "Black Friday." The
American dollar had depreciated in value 14 per cent from
the time of the surrender of Lee, April, 1865, until the collapse of "Black Friday," and gold was bringing a heavy
premium. It was then that Jay Gould, with his associates,
conceived a scheme to corner the country' supply through
manipulation of the market. They proceeded to buy up all
the gold possible, the one influence feared being the Govern-

ment, which had in its treasury about $100,000,000 in gold. Gould had formed a friendship with A. R. Corbin, of New York, who had married a sister of President Grant, who frequently visited Corbin's home and in this way became acquainted with Gould.

General Grant was not a good judge of character, but if he liked a man he trusted him entirely, and would believe nothing evil of him. In these private conversations with Grant, Gould made a good impression; he talked a great deal about the necessity of prosperity at such a time and how important the prosperity of the farming class was. He tried then to show that all this depended on maintaining the high price of gold, or even on raising it higher. The point of all this, of course, was to prevent the Government from paying out gold, and thus spoiling Gould's plans.

Grant let things run along without committing himself. Meanwhile Gould was buying up all the gold that he could, but he had to purchase enormous amounts before he dared to advance the price. In the early part of September, 1869, gold stood at 132. Gould's agents had managed affairs so well that they had ensnared certain government officials and had induced them to speculate in the gold market. Then came the famous "Black Friday" which brought on the panic of 1869. Scores of writers have drawn vivid word pictures of this famous financial tragedy. A typical and well written story is that by Moore:

"By the middle of the month it became known that Gould and Fiske were trying to corner gold coin. And then the scramble began. Legitimate business was lost sight of in the mad speculation that came to its climax on Friday, September 24, 'Black Friday,' the most disastrous day our business world had yet seen. On September 20th gold had risen to a fraction over 137, and with this rise the speculators made a false step. The tremendous burden that they were carrying had made them nervous; they had bought millions in gold, which was safe enough if they could sell it for more than they had paid for it, but if the market broke and they had to sell for less than they paid their losses would be enormous. Many of their sales were for future delivery, and if they should be forced to meet these demands they would be ruined. The greater their purchases, the greater the risk they ran, and even Gould, accustomed as he was to speculating, became frightened. He got Corbin to write to Grant, urging on him the supreme importance of keeping the Government's gold supply intact. Though Grant did not understand this letter (received September 19th) he was sure that something was wrong, and he did not want to be involved in any sort of financial crookedness. So he had Mrs. Grant write to Mrs. Corbin, telling her that it was imperative that Corbin should get out of the gold market and sever all relations with the Gould interests. Although this cost Corbin a pretty penny, he was so impressed with the gravity of the situation that he did cut loose entirely from speculation in gold (September 23). Gould took warning at this, and continued quietly to sell all that he could. Fiske, however, plunged even more recklessly. When the close of business came on Thursday gold had risen to 144. Thursday night and early Friday morning the excitement became intense. Tremendous pressure was brought to bear on the Secretary of the Treasury from all quarters, urging him to pay out gold to save the business world from ruin. The speculators calculated that business men must buy gold, no matter what it cost them, because they could do business only with gold. When the price went so high that they could not buy it, then they must fail. With the price at 144 and still rising, thousands of men were near to bankruptcy. Yet, without the sanction of the President, the Secretary of the Treasury could not change the policy of the Government and pay out gold. When the market opened on Friday, September 24th, Fiske's party assumed control. They rushed the price up to 150 almost at once. The uproar was frightful. Increase a thousand times the excitement of a pennant baseball game, shut it up in a small hall, and you may imagine the scene of Friday morning. By noon the price had risen to 160, and a few moments after 12 it reached 162. Just then came word that after a long consultation Grant and his secretary had determined to relieve the situation by selling gold, the amount of the first day's sales to be $4,000,000. This indication of a change in policy by the Government brought people to their senses, and the price of gold dropped almost at once from 162 to 135, only a little higher than it had been two months before. The reaction was terrible; the blind rage of mob violence seized the throng of brokers and onlookers, and Gould and Fiske, who were known to be operators of the scheme, had to hide for their lives.

"The results of Black Friday were two; one moral, the other financial. Such a time presents peculiar temptations to get rich and to cover up financial sins; the great number of dishonest transactions at that time shows the disastrous effects of such occurrences on public morals. The financial effect of this day's work was the great number of business failures that resulted. The whole business life of the country had been at a standstill while the last scenes of the conspiracy were being enacted. This in itself represented a great loss; moreover, these merchants were obliged to get gold or else suspend business. It was not a question of a large or a small sum; every man who owed money was in an equally difficult situation. If no gold could be had, failures must follow in many cases. Friday morning, when the price was up at 160, the failures were to be counted by thousands, and even after the day was over bankruptcies continued. So involved are the relations of the business world that one bad failure often carries others with it, even in good times; but when panic is in the air, the result is doubly disastrous."

A humorous story is told of an Israelite who traded on Wall Street and who had a large supply of the precious metal. When he learned of the break in gold from 160 to 140 he fainted, and after first-aid had been administered for several minutes he recovered. As soon as he opened his eyes he asked, "What ish the prizh now?" When told that it had gone still lower he fainted again, and before the debacle was over he was ruined.

The Garfield Committe in Congress later investigated the whole transaction. Little came of it, but a part of the report read: "The wicked and cunningly devised attempt of the conspirators to compromise the President of the United States or his family utterly failed." When the conspiracy was discovered eye witnesses say that a riotous crowd gathered outside of the office of Jay Gould bent upon lynching that gentleman, but their bird had flown by a rear passage. Gould was later arrested.

Hundreds of firms engaged in business and industry were wholly ruined or seriously crippled. Importers of foreign goods were for many days at the mercy of gamblers and suffered heavy losses. For weeks the business of the entire country was at a standstill; a vast volume of money was drawn from the channels of trade and held in the grasp of the conspirators. The foundations of business morality were rudely shaken, and the numerous defalcations that followed are clearly traceable to the wild spirit engendered by speculation.

The scandals of the Erie Railroad first came to light this year. The Erie stock was in its day much sought after. The numerous pools organized between London and New York fought for control, and the memorable contest between the directors of the Erie Railroad waged between Commodore Vanderbilt on the one side and Gould, Fiske and Drew on the other, was one of the disgraceful occurrences of the period. Vanderbilt, in his attempt to corner the stock of the Erie, spent nearly $16,000,000 in buying stock, which his opponents were issuing fraudulently. The Wall Street fight was carried to the courts, and here injunctions and counter-injunctions resulted in no definite action. The matter was then transferred to the Legislature, where the outcome apparently depended solely upon which side would pay the most money for the votes of the legislators.

Since the outbreak of the war the country had revolutionized its methods of government and business. Truly the Civil War marked the greatest epoch in our history, not only political, but economic: a new monetary system had been created, the policy of extreme protection to our industries inaugurated, and for the first time in our history the system of direct taxation. All of this had its effect on business, although the statesmen of the time carefully safeguarded the interests of business whenever possible.

Failures numbered 2,799, with liabilities increased to $75,054,000. The number of immigrants increased to 352,768. In 1868 fourteen national banks had failed and been placed in the hands of receivers, and a number had gone into voluntary liquidation. The business of the country slowed up only temporarily, and was soon going ahead by leaps and bounds, only to be retarded by the shock of 1873.

CHAPTER XVII

THE DEPRESSION OF 1873-75.

Speculation with all its attending evils was the primary cause of the depression of 1873. Every line of industry had been stimulated beyond its needs in anticipation of still greater profits. Borrowers went heavily into debt, paying high rates of interest, to develop new industrial enterprises with the inevitable consequences of over-production. The depression was marked by failures and bankruptcy of many banks and business houses all over the country. It lasted for three years. This was a world-wide depression. It began in Vienna in May, 1873, spreading through Europe, particularly to London, and then to the United States. It affected Austria-Hungary, England, Germany, Italy, Russia and South America. This country was quickly affected by conditions in Europe because we were unable to market further securities in the Old World, principally railroad stocks and bonds.

The country had incurred a heavy foreign indebtedness, having during the years 1861 to 1868 borrowed abroad on her national, state, railway and other securities, an amount estimated at $1,500,000,000. In consequence of this credit we incurred an annual interest charge estimated in 1868 at $80,000,000. In addition, payments made by American travelers abroad and for freights in foreign vessels brought the total annual tribute, not counting payment for ordinary imports, up to $129,000,000.

The panic started on September 13th, when a rubber house failed in New York. This was followed a couple of days later by two large banks, and by the 20th excitement was intense and runs were made on several other banks. The Stock Exchange closed its doors for ten days, while the clearing-house issued certificates, thus enabling the banks to retain the specie in their vaults. Payment in gold and silver was partially stopped by all banks in New York. Manufacturing, agriculture, transportation and banking lay helpless in the path of the storm. Railroad building had come too fast to be healthy, and such failures as the Erie and the Credit Mobilier hastened further demoralization. A number of Congressmen were given stock in the Credit Mobilier for their influence in legislative matters, and two members were later expelled from the House for bribery in connection with this company. Others were censured and an effort was made to impeach Vice-President Colfax. The import duties of 1872 had been so lowered that foreign competition was sufficient to capsize the already overloaded enterprises which were unable to market their stocks at anything but a ruinous price, with the result that thousands of business firms failed to meet their obligations and went into bankruptcy. The banks were slow in taking concerted action, but even had they done so with greater promptness it is a question whether the panic would have been averted. Deposits in the national banks fell from $641,121,775 on June 13, 1873, to $540,510,602 on December 26.

At the height of the panic money could not be had at any price; some few loans were made at 1½ per cent per day. The banks passed the most critical period by October 14th. Out of 32,278,000 legal-tender dollars at the beginning of the panic, only $5,800,000 remained on hand. According to the statement of the Comptroller of the Currency, "paper discounted decreased between the 12th of September and the first of November from $199,000,000 to $169,-000,000."

An incident of interest might be mentioned here in that it was the first time the expression "frenzied finance" was used, a phrase that we read a great deal about in later years. This period brought forward a new type of American business man. The sober, conservative worker of the antebellum period was replaced by men who delighted in taking big risks, many times blazing across the financial skies like a comet, often making a fortune in a single night. If they made good they were lauded and praised, and if they failed it was little trouble to escape jail. That figure has been with us for some years, but it is probably now passing in favor of the type that is called aggressively conservative.

Railroad construction had gone ahead beyond reason. Five years preceding the depression 32,000 miles of railroads had been built, involving the sum of over $2,000,-000,000. Large sums of this money could not possibly bring an immediate return and scores of the new railroads, unable to meet the interest on their bonded debt, were forced into bankruptcy. Among the important houses to suspend was Sprague, Claflin & Co.

The previous year was a presidential election year, and the notorious Tweed Ring, bent on electing Horace Greeley over General Grant, arranged that a panic should take place simultaneously with the State election in Pennsylvania, so as to illustrate the evil results of Republican rule, and turn the influence in favor of Mr. Greeley's election. The plot was discovered and the news sent to Washington. When the Secretary of the Treasury was convinced of the correctness of the move he arranged to purchase $10,000,000 of bonds and the sale of $10,000,000 of gold for the purpose of thwarting the Tweed conspiracy. The sum of $20,000,000 was deposited in New York banks and placed in circulation, promptly defeating the machinations of the Ring, but it afterward proved that this only postponed the hour of reckoning until the following year.

Many writers insist that the crisis of 1873 was a rebound from the Civil War. We escaped the great European crisis in 1866 because we had become economically independent during the war. The short depression of 1869 might be more properly classed as a reflex of Civil War conditions. Just how the depression of 1873 could be connected with the Civil War is not apparent. It was eight years following the close of the war. The national banking system had been firmly established, and preparations had been made to carry the war debt over a period of years. No trouble was seen ahead in meeting interest payments as the principal was gradually retired. For a country as large as the United States, its national indebtedness, as well as its per capita indebtedness, was not abnormal in the year 1870. Statistics again offset these claims because they show that the absorption of capital in the expanding enterprises of the country between 1866 and the crisis of 1873 was as large as the cost of the war itself. Therefore, it is clear that such inflated credits for peace enterprises was due to come to a sudden halt.

This was the tenth year of the existence of the national banking system and there were 1,980 banks in operation. Coincident with the failure of Jay, Cooke & Co., New York, was the failure of the First National Bank of Washington and the National Bank of the Commonwealth, New York. The widespread distrust brought depositors to demand their money and the country banks drew upon their city reserves. "Between September 12 and December 26 the aggregate individual deposits were reduced from $622,-685,563 to $540,510,602, and amounts due from reserve agents from $96,134,120 to $73,032,046. The New York clearing house issued certificates upon the bills receivable and other assets of its member banks, thus following a precedent first set in 1860. These certificates took the place of cash and allowed the banks to retain cash in their vaults. With some exceptions they were accepted by the public, and the measure was effective as a whole." There were no other failures, and in New York within two months the runs had ceased.

The country banks suffered materially and business was generally prostrated. The terrible distress prevalent impressed the public mind to such an extent that the causes of the catastrophe were earnestly looked into. Speculation was commonly accused of being at the bottom of it all. From a banking standpoint the view was taken that "the provisions of law requiring or permitting national banks to keep a large proportion of their reserves in the financial centres collected a larger proportion of the currency there than could be used for legitimate business. Moreover, the city banks in competition among themselves bid for these deposits from the outside banks by offering to pay interest upon them. In order to make a profit the banks were forced, in the absence of other opportunities, to loan to speculators, and thus the overtrading and speculation which are so apt to end in financial disaster were encouraged. Even the New York Clearing House Association, seized with a "spasm of virtue," as one writer put it, appointed a committee to make recommendation to prevent the repetition of such panics. This committee brought back resolutions "against the practice of certifying checks where there was not a corresponding credit to the drawer," a widespread practice in those days, and against all the well known rules of banking. Others thought the crisis could have been avoided by requiring prompt redemption of national bank notes so that the banks would have to keep their reserves in their own vaults for that purpose instead of sending them to larger centers to get interest. The agitation led to the banking law of 1874, which "permitted the banks, whatever their capital, to withdraw their bonds down to a minimum of $50,000 by depositing lawful money with the United States Treasurer to retire their circulating notes." This law had immediate effect in inducing the voluntary retirement of a large amount of circulation by banks. There was at this time a premium of over 12 per cent in currency upon the 6 per cent United States bonds deposited by the banks as security for their circulation.

The Homestead Act had contributed its full share to the craze for investment. The pioneer farmers, eager to improve their new farms, borrowed from eastern capitalists, mortgaging their lands to them. They, like the railroad companies, made the mistake of investing in improvements more money than they could make good out of their surplus products for years to come. The eastern money-lender was loath to foreclose the mortgage and take the land in lieu of payment—an asset that could not readily be converted into cash. Thus, as Coman puts it, "A Kansas mortgage became the synonym for a losing investment"

Congress met in December of that year, and the intense excitement prevailing was reflected in the deliberations of that body. Over sixty different bills and resolutions were referred to the Senate Committee on Finance. Methods and proposals of various sorts were put forward to relieve the prevalent distress and provide against repetition in the future. The various legal tender acts had authorized issues of $450,000,000 of legal tender notes, on which amount $50,000,000 had been maintained as a reserve for the redemption of temporary loans. They had been permanently retired when the temporary loans were funded, so that the legal tender issues stood at $400,000,000. This amount had been diminished to $356,000,000 when further contraction was stopped. In addition to these legal tender notes, the law allowed an issue of $354,000,000 in national bank notes, most of which were in circulation. Pressure was brought to bear on the Secretary of the Treasury to treat the $44,-000,000 of retired legal tender notes as not permanently retired but as a reserve, and yielding to this demand the greater part of this sum was put back into circulation to relieve the strain. As usual, in the troubles of those days, a great many blamed the currency system. It was afterward obvious that there was ample currency, but too much of it was tied up in speculative channels instead of in productive trade. But cheap money agitators have always been the most clamorous because their ideas appealed to the public which was not educated on the question.

The scarcity of money was most severely felt in the West

and South, and banks in those sections claimed that they had not received their full share of the distribution of circulation, so that these sections were eager to take up the cry of more circulating medium. These people pointed out that currency actually contracted by the retirement of legal tender notes in the face of greatly expanded business, manufacturing and agriculture, railroads, etc., and increased population. They claimed the money circulation should keep apace with increase in population and the growing demands of the people. At that time the per capita proportion of the United States was much under the per capita in France and England. The opponents of the plan pointed out that increased circulation only tended to raise prices, make the cost of living higher and worked a hardship on the poorer classes; that a reasonable amount of money was provided by the present law, if it was taken out of unproductive channels which brought no immediate return and placed in active producing channels. It also was pointed out that railroad building had been overdone. Large stocks of manufactured products were on hand and the capital was tied up in speculative investments which locked the money up until it could gradually be released. They pointed out also that further inflation of money would only bring another day of reckoning and that the period of deflation must be allowed to take its course. This class advocated the return to specie payment, which became an issue in the following years. Those favoring a still larger issue of legal tender currency organized the Greenback Party, while those demanding a return to specie payment remained in the old parties. That the money stringency was not as bad as the inflationists made out was shown in the voluntary retirement of their currency by the national banks of the east and withdrawal of bonds during the period.

The Republicans had demonetized silver and the depression hit particularly hard those men who were interested in the mining of silver, for although silver had formerly been so high that the metal in a silver dollar had been worth a few cents more than a dollar, the discovery of new sources of supply threatened to overturn the price of this metal in the market. "The silver producers, being human, tried to find some reason for their distress other than their own thoughtless action in producing more silver than the market could absorb. Perceiving that the Government might be a good customer if it were coining silver dollars, the silver men immediately charged the leaders of the Republican party with having conspired secretly to cut out the coining of dollars purely out of spite against certain western states, whose chief product was silver. The charge of conspiracy was absurd, and the whole accusation is very plainly a case of trying to shirk responsibility. Hence the phrase "crime of '73" was fastened upon a very innocent and unoffending law."

It was during this period that the agitation started for the free coinage of silver which continued for twenty-five years, being favored, alternately, by both parties until the question was finally settled by the election of 1896.

Hyndman, an European writer, describing money conditions in America after the depression, said: "As usual in all countries after a crash, instead of looking into the methods of production, and the unregulated maladministration of capital, the rich and their governments began to overhaul the banking system and those currency arrangements which, however defective they may be, cannot by any possibility create an industrial crisis, though they may and do intensify one when it comes."

Some writers claim that had there been prompt and united action on the part of the bankers with the United States Treasury the worst of the money difficulties of this year could have been avoided. Henry Clews charged bank managers with having acted "without judgment and almost entirely without any well defined plan of action. There had been an astonishing lack of vigor in their methods and purposes, which were weak and vacillating in their character—frequently more like the acts of children than those of business men."

Various other causes have been given for the panic. Among them were:

(1) Over expansion of the railroads. A large amount of money being sunk in property which could not pay an immediate dividend because of the undeveloped state of their traversed territory. When stockholders found the promised dividends were not forthcoming, they naturally grew wary of further investments, bringing financial embarrassment to new and uncompleted roads.

(2) The money question, the demonetization of silver causing fluctuation in the value of our currency.

(3) Over-extension of credit by the banks to the people, in general resulting in over-expansion of the business beyond the capacity of the financial system to handle.

(4) Some writers refer to the Chicago and Boston fires and their attendant heavy losses as one of the causes of depression.

Another feature that added to the distress was the repudiation of bonds by southern states. The sovereign State of Georgia in this year repudiated the bonds issued by the "Carpet-Bag" administration.

Effects were seriously felt in California by the suspension of the National Gold and Trust Company of San Francisco. Nine national gold banks were operating in that State with a gold note circulation of $2,630,000. These notes were hurried in for redemption, having had bad effect upon business in that section. Gold was popular anyhow in the western states and more or less prejudice existed against paper currency, although such paper today would be eagerly taken in preference to the gold. The first year following the panic saw 5,183 failures, with a loss of $228,-500,000, and during the three-year period of depression over 20,000 failures were recorded with a money loss totaling nearly a billion dollars. Three million men were thrown out of employment with a consequent curtailment of demand for goods. More than 450,000 immigrants came into the country in 1873, which greatly augmented the unemployment.

CHAPTER XVIII

THE DEPRESSION OF 1878.

The business depression of this year was brought about through the uncertainty of the financial situation. In 1875 Congress had passed a law giving the banks four years in which to prepare to resume specie payment, the date of resumption being fixed at January 1, 1879. Business slowed down to see if the banks would be able to comply with the law. As the time grew near there was considerable agitation for the repeal of the law. Conditions of the country were described as full of "desolation and anxiety, and actual want, that reign in hundreds and thousands of households throughout the length and breadth of the land, wrought by this infamous resumption robbery." Time proved that the public was more frightened than hurt, but business was suffering because of the uncertainty. General Garfield insisted that the country was fundamentally sound and underlying conditions satisfactory. He favored resumption. Opponents of resumption claimed that business would improve if the act was repealed. They argued that the national banking system was the main cause of the distress that existed and advocated a free issue of national currency, known at the time as "greenbacks." It was during this agitation that the Greenback Party arose to prominence.

Resumption talk was on every tongue. Horace Greeley, deploring the resulting chaos and uncertainty insisted, "The way to resume is to resume."

In the year previous, 1877, a panic, confined wholly to the savings banks, began in New York and swept over the country. The uncovering of some unsavory methods had led to the general distrust in these institutions. Even the strongest of these banks were put to a crucial test. So great was the distress that most of them were obliged to require notice from depositors. This started the first agitation for laws which are now general, requiring sixty days' notice for withdrawal of savings funds.

Desperate efforts to repeal the resumption act failed, and on the day of resumption the Secretary held $135,382,639 of gold coin and bullion, and, in addition, over thirty-two millions of silver coin and bullion ($32,476,095), the gold alone being nearly 40 per cent of the United States notes then outstanding.

Ex-Comptroller Knox said: "The banks of the country at the date of resumption held more than one-third of the outstanding Treasury notes; but they had so much confidence in the ability of the Secretary to maintain resumption that none were presented by them for redemption. The people also, who held more than three hundred millions of the issues of the national banks, based upon the bonds of the nation, preferred such notes to coin itself. There was, therefore, no demand for payment of the notes of the Government, and the gold coin of the treasury increased more than thirty-six millions in the ten months succeeding the date of resumption."

It can be seen now that the greatest evil of that day was the delay in putting the law into effect. The uncertainty had lessened production and led to stringent money conditions. Too much importance was given to the resumption law and to the contraction of legal tender notes. Business was simply languishing from the effects of the panic of 1873; it had started to recover, but sank back into decline when the agitation started on the resumption question.

Thus, after a great deal of needless stress and agitation involving the failure of business concerns in the short time previous, amounting to $500,000,000, the country passed on to a period of prosperity on a sound financial footing. The economy that prevailed during the depressed times

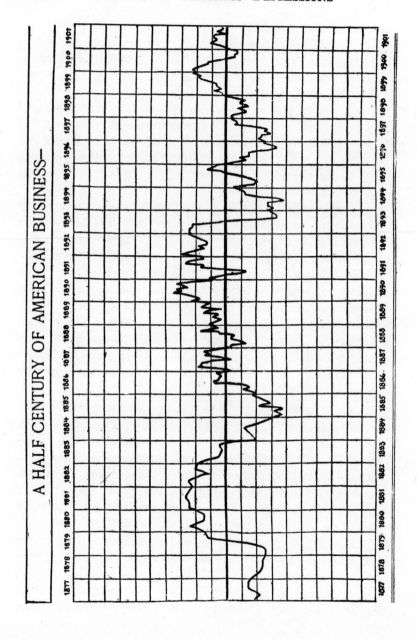

A HALF CENTURY OF AMERICAN BUSINESS—

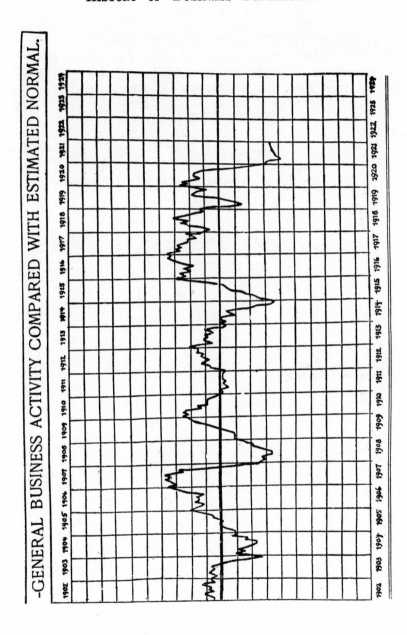

-GENERAL BUSINESS ACTIVITY COMPARED WITH ESTIMATED NORMAL.

made prices of agricultural and manufactured commodities cheap and we exported large quantities, bringing a favorable trade balance and an influx of gold. All of this helped to bring about favorable conditions at the time of resumption so that the various dire predictions did not mature.

CHAPTER XIX

THE DEPRESSION OF 1884

The collapse of 1884 occurred suddenly and with only a short preceding depression. In August of 1883 a rumor started that the failure of a firm of brokers had involved the Wall Street National Bank. An examination by the authorities showed over-certification of checks. The amount was nearly $200,000 and the bank, in order to avoid receivership, went into voluntary liquidation. This was the beginning of the crisis of 1884, the number of mercantile failures in the latter part of 1883 having precipitated the crisis. The year opened unfavorably with the appointment of a receiver for the New York and New England Railroad. Shortly after came the troubles of the Oregon and Transcontinental Company and the North River Construction Company. In February, March and April commercial failures followed. Stocks and securities fell rapidly. On May 6th the Marine National Bank failed, involving houses that were connected with it, one of which was Grant & Ward, with $17,000,000 of liabilities, and a few days later the president of the Second National Bank of New York checked up $3,185,000 short. This institution, however, did not fail because its directors immediately made good the defalcation. In one week three New York banks failed, the Second National, the Marine and the Metropolitan, due to mismanagement and unwarranted speculation. The stringency existing in the money market was occasioned by the displacement of gold, by the newly coined silver, and by draining of reserve which had gone into railroad development and other speculative enterprises. Confidence was shaken to its foundations, however, and institutions of every kind that were not in a strong position suffered embarrassment or complete failure. May 14 the Metropolitan National Bank failed, together with several private bankers and brokers. The same day the Newark Savings Bank, Newark, N. J., suspended, followed in rapid succession by big institutions, such as the West Shore Railroad, the Philadelphia and Reading and many others. The failures caused great excitement. It was practically impossible for banks to collect their call loans as the borrowers could not obtain money by the sale of their securities except at ruinous sacrifices. The New York clearing house again issued certificates which found ready acceptance among the business people and assisted in allaying the excitement and stopping the heavy withdrawals. The country banks experienced similar difficulties. Eleven New York banks were placed in the hands of receivers during the year and more than one-hundred state banks and banking firms throughout the country failed with liabilities exceeding $32,000,000.

Smaller institutions failed in every state, but there was no suspension of gold and currency payments at any point, and the issue of loan certificates was confined to the banks of New York City, and these banks were soon enabled to collect their loans and made good their reserves. Specie payment had been resumed in 1879, since which time no form of United States currency has been at a discount. International bimetalists of repute and authority attributed the bitter experience of trade and industry in 1884 "to the wanton mischief perpetrated by Germany between 1871 and 1875 in demonetizing silver."

The country was now on a silver basis, a total of $369,-400,000 silver dollars having been coined and put into circulation. In 1880 the per capita circulation was $22.82. While this large amount of silver was put out gold was leaving the country, $32,000,000 in gold being exported in 1882 and $41,000,000 in 1884. Silver superseded gold in payments on government obligations as well as in private exchanges. The depreciated value of this money helped largely to bring on the crisis of that year.

*"In the year 1883 the contraction of the National Bank circulation, due to the rapid payment of the debt of the United States, began to be very noticeable. During the year ending November 1, 1883, more than one hundred and five millions of the public debt were called in and paid, and all of the remaining 3½ per cents were called for payment and had ceased to bear interest. Nothwithstanding the fact that 262 new banks were organized with a capital of $28,-654,350, depositing $9,375,550 of bonds as security for circulating notes, the aggregate amount of bonds on deposit for that purpose had diminished from $362,490,650 to $352,907,300, a reduction of $9,583,350. More than forty millions of 3½ per cent bonds held by the banks the previous year had been withdrawn or called for payment, the 3's had increased less than twenty-two millions, and the 4's and 4½'s less than nine millions."

Among the characters prominent in this disturbance were Ferdinand Ward, James D. Fish, George I. Seney, and John C. Eno. It is said that the Metropolitan Bank, the largest failure, was due to Seney's misfortune in speculations. Seney was the president. He also owned various railroad stocks. The system of operating was unusual even for Wall Street. After organizing railroad enterprises, instead of starting with a moderate stock issue, he boldly proceeded to water them lavishly with unvarying exception.

Future prospects of the properties were painted in glowing colors and the public bought freely, probably for the reason that they at once became active stocks on the market. It was later found that this was done through the system of "wash" sales, through which orders were executed to buy and sell both by the same man, which in this case was Seney himself. This process was costly in commissions, and yet that was insignificant to the advertising of the stocks

---

*Knox, "History of Banking."

and their constantly enhanced value. Seney was able to keep up this practice over a period of years largely because of his philanthropic activities.

John C. Eno was in some respects the most spectacular comet that ever blazed across the financial heavens. He was only twenty-six years of age and was president of the Second National Bank, although it must be said that this position had not been acquired through his own efforts, but through his father, who was a very wealthy man. Young Eno was very rash and classed as one of the reckless youths who plunged into speculations without regard to consequences. Speculative tendencies and constant losses caused him to loot the Second National Bank of practically all of its currency. When this was discovered John Eno left for Canada, and naturally trouble followed for the bank, although his father made good practically all of the $4,000,000 which his son had stolen.

Ferdinand Ward was a financier and made a partnership with General Grant, then President, under the firm name Grant & Ward.

Henry Clews writes: "The transactions of the four prominent speculators who played the most conspicuous part in the events which resulted in the panic of May, 1884, should be preserved for reference, as a guide when similar cases arise, for in spite of the deep disgrace, shame and misery that have followed in the wake of their enterprises, these men will have hosts of imitators for many years to come. Ward, Fish, Seney and Eno, with probably the one exception, Fish, are, by many, considered smart men, who simply had the misfortune to become involved, but who had a fair chance of coming out of all their troubles great millionaries and publiciy honored for their ability and success."

There had been administrative mismanagement of important railway companies, an excessive construction of railways, and a wasteful investment of capital in non-paying enterprises. Iron and steel industries were consequently seriously affected, and this in turn extended the circle of disturbance. Many mines were shut down, and for a time there was a large army of unemployed. The presidential campaign was on and the expression "pauper labor" was created as an issue in the campaign.

As an indication of the depressed conditions at the time, it may be noted that wheat fell to 64 cents a bushel, one-half its normal price for that period, thus causing enormous losses to farmers who were unable to pay their loans to banks and eastern capitalists.

Describing the condition of the farmers in Kansas following the depression of 1884, Mr. Frank Wilkeson wrote in the New York Times as follows: "It is a financial impossibility in this era of agricultural competitive warfare for a farmer of average intelligence and skill who tills a farm of one hundred acres of land, except corn land, to lift a mortgage of say $1,000 with money earned by growing staple crops. And nine-tenths of all the uplands lying west of the 97th meridian are utterly unfit to produce corn, excepting in excessively wet seasons." The picture given of life on Saturday in a Kansas town is certainly a startling one. "It matters not how dull the town has been during the week, on Saturday the streets are crowded with people; on that day chattels are sold to satisfy the overdue mortgages. At present these sales are numerous in the West, outside of the corn belt, and a very large portion of these do not realize sufficient to pay the mortgages."

The situation gave evidence of underlying strength, and, notwithstanding the high rates of money and a tremendous drop in prices, there were only a few bank failures. At the close of the year equilibrium was re-established, although the losses had risen to $240,000,000. These losses, it is true, were largely borne by financiers and speculators, rather than by manufacturers and traders. During the fiscal year

1884 the excess of exports over imports of gold amounted to $18,250,640.

Causes of the crisis and depression were a scarcity of money bringing the numerous business failures, decline of prices, and underlying fear that the United States Treasury might find it necessary to resort to payment in silver.

CHAPTER XX

THE DEPRESSION OF 1889-90

In this year we had an instance of depression setting in first, followed by a panic. Agricultural interests were in an unsatisfactory condition and the outlook was unfavorable. The only activity recorded during the year 1889 of any consequence was the completion of railroads which was being prosecuted with unusual vigor, apparently because it was obvious that trouble was ahead. Immense sums of capital of New England had been loaned in the Mississippi Valley and Pacific Coast states on securities which in many cases were not even paying interest. The depression was felt principally in the West and South, due to poor crops and an enormous outflow of money to pay high interest rates which, in the face of low prices of products, was a burden that thousands of farmers could not carry. A large movement of capital to this section had made money stringent in the East. Various banking institutions found themselves with low reserves at the end of 1889. Capital had been so attracted by the new enterprises in the West that eastern business men were unable to obtain accomodations and a severe depression spread over that section. When it was evident that western investments would not materialize favorably, it was felt that there was trouble ahead and preparations were made for the expected collapse. Europe was passing through a period of liquidation and loss consequent upon the failure of the Panama Canal Company in France and unfavorable South American investments in England. In order to strengthen the cash reserves gold was shipped from this country, causing still further weakness in our own situation. The depression lasted the whole of 1889 and well into the year 1890.

The noted Baring Brothers' failure in England in 1890 was reflected in this country. The embarrassment of this firm shook the financial foundations of Great Britain and the Bank of England, in order to avert widespread trouble, guaranteed the Baring Brothers' liabilities to the extent of $75,000,000. The Bank of England was forced to borrow £3,000,000 in gold from the Bank of France and £1,500,000 from Russia.

The financial storm spread to this country, causing a short panic on Wall Street. Probably our banks would have pulled through this crisis had it not been for the large withdrawals of gold previous to the Baring failure.

The Secretary of the Treasury threw the resources of the country into the breach, purchasing over $99,000,000 worth of United States bonds in three months and almost exhausting the available surplus in the treasury. The banks of New York, Philadelphia and Boston were sorely pressed, and the issue of clearing house certificates was again resorted to in order to relieve the stringency. The New York clearing house issued $16,645,000 in certificates, Boston issued $5,065,000, Philadelphia $9,655,000. In that city the Keystone and Spring Garden National Banks failed. Some new silver certificates were also issued and, while this brought on the renewal of the debate on the money question, it relieved the situation for a time, until the great panic of 1893. It was the act of July 14, 1890, designed to relieve the money stringency, that authorized a new kind of paper money called Treasury notes. These were to be used in the purchase of silver bullion at its market price, at the rate of 4,500,000 ounces per month.

The gross deposits of forty-six national banks in the city of New York showed a falling off of $44,831,356 between February 28th and May 17, 1890. Messrs. Charles M. Whitney & Co., David Richmond, J. C. Walcott & Co., Mills, Roberson & Smith, Randall & Wierum, Gregory & Ballou, P. Gallaudet & Co., failed in New York, the North River

Bank of that city was thrown into receivership, and in Philadelphia the failure of Barker Brothers was followed by a number of others. Business was further adversely affected by apprehension, due to changes in the tariff schedule. Business men entertained uneasiness as to the future, and precaution was deemed necessary in all transactions. This depression was almost entirely confined to the East and the Middle West, and was not felt at all in the Pacific Coast states.

Farm and home proprietorship and indebtedness were made the subject of statistical investigation in the Eleventh Census by special act of Congress. No previous census had undertaken a similar work. It was due primarily to the efforts of Mr. B. C. Keeler, of St. Louis, Mo. In 1889, at a meeting of the St. Louis Single Tax League*, he offered a resolution requesting the Suprintendent of the Census to undertake the investigation covered by this report. The idea was at once taken up, and various farmer and labor organizations invited to co-operate in the work.

The report showed that the farms cultivated by owners and subject to incumbrance numbered 886,957, and the value, as reported, was $3,054,923,165. New York had a larger aggregate value of such farms than any other state, totaling $309,352,398; Iowa was second, with $305,658,669, and Illinois third, with $285,706,170. More than two-thirds of the value of this class of farms in the United States was found in the North Central division, and only 4.63 per cent of the total value in the South Atlantic and South Central divisions. Upon the owned and incumbered farms there was an incumbrance amounting to $1,085,905,960, and there are two states in which the amount was at least $100,000,000, namely, New York, with $134,960,703 and Iowa with $101,-745,924. There was an incumbrance of $98,940,935 in Illinois, and an amount not less than $50,000,000 nor more

*Nourse Agricultural Economics pp. 716-717.

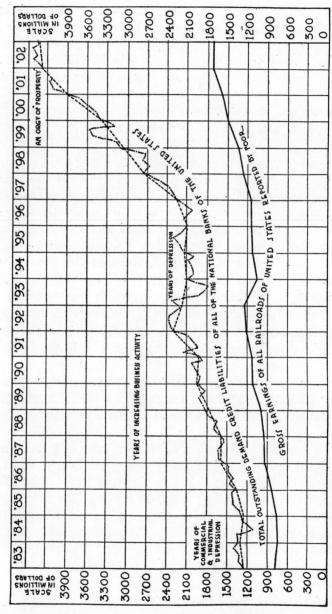

A Typical Span of Two Decades in Our History showing the gradual Upward Climb Halted by Periods of Industrial Depression.

than $75,000,000 in each of the states of Kansas, Michigan, Missouri, Ohio, Pennsylvania, and Wisconsin; 30.91 per cent of the incumbrance was concentrated in the three states, Illinois, Iowa, and New York; 51.01 per cent in the six states, Illinois, Iowa, Kansas, New York, Ohio, and Pennsylvania; and 71.37 per cent in the ten states, Illinois, Iowa, Kansas, Michigan, Missouri, Nebraska, New York, Ohio, Pennsylvania, and Wisconsin. The smaller amounts are found in the Southern States and the Rocky Mountain region.

CHAPTER XXI

THE DEPRESSION OF 1893-95

The crisis of 1893, unlike others, notably those of 1837, 1857 and 1873, did not follow a great wave of prosperity. It cannot be said that the eight years preceding 1393 were any better than normal at the most. The slow times that set in during Cleveland's first administration continued to some degree during the whole of Harrison's, and while they could not be called depressed times, yet they were years in which very little headway was being made. The crisis started with the failure of the Philadelphia and Reading Railroad, February 20th, which occasioned widespread alarm and brought uneasiness to bank depositors. It was known that the banking institutions in New York were heavily involved with speculative investments and their facilities were being strained. Depositors in rural sections began to demand their cash, causing rural banks to call upon their depositories in the large centers. In many cities clearing houses issued certificates, notably, New York, Boston, Philadelphia, Baltimore and Pittsburg.

The depression which continued during 1894 was extremely severe on account of our large and growing industrial population, causing greater loss and more suffering than ever before in the history of the country. The West and South were particularly demoralized. Gold brought a premium of 4 per cent. Commercial failures numbered 8,105 during the six months, April 1st to October 1st, 1893, with liabilities of $284,664,624; and for the year numbered 15,242 with the loss of $346,779,889. Depression extended to every industry. Silver mines which had been prosperous in the previous days of inflated silver closed down because of the low price of that metal. Production of all mines and mills fell off greatly on account of the lessened demand. The farmers became involved on account of the combination of low prices and crop failures. Distress was general and want and even hunger widespread. The panic was followed by the Chicago riots and other disturbances caused by unemployment. Coxey's Army marched in protest from Ohio to the Capitol.

The Baring failure in 1890 frightened European investors regarding American investments, even though North American credits were based on far more substantial securities than in South America. European investors were, in many cases, demanding the return of their principal and were refusing to reinvest the interest, which, in itself, was an important item. In years past American investments had as a whole proven profitable for Europeans, many times enriching the holders in a few years. Under such conditions little money left the United States, as in most cases the interest was reinvested. But with the withdrawal of this capital, which began in 1890, even the interest payments called for enormous amounts of specie to be shipped abroad without compensation in return. It is estimated that the annual interest payments to Europe alone were $350,000,000 a year, and the principal of the debt upon which interest was due was computed at not less than two billions of dollars, these figures being estimates published in the New York Journal of Commerce.

Further cause for the withdrawals was the Sherman Silver Act, which caused Europe to fear the United States was going on a silver basis and abandon the gold standard.

Fuel was added to the flames by this agitation which led to a run on the gold in the United States Treasury till the amount dropped to less than twenty millions, while the amount in the Sub-Treasury in New York was reduced to only about $8,700,000. It was then—in February, 1893—that President Cleveland made his famous gold purchase of

3,500,000 ounces of gold for $62,312,500, giving in exchange United States bonds to the Morgan-Belmont syndicate. This stopped gold exports and replenished the supply of gold in the Treasury, and so restored confidence. The run ceased and after that the greatly increased customs duties began to bring more gold to the Government that it had ever held before.

The 1893 crisis largely revolved around the money question so that a review of the financial and currency problems of the period gives the cause and effect of the depression. The year 1892 had been one of artificial prosperity, due to the infusion of paper into the currency. The paper money was taken freely, and for a short period speculation ran high. Various speculative enterprises were started; new towns were laid out; further manufacturing developed and the general boom was on, but it was the shortest boom we ever had in our history. On December 31, 1892, R. G. Dun & Company's Weekly Review of Trade said: "The most prosperous year ever known in business closes today with strongly favorable indications for the future."

During the years 1891 and 1892 the western banks' deposits of reserve funds in the East increased one-third. During the same period western deposits in New York City were doubled. At the close of the year 1892 the deposits of interior banks in eastern centers amounted to $204,000,-000, all payable on demand. When the run of depositors upon western and other interior banks began in May, these institutions, in order to meet the urgent demands for cash, at once recalled their reserves and other funds which they had on deposit in the East. During the latter part of June the rates for call loans in New York ranged as high as 74 per cent. On July 28th the rate was 72 per cent, and on August 4th 51 per cent was demanded. During the height of the panic there was a tremendous shortage of currency, and many expedients had to be resorted to for the purpose of supplying even the bare necessities of the country for a circulating medium. In this crisis the loan certificates issued by New York banks alone reached $38,280,000, and by the banks of the entire country $63,152,000. It was apparent that the banking facilities were too weak to support the volume of business in the country entirely outside of the money question. Had there not been an over-expansion of credits the money question would probably not have entered into politics and economics at that time.

An attempt was made to solve the problem by establishing 371.5 grains of silver as a standard of payment for existing liabilities and for the valuation of assets. This device would have doubled the proportion of assets to credit liabilities and would have temporarily been an easy solution of the problem, but a large element who thought it would lead to further trouble insisted on the gold standard, which was later adopted in the election of 1896, after which credit was entirely liquidated and the country continued on a sound basis.

"Before the depression began," writes Cleveland, "the capital, surplus, and undivided profits of national banks amounted to $1,041,807,066.87. September 15, 1902, immediately before the October money and credit stringency of that year began to be felt, the total of capital, surplus, and undivided profits was only $1,201,145,882.69, a decrease of nearly $11,000 per bank doing business. There had been an increase of $1,561,335,896.44 in obligations to depositors, while the gross increase in capitalization available to support this increase in demand liabilities was only $159,338,815.82, about 10 per cent. The average net increase in deposit liabilities was $282,418; the net decrease of capital was $10,951 per bank doing business."

The passage of the Sherman Silver Law, while not a direct cause of the panic, contributed indirectly to it because it brought on withdrawls of gold from the treasury almost from the moment it was enacted. On June 30, 1890, the total gold in the treasury was $321,612,424. It gradually shrank until by June 30, 1893, it had fallen to $188,455,432. The gold certificates in circulation June 30, 1890, amounted to $131,380,019; on June 30, 1893, to $92,970,019, leaving a net gold reserve on June 30, 1890, of $190,232,405, which dwindled in three years to $95,485,413, and this was the total gold reserve that the government had on hand to combat one of the greatest panics of our history. Gold exports began in large volume the month the Sherman law was approved and reached a total in the fiscal year 1891 of $86,-362,754; in 1892 of $50,195,327, and in 1893 of $108,-680,844.

On June 1, 1893, the banks of New York held $21,000,000 in excess of their legal cash reserves. The national bank notes then outstanding were about $177,000,000. The exceptional demands for currency had drawn down the reserves of the New York banks, on August 1, $14,000,000 below the legal minimum.

President Cleveland made an earnest effort to secure the repeal of the Sherman law in order to convince the world that American money was sound and that she was ready and able to meet all obligations. A meeting of the cabinet was held on June 30th, at which the increasing number of failures and suspensions of banks and the paralysis of business were fully discussed, and the President determined to summon Congress in extra session on the 7th day of August. The call came none too soon but did little to stay the progress of the panic. Banking institutions, national, state and private, were daily suspending; depositors were withdrawing their cash from the banks whenever possible, and industrial enterprises were closing down. Twenty-five national banks suspended in June, a number never before exceeded in an entire year; seventy-eight suspended in July, and thirty-eight in August. The collapse of private and state banks was even more alarming.

For some years the United States had been trying to get united action by the nations of the world in making silver the universal basis of money by free coinage. The International Monetary Conference held several sessions at different capitols, but in no case was an agreement reached. Italy, France and Spain had formed a monetary alliance known as the Latin Union, which was able to maintain the value of silver at a fairly uniform price retail. Bismarck, then Chancellor of Germany, was persuaded to the demonetization of silver. A large amount of the metal from that country was then thrown into the Latin Union countries and overflowed into the United States in great abundance. The European countries first limited their coinage of silver and finally suspended it. This put the price down to its commercial value and caused consternation in the United States, where it naturally depreciated.

America stood almost alone for bimetallic coinage. Just at this time the Indian Currency Committee officially announced the closing of the mints to the free coinage of silver. This news of the action of the British Government caused a profound sensation in the United States and in-creased the tendency to unreasoning panic. After a hard fight in Congress, in which party lines were divided, the Sherman law was repealed. The business public accepted the suspension of payments without complaint and certificates were gladly taken in order to transact what business was done.

Flooding the country with the immense amount of paper money authorized in 1890 was bound to lead to trouble. It was beginning to be realized then that the previous stringency in 1890 was not caused by lack of circulating currency but entirely from other causes, such as crop failure, large importation of foreign goods, causing an outflow of gold, and too much money tied up in speculative channels. Had the government refrained from purchasing silver the national banks would have increased their circulation up to a much higher point and the situation would eventually have been relieved on a sound basis. On the strength of the large amount of paper money issued new banks were rapidly organized.

In 1892 one hundred and sixty-three new national banks commenced business with a capital of $15,285,000. All this was the forerunner of one of the most disastrous panics the country ever experienced. Business began to be depressed because of the prevailing doubt as to the power of the government to maintain gold payment of all this paper money if presented for redemption. The banks themselves were the first to become wary. Back of it all there was really a lack of confidence in the Treasury. Depositors began withdrawing money in specie and putting it away. Practically every savings bank in the country was menaced and for a few months it was not thought possible that even the strongest institutions of this kind could weather the storm. Unemployment was so general that withdrawals were made even by those who had confidence in the savings banks. Fear was in the minds of the people that we might fall to a silver standard because of our low gold reserve and the large ratio of silver being coined.

An idea of the reduction in exchanges caused by the panic may be gathered from the shrinkage of the transactions of the New York Clearing House from $34,421,380,870 for the year ending October 1, 1893, to $24,230,145,368 for the year ending October 1, 1894. The comparison for the prosperous month of October, 1892, with the same month in 1893, showed a shrinkage in the clearing transactions of the leading cities of the United States from $5,501,901,592 to $4,-043,510,662. The clearings throughout the leading cities of the country showed a shrinkage from $58,880,682,455 for the year ending September 30, 1893, which included a part of the period of panic, to $45,017,960,736 for the year ending September 30, 1894. The failures throughout the country increased from 10,270, with liabilities of $108,500,000 in 1892 to 15,560, with liabilities of $402,400,000 in 1894.

During the year 158 national banks suspended business,

the capital stock aggregating $30,350,000. In all the large cities clearing houses issued certificates. State banks, private banks and trust companies to the number of 415 failed. A careful compilation of the records show that over 900 banks of all classes were in difficulties. A portion later reorganized and resumed. Deposits in the national banks declined in a few months from $1,764,456,177 to $1,451,-124,330. The net earnings of the national banks that year was only 5.6 per cent, with two exceptions, that of 1878 and 1879, the lowest on record. Banking institutions were consolidated in many cities in order to preserve their resources.

July 26th was a day of great strain in New York. Rates for money, which were normal in the morning, rose to 75 per cent per annum before the close of business. An appeal was then made to London and $10,000,000 in gold was engaged. By August 5th the reserves of the New York banks were $14,000,000 below the limit.

For fourteen years, 1878-1892, only an insignificant amount of gold was paid out by the treasury in the redemption of legal-tender notes. The total amount of gold in the treasury increased almost steadily and continuously from $140,000,000 on January 1, 1879, to $300,000,000 in 1891. A new issue of treasury notes in 1890, together with demands in commercial channels, placed heavy burdens upon the reserve, the rapid diminution of which is shown in the following figures:

Date	Net Gold Reserve
June 30, 1890	$190,232,405
June 30, 1891	117,667,723
June 30, 1892	114,342,367
June 30, 1893	95,485,413
June 30, 1894	64,873,025

The reasons of the fall in the gold reserve are various and complicated, but among them might be given the withdrawal of gold by Europe following the Baring failure, the hoarding of gold in this country by individuals, and its purchase by banks who feared the results of the Silver Purchase Act.

"The Treasury had been weakened," explains Dewey, "by the reluctance of Secretary Windom to deposit government funds in national bank depositories, and by his preference to rely entirely upon the purchase of bonds for getting money back into circulation. In the earlier years of Harrison's administration bonds were purchased freely, too generously in view of the impending strain upon the resources of the treasury."

The failures for the year 1893 are given in this table and figures for the year 1892, a normal year, are given by way of comparison:

*MERCANTILE AND INDUSTRIAL FAILURES 1892-93

1893	First Quarter	Second Quarter	Third Quarter	Fourth Quarter	Total
Number......	3,202	3,199	4,015	4,826	15,242
Liabilities...	47,338,300	121,582,539	82,470,040	95,389,010	346,779,889
1892					
Number......	3,384	2,119	1,984	2,857	10,344
Liabilities...	39,284,349	22,989,331	18,659,235	33,111,252	114,044,167

Bank failures are given below as shown from the table compiled by the Comptroller of the Currency:

BANKS, ETC., WHICH SUSPENDED, JAN. 1 TO SEPT. 1, 1893

Class	Number	Assets	Liabilities
State Banks_____	172	$41,281,848	$36,903,266
Savings Banks _____	47	17,673,938	16,830,809
Loan and Trust Cos.___	13	14,337,500	22,354,000
Mortgage Companies__	6	760,803	1,790,000
Private Banks _____	177	20,237,259	19,315,455
	415	$94,291,348	$97,193,530

The following year, 1894, really saw the worst of this depression. Great poverty existed in the cities; factories were closed and distress was felt everywhere. The Chemical National Bank of Chicago, with a capital of $1,000,000, closed its doors on May 9th, and was followed two days later by the Columbia National Bank of Chicago, with a

---

*Figures from "The Commercial and Financial Chronicle."

capital of an equal sum. The Distillers and Cattle Feeders Company was another large concern which was involved, its shares falling from $70 to nothing. In 1893, the proportion of loans to deposits rose to about 109 per cent, and proportion of specie to loans declined to 13 per cent. The average price of twenty prominent stocks reached about $47 per share. The number of failures for the year exceeded 15,000.

*"Aggregate liabilities of bankers and banking institutions in the United States failing in 1893 and the two succeeding years:

1893 (year of crisis) _____		$170,295,698
1894 (year of depression) ___	$13,969,950	
1895 (year of depression) ___	22,764,000	
Average for the years 1894 and 1895 _____		18,366,975

Excess in 1893 (year of crisis) over average
    for 1894 and 1895 (years of depression) $151,928,723

    or 827 per cent."

*"Aggregate liabilities of all others, including merchants and manufacturers:

1893 (year of crisis) _____		$231,704,322.
1894 (year of depression) __	$135,030,050	
1895 (year of depression) __	136,236,000	
Average for the years 1894 and 1895 _____		135,633,025

Excess in 1893 over average for 1894 and
  1895 _____ $ 96,071,297

"Excess of liabilities from failures of merchants, manufacturers, and others in 1893, year of crisis, over average for two ensuing years of depression, slightly less than 71 per cent."

"It thus appears that the percentage of excess of liabilities in the crisis year over the average for the two succeeding years of depression was nearly twelve times as great (827 to 71) in banking failures as in mercantile, manufacturing, and all other failures."

This revulsion witnessed the distress incident to a financial collapse of the ordinary type, intensified by the depletion

---

*Figures used by Burton.

of the gold reserve in the Treasury and the perils which threatened even the gold standard.

The range of leading industrial stocks on the New York Stock Exchange in 1893 is shown as follows:*

Miscellaneous	Opening	Lowest		Closing
American Sugar _____	111	61	July 26	81
American Tobacco Co._____	121	43	July 31	70
National Cordage _____	138	7	Aug. 25	20
Pacific Mail Steamship_____	27	8	July 27	14
United States Rubber Co._____	46	17	Aug. 17	42
Western Union Tel. Co._____	96	67	July 26	82

*Figures used by Lauck.

CHAPTER XXII

THE DEPRESSION OF 1903

The year 1903 may be characterized as the culmination of that long period of prosperity which had its inception in the sound money triumph in the presidential election of 1896. Wonderful strides had been made by the nation if we may judge by the largest three industries. The iron and steel industry was never so busy, the railway industry was burdened with all the freight that it could handle, while the agricultural interests of the country were favored by enormous crops. If these three industries are a reflector as they usually are, the prosperity of the nation was such as to stand almost without a parallel. We might expect, therefore, that the prices for securities representing large industrial concerns would be quoted at a very high level. And we might also expect a reverse in the upward swing, characterized by conditions in the stock market approximating a panic. It was a year marked by fluctuations in stocks. In a single day Pennsylvania Railroad stock was quoted at the low and high extreme of 110¾ to 157⅜.

There was a period of sharp increase in money values. All stocks lost heavily through the resulting liquidation. As the speculative period had apparently ran its course it was to be a year generally of declining prices which periodically comes, at which times weaker stocks suffer and companies are often taken over by more powerful corporations. The Northern Securities suit of that year undermined confidence because of the publicity given to unsavory financial methods. The shrinkage in the value of stocks was so pronounced and so continuous that it may be said to have had few, if any, parallels in stock exchange history. The extent of the decline may be understood by the quotations of a few high grade stocks. Pennsylvania Railroad stock dropped in January from 128⅝ to 110¾ in November. It again rose to 140 in 1904. New York Central fell from 156 in January to 112⅝ in July. It again rose to 145 in 1904. Chicago and Northwestern declined from 224½ to 153 during the year, but again rose to 214. Union Pacific fell from 103⅝ to 65¾ but again rose to 117 in 1904.

The depression, affecting mostly investors and speculators in stocks, started through the collapse of large corporations which had been over-inflated and watered beyond reason. Over $6,000,000,000 worth of securities had been floated in the few years preceding, many of which were of questionable value but which were bought eagerly by the investing public who had been duped with stories of immense fortunes having been made in industrial lines, the outstanding example of which was Andrew Carnegie. The shipbuilding trust, as it was called, was the first to collapse, revealing as it did some of the evils of high finance which permeated the period. Disillusioned investors threw every kind of stock on the market, resulting in severe declines and a reaction of public sentiment against industrial stocks. This followed the day of rapid organization of trusts and combinations. One hundred and eighty-five had been formed within a few years of this time, taking in from four to as high as forty plants in a given industry with a total capitalization of $1,436,625,910. Some of them did not meet with the success that was anticipated and these followed the shipbuilding trust in collapse, due to over capitalization and stringency in the money market.

The barometer, as indicated by the iron trade, was still rising at the opening of 1903. Good crops had been gathered and were being sold at good prices; railway earnings were large, and railway companies were making heavy expenditures for new equipment and improvements, and every department of business and manufacturing industry seemed prosperous. So heavy, indeed, was the demand for iron and steel that the capacity of the plants was unequal to it, and we were importing iron and steel to some extent, as we had been in 1902. Then in June the iron industry experienced one of its well-known quick changes. The figures suddenly registered a severe drop. The demand subsided with surprising celerity in all lines, and by November prices in some lines were 50 per cent lower than in January. The boom in the iron trade which commenced in 1899 was at an end.

Before the end of 1903 liquidation on a large scale in stocks had run its course and exhausted itself, and the market quieted into comparative steadiness.

In this same year Canada made material progress, more so than in any previous year of her history; money was plentiful, crops good, and 150,000 emigrants had entered the Dominion.

The depression affected the United States Steel Corporation to such an extent that, for the first instance in its history up to that time, the wages of the men employed in the plants were reduced. Gross sales for the year were only $444,405,431, and net profits $73,176,522. No special appropriation for new construction was made and, despite the small profits, the corporation managed to show a surplus of $5,047,852 after the payment of the full preferred dividend.

Bank clearings showed a reduction of $9,000,000,000 as against the previous year. During this period several bills were introduced in both houses of Congress aimed at correcting the financial system so as to avoid recurrence of crises.

At this time we heard the first serious discussion on the question of taking the center of the national finance away from Wall Street and establishing reserve cities so as to distribute financial centers throughout the country.

CHAPTER XXIII

THE DEPRESSION OF 1907-08

This depression followed a financial panic which broke in November, 1907, almost without warning. The business depression following it was of comparatively short duration, lasting only through 1908, or about fifteen months. The crisis proved to be a blessing in disguise, as it demonstrated the weakness of our financial system and awakened us to the need of urgent action, finally bringing about the passage of the Federal Reserve Act. The causes of the disturbance were the weak financial system and unrestrained speculation, although a number of other theories have been advanced. On the whole there had not been extensive over-production or construction work beyond immediate needs. Neither was there undue inflation in real estate values.

On the surface the events of 1907 were more startling, more spectacular and more unexpected than the events of either 1873 or 1893. No word had gone out to the public about dangerous underlying conditions that existed in the financial world. Since the facts have come to light, the crisis that was developing during the whole of that year has become known as the "silent panic."

This panic would have broken in March, 1907, had it not been for prompt relief from Washington. Previous months had witnessed high tension in the financial center. Call money in December, 1906, commanded from 9 to 15 per cent. During a few days in January as high as 50 per cent was paid for call money. By March the situation had become so bad that the banks were forced to call loans, and securities dropped in a single day five to twenty-five points. General prosperity ruled throughout the country and there seemed to be no fear on the part of the public of an impending disaster. Relief measures taken at Washington remedied matters somewhat and had proper precautions been taken perhaps the panic which came in the fall could have been averted. However, everybody was making money, sales were good, bank clearing the highest on record, and nobody wished a halt in the good times. Those with their ear to the ground saw, however, that inevitably something must happen.

Financial leaders should have demanded a gradual contraction, or at least no further expansion, confining loans to what were absolutely necessary to protect the solvency of the borrowers. But the banks apparently went ahead unchecked, and when the emergency came they called on the treasury as they were in the habit of doing. In May of that year the banks called for help and again in August, when additional relief was rendered, but all this did not suffice. It left the ever increasing weight of obligation still on the banks, and when rumors of the weakness of certain banks persisted runs started and the crash came.

It is now conceded that the officials at Washington made a mistake. Instead of calling attention to the capital weakness of the banks, the Government permitted them to continue to use the large treasury balance without interest.

It was a period of confidence, large crops and ample business. All the leading influences contributed to make it a period of unexampled activity. The railway industry and the iron and steel industry were favored to an exceptional degree.

Bank clearings in New York were $29,350,894,000 in 1896 and increased in 1907 to $95,315,441,000, and for the entire country the increase was from $51,935,651,000 in 1896 to $154,662,515,000 in 1907. The volume of money in circulation rose from $1,506,434,966 in 1896 to $2,772,956,455 in 1907. In the five years from 1903 to 1907, inclusive, the world's output of gold was $1,855,421,300. The country made rapid strides in every line—agriculture, manufactur-

ing, banking, etc. Par value of outstanding securities in
the United States in 1905 totaled $35,000,000,000. Money
rates continued reasonably low until the latter part of September. The activity and tremendous rise in prices which
marked the year 1904 were hardly a circumstance to the
extraordinary buoyancy and unrestricted optimism that developed in 1905, '06 and '07. As the Commercial and Financial Chronicle stated:

"Unfavorable developments were completely ignored and favorable features long seemed to count,
yet this year was marked by some very severe
breaks subject, however, to almost immediate recovery. Thus in January there were rumors of an
early settlement between the Harriman and Hill
factions. There were also rumors concerning a
combination of the Union Pacific, Standard Oil,
and Vanderbilt interests. Largely because of these
rumors, and other circumstances, the price of
Great Northern jumped from 236 to 254. Northern
Securities rose from 113 to 123. As a matter of
fact, nothing came of all these rumors except that
there were some changes on the directorates of
these corporations which made for greater uniformity of management. Yet in spite of these
conditions the last few days of the year showed
a tremendous decline in the value of almost the
whole list of securities, and the market on the
closing day of the year was practically on the
verge of a panic. Great Northern dropped from
335 to 270; Union Pacific from 137 to 118; New
York Central from 163 to 141; Milwaukee and St.
Paul from 187 to 170; Ontario and Western from
63 to 49 and Pennsylvania Railroad from 144 to
137."

This decline in the value of these securities while their
earning power continued undiminished—and the condition
of their business was as favorable as could be desired—
serves as an illustration of the effect of extraneous forces
upon the security market.

Amalgamated Copper took a turn downward in the summer, thence leading up to the fall crash. Steel and other stocks were moving down without any apparent cause. Lord Rothschild gave an interview in London, which, coming from the source it did, was ominous. He said New York was hoarding money. Apparently, it was the insiders who were selling and holding the money in order to buy back cheaply. This feature has been referred to as the "Conspiracy of 1907." Alvin S. Brown, a New York man, issued a pamphlet of that title; he gathered in a unique collection of clearing house certificates issued in various cities in the United States.

The reversal came quickly and dramatically. Starting in November it overwhelmed banks and industrial corporations, the most important of which was the Tennessee Coal and Iron Company. The Morgan interests seized this opportunity to take the property over as a part of the United States Steel Corporation. This was the most important instance of a tendency that had sprung up during recent depressions of powerful corporations to absorb the weak. That does not, of course, mean that large corporate interests have any great liking for depressions. Rather, they have a great deal to fear because of the heavy overhead involved in keeping the many plants in running condition, thus taxing their resources to the limit. Corporations that are sound and have strong banking connections weather these periods and even take over their smaller competitors, but an independent plant, if in sound financial condition, and properly managed, has the advantage in years of depression because it is able to more quickly and effectively curtail expenditures. Large companies, commonly known as trusts, have a further disadvantage in that they are looked to in setting the market prices of the commodity they control. With large stocks on hand they are not able to make the quick reductions necessary to stimulate business in times of depression, because of the loss they would have to take which would often weaken them and bring their finances to an unstable condition.

These corporations invariably make worse rather than improve depressed periods by draining the resources of the financial world. Unless they followed this practice they would be forced into bankruptcy, with its attendant ruin, so that it is necessary to sustain them until they can decrease their stocks and readjust their costs. On the other hand, small independent concerns do not require such large financing and are more able to make a quick readjustment. These corporations have banking institutions closely affiliated with them in order to protect them when no call money is to be had. Sometimes the resources of the banks are strained to support the large corporations, so that the average business man and investor is without resources to tide him over. This was the case in the depression of 1907 and '08.

This panic has been called the "rich man's panic". A writer who lived in the day of the Great Chief, and was probably numbered among his enemies, has attempted to brand it as the "Roosevelt Panic." Still another even goes so far as to record on the sacred pages of history the statement that Roosevelt's speeches were the main and principal cause of the panic and depression. What "malefactor of great wealth" this writer was interested in is not known!

Adolph Edwards, a long forgotten writer, wrote a book entitled "The Roosevelt Panic of 1907," in which he started off thusly: "In the course of time a man in clerical garb will stand before the earthly remains of Theodore Roosevelt and repeat the familiar words, 'Dust to dust and ashes to ashes,' and the gaping multitude will look on, as it always does, dumb, stolid and unflinching, before the last and greatest mystery of human existence. 'The evil that men do lives after them,' and the unmoved and inexorable historian shall submit to the judgment of unborn masses the record of the achievements of this unique figure in the annals of American history. The ruin he may have caused, the homes he may have wrecked, the unspeakable misery of want and starvation, or the dread of them he may have inflicted, the reckless blunders, the wanton lack of judgment and deliberation, of which a nation of eighty millon, nay, the whole world, has suffered the inevitable consequences —all this shall be written, not in the heat of passion or under stress of suffering, but coldly and with relentless deliberation."

Fourteen years have passed since this was written and Theodore Roosevelt has passed on, but even after this short space of time no living soul would hold him responsible for the panic of 1907. Yet, at the time, there were thousands who, probably conscientiously, held the opinion of the author quoted.

It was fashionable in those days to blame Roosevelt for everything, and some scored him who now are haunted by their words. Had President Roosevelt not taken the bold stand he did against the flagrant abuses of those times we would have had a worse day of reckoning than we did in 1907. Roosevelt saw plainly where those practices were leading us and he knew that there had to come a shock in facing it, at one time or another, and he must be given credit for having the courage to face it himself and not leave it over to his successor. As time goes on we see that his course was timely and providential.

Attorney General Bonaparte facetiously said "that there was a fine covey of game among the large capitalists in control of corporations, and that it would be a poor marksman who would not bring some of the birds down." All of this had the wrong-doers in a very nervous state. However true it was that the panic was a "rich man's panic," it affected seriously the business of the whole country and some claim that we did not fully recover until the World War. It is true that we did not have any further boom times, but 1909 was a normal year according to all statistics, and normal years continued with the exception of the depression of 1914-15.

The insurance scandal unearthed by the Hughes investigation had already undermined confidence in the financial structure. Coman gives this as the cause of the general weakness of American financial organizations: "Undoubtedly, the antics of the big people caused investors to be wary, with the result that the corporations were not able to market securities readily and resorted to the heavy use of their borrowing power, thus draining the money market, so that ordinary concerns who were in pressing need were driven to failure." When New York banks found difficulty facing them, particularly the Carnegie Trust Company, with which, incidentally, Andrew Carnegie had no connection, they were unable to obtain immediate help because of already lowered reserves in other institutions.

As that disaster was well within the memory of most of us now living, what can be said here will be taken only as the opinion of an individual. Others might have a different diagnosis. It is known that the match that lit the conflagration was the single incident of a scandalous bank failure at the opportune time, when a slowing up was very much desired, if not past due. When the first bank failure came along it caused other banks to call loans and a contraction resulted in general fright. After it was under way the enemies of Roosevelt who swarmed from Wall Street and from other high places quickly seized the opportunity to "wrap the child in their own soiled garments and lay it on Roosevelt's doorstep." Three great trust companies of New York failed, bringing fear and distrust into the minds of the people throughout the country. Clearing house script was in vogue in all large cities. Laws were quickly passed by legislatures in session allowing savings banks as much as sixty days' time in meeting withdrawals. Agricultural districts were not affected so much, since the depression was

quickly over, and the end of 1908 found the country ap-
approaching normalcy.

"In 1890, according to statistics compiled by the director
of the mint, the world's supply of gold available for momen-
tary use was less than $4,000,000,000. In 1907 it exceeded
$7,000,000,000. At the same time, based upon this gold,
there was a gigantic expansion of banking credit. In the
United States bank deposits (including those of savings
banks) increased between 1890 and 1907 from $6,000,000,-
000 to $19,000,000,000, and practically all of this expansion
took place after 1897. According to compuations made by
the Comptroller of the Currency the item of individual deposits in national and state banks increased from $7,000,-
000,000 in 1900 to $13,000,000,000 in 1907. During the
same period—the advance beginning in 1897 and ending in
January, 1907—the average prices of commodities in gold-
standard countries rose some 40 per cent. In the stock
market the upward movement of prices during those ten
years was still greater. According to computations made by
Mr. James H. Brookmire, of St. Louis, who bases his calculations on the quotations of twenty representative railroad
stocks, the lowest point was touched in December, 1896,
when the average price was 41. From then until the end of
the Boer War in 1902 there was an irregular advance to 130.
In the Fall of 1902 began a decline in stocks which continued
until September, 1903, the lowest point which these stocks
touched being 88. Then began a more rapid upward movement continuing through 1904 and 1905, the highest point,
138, being reached in January, 1906. Throughout 1906 the
prices of these stocks barely held their own. A rapid downward movement began in January, 1907, until in March
they touched 98; then they advanced until July, when a
decline began which finally carried them during the October
panic down to the lowest point of 82."

"It is very difficult to escape the conclusion that all this
advance of prices and expansion of credit must in the main
be attributed to the great increase in the world's stock of
gold. This prosperous decade had much more than its share
of untoward events which were calculated to restrict enterprises and hold credit in check. There were, for instance,
our own war with Spain in 1898, England's war against the
Boers in 1900 and 1901, the Russo-Japanese War and in

1904 and 1905, the anthracite coal strike in 1902, and the Baltimore and San Francisco conflagrations. Despite these events and others of a similar character, which tended to waste capital and destroy the confidence of conservative men in the business outlook, the tide of prosperity rolled on almost without check until the beginning of 1907, prices advancing, the stock market booming, bank clearances swelling, the average man convinced that good times, being deeply rooted in natural conditions, would persist so long as the sun shone and the rains fell. This prosperity was by no means confined to the United States. It existed in Canada on the same scale as here, and in a lesser degree throughout Europe and in the countries of South America, in which large sums of European capital were invested. For example, the loans of Canadian banks rose from $225,000,-000 in 1896 to $712,000,000 in 1907. The total bank clearings of the United States increased from $51,000,000,000 in 1896 to $160,000,000,000 in 1906; clearings at London rose from £7,500,000,000 to nearly £13,000,000,000, and the Paris clearing from 7,000,000,000 to nearly 18,000,000,000 francs.

"In 1897 prime commercial paper sold in New York City at from 3 to 3½ per cent. In 1904 it sold at from 4 to 5 per cent. In 1906 and 1907 the rate was often 7 per cent and the average was fully 6 per cent. The bank of England, except for brief intervals, has maintained rates ranging from 4 to 6 per cent for the ten years, but finally in 1907 it advanced its rate, as the result of the panic in the United States, to 7 per cent. The rates of interest at other European financial centers were correspondingly high. The most spectacular evidence of the shortage of investment money in Great Britain was furnished by the decline of consols to 83."*

General speculation was the order of the day, and when the year 1907 opened it was apparent among far-sighted financiers and business men that inflation had been carried to extremes and conservatism must prevail to avoid serious difficulties, but the public would not have it that way. In the early part of 1907 old time traveling salesmen said they never had such a bonanza; everybody bought liberally. To those who did not have their fingers on the pulse of the

---

* Quoting Laughlin.

economic situation it looked like the good times would continue perpetually. The short collapse in the stock market in March only caused the rest of the country to sit back and grin. They saw no trouble ahead and felt secure against the evil influence of Wall Street.

The year before the United States Treasury held $816,-354,352 in gold, the largest amount held up to that time by any government or institution in the world. Other causes advanced for the panic were the agitation against the railroads and the decision of Judge Landis against the Standard Oil Company, inflicting a fine of $29,000,240, which frightened capitalists and investors. The speculators became excited and reasoned that if one corporation could be fined $29,000,000 there might be no end to it and bring ruin to many. With this idea they outdid each other in selling their holdings. Some claim the financial stringency was caused by the San Francisco earthquake, which took $350,000,000 out of the money market in order to pay the losses. There was also the revelation of scandals in the life insurance business by the Hughes investigations, and the New York State Utilities Bill which caused street railroad stock of New York City to fall from $127 to $20 per share, playing havoc among investors in New York City. The connection of these corporations with some of the picturesque but unsavory incidents of then recent Wall Street history caused uneasiness in powerful circles. In addition it was felt that the complete reorganization of the insurance companies was inevitable, that restrictive legislation would follow which would prevent them from participating to the same degree in underwriting operations, and that it was within the range of possibility that they might be forced to sell large quantities of securities which they had in their possession, which were also held to a large extent by speculative interests. Probably no one of these caused the panic, but rather a combination of all of them.

Business had reached a high water mark and the country's

currency had been stretched to the last point. A contraction was due, and there was little doubt that there would have a business depression in 1908 even if the panic of 1907 had been averted. Probably the first failure was the Heinze crash which involved the United Copper which F. A. Heinze controlled. Commercial failures increased 60 per cent the last few months of 1907 and early in 1908. Money had been overused. Interest rates were extremely high and failures were frequent everywhere. The Westinghouse companies of Pittsburg were placed in the hands of receivers for inability to meet maturing obligations. The exchanges of the country were thrown out of joint. On October 29 Chicago drafts on New York were quoted at $2.50 per $1,000 discount. In other places the usual country balances in New York had been so far drawn down that the banks in the interior, although having plenty of cash in hand, could not sell drafts on New York at all. Most of the cotton, woolen and other mills of New England and the East shut down for a period or ran on part time only.

In several western states holidays were declared by the authorities in order to give the banks a breathing spell and allay distrust. Between October and December $100,-000,000,000 in gold was imported from abroad which filtered through New York to all parts of the country. Arrangements were started to secure gold from the Bank of France, but the French Bank, when approached in behalf of America, responded that as there was no central bank in America similar to the Bank of England, it would be glad to help, but through the United States Treasury, which could not be done.

Our exports had fallen off that year. Europe wanted nothing but our gold because they were overstocked with goods themselves. England was suffering from the result of the Boer War and her consols sold as low as 81, the lowest price since 1848. Germany was particularly overstocked and the Berlin stock market was going through a depression of its own. Even the city of New York was embarrassed in placing a new issue of municipal bonds. Abroad there were abundant evidences of difficulty, extending to Egypt, Japan, and Chili. Some bourbon English writers attributed the stringency of money in England in 1907 to the "labor socialistic" government under Lloyd George, whom they called a "fresh up-start." Interest rates were higher all that year all over the world; there was not an easy money market anywhere and 4 per cent issues could not be marketed in any country. The trust companies had been making inroads on the business of the national banks, thus weakening the national banking system. It was the trust companies, which had extended their business to commercial banking, that engaged in operations far beyond the limit of conservative practice. They particularly did not protect their deposits by adequate reserves.

Our neighbors in Canada avoided the worst of the cataclysm, probably because they had a better banking and credit system. Canada has often had trade declines and depressions, but seldom has she been involved in panics. With bad crop conditions in 1907 and stringent money she faced difficulties. At the grain growers' appeal for assistance the Government finally decided to exceed her legal minimum of note issues in order to place currency at the command of the farmers. This plan carried them through the depression without serious consequences.

The crisis of 1907 was much less prolific in bank failures than its larger predecessors. The reference to the "Rich Man's Panic" is largely true, because at that time the savings banks were full of money and the average citizen throughout the country was fairly well fixed. One New York City institution, the Bowery Savings Bank, held over $100,000,000 of deposits. Wall Street capitalists no doubt envied their poor brethren who possessed this cash. The following year, 1908, history repeated itself; money accumulated in the banks, interest rates fell, and securities steadily advanced. In all leading commercial countries industrial revival quickly proved that the catastrophe, although severe while it lasted, was of shorter duration than previous ones.

The banks of the country, New York particularly, took a wise course, making necessary loans liberally where urgent and furnishing funds to other parts of the country. The week ending November 9th saw their lawful reserves declined $51,000,000 below the legal limit. But imports of gold were flowing in to take their place.

At the height of the crisis rumors spread that the Trust Company of America was in difficulties. This institution had a capital of $3,000,000 and resources of $74,000,000, including $12,000,000 cash in its vaults at the time. Under normal conditions it was perfectly solvent and able to meet its depositors' claims, but that it was not in position to withstand a prolonged run was proved by subsequent events. Realizing that the failure of the Trust Company of America would make the crisis far more acute, Mr. Morgan and his associates resolved to come to its assistance, provided it could prove that its statement of conditions were correct.

A contemporary describes the scene as follows: "In vain did the officers of the company put seven tellers to work instead of the usual one, in vain were all deposits paid promptly and unhesitatingly. Denser and denser grew the crowd of depositors, and it became obvious that the millions that had been passed over the counters in the morning hours would not suffice to stem the tide. Thorne hurried over to the Morgan offices and there succeeded in obtaining $2,-500,000 immediately. This loan was subsequently augmented by another of $10,000,000 made a few days later and a third of $15,000,000 made early in November. On this one day, October 23rd, $13,500,000 was paid out over the trust company's counters! But this was not enough to stem the run. As near as can be estimated something between $30,000,-

000 and $35,000,000 was paid to depositors. But the Trust Company of America was saved. It has been claimed that the price of its salvation was the surrender by its president of some 5,500 shares of Tennessee Coal, Iron and Railroad stock which he owned.

"The whole financial community had turned to Morgan as its Joshua to lead it out of the desert. Upon his shoulders fell the burden of saving the country from financial ruin. The Morgan library looked like the headquarters of an army. Here were congregated at all hours of the day and night bankers, brokers, business men of all kinds, both those who needed help and those who could assist the banker in the work he had thrust upon him and the ardous duties which he had assumed. Men rushed in and out of that library, pleaded for help, begged for information and, awaiting their turn, even slept in its luxurious chairs. The task that Morgan and his associates had undertaken was one of exceedingly great difficulty. Despite all that had been done to dam the torrent of financial disruption and the fact that each weak spot was strengthened as soon as discovered, the banker knew that his herculean efforts might be brought to nothing by one big failure which would let, loose the panic fears it was sought to allay."

As we have now had fifteen years to look dispassionately into the causes, it is apparent that steel had a great deal to do with this debacle. The United States Steel Corporation was apparently determined to absorb the Tennessee Coal and Iron Company, its strongest competitor. The latter company had been making big inroads into the business of the larger concern, which felt that it should either destroy or absorb its rival. "The friends of the corporation, on the other hand, are equally emphatic in asseverating that the competition offered by the Tennessee company was not such as to cause anxiety to the management of the steel corporation, that it was not a very valuable property and that the corporation purchased its stock only upon solicitation by

the interests controlling the company and their assurance
that a refusal to do so would result in the failure of an important security house, which would add greatly to the
severity and danger of the panic. They claim further that
the price paid was more than the actual value of the stock
and that, far from using any advantage it may have had to
squeeze the smaller concern, the steel trust, against the better judgment of its management and with the single purpose
of alleviating the panic dangers, paid for the securities it
took over something like 60 per cent more than good business
practice seemed to warrant."

Cotter in his "History of the United States Steel Corporation" says: "If the claims of the first are correct and
the corporation did use its power to force a competitor to
the wall, regardless of the fact that in so doing it was
bringing misery and calamity to the ninety millions of
people of the United States, this act alone must be more
than sufficient to convict it on a more serious charge than
'monopoly in restraint of trade'—of high treason and betrayal of the trust which big business, willy nilly, under-
takes. But if the corporation, through its directors, put the
national welfare before all other considerations this, conversely, should prejudice public opinion, properly informed,
in its favor.   And this is why the year was by far the most
important epoch in the corporation's history and its events
are worthy of careful consideration."

An officer of the Tennessee Company later said: "The
sale of the Tennessee Company was an incident arising in
the course of the panic, not a cause. The corporation was
offered a chance to get what I consider a valuable property
and seized it.   But let me tell you,'" he added, "the corporation did not get the property cheap."

On the other hand, other members of the Tennessee organization did give damaging testimony against the United
States Steel Corporation in the suit brought by the government to dissolve the corporation. The story is told that the

Tennessee Company secured an order from E. H. Harriman for 150,000 tons of steel rails early in 1907 and this angered the steel corporation to such an extent that plans were set under way to put the Tennessee company out of competition. Whether the steel trust actually and premeditately planned and brought on the panic, or whether they waited for a financial storm of its own making to bring them their opportunity is a mooted question. Banks often get in trouble and are helped by others, and some claim that the Knickerbocker Trust Company under ordinary circumstances would have been helped by Morgan. The father of the steel trust passed up help, looking in the direction of the Trust Company of America, against which also rumors had started and whose officers were controlling stockholders in the Tennessee company.

George B. Cortelyou, Secretary of the Treasury, had hurried to New York on the night of October 22nd and went into conference with Morgan, Geo. W. Perkins, Jr., James Stillman, and Henry B. Davidson. They later summoned Oakley Thorne, president of the trust company, and agreed to assist his institution. The next morning, however, the run started and a clamorous mob surged through the doors and demanded its money.

After the storm had lulled Judge Gary and Henry C. Frick, representing the steel trust, went to Washington and obtained an interview with President Roosevelt, who had with him William Loeb, Jr., and Elihu Root, Secretary of State. Roosevelt was asked for his approval of the taking over of the Tennessee company by the steel corporation. Under the circumstances Roosevelt said he would put no obstacle in the way of the completion of the transaction, although he had no power to give it any official sanction. Two points stand out in the whole transaction that allow the reader to draw his own conclusion. First, the Morgan interests which controlled the United States Steel Corporation did save the Trust Company of America, but after they had in their possession controlling shares in the Tennessee Coal and Iron Company. Second, while Roosevelt unofficially acquiesed in the merger, the fact is that the deal was already closed and would have been consummated whether or no. However, had the administration been antagonistic, the Government might have had a better chance to win its suit of dissolution later.

A peculiarity of the situation also, was the fact that Moore and Schley, leading brokers of Wall Street, became embarrassed to the extent of several million dollars. Affairs of this concern were deeply mixed with the Tennessee company, one member of the firm being one of the syndicate that controlled the Tennessee company and the firm itself had marketed a considerable proportion of the securities of the Tennessee company. This firm was also saved by Morgan by the surrender of Tennessee securities which it held.

Another reason for the steel company's supposed fear of the Tennessee company was that the latter, being located in the South, would be in a position to capture not only the business below the Mason and Dixon line, but would have a distinct advantage in exporting steel to Latin America. The steel trust always claimed that the merger saved the financial situation and stopped the panic.

Following the successful merger which so pleased the steel corporation, Judge Gary, it is said, gave on November 20th the first of the famous dinners which were later widely criticized in the newspapers. The stated object was to get all the steel operators together for the purpose of devising ways and means to meet the exigency arising out of the panic then existing and to prevent further calamity to the industry. The ways and means devised consisted of nothing more than an agreement to hold prices firm, to keep their heads and avoid the consequence of reckless price cutting. While this was practically an agreement in restraint of trade among the steel people, yet it no doubt helped greatly to alleviate the panicky conditions and get business back to normal. While all circumstantial evidence shows that there was a deliberate attempt on the part of the steel corporation to bring its competitors to terms, resulting in its success as incident to the panic, yet there is no telling after the panic was on where the end would have been had the merger not taken place.

The effects of the depression on the United States Steel Corporation were reflected in the last quarter, earnings for those three months, net for dividends, being only $18,614,-416, compared to $28,758,142 for the three months preceding. But it was not until 1908 that the full force of the storm was to be seen. In the first quarter of this year net profits applicable to dividends dwindled to $8,854,297.37, compared with $27,031,008.20 a year previous, and second quarter profits were $9,042,027.55 against $30,843,512.61 in the same period in 1907.

At this time Thomas A. Lawson, running a series of articles in a magazine, exposed "the system" and among the panic producers must be recognized these vitrolic articles.

Few railroads were forced into bankruptcy, and the proportion of business failures was not so high as after the crisis of 1893. It was largely a rich man's panic in a true sense, the effects being mostly confined to the stock market and credit operations. There was no appreciable decline in prices, wages, land values, or railroad earnings.

The Postal Savings Bank System was created in 1910, the agitation for it having started in the panic of 1907. It was pointed out that small depositors had a tendency to withdraw their deposits from the savings banks in the times of financial crisis and it was proposed to establish postal savings banks in order that the small depositors could leave their money with the Government at a small rate of interest. Thus the memorable panic of 1907 again served a great good after all the suffering it brought.

CHAPTER XXIV

THE DEPRESSION OF 1914

The money crisis at the outbreak of the World War, while of short duration, was of unequaled intensity or extent. Practically every stock exchange in the world was closed, but the needs of the day were so imperative that business soon resumed after the immediate effects of the shock. The world financial system held its equilibrium, but business suffered according to the relations of the various countries with those at war. Some claim that world events could be forseen as early as 1912.

According to Hull "the business world seemed merely to be hesitating, to be timorous about making new ventures, to question the future as if ripening for the great war, for although conditions over the end of 1912 and into 1913 were good, this hesitancy was still in evidence, something ominous seemed to hang over the world of business and finance. Probably then some of the leaders of finance foresaw, even though dimly and uncertainly, the trouble that was brewing. The depression really started in 1913. When the war broke out July 30th, 1914, disastrous results followed in the business world. Industry was just beginning to struggle out from the depression that had begun in the latter half of 1913, when the sudden clash of arms paralyzed world money markets, closed the stock and other exchanges, closed or restricted operations at hundreds of plants of one kind or another, and threw thousands of workers out of employment. The demand for steel, never very active at any time since about July, 1913, fell almost to a vanishing point, and earnings of the United Steel Corporation, in the last quarter declined to the lowest point in its history—$10,935,635.36 Total earnings for the year were only $71,663,615.17, and although the dividend rate on the common stock was reduced from 5 per cent to 2 per cent annually in the third quarter, and the dividend for the last quarter was passed, earnings were not sufficient to meet charges, and a deficit of $16,971,983.83 was reported. The company passed all dividends for the first time in its history."

At that time we owed a large sum of gold to Europe and her banks hastened to recall it because of the needs of war, but it soon flowed back in payment for the phenomenal exports of war material.

An account of this crisis coincides with the history of the inauguration of the Federal Reserve System. This law was drawn up in 1913 by the House "Banking and Currency Committee" of the Sixty-second Congress. Honorable Carter Glass, of Virginia, later Secretary of the Treasury, was chairman, and it was enacted as a law just in time to save us from a great financial catastrophe. At the outbreak of the war in the Summer of 1914, Europe began withdrawing gold in enormous quantities, and it was at once evident to all that very striking changes would result in every department of business life. The closing of the principal stock exchanges of the country almost immediately upon the definite announcement that the war was unavoidable was thus dictated by two considerations. First, the belief that prices for stocks and other securities would be reduced to a point so low as to bring about the repurchase of the securities by Americans, who would then be obliged to pay for them in gold; and secondly, the belief that, in consequence of this reduction of prices, many bank loans based upon securities would have to be "called," thereby bringing about failures and incidentally assisting in the movement of specie out of the country. The exchanges had closed in previous years, but never for the reasons which now controlled them.

Laughlin writes: "That they should close because of the fear of failure and the loss of gold implied a serious danger of disaster which appealed powerfully to the public mind, and which presented a problem that could not be explained away. The fact that, coincident with this closing of the exchanges, international trade was practically suspended for several days, and was seriously interrupted for several weeks, until British vessels assumed control of the North Atlantic, tended greatly to increase the public anxiety. It formed, apparently, good ground for the suspension of business operations and for the non-fulfillment of contracts, even when the very difficult conditions did not themselves compel a recourse to such methods. The fact that foreign countries had adopted legislation deferring the date when debts need be paid or contracts fulfilled, although not paralleled here, produced a sympathetic influence upon business in the United States, which practically resulted in the partial or tentative adoption of a somewhat similar relaxation of commercial requirements in many industries and branches of trade. Europe was throwing American securities on the market by loads, and when the exchanges opened the banks still found themselves under great strain to meet the situation. The national currency associations, which had numbered only eighteen up to the beginning of the European war, rapidly increased until they aggregated forty-four, and prompt preparations were made in Washington for supplying emergency currency, under the terms of the Federal Reserve Act, to any such association as might need the notes. At the same time, practically all of the clearing-house associations of the larger cities arranged for the issuing of certificates."

Congress amended the measure lowering the rates of taxation upon emergency issues and giving wider latitude for the issuing of currency. Under this act a total of $380,-000,000 was put into circulation, together with clearing-house certificates of $211,000,000, a total of nearly $600,-000,000 of new money that went into circulation in this country within a few months. Apparently, no need could be had for such sums unless there were withdrawals in other directions. No doubt this is what occurred, banks hoarding the cash by withholding it, so far as possible, both from one another and from the public; while the public hoarded lawful money by retaining it as it came into its possession, and applying to the banks for more supplies of circulating media.

Foreign exchange rates soon became prohibitive, and for a time trade between this country and the Old World was

practically suspended. "The breakdown of trade with
Europe through the inability of vessels to run regularly at
the outset of the war, and through the reduction of buying
power, due to the interruption of all regular industrial,
commercial, and financial operations, meant that in the
absence of some restoration of the normal course of business it would be necessary to find other means of liquidating
our obligations to foreign countries." In order to relieve
the situation and keep the money at home the Federal Reserve Board began an investigation to ascertain the extent
of international indebtedness, so that a means could be had
to liquidate without sending more gold abroad.

The Allies were very desirous of keeping the good will
of business interests in the United States and after a few
months pressure was greatly lessened from that source.
In a short time the urgent pressure for note accommodation
passed away, gold reappeared in circulation, clearing-house
certificates were retired, and practically the whole of the
emergency currency was taken up within ten months from
the beginning of the crisis.

The closing of the stock exchange affected business in
every direction, despite the great issues of temporary
clearing-house certificates. Several enormous failures occurred in June and July, including the Claflin catastrophe.
Bank clearings for the whole country fell to $155,000,000,-
000, from $170,800,000,000 in the previous year. Liabilities
of failures touched nearly $350,000,000, the heaviest mor-
tality for twenty-two years, involving over 1 per cent of the
total number of firms in business.

A writer on the steel and iron industry says: "So acute
was the depression that it was decided to stop construction
work at the new Duluth plant of the United States Steel Corporation in the Fall of the year. Expenditures for this account for 1914 amounted to $4,094,363.97. In December,
1914, production at the corporation's plants fell to the lowest
point ever recorded. The general average of operations was
reported to have been about 25 per cent but this is probably

somewhat overstated, as two of the largest. subsidiaries reduced operations as low as 15 per cent in one case, and 18 per cent in the other, during the last fortnight of the year. Never did a year dawn blacker for the steel trade than did 1915. The financial upset that followed the outbreak of the great war paralyzed industry, and the effect was felt in steel, the barometer of trade. Closing 1914 with operations at the lowest point in years—perhaps on record—and with no actual sign of early betterment, it was small wonder that all except the perpetual optimists faced the future with some dread. And the events of the early part of the year seemed to justify this dread. In the month of January the steel corporation's earnings fell to the lowest point on record, $1,687,150."

Cotton fell to the lowest point it had reached for several decades, bringing five and six cents on the plantation. The distress was so severe that the "Buy-a-bale" movement started and spread over the country. Northern wholesale merchants and investors bought a bale in order to relieve the South, and the wealthier classes throughout the cotton growing states bought what they could to take it off the market. Many who did so, and held it, sold that same cotton later for upwards of thirty cents.

The Underwood tariff had begun to hurt. Manufacturers feared a great influx of imports that would adversely affect their commodities. The depression from this cause had already set in and even before the war broke out it was generally expected that a period of hard times was ahead.

While this depression was of comparatively short duration, it is surprising to note that the number of failures was greater in proportion than in the depression of 1920-21. The depression lasted well into 1915, when orders from Europe began pouring in and a period of abnormal conditions followed.

CHAPTER XXV

THE DEPRESSION OF 1920-21

Chas. Duguid in his "Story of the Stock Exchange" is the only prophet we can find who might lay claim to having predicted the depression of 1920. After referring to the South Sea Bubble and the Mississippi Bubble of 1720 and the world-wide depression of 1820, starting in this country in 1819, he said, "The history of 1720 repeated itself in 1820, as it may—who knows?—repeat itself in 1920."

The causes which may be given now from the best judgement later may be proven wrong. Certainly in economic affairs as well as in romance "distance lends enchantment." That is shown in perusing the newspapers and periodicals published at the times of our various crises. Time proves that writers apparently see things from too close a viewpoint. They are prone to take a narrow view. Many articles written at the time of the various depressions, ascribing different causes, have later proved to be wrong; indeed, many of them ridiculous. As time goes on, the small and minor details of crises that are often magnified are lost to view and the main causes uncovered by time itself. At the time we invariably find politics given as the paramount cause of business depression. The administration in power is always condemned. Jackson was blamed for the crisis of 1837, Cleveland for that of 1893, Roosevelt for that of 1907 and Wilson for that of 1920.

The central buffer which receives the ultimate shocks of depression is, of course, finance. Most of our crises and depressions have revolved around the question of money or the medium of currency. The depression of 1920-21 is an exception to the rule, being one of the first depressions in our history in which the question of money or currency did

not enter either in cause or effect. It is true there was some
demand for a more liberal policy of rediscounting by the
Federal Reserve Banks, as it was the curtailment of credits
that largely brought on the depression.

A violent quarrel started between politicians and the officers of the Federal Reserve Board regarding the advis-
ability of a more liberal use of Federal Reserve notes
and a reduction in the discount rate. Governor W. P. G.
Harding, of the Federal Reserve Board, in a letter to Senator Sheppard, of Texas, said that wild speculation might
result from such action. "If our present large gold holdings were deliberately made the basis for an undue extension of domestic credits, as might well be the case if our
discount rates were made so low as to offer an alluring
profit to banks," Governor Harding wrote, "there might
develop a very dangerous condition in the United States.
No small part of the responsibility of the Federal Reserve
system is to make sure the consequences of this flood of
gold is not wild speculation and unsound banking practices."

Terrific price declines were the rule of the day, and these
so shocked the industrial system that there is little doubt
that but for the Federal Reserve System an unprecedented
panic would have ensued. The Federal Reserve Board may
have justly deserved some of the criticisms directed against
it because of its policy of too sharp action. Mistakes were
made, no doubt, and it since has been admitted that the same
result could have been accomplished by a more gradual deflation attended with a lesser degree of loss particularly as
regards to agriculture. On the other hand, Governor Harding and other members of the Board give as their defense
the fact that they repeatedly warned business and finance
to start deflation. They claimed, and it is true, that their
warnings were disregarded, and not only was there no start
made in deflation, but inflation continued. It is further
known that even after the Federal Reserve Board absolutely
shut down and deflation had set in, bringing depression in

many lines, yet thousands of business men refused to believe that a reversal was coming. Many went straight ahead,
using up the round sums they had made during the war
period and continued expansion beyond reason. The people
as a whole continued their extravagant habits, feeling that
the depression would be of short duration.

In looking back it is apparent now that there could have
been a middle ground; that the deflation could have come
more gradually by the proper use of resources at our command through the Federal Reserve System. Let us not overlook the idea that business has its rights the same as banks.
The banker would not like it if he were forced to liquidate
too quickly. He simply could not do it. Yet the banker
takes a notion all at once that business must liquidate. Instead of giving business the same time that banks would
require he proceeds to force things at the drop of the hat.
Liquidation and deflation should have been stretched out
over a period of three or four years, and we could have
returned to normal without the great shock of depression
that we are passing through. We did it after the Civil War,
assuming that the panic of 1873 had nothing to do with the
war period. I know what my industrial friends will say in
answer to this. They will answer it by asking the question,
"How could we have liquidated labor without the depression?" Admittedly that is the hardest question that could
be put to me to answer, because no man can tell what the
attitude of labor would have been. The probability is that
labor would have balked. Though their leaders may have
tried to lead them aright, yet these leaders themselves know
only too well how difficult that is.

"What might have occurred during that period without
the facility of Federal Reserve note issue is impossible to
surmise," says Laughlin, "but the magnitude of the problem is indicated by the fact that money in circulation increased from $3,419,000,000 on July 1, 1914 to $6,393,000,-
000 in November, 1920, when the peak was reached, during
which period the net increase of gold held in the country

was only $848,365,000, and that gold constituted the reserve base for probably ten times that amount of credit created in the process of the Government's financing its war expenditures. On December 23, 1920, they were outstanding in the total amount of $3,404,931,000 as compared with $2,420,831,000 on November 9, 1921, a decrease of $984,-100,000 in eleven months.

"During the war we did the unbelievable. The people furnished in taxes and loans to the Government the stupendous sum of $34,000,000,000 to carry on the war, and besides that we carried on unprecedented enterprises, much of it on a credit basis. But at the end of 1919 combined demands of both these factors brought us to the limit of our banking power. The way we were going it is a question whether we realized that there was such a thing as a limitation of credit. We now see where we made many mistakes in our wartime finances. It was a time of enormous profits, and the discount rate should have been raised on both war and commercial paper, as borrowers could have well afforded to pay for it. It is also now seen that expansion should have been penalized at its source by automatically adding a sliding scale or commission to the rate of discount to member banks as their re-discounts rose relatively to their capital. We had an abundance of gold concentrated in the hands of reserve banks, but it created a dangerous over-confidence. This high funded gold encouraged expansion and deposits and notes rose to such figures that no great margin of free gold was left. The halt should have come before it did, because it was plainly evident that a sudden reversal in international trade would call for gold exports and leave us in a serious predicament."

The victors in the Great War suffered more, economically, from the aftermath than did the defeated. The peculiarity of war is that often the victors, attaining the objects of the war, find themselves in as severe internal difficulty as the loser. This was the case in the Napoleonic wars, when the victors suffered through depression as much as the vanquished, and again in 1870 when Germany experienced a violent crisis and depression after her victory over France, while the latter prospered. Half in humor and half in earnest, a German comic newspaper said at the time: "Let us have another war; let us be beaten and pay an indemnity and then we shall be prosperous again."

The depression in Great Britain was equally as great proportionately as in this country. France also suffered a depression because of the readjustment of war prices, but not to any such degree as in Great Britain and America. The other allied countries suffered severely—Italy, Japan, Greece, and the smaller nations. The repudiation of the Russian debt, in some respects, counter-balanced the enormous indemnity exacted from Germany. This is the second time in history that Russia has repudiated her national debt. In 1843 the empire declared itself bankrupt and paid two-sevenths in a new issue of currency for the old issues that were outstanding. The Italian Government met the problem of unemployment and depression heroically. The sum of $32,000,000 was voted for public works and land reclamation. The water power and natural resources of the country were developed and $6,000,000 more spent for laying cables to Spain, Greece as well as South American countries, rendering Italian trade independent of foreign cable lines.

We have heard much adverse criticism of the paper currency regime in Germany. Dire predictions are made as to the outcome. But while we are making these predictions let us not forget that our own country went through the same periods of paper currency, not only once but several times, and we have come out whole.

After the depression set in in 1920, and including the first three-quarters of 1921, failures numbered 6,503—involving $202,532,000—August 1921 showing the greatest number of defaults, a total of 1,562. Unlike most previous depressions the West was the least affected. Only 565 failures were reported from the Central West, with $7,740,727 of liabilities as against 1,695 in the Middle Atlantic, with $46,406,944 of liabilities. Altogether 17,000 concerns, large and small, were forced to go out of business in 1920 and 1921 and a large number of others no doubt suffered enormous losses.

When the depression set in people started saving. Everybody had spent wildly, getting little value for their money, until the buyers' strike came and men were thrown out of employment. Then they started saving.

Preceding the depression prices of average commodities were higher than ever before known in the memory of people living. However, they did not reach the prices that prevailed during the Napoleonic wars, the price peak of all our national history having been reached in 1815.

Whatever differences of opinion may exist as to the main and principal cause of this depression, all admit that the buyers' strike had a great deal to do with it. The public had gone its limit and refused to put up with further profiteering. There was the wholesaler and other middle men, each taking a long profit. Figures indisputably show, however, that the retailer was the greatest profiteer and of all hands through whom merchandise went on its way to the consumer the manufacturer was the "gamest." That substantiates the best theory of all economists for decades back. There is less proportionate profit in manufacturing than in any end of merchandising. All available records show the predominance of wealth in mercantile communities over manufacturing communities. The greatest wealth invariably goes to the selling center rather than the manufacturing center, proportionately speaking.

A certain merchant liked to make excuses for his profiteering by telling about how he sold shoes. He placed ladies' shoes on sale at $7 and at the side of those the identical shoe, excepting a different style, for $12. He boasted that nine out of ten purchasers would by the $12 shoes. That merchant may not know it, but such instances is what helped bring on the depression of 1920. His customers eventually found out that they had been tricked. It was not smartness on the part of the merchant that caused

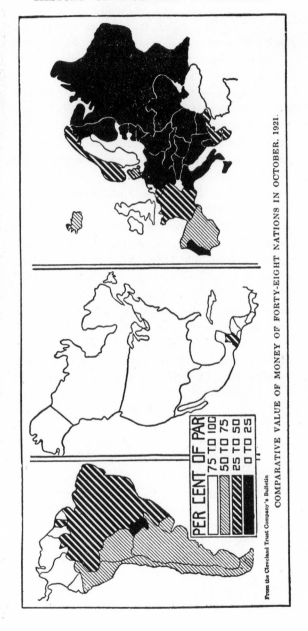

COMPARATIVE VALUE OF MONEY OF FORTY-EIGHT NATIONS IN OCTOBER, 1921.

From the Cleveland Trust Company's Bulletin

PER CENT OF PAR

75 TO 100
50 TO 75
25 TO 50
0 TO 25

the customer to buy the $12 shoes. Times were prosperous, the customer had money, could afford the best and wanted the best. When they bought $12 shoes they trusted the merchant to give them $12 values, not being leather experts themselves. When the customer found that the merchants were taking advantage of their trust, easing their conscience with the thought that "everybody is doing it," they revolted, bringing on what was called the "buyers' strike."

In the far background the failure of America to enter the League of Nations was another cause of the depression. This opinion is held by Republicans and Democrats alike, by supporters and opponents of the father of the League. That body offered a medium through which we could get our heads together with other nations upon whom we are more or less dependent and help them solve their problems. By admitting Austria and Germany the League could have established a monetary commission which would have devised ways and means of stabilizing exchange, of funding the international indebtedness, and general promotion of international commerce. The world will come to see the day when it realizes the price we have paid for the stubbornness of one man and the spite of a group of others.

Confidence in our money system was a bright feature of the 1920 depression there being no runs on banks of any consequence. There were no outstanding failures, no spectacular panic, although in various parts of the country smaller banks closed their doors and some consolidated with stronger institutions in order to pull through the stringency. There were a large number of failures, but mostly superfluous concerns which had no good reason for existence. There were no restrictions on withdrawals of deposits, no moratoria, no stock exchanges closed. We had in our vaults 50 per cent of the world's gold, which was a bulwark against loss of confidence.

In 1920 there was a grocery store to every 218 persons in the United States, or one to every forty-eight families, according to Alvin E. Dodd, manager of the Department of Domestic Distribution of the United States Chamber of Commerce, who intimates in an article in the *Nation's Business* that there may be too many retailers. On the basis of the estimated average family budget the average grocer in the United States would have an annual turn-over of only $9,400. This is too small to permit him to obtain a living, and the result appears in the high mortality rate in this trade. In 1920 there was one failure for every two hundred grocers in the country, and in the past five years, although during this time the country was highly prosperous, retail grocers succumbed at the rate of about twenty a day. "This, of course, only means that competition is simply weeding out the unfit and that economic laws will not be thwarted."

Our population was practically double in 1920 the population at the time of the depression of 1873, at which time three million workers were thrown out of employment. According to figures given out by President Harding's unemployment conference the unemployment reached six million. From that angle the depression of 1920 was equally as bad as any on record. However, economists point out that in 1920 perhaps two and one-half million were counted among the unemployed who were not heads of families or needed wage-earners, but who had been pressed into the ranks of workers during the war.

History repeats itself with uncanny regularity in cycles of business depression. Referring back a hundred years to the depression known as the panic of 1819, but at its worst in 1820, a writer in Niles Register says; "Mail robberies and piracies are the order of the day." How like our own times!

In 1921 mail robberies were so numerous that Postmaster General Hays and Secretary of the Navy Denby placed armed marines on mail trains and at stations where mails were handled.

One of the big factors of the depression, and the one which undoubtedly prolonged it, was the enormous issue of tax free bonds. In order to avoid excessive war taxation on incomes investors bought tax free state, county, and municipal bonds. Such issues ,were eagerly grabbed up on the market, creating an orgy of public spending at exhorbitantly high prices and taking the wealth of the nation out of the channels of trade and industry. Money used in public work goes through a slow process in getting back into the channels of commerce. It often is injudiciously used and the large amount of money spent in this direction retarded business activities because of tied up credits in channels of slow liquidation. "As a rule," says John Mills, "panics do not destroy capital; they merely reveal the extent to which it has been previously destroyed by its betrayal into hopelessly unproductive works."

Steel and iron people claim that the depression of 1914 was worse than 1920-21, claiming the percentage of unemployment was not so great and there was plenty of money to be had in the recent depression, whereas in 1914 money was very scarce.

President Harding, upon coming into office, found a deplorable state of affairs with increasing distress and unemployment. As winter approached a conference of industrial and labor leaders and well known economists was called under the leadership of Herbert Hoover, Secretary of Commerce. This conference attempted to devise ways and means of alleviating unemployment. Many plans were proposed and discussed, but the outgrowth of it all was that there was nothing to do but to go to work. The President in an address made it plain that the public treasury would not be used in giving out alms. This attitude was approved in general by press and public. In Canada, where the English idea of doles was growing, the President's attitude was given outspoken approval. The Montreal Gazette said; "The United States is still the most individualistic of the great nations, and is likely to remain so. It grew great by the work of men who, when in need, turned to and did whatever their hands could find to do. The Government's attitude may seem hard, but it is in keeping with the country's record. The giving and taking of doles does not make for manliness or self-reliance."

The President's conference was at first inclined to outline an educational program to show individuals how to prepare for their own protection against recurring depressions, but Secretary Hoover declared the Conference to be entrusted with the duty of relieving present evils and doing some-thing of a definite nature to relieve unemployment and help industry back to its feet. The final recommendations of the conference show that this idea finally prevailed.

In the Fall of 1921, unfortunately just at the time of the Washington Peace Conference, financial panic broke out in China and spread over the Republic. Some observers say that Japanese plotters instigated the panic for the purpose of showing that China was unable to handle her own financial affairs without help from outside. Whatever truth may be in that it is known that China's Government did default in payment of loans to the Continental and Commercial National Bank of Chicago. The panic halted, however, before great damage was done.

Various leaders, among them Postmaster-General Will Hayes and Secretary of Commerce Herbert Hoover, were sure that prosperity was just around the corner from 1922. Others, such as Secretary of Agriculture Wallace, said in a speech in Chicago that the depression in agriculture was the worst known in history and it would take five years to recover. Ex-Senator Beveridge, before the New York Chamber of Commerce, said that the return of prosperity was still a long way off. If we can go by the past, however, striking an average, we will find that depressions run their course in two or three years. Business has never remained below the normal line for longer than three and a half years.   Our longest depressions were 1837 to 1840, 1873 to 1876 and 1893 to 1896.

The U. S. Department of Commerce furnishes a table of 1921 prices with approximate index numbers based upon 100 for 1913.

Cost of Living:	Index Number
Department of Labor (May Survey)	180
National Industrial Conference Board	165
Average price to producer, farm crops	109
Average price to producer, live stock	113
Average wholesale price, foods	152
Average retail price, foods	155

Wheat and Flour:

Wheat average to producer	128
Flour, wholesale, U. S. average	173
Bread, retail, U. S. average	173
Freight rate flour, Minneapolis to New York, domestic	187

Live Stock and Meats:

Pork—

Hogs to producer	116
Retail ham	197
Retail sliced bacon	162
Wholesale short side	108
Wholesale pork chops	184
Retail pork chops	181
Retail lard	115

Beef—

Cattle, average to producer	91
Wholesale carcass beef at Chicago	124
Retail, sirloin steak	157
Retail, round	160
Retail, rib roast	147
Retail, chuck roast	130
Retail, plate beef	112
Wages in meat packing (Dept. of Labor Investigation)	186
Freight rates, dressed beef, Chicago to New York	214

Hides and Leathers:

Hides, green salted, packers, heavy native steers (Chicago)	76
Hides, calfskin No. 1, country, 8 to 15 lbs (Chicago)	86
Leather, sole, hemlock, middle No. 1 (Boston)	120
Leather, Chrome, calf, dull or bright, "B" grades (Boston)	195
Wholesale boots and shoes, men's vici kid, blucher-campella	225
Freight rates, shoes, Lynn, Mass., to Chicago	210
Wage scales in shoe industry (Massachusetts), about	200

Cost of Living: Index Number

Cotton:

To producer _____ 105
Yarns, carded, white, Northern mule, spun, 22 cones
(Boston) _____ 107
Wholesale sheeting, brown, 4-4 ware, shoals LL, N. Y. 118
Wholesale printcloth 27 inches, 64 x 60, 7.60 yards to
pound (Boston) _____ 137

Wool:

To producer _____ 92
Wholesale worsted yarns 2-32, crossbred stock white
in skein (Philadelphia). _____ 148
Wholesale women's dress goods, storm serge, all wool,
double warp, 50 inches, (New York)_____ 157
Wholesale suitings, wood-dyed, blue 55-56, 16 ounces,
Middlesex (Boston) _____ 183
Freight rate clothing, New York to Chicago_____ 210
Wage scale in mills, about _____ 200

Building and Construction:

Prices—

Lumber, average southern pine and Douglas Fir (at
the mill) _____ 128
Brick, average common, New York and Chicago_____ 199
Cemet, Portland, net, without bags to trade f. o. b.
plank (Buffington, Ind.) _____ 175

Freight rates—

Brick, common, Brazil, Ind., to Cleveland, Ohio_____ 204
Cement, Universal, Pa., to New York_____ 179

Building labor:

Union scale, simple average, 15 occupations_____ 190
Union scale weighted average, 8 occupations, frame
houses (3) _____ 197
Union scale, weighted average, 8 occupations, brick
houses (3) _____ 193
Common labor _____ 130

Construction costs: Cement building (Aberthaw Const.
Co.)

Coals:

Price bituminous, Pittsburg _____ 186
Price, anthracite, New York tidewater_____ 198
Union wage scales about _____ 173
Non-union scale, about _____ 136
Freight rates _____187- 209
Metal trades, union wage scale: Simple average, 19
occupations _____ 218

Cost of Living: Index Number

Metals: Prices—

Pig Iron, foundry No. 2, Northern (Pittsburgh)___   137
Pig iron, Bessemer _____   128
Steel Billets, Bessemer (Pittsburgh)_____   115
Copper, ingots electrolytic, early delivery, New York   75
Lead, pig, desilverized, for early delivery, New York   100
Zinc, pig (spelter), Western, early delivery, New York   80
Day labor, scale U. S. Steel Corporation_____   150

Printing and publishing:

Book and job, union wage scale _____   194
Newspaper, union wage scale _____   157
Railroad, average receipt per ton-mile_____   177
Bureau Railway Economics estimate of railway wages
  based on average annual compensation, third
  quarter _____   226
General estimate all union wage scales by Prof. Wilson
  _____   189

NOTE—The wage indices refer mostly to wage scales, not the earnings, which necessarily depend upon regularity of employment.

The figures show that agriculture has liquidated to a greater extent than any other product, and also that for the first time in our history we have gone through a depression with commodity prices higher than the average for the preceding period.

CHAPTER XXVI

MINOR DEPRESSIONS

A number of lesser depressions affecting certain industries or sections have occurred in the intervening years
which had little effect on the country as a whole, and no lessons are to be gained from them other than that can be
gained from general depressions, so that but brief space is
given them here.

In 1798 the country experienced a short panic and depression when we were quarreling with France, who insisted that we help her in her war against England. In
that year news of Napoleon's victories had reached England
and a panic ensued; it was reflected in this country. The
prisons of Philadelphia were filled with debtors, formerly
honorable men of good standing. This panic was soon over
and peace was made with France.

There occurred in 1828 and 1829 an accidental and very
brief scarcity of cash. This depression marked the beginning of the agitation against the Second National Bank,
causing uncertainty in financial circles. The cry was taken
up by an element of politicians who wanted the State Bank
system, which they thought would help more to develop new
lands in the South and West. Defenders of the National
Bank pointed out that its notes were accepted the same as
gold in every part of the country and practically at their
face value in all the financial centers of the world. The
parent bank at Philadelphia was housed in a marble palace,
with hundreds of high-salaried clerks. There were twenty-
five branches in different cities of the Union. A large export of specie was taking place at the time, and when it
became known that the volume of paper currency was so
large against the specie in the vaults of the banks general

distrust swept over the country. A committee of the Senate reported in 1829 that the soundness of the bank was unquestioned and the uniformity of the currency satisfactory.

The crisis which occurred in 1833 was of short duration and felt but little in business circles. It was precipitated largely by the hostile attitude of President Jackson against the United States Bank. The bank felt compelled to contract its discounts suddenly, causing confusion among borrowers, who quickly retrenched, and the stringency was short lived. At this time President Jackson withdrew the government deposits from the Second National Bank. The year 1833 was one of contraction of credits and decreased business, mostly on account of uncertainty and the crop failures of 1832, but business soon emerged into the great boom that preceded the panic of 1837. The expansion of the West demanded so much capital that there had to be a temporary let up, but the West would not down and insisted upon riding ahead ot its fall in 1837. When the contraction had set in Jackson's friends led him to believe that the Second Bank was bent on causing a prolonged depression so as to injure his administration. Jackson then set about to start good times, and this resulted in inflation. Jackson felt very triumphant in that he had forced the Second Bank to "abandon the system of curtailment and extend its accommodations to the community."

An incident of this crisis was the failure of the Bank of Maryland, then an important institution. Bitter feeling arose between the directors and the stockholders and depositors, and, after the trustees had not rendered an accounting for seventeen months, the depositors became so exasperated that they mobbed the houses of all the parties concerned in the partnership, resulting in considerable destruction of property. The mob held sway for five days. Upon petition to the Legislature an indemnity of $102,550 was granted to those who suffered by it.

The year 1851 marked a short period of depressed business described in typical language by a writer as follows:

"A bad credit system has been in vogue, trade with California had not met expectations, imports had been large, exports of gold heavy, cotton declined in Europe, the banks contracted, property was sacrificed to raise ready money, mercantile credit was disturbed everywhere, and distress was general in all cities. In Wall Street large blocks of stock were unloaded and the market was broken. Erie went down from 90 to 68¾. Later in the month money became easier, prices advanced, and the market resumed its ordinary aspect."

The depression of 1882 was inconsequential and probably a reflection of the crisis in France of that year; 1867 probably also was purely a reflection of the great European crisis of 1866.

A short depression came in December, 1895 at the time of President Cleveland's "Venezuela Message." A panic was precipitated in Wall Street, and iron production dropped off about 25 per cent. The trouble passed over, however, within a few months and conditions returned to normal.

The year 1901 witnessed a remarkable performance in Wall Street. It was the year of the Northern Pacific corner, which dazzled the boldest speculator that ever entered the Street, and it is now admitted that had there been other disturbing elements at the time it would have caused a panic equal to that of 1907. The incident did not disturb business as a whole, and it is entitled to little space here, but Wall Street was severely shaken and many fortunes lost in a single day, while "the rest of the country stood off and literally laughed."

The flurry of 1900 was purely financial and did not affect business. Industrial conditions were encouraging; foreign commerce was expanding, and harvests were generous, so the Wall Street excitement reflected only slightly on the rest of the country. The year 1918 had a breathing spell of about sixty days following the armistice, when hundreds of thousands of workmen were let out of war industries.

Other minor depressions or short financial crises are recorded in the years 1846, 1855 and 1882. Still other financial panics have been confined to Wall Street and had little or no effect upon the country, and can not be included in a list of business depressions.

CHAPTER XXVII

OUR RELATIONS TO FOREIGN DEPRESSIONS

It has been seen that depressions afflict other countries as well as the United States. Sometimes they are world-wide, at other times they spread to a group of nations, and again only one country may be affected. In many cases reverses in one country spell profits to another. "It's an ill wind that blows nobody good" is a saying that obtains in the world of business and finance as in everyday affairs. A general world depression is the exception rather than the rule, although with the increasing intercourse between nations disaster in one has a growing tendency to affect others. It is claimed that the entire world was passing through a period of lethargy previous to the recent war.

Arnold Toynbee in his book, "The Industrial Revolution," said that depressions in England were generally associated with bad harvests, although free trade had lessened their force, because when they had bad harvests there they got plenty of corn in America, but admitted that trade depressions were then getting to be of international scope and of more widened area, as "a bad harvest in Brazil may prejudice trade in England." We have been having business cycles regularly in this country ever since we have been a nation, and England has had them ever since the beginning of the mercantile period. In former years crises in England developed into the worst kinds of panics, until in 1866 they developed a plan of panic financiering. This included the adoption of a centralized banking system, the vital feature of which was to give practical assurance that every business enterprise not actually insolvent can, by paying a stiff rate of interest, obtain bank loans to meet its liabilities. This act tended to stave off panicky runs and retain an element

of confidence in business and finance, no matter how dark
the outlook. It is true that England has had crises since
this time, but they have lost their dramatic intensity and
the nation has come through some very trying times, while
the system held true. England was fifty years ahead of us
in taking steps to avert panics. Our Federal Reserve Act,
no doubt, kept us from having a panic in 1920, and will
probably be a bulwark against them in the future. However, we, like England, will for some time have recurring
business depressions, and since we are now practically secure from panics our thought should next be developed into
mitigating the violence of deflation and resulting depression.
We have been affected by England's crises and depressions
and she by ours, more than any other two countries, because of the close inter-relationship of our financial and
commercial systems. Seldom have we felt the effects of a
foreign depression other than England's, unless it was in
1884. This, some think, was a reflection from France's
trouble of 1882. We have, however, felt world-wide depressions along with most all other countries.

In the early part of the Nineteenth Century, from the
years 1801 to 1804, France suffered a financial reaction. The
most important reason for this was no doubt the disturbance caused by the continual wars in which she had been
engaged, both foreign and internal, rendering the paths of
industry precarious in the extreme. During these years
America prospered from supplying the warring nations of
Europe.

The depression of 1819 was general in all the western
world because of a general crash following the Napoleonic
wars. It spread to America. Our 1825 depression was
nothing but a reflection of the English and French crises
and depressions of that year. Our domestic situation was
sound and it had little effect upon us. India had notable
depressions around the years 1830 and 1866. We felt
neither of them. In October, 1836, a financial crisis over-

whelmed Great Britain. While our panic a year later cannot
be wholly and definitely attributed to the crisis in England,
yet one had considerable bearing on the other.

In 1841 Great Britain experienced a financial crisis which
brought many failures among mercantile houses and wide
distress among the working classes, but had no effect on
this country.

In recent years, up to the Great War, Germany has been
very fortunate in avoiding serious commercial depressions.
She had suffered very severe financial reverses from the
revolutionary movements in 1848 and the various disturbances as an outgrowth of quarrels in welding the various

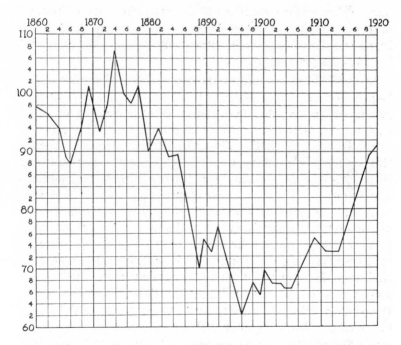

Prices of English Food Commodities as a Whole Since 1860. Prices
Reached a Lower Level Throughout the World in the Depression of
1893-4 than for a century previous. The Comparatively Low Level of
the War Period 1914-1918 was Due to the Government Purchases of
Food Stuffs That Were Sold to the People Below Cost.

states together. Her crisis of 1848 was echoed in this country. After the lull following the Franco-Prussian War she went forward in great strides, few depressions of widespread consequence being recorded. The story of the growth of Hamburg compares well with that of the great and rapid rise in Chicago.

The crisis of 1857 affected England and America. In 1864 Brazil and Australia were both affected by severe business depressions, neither of which were felt in America. That of 1873 swept over the continents of North and South America and Europe. Silver was very high and the amount of silver in a silver dollar was worth several cents more than par. When great quantities of German silver were dumped onto our market at these prices, a tremendous decline set in, augmenting the already precarious state of affairs, merging into the general panic.

In 1886 Great Britain appointed a Royal Commission on Depression in Trade, which carried on an extensive investigation of underlying conditions. Our depression of 1884 was over by that time. All of South America was affected in the troubles of 1890. The difficulties centered in Argentine, quickly spreading to other Latin-American nations, thence to Europe, causing the Baring failure in England, and finally to America. Our depression of 1893, terrible as it was, affected us almost alone. India had a panic and depression that year, though it probably bore no relationship to ours, except the re-echo of the demonetization of silver in that country. Acute commercial conditions also existed in far-away Java and the Straits Settlements in 1893. In 1907 the whole world, including the Orient, felt the crisis. It seriously affected business in Latin-America. At the outbreak of the World War in 1914 every country on the globe was affected for at least a year. Again in 1920 scarcely any country escaped.

Our depression of that year followed the severe Japanese panic, which caused numerous failures on the Pacific Coast of our country. A depression had also set in in England and Italy and to some extent in France. On the other hand, Germany and Belgium were prosperous—Germany because her people were going back to work, willingly taking depreciated money; Belgium because the first Germany indemnity payments went to her.

There have always been small local depressions in the different countries and depressions affecting individual industries in a single country. But it can be seen that as the nations of the world engage more and more in commercial intercourse the major depressions of the future are bound, to some extent, to affect them all.

Years Of Depression In United States And Other Countries.

Other countries mentioned had various depressions not noted here. Those are given which had relationship to our own.

United States	England	France	Other Countries
1785		1785	
1808	1808	1808	Ireland, Holland.
1814			
1819	1819	1819	Entire Europe.
1825	1825	1825	
1837	(1836)		
1848		1848	Germany, Austria.
1857	1857		
1860			
1869			
1873	1873		Austria, Russia, Latin-America.
1884		(1882)	
1890	1890	1890	Latin-America, Germany, Turkey, India, Java, Australia.
1903	(1902)		
1907	1907	1907	Orient, Europe, Latin America.
1914			Entire world, except Europe.
1920	1920	1920	Entire world.

CHAPTER XXVIII

CAUSES OF DEPRESSIONS

Theoretical Causes.—In the early part of the Eighteenth Century British merchants and financiers spent much time worrying over their relative cash basis as compared with other countries, and sometimes studied that matter so intensely that they lost all sense of the real proportion of things, and thought that the nation was being ruined because the importation of gold and silver was hindered or stopped. Wise old Joshua Gee, who wrote (1730) "The Trade and Navigation of Great Britain Considered," ended his book with this paragraph: "The trade of a Nation is of Mighty Consequence, and a thing that ought to be seriously weighed, because the Happiness or Misfortunes of so many Millions depend upon it. A Little Mistake in the Beginning of an Undertaking may swell to a very great one. A Nation may gain vast Riches by Trade and Commerce, or for want of due Regard and Attention may be drained of them. I am the more willing to mention this because I am afraid the present Circumstances of ours carries out more Riches than it brings home. As there is cause to apprehend this, surely it ought to be look'd into; and the more, since if there be a wound, there are Remedies proposed, which, if rightly applied, will make our Commerce flourish and the Nation happy." He had studied the trade for the year 1723, and had found that he could trace the export of more than a hundred and seventy tons of silver and about eleven tons of gold. In another place he says, "yet so Mistaken are many people, that they cannot see the Difference between having a vast treasure of Gold and Silver in the Kingdom, and the Mint employed in coining money, the only true token of Treasure and Riches, and having it carried away; but they say Money is a Commodity like other Things, and think themselves never the poorer for what the Nation daily exports."

Investigation of trade cycles and causes of depression bring on an interesting study. In late years it has been demonstrated, notably in 1901, 1905 and other instances, that Wall Street can have a regular old-fashioned panic and the rest of the country go on unaffected to any degree. Such might be called "financial hysteria" and be confined to the "Street." On the other hand, we may have business depression, such as came in 1914, resulting from uncertainty due to the outbreak of the European war. At that time Wall Street prospered by making foreign loans at usurious rates, while the business of the rest of the country was stagnant. Wall Street panics are usually brought about by the selling of securities by holders who feel that the peak has been reached, particularly when some untoward instance happens which might look like a setback was ahead. A large number of sellers appearing at the same time naturally causes the market to recede. A few days of sharp drops causes the holder to become frightened and a general unloading ensues, and the legitimate investor often follows the speculator, but too late. By the time he has awakened to the fact that a genuine stock panic is on the value has sagged considerably. Such declines are caused by or are followed by stringency in the money market, and others are forced to sell because their margins are exhausted. The decline continues with disastrous effects until a point is reached where many times the stock becomes an actual bargain and it is picked up by that element of fortunate people who always have money through steady incomes or are able to borrow under any circumstances.

A friend, during a game of cards where the luck of the players was going bad, used to say: "Never mind, your luck will change bye and bye—and get worse." That well describes some of the depressions we have had. The de-

pression of 1848 did not follow any particular period of
inflation or expansion, but came on during very normal
times. Likewise the depression of 1884. The depression of
1893 also followed a period of six years which were below
normal rather than above normal. In other words, bad
times got worse. A class of economists hold to the doctrine that trade cycles follow the fluctuations of precious
metals. They attempt to explain that scarcity of gold means
retrenchment and a stagnation, and that a great output
of gold brings expansion and prosperity. How, then, do
they explain the depression of 1920 in the United States,
which had over half the world's gold, and a depression of
equal volume in Great Britain, which had the next largest
gold reserve, as against the unprecedented prosperity in
Germany, which had very little gold? Another school of
writers claims that depressions are caused by unsound
money, in the form of too large coinage and circulation of
silver. That theory has been generally accepted in this
country because of the unfortunate experiences we have
had with silver money. But, on the other hand, we can
point to many countries that are and always have been on a
silver basis, and they have suffered less from severe depression than have we in this and other gold standard nations.
The money of Spain, known as a silver country, brought a
premium during the World War, and on the western continent up through history Spanish silver money has always
been at par and usually brought a premium. Thomas Jefferson favored putting this country on a silver basis, pattern-
ing our currency after the Spanish coins, which circulated
freely and were in great demand in some of the colonies for
thirty years after the Revolution. The examination of financial history shows that there is no reasonably close relation
between depression and the output of precious metals,
either gold or silver. It is known that the decade ending
with 1850 shows the output of gold doubled, compared with
the previous ten years, yet that decade was marked the

world over by financial reaction. Our panics of 1857, 1873 and 1907 all occurred during periods when there was a great inflow of new gold.

Still again there is another group that sticks to the money question as the root of the depression evil. These probably come nearer to a correct diagnosis than the others.

The issuance of paper money of unsound backing has undoubtedly caused several serious depressions. The use of this money led to extravagance, over-expansion and wild speculation, so that a halt was bound to come. The issuance of paper money within reason as a circulating medium is necessary. We are so used to paper money that in these days the tendering of a silver dollar causes curiosity if not resentment. We have already entered the Paper Age. We are reaching a point where we realize there is something of basic and intrinsic value in the world besides gold and silver. These metals may always be used as a basis of money issues simply because of their rarity, but they will grow less and less in importance. The Bolshevists of Russia tried the age-old theory that money is unnecessary, and they will find to their own surprise and to our chagrin that they are half right. When we are further along money will be necessary only as a paper medium to represent recognized essentials of mankind upon which it will be based. Our Federal Reserve Act provides that we may issue paper money on something besides gold and silver and the notes still be more than a mere promise to pay. Our Federal Reserve notes are based on certain approved securities which are far more necessary to the progress and welfare of mankind than gold and silver. True, these notes are redeemable in gold, but it is well known that the issues outstanding are ten to twenty times as great as the gold reserve back of them. As we go along the Federal Reserve Act will probably be so amended, and at the same time strengthened, that our money will represent the accumulated wealth of our brains and our toil, which is the finest intrinsic value that God has created.

There have been minor depressions in our country that are really hard to analyze, with no apparent causes. In the case of our major depressions, however, the causes may be well defined. At different times various governments have attempted to analyze depressions and if possible find a remedy. Among these are the United States, Great Britain, France, Belgium, Germany, Switzerland and Italy. A variety of causes have been advanced by scores of writers, economists, investigators, financiers and business men. Some are old and have been eliminated by the march of time. Some are obviously of little consequence, while others are very apparent causes and these are defined later. Among the causes that have been advanced at different times are:

Underconsumption.

Large Exportations of Gold.

Large Importations of Goods.

Effects of Fear of the Tariff.

Weak Banking Systems.

Presidential Elections.

Unpopular Taxation.

Lack of Foreign Markets.

Unemployment.

Want of Confidence.

Inflation of Values.

Variation in the Cost of Production.

Unpopular Legislation.

Unreasonably High Prices.

Centralization of Capital.

Manipulation of Money Power.

Depreciation of Currency.

Withdrawal of Money from Circulation.

Contraction of Currency.

Inflation of Currency.

Suspension of Specie Payment.

Disturbed Value of Gold and Silver.
Lack of Fixed Policy in Governmental Affairs.
Extravagance, Public and Private.
Inefficiency of Labor.
Large Immigration of Pauper Labor.
Speculation.
Depressed Value of Farm Products
Exhorbitant Transportation Costs.
Artificial Stimulation.
Timidity on the Part of Money Lenders.
Bank Failures.
Conflicts between Capital and Labor.
Buyers' Strikes.
Enforced Economy, Public and Private.
Starting Needless Enterprises.
Political Distrust.

At different times various causes, more or less absurd, have been ascribed, many of them of course having little bearing on the question. Among them are:

"Withholding Franchise from Women."
"Want of Training of Girls for Future Duties."
"Faulty Laws Relative to the Guardianship of Children."
"The Custom of Issuing Free Railroad Passes."
"High Telegraph Rates."
"The Use of Tobacco."

Professor Frederickson, of the University of Copenhagen, earnestly believed his theory that depressions "were due to the minds of men" or the result of "mental process."

Many of these theories have been disproved, as for instance, that relative to the exportations of gold. Let us refer to the case of the French nation, which in 1871 paid Germany a large indemnity in gold. Yet depression followed in Germany in two years, while times were normal or good in France.

Sun Spots.—Some years back Professor Jevons advanced

a theory which attracted considerable attention and many believers, viz., that cycles of depression followed the appearance of sun spots. He sought to prove that sun spots occurred in the history of England during the dates of her financial crises which he named as 1701, 1711, 1731, 1742, 1752, 1763, 1772, 1783, 1793, 1804, 1815, 1825, 1836, 1847, 1857, 1866, 1878. In seeking an explanation of this strange coincidence the Professor claimed that sun spots caused defective harvests which, in turn, brought on industrial disaster. Both astronomists and biologists, however, failed to agree with the Professor and the theory has long since been discarded.

Over-Population.—It has been held in Europe for some time that depression was caused by over-population; that there was not sufficient employment and too many had no buying power. Yet we have had depressions in America of still greater severity when the country was sparsely settled and even now it certainly cannot be said that this country is over-populated.

Over-Production.—The cry of over-production goes up, particularly among theorists, as a cause of business depression. Yet there has never been a time, even in our most prosperous years, when there were not thousands in need who would gladly give labor or its equivalent for the very articles that were claimed to be over-produced. Many students of economy laid the distress of 1920 to over-production, as was the case in many previous depressions. This was a quick change of front from a year preceding, when all the professional economists told us that we must have greater production in order to relieve high prices and profiteering. In 1919, in the face of the fact that prices were then outrageous, salesmen went up and down the country with the stereotyped phrase that they were doing the customer a favor by selling at prices quoted and that the next order would cost more because prices were sure to rise still higher. They claimed there was an under-production and that raw material and labor could not be obtained to supply the demand. Then came the buyers' strike, and almost over night we switched the blame for our predicament from under-production to over-production. Over-production is responsible, more or less, for our temporary depressions and set-backs, yet that is a wrong diagnosis of the primary causes for the sickness of America in 1920. Stimulated by universal demand manufacturers, and farmers in particular, produced abundantly. Of most commodities we always have a surplus, and what surplus we had could easily have been taken care of had international finances been anywhere near normal. Foodstuffs were rotting in this country while China and half of Europe were starving. Europe also had urgent need of the products of our mines and mills, and our surplus would ordinarily have been shipped there had not their finances been strained to the breaking point.

We had a surplus, not from any cause of over-production, but because of our time-worn custom of producing a surplus, and the use of the word "surplus" in this connection gives the unthinking man an entirely erroneous impression, for it gets the cart before the horse. It implies that foreign trade is a device to get rid of a surplus product, whereas the so-called "surplus" was brought into existence because of the demand originally created by foreign trade.

Excessive Saving.—Several writers have come forth with articles taking the stand that excessive saving is a cause of depression. These writers put forth earnest efforts to show the fallacy of saving, but their arguments are without merit. We know that money saved is not taken out of circulation at all, but the savings institutions lend it to borrowers and it is put to work in production just as if the original owner had spent it. The only time the question of excessive saving might enter into depressions is when the depression is at its height. When banks are liquidating to an extreme and people are saving to an extreme, a bad situation is certain to be created.

The solution is that people must save more in good times
and the banks must lend more in bad times.

Foreign Investments.—We are facing today a new situation that might in the future be agitated as a cause of depression in this country. This factor is the large investment
of American capital in foreign countries. English economists of fifty and a hundred years ago complained that their
industrial conditions were depressed because of enormous
investments of British capital in foreign countries. No
doubt that did drain England of money for the time being,
although in later years those investments were a source of
great wealth to England. It is easily possible to see that
in this country the matter of foreign investments can be
overdone, bringing temporary detriment to business in this
country. Some insist that we are still a new country, that
in every locality there are great possibilities for development and a need for investment capital. Yet enormous sums
of American wealth during the depression of 1920 and
1921 were invested in buying the Hapsburg estates in Austria and Hungary, in South American oil fields, in Russian
concessions, in Cuba, Mexico and the Orient. It is pointed
out that these investments were necessary to secure future
supplies of oil, rubber and other raw materials, and probably we missed the money less in 1920 and 1921 than we
would in normal times, because of the great wealth poured
into this country during the war. Most of these investments
were made as a result of exchange of loans already owed us,
and will no doubt benefit us in future years. In 1846 John
MacGregor in his "Commercial Statistics" described the
condition of Holland during the progress of her decline. He
called attention to the fact that a great part of her specie
and capital was then being diverted into investments in
the manufacturing trade and securities of foreign countries,
which permanently exhausted and weakened the power and
energy of Holland. It was soon found that where a man's
money went he eventually followed, so that not only the

money but the life blood of Holland went to other countries; not only to her colonies, some of which she later lost, but to many other countries. American investments abroad may not cause our best business men to follow, but unless it is a gradual process it is certain to be reflected in our domestic industrial welfare.

Falling Prices.—Carroll D. Wright, former United States Labor Commissioner, gives falling prices as one of the chief causes of depressions. His report made in 1886 on this subject is interesting and shows thorough investigation of a practical nature.

As a cause of depression falling prices is secondary, because they, in turn, are brought about by more fundamental causes. Rising prices have a psychological effect. They stimulate hope and courage, whereas falling prices cause caution, fear and depression. Falling prices may follow a financial crisis or may precede a general depression. In 1920-21 the depression could have been largely avoided if prices could have been gradually reduced in proportion to a decline in cost of production. In such a sharp fall of prices as we have recently witnessed great losses must take place and depression will follow until these losses can be made up or overcome. Low prices naturally bring depression in values of property and stocks on hand.

Mr. George Grubb, National Secretary of the Marine Engineers' Association, claimed the depression was brought about by a concerted effort of employers who wanted to squeeze labor. No doubt there was a general desire on the part of employers to discipline labor because of alleged inefficiency, although no evidence is at hand to show that this movement was organized. If it is true that the depression was deliberately brought about, which is extremely doubtful, then the employers badly mismanaged matters when they let the movement get away from them. It is certainly plain that the employers lost enormous sums of money when the buying power of millions of workers was curtailed, as well as through the depreciated value of their own enterprises arising from curtailed earning power. For instance, a manufacturing institution might easily be worth a million dollars as a going concern, if its output is being consumed and it is earning healthy dividends. Yet it is also possible that the value of that same plant might depreciate to half that amount through lack of orders, stringent credits, decreased earnings and disorganized employees. In the face of these facts what would the employer gain by a concerted movement to shut down? Thus decreased earning power will cause falling prices entirely outside of the natural order of supply and demand.

Changes which take place in the prices of commodities may be due either to changes which affect the commodity only or, since price is the relation of the commodity to money, to changes which take place in the value of money. Change in price may therefore arise from a change in (1) the demand for, or (2) the supply of the commodity. Changes of this nature are reflected in the prices of one commodity as compared with another; their positions in the price scale change. It may be noted that when prices change "by reason of differences in the demand for, and the supply of commodities, some commodities may rise in price while others fall. Such readjustments in prices of commodities are constantly taking place. On the other hand, should price changes be wrought by changes in the value of money we should expect uniform action upon prices—a general rise of prices or a general fall.

"The study of prices has long been a subject of particular solicitude, not only to the men actually engaged in business but to the students of business affairs. To separate the general from the particular, economists have invented what is known as the index number. The purpose of this device is to ascertain the average change in prices of a group of commodities. The prices of a given period or a given time are selected as a base, and the price of each commodity is determined," says Joseph French Johnson, dean of New York University School of Commerce, Accounts and Finance, who tells in "Economics of Business" how the method of tabulation arrives at a scientific price barometer. "The advantage of taking as a base the average price for a series of years is that this course makes it possible to eliminate as far as possible the influence which, in a shorter period, unusual conditions might have had on the price of a particular commodity. When the base price is ascertained other prices during, before and after the period of the base are expressed as percentages of this base. Commodities A, B, C and D will each have a different base, but when the base is turned into a percentage it becomes uniform for all, namely, 100. We may suppose that at a later period A is represented by 110, B by 106, C by 102 and D by 98. Now, if these figures be averaged the result is 104, and this represents for the group an average rise in price of 4 per cent over the base. One of the commodities indeed declined in price, but this does not alter the fact that the general tendency is to advance the price. In following the method, briefly indicated, of constructing an index number, each article has been given an equal importance in determining the change. If instead of abstract designations, A, B, C and D, concrete articles had been named, such as wheat, iron, wool and indigo, there might be some doubt as to the propriety of giving each an equal importance in fixing the result. To avoid such questionings various methods have been devised to give an appropriate weight to the different articles, such weights being arranged in accordance with the foreign trade, or with the estimated national consumption, or the expenditure of workingmen's families."

None of these highly complicated methods have, however, led to substantially different results from the simple arithmetical average. It is clear that if each article moved upward in price exactly 5 per cent it would not matter how many articles were added to the list or how they were com-

bined, and one could not get any other general result than
a 5 per cent advance. If some articles increased 4 per cent
and others 6 they would, if equally divided, show an average of 5 per cent, but no method of combination could make
the advance less than 4 or more than 5 per cent. In other
words, in a group of prices the general tendencies outweigh
the particular ones, and no combination of different results,
according to any plausible system of weighing, will empha-
size the particular tendencies at the cost of those which are
general.

Economists agree that there is not a level of prices,
whether it be high or low, which causes either prosperity
or distress, but it is the conditions brought about by either
that brings the need of readjustments. In case of falling
prices being the direct cause of depression in a given industry where production costs have been high and losses
entailed, lower prices do not of course necessarily mean
depression. If production has been large the reduced cost
lowers prices and sometimes stimulates trade because of
greater consumption. Through a period of depression
prices gradually decline until the bottom has been reached.
Sometimes prices go down beyond reason because of the
panicky feeling among buyers, in which case production
must stop, bringing sharp reaction. For instance, in 1920,
when cotton went far below cost of production, the result
was a curtailment of acreage amounting to 40 to 50 per
cent, bringing the following Fall sharp upward reaction in
prices to the extent of 80 per cent. After it is apparent
that the bottom has been reached prices will start an upward climb, bringing a feeling of hopefulness and activity.
Buyers will not buy on a falling market for more than immediate demand, but they will buy liberally on a strong or
rising market, because of the speculative chance to make
more than a normal margin on the purchase.

Falling prices are also brought about by the recurring
necessity for adjustments of credits. When the cycle of

liquidation comes manufacturers and merchants hasten to turn stocks into money in order to meet loans coming due. Many times these stocks, if held and marketed in an orderly way, would bring normal prices, but when loans are called money must be secured and stocks are sacrificed at reduced prices. This has a tendency to break the market. Forced credit liquidations are an important factor in producing falling prices and consequent depression. Banks are, however, more and more willing today to carry the borrower until such time as he can market without too great a sacrifice. It has been calculated that the loss on industrial stocks during the depression of 1903 exceeded $3,000,000,000. The depreciation of securities of 1907 and 1920 was much greater, and if stocks or raw material and merchandise were taken into consideration the total would be very greatly increased. It was too much inflation in flush times that brought conditions where falling prices were inevitable.

Exports of Gold.—Gold is, of course, being more or less constantly exported to settle balances, but a large and continuous outflow of gold denotes an unhealthy condition back of it. It is likely to mean a money crisis ahead and probably ensuing depression. When the export of gold is attended by a scarcity of money and a marked increase in the rate of discount, it is a decidedly unfavorable indication. Unless the flow stops and the tide turns it may be taken for granted that a crash will follow. The big financial centers watch the gold situation very carefully, and money conditions are very sensitive to the gold situation. Financiers who are in a position to watch gold movements often have the inside track, so to speak, and are able to cover before a crisis. It is these "gold sharks" who are invariably found to be the men who profit from depressions. In other words, they are experts in buying cheap and selling dear. Gold has a close bearing upon our business life and the average business man should watch its trends closer than he does.

Bad Banking.—This should properly come under the head of speculation. Unsound banking has caused a great deal of difficulty for business, and this is not altogether the fault of the banker. On the whole he is generally conscientious in desiring to aid in the development of the country. Newspaper files of our periods of depression show that almost invariably the public press attacked the banks as the cause of all the difficulties. In 1920-21 business men claimed that they were left to shift for themselves while the bankers watched and preserved their own interests.

In times of prosperity men become optimistic beyond reason and enter into transactions far beyond their means. The mania of taking a chance becomes widespread. Then the banker finds out that notes are not being met and a large portion of his customers have been borrowing for speculative purposes. Often they are found dividing profits with the banker himself. The situation reveals itself the country over and contraction sets in. Then is the time for business men and investors to sail close to shore, to sell, if possible, keep stocks low and quit taking chances for a while.

We have read a great deal about bad financing during the Nineteenth Century. The early part of the present century has seen great strides made in halting the destructive pendulum swing back and forth from extravagant prosperity to panic. In former days when any financial center got into difficulty it was left to its own resources. Now, even its enemies come to its rescue because it is well understood that a run on a bank's neighbor is likely to lead to its own disaster if allowed to go its full course. Down through the years of history, as every cycle of depression is examined, we find the same old story of bad banking. It is found that the banker has invariably dipped his finger in the attending over-speculation. The promoter is smooth enough to arrange a division of the excessive profits with the banker and the banker often makes injudicious loans when this division is hung out as a temptation. Then when the bubble bursts the banker goes to the other extreme and his tendency is to be parsimonious, often from a very narrow viewpoint and against his own interests.

Poor Crops.—While crop conditions have a certain effect on business, it is often localized and does not affect the entire business system to the extent generally believed. Let us take the year 1900. Statistics of the Department of Agriculture show that we had an area planted amounting to 83,320,872 acres, producing 2,105,102,516 bushels at a farm value of $751,220,034—an average of .357c per bushel or $9.04 per acre. The following year, 1901, a greater area was planted, 91,341,928 acres, but production was less than the year before, being 1,522,519 bushels, but with a greater farm value, $921,555,768, a per bushel value of .605c and a yield per acre of $10.09. That is a usual instance because the law of supply and demand insists that in a year of short crops the price is higher, bringing as much money to the farmer as a big crop with lower prices.

Foreign Exchange.—Foreign exchange is a barometer of world trade conditions. It is a study in itself, and all that could be written about it would fill an ordinary library. Every business man and investor should study the question, because as we progress in our commerce and it becomes more interlocked with that of other countries conditions in those countries will more and more affect our every day business life here. This subject is one of growing importance.

We do not carry on our foreign trade the same as we do the business among ourselves. Within our own borders a simple check and draft system suffices, because funds in Blaine, Washington, are on a par with funds in Key West, Florida. But when a merchant in one country trades with a merchant in another country, there must be a medium through which payment is cleared. This is known as foreign exchange. In principle foreign and domestic exchange are the same, the difference is in the value of the money of one country as against another. Where the value of the standard money in one country is high it brings a premium, whereas the money of another country may have depreciated for various reasons and it is penalized. Where exchange is steady money in the leading countries is around par, as during the normal times preceding the World War. Then trade flows fairly evenly and there is little to fear from difficulties in that direction, outside of the ordinary business hazards. But in times of distress in different countries, brought about by political or economic reasons, foreign exchange has an important bearing on the study of business depressions. Foreign trade is done on a basis of payment in London or New York exchange, or between bankers themselves in gold specie. If by watching the daily newspaper quotations it can be seen where money of a certain country that buys a large portion of our products is depreciated, there is almost certain to be a falling off in demand from that country and, unless some other country is taking the difference, depression in those commodities will likely result. Sometimes this condition may be general. For instance, in 1920-21 the American dollar became so high that foreign countries could not afford to buy dollars in order to pay us in our own money, which we demanded. This augmented the depression because we were unable to ship our surplus out of the country to as large an extent as formerly. In normal years when trade flows back and forth in its regular channels and exchange is around par, trade balances tend to adjust themselves in the same manner that a local clearing house clears checks through a system of debits and credits, one against another. We are going to be more affected by foreign exchange in the future than ever before, because New York is now the world's financial center. To the extent that we are called upon to finance the world we are going to feel the reflection in our own business life, and foreign affairs are going to more largely enter into our trade revivals and depressions.

Exchange between two countries is at par when a demand draft on either country sells in the other at its face value. For instance, an English pound sterling in mint value is $4.8665. Exchange therefore at par would bring $486.65 on a draft of 100 pounds, less the small banking charge. If, however, conditions bring about a change in the par value of either standard of money, the exchange rates would immediately reflect that fact. If a business man is shipping goods to England, or is dependent on customers who ship there, and a dollar is quoted at a premium over the pound, then he can expect a slowing up of orders from England until the exchange is more favorable. Thus it will be seen that foreign exchange not only affects the exporter and importer, but all of us who are dependent more or less on them. When foreign exchange is continually against us, as in 1920-21, we may expect general depression to some extent.

A premium on the dollar, as was the case in 1920-21, means that there is an abundance of gold in this country to back up the dollar, whereas a depreciating pound sterling or German mark would mean that gold reserves were either depleted in proportion to the depreciation or there was an over abundance of fiat money in circulation in those countries. Another element that enters into the trade situation is the fact that when the exchange rate is against us, that is, when the dollar is at a premium, we are likely to not only export less but to import more, because countries with depreciated money will make extraordinary efforts to export in large quantities in order to establish a trade balance and get the gold flowing back to them. Ordinarily, if we loaned a great deal of money to France, for instance, or purchased their securities, there would be a great outflow of gold from this country to France. But during the recent war period when we loaned heavily to Europe we loaned through a process of giving bank credits in this country with the understanding that credits were not to be transferred to Europe but were to be used for purchases of supplies in this country. Thus the exchange later worked against us, whereas had we sent the gold it would have been in our favor. In this way also we became a creditor nation and at the same time kept the gold here.

The question of discount rates also enters largely into the matter of foreign trade, but does not necessarily bear directly on trade depressions in this country. When there is a panic in one country it will immediately be reflected by the exchange rates. With distrust growing in one country and reserves depleted banks will raise their discount rates, which will be followed by like action by banks in commercially related countries.

In such times the banks of a country in distress draw to the limit on their reserves in other countries, and those countries are often taxed to meet them. It is through this medium that one country is directly affected by panic in another. It does not follow that all countries are to be affected by a panic in some one country, but only those groups of commercially related countries which depend largely upon one another. Even then, with a good banking system, one country need not necessarily be greatly affected by a crisis in another, no matter how closely related.

In 1920-21 people in necessitous countries hoarded large amounts of foreign money, due to the huge profits they saw accumulating daily through the continuous depreciation of their own currency. Depression can only be remedied by finding a means of stabilizing exchange. This may be done by making loans to countries whose exchange is depreciated and help them to restore confidence, or to buy sufficient of their goods to give them a favorable trade balance, causing the flow of gold into that country. Most nations are not willing to import goods, because it destroys home industry. But they are more willing to make loans if certain of payment at maturity. These loans simply help in the transition stage, and in time the situation will work itself out. Unfavorable exchange prolonged for more than a short time will cause the creditor country to feel the effect as much as the debtor country. When exchange is stabilized the vicious cycle is broken and economic conditions, all other factors being satisfactory, will quickly return to normal.

In times of war some countries still resort to the mediaeval practice of prohibiting the export of gold. This causes a still wider fluctuation in exchange. Exchanges are affected by the constant flow of gold and goods. This has its effect on trade in this country because exchange being against other countries they naturally can afford to buy only as little as possible, whereas the premium on our money makes it favorable for us to buy what we like. All this causes the agitation for American valuation in the tariff. The tariff schedules enacted in normal times become a mass of confusion and have effects far from their original intention in times of abnormal exchange.

Exchange can be brought to par by the simple expedient of shipping gold. But in times of stress some countries do not have the gold to ship or, as a matter of self-protection, do not wish to ship what they have. In such a case foreign exchange must be carried on through the draft system, which is generally used between countries that have a very even balance of trade. All countries do business through New York and London drafts, and these drafts can be cashed above or below par according to the gold situation and the trade balances in the different countries. The high price of drafts in Germany would encourage and stimulate the sale of American goods in Germany and would encourage buying in Germany. Likewise, high prices of drafts in the United States would encourage and stimulate the sale of German goods in this country and discourage them from buying from us. It is evident then that a favorable trade balance, such as we experienced during the war, could not keep up indefinitely. The tide must flow out, and this is often accomplished by a period of depression.

Mr. Frank Vanderlip has proposed a billion dollar international bank for the twofold purpose of regulating foreign exchange and promoting international trade. This idea is undoubtedly good, and if put into execution would go a long way toward solving the knotty problem of foreign exchange.

Strain of Credit.—Through the agency of credit a great number of obligations payable in money are created. It would, of course, be impossible to redeem them all at one time. Against these credits there is kept a certain amount of gold as reserve. If demands for redemption lessen the quantity, it must be replenished. These demands now arise mostly from foreign sources. It can be replenished only by curtailing credits. Such a process does not lessen in any degree the amount of existing wealth, but none the less it may necessitate painful readjustments in business. Those who had counted upon the continuance of credit accommodations are forced to curtail or even abandon their operations.

"If the demand for a liquidation of outstanding credits is widespread, panic and business depression ensue. Wealth is not destroyed. But the control of wealth passes more and more into the hands of those who own the wealth, and its activity is lessened. Capital or wealth used in production is diminished, and with the decrease in capital the creation of new wealth slackens. On the other hand, in times of reviving business, the prospect of gain lures wealth into productive uses and through credit the available capital is increased." Thus back of all the alternate periods of prosperity and depression lies the question of credit. No plan has yet been found effective which will prevent these fluctuations, nothing which will give credit freely when credit is most wanted. But through a wise adjustment of credit agencies much can be done to mitigate the severity of periods of stress and strain.

A time must come when there must be a contraction of over-expanded credit. At times we find the capital of the nation largely tied up in the hands of speculators who have practiced the unbelievable process of borrowing the people's money in order to increase the prices of their own necessities. As the periods come along when we work out of depressions into good times the speculator gradually starts to borrow money because he is smart enough to know that things are on the upward grade. He picks commodities on which prices are well declined and are bound to rise with greater demand. As time goes on he makes fair margins, thus encouraged he increases his holdings through greater borrowing. This continues for several years, all the time the rising tide of prosperity increases the fury of speculation when finally the peak is reached. Some unforeseen incident brings sharp reaction or a revolt on the part of the public against the ever increasing prices. Bank reserves become low from the large borrowing and then the banker becomes wary and begins to call loans. When this time comes great sums of money are found in the hands of speculators. Some of them hurry to unload if possible, taking a small loss out of their already large gains and laying low until the depression blows over. Others have to be carried by the banks until the security can regain its value and passed on to others. Thus speculation is not only responsible in bringing on our crises and depressions, but it invariably prolongs them because of the long, painful spell that is required to get conditions back to normal. During all this time we hear the constant cry: "Liquidate! Liquidate!" and the average legitimate borrower and business man and farmer are forced to liquidate many times at a sacrifice while the capital of the country and their own deposits are used to hold up speculators, non-producers, who have over-borrowed and if allowed to fail would often endanger the solvency of the banking institutions themselves.

An English View.—Mr. J. M. Keynes who was in charge of all loans made by Great Britain during the war and author of "The Economic Consequences of Peace," gives a view on the world wide depression from the British standpoint. "The causes of these 'cyclical fluctuations' are various and disputed. Like its predecessors, the recent depression has been of complex origin. But a bad season in Asia and the miscalculations of merchants have played the biggest part. No doubt the war has been indirectly responsible, because the severity of the crisis has been due to the exceptional range of miscalculation, which the terriffc fluctuations in prices consequent on the budgetary policies of governments have brought about, and also by the inapplicability of pre-war standards as a guide to what was normal. These helped business to lose its bearings and to drift far out of its course. If we look back eighteen months, it is obvious how greatly .the troubles of traders have been due, not so much to the intrinsic situation as to grave miscalculations about it. The crisis commenced, not in Europe, but in Japan. Thence it spread to the United States; next to England and last of all to continental Europe, which has not, at any time, experienced its full severity. What upset British business was the sudden drying up of the Overseas markets, India, China, Australia, South Africa and South America; and it was the collapse of the exchanges between London and many of these centers, rather than of those between London and the continent of Europe, that threw out the calculations of the business world.

There were two other factors also which multiplied the stream of commitments. Many markets had been starved by the war of their usual supplies, and were replenishing stocks. But it was difficult to know how much current demand represented such replenishment and how much of it was covered by current consumption. Lastly, the abnormal demand stimulated by all these influences was yet further exaggerated, because merchants, experiencing an unusual difficulty in obtaining deliveries began placing orders on an even larger scale than they really wanted, in order to make sure of obtaining at least a proportion. For all these reasons merchants and middlemen in all quarters of the world over-ordered enormously. That is to say, they entered in advance into commitments on a scale greatly in excess of the current rate of consumption and at a price level above that which the currency systems of the world could support, hugely inflated though they were, when once the actual goods were coming into existence and needing finance. This necessarily resulted in an excess of stocks and, when the value of the stocks exceeded the amount of wealth which the world was voluntarily prepared to set aside in this form, the bubble burst."

Political Uncertainty.—H. Gordon Selfridge, in his admirable book "The Romance of Commerce," says: "There are enough mistakes made and poor judgment shown, as we all know, in that field of activity called Commerce; but if one-tenth of the foolishness had been employed there that has been exhibited by those who have undertaken to govern, all commerce and everyone connected with it, would have been bankrupted many times over and have sunk long since in the seas of oblivion."

Political uncertainties often retard industry. The statesman (a dignified name for politician) is often unmindful of the injury he is doing in bickering and delay. How many times has trade been halted waiting the leisurely action of the legislators! The old bugaboo that we cannot change political administrations without accompanying depression was long ago exploded. Time has proven that depressions come under the administration of one political party as well as another and it would be a sad and evil day for the American Republic if the threat were constantly held over us that we had to vote one way or have our bread and butter taken away from us.

Presidential Elections.—It is rather old-fashioned now to ascribe business depressions to presidential election years. That has been so overdone in the use of politics and proven to be so utterly without foundation that it is worth but little space. By way of information, however, the accompanying table will show the presidential election years since 1800 and the years of depression, showing that only five depressions have occurred in our history during presidential election years, two of them being minor depressions.

Presidential Election Years

1800	1816	1832	1848	1864	1880	1896	1912
1804	1820	1836	1852	1868	1884	1900	1916
1808	1824	1840	1856	1872	1888	1904	1920
1812	1828	1844	1860	1876	1892	1908	

Depressions falling in these years are:

1808   1848   1860   1884   1920

In one of these, namely, 1884, the depression was an issue in the campaign. In none of the others was there much connection between politics and business, although the depression of 1860 was obviously from political causes on account of the threatening Civil War.

Excessive Taxation.—High taxes are going to be more and more a cause of depression in this country in future generations. In our early history the government was rich beyond compare because of the enormous amount of public lands. From the sale of these the Federal treasury not only received sufficient to run the government, but divided great sums between the States. Following this period under the protective regime we collected sufficient from that source together with such internal revenue taxes as were obtained from tobacco and liquor to run the government. Then as we went into the Twentieth Century our expenses were so enormous that we began to devise means of direct taxation and the income and corporation taxes resulted.

Under our present laws, on incomes of $200,000.00 and over we exact fifty per cent. All of this, no doubt, has its effect because the incentive is taken away to some extent for large capitalists to make an effort because half of the effort, they feel, goes for naught. Let us turn to the history of the Roman Empire and examine into the causes of its decline. We will find that "the pressure of public burdens was an increasing disability that ate the very heart out of the capitalist and the labourer alike; there was no hope to inspire energy or encourage enterprise and the gradual decay culminated in an utter collapse." The exorbitant taxes collected to maintain an expensive government started the decline of the commercial life of Rome. Will history repeat in Europe and America? Money spent for taxation does not reproduce and unless we can keep money in productive channels we are bound to have depression in trade.

Dumping.—This subject is one of the utmost importance during depressions. After the Revolution when we had no organized central government, our trade was severely depressed by dumping of English goods on our market. Our infant manufactures had to close down and the trade balance was enormously against us.

Our great depression of 1819 was brought on as a direct cause of dumping European goods in this country. It was then that Lord Brougham made his famous speech in Parliament: "It was well worth while to incur a loss upon the first exportation, in order, by the glut, to stifle in the cradle those rising manufactures in the United States which the war had forced into existence, contrary to the natural course of things."

While a protective tariff law had been enacted in 1812 which gave some protection during the war, it was entirely inadequate and when peace came in Europe in 1815 followed by very terrific depression and low prices in 1816, this country became flooded with their surplus which was disposed of by the well-known "auction" system. European exporters were willing to sell at almost any price; first, to get cash; second, to destroy the rising American manufactures. Considerable agitation swept over this country against the "auctions;" yet they multiplied and in one year $14,685,399 worth of merchandise was auctioned in this country, which was double the normal needs of the people. No wonder prices in this country fell swiftly. Imported goods were drawn into every nook in the country, causing stagnation to the American manufacturer. Merchants and farmers bought these goods eagerly, because they were cheap, but in doing so they undermined the prosperity of their own country.

The dumping of this period of "auctions," as it was called, was a nightmare to American merchants and manufacturers for many decades. Prices fell so low that merchandise brought little more than the duties. Auctioneers increased in number, wealth and influence. It was a common custom, and one well understood by merchants, that many foreign importers residing here, and who sold their goods mostly by auction, were in the constant habit of receiving two invoices for each parcel of goods. One of these was made out at a very low rate and was used to enter the goods; "the other contained the actual cost." Of course, the government was injured by losing the revenue justly due it, while American manufacturers and importers suffered materially. Of the many industrial enterprises which had been launched during the war with so much confidence, only a few had had a prosperous history. Many had been hopelessly wrecked; while others were thumping against the rocks and threatened with speedy ruin.

After the Civil War we were saved because of protective duties against dumping and naturally this subject is related to the tariff. Traders of all countries do this. We are as guilty as the others. For years our manufacturers have sold the surplus abroad at less than in the domestic market. But practically all countries are now providing against it. Following the World War our rich market and high prices were prey for the foreign trader with a surplus. Everything was dumped on our market that could be found in foreign countries, particularly food stuffs, affecting the farmer very adversely. This was one of the primary causes of the 1920-21 depression. Had we a protective tariff or even an anti-dumping law our commodities would have been given a chance to seek their normal level gradually. When our farmers and manufacturers cannot have their home market it is bound to mean depression, unemployment and far-reaching distress. In 1920 we were as thoroughly at the mercy of foreign cheap labor as we were in 1819.

The American valuation plan is now agitated as an anti-dote to dumping, but this plan is not new. It was first known as the "Home Valuation" principle and was advanced by John Quincy Adams when he was a member of Congress in 1832.

Hoarding Money.—In former years the practice of hoarding money no doubt augmented depressions to a large extent. It is said that French peasants in the 19th century universally hoarded their savings, many times causing severe stringency. Hoarding was also practiced in America during the 19th century, particularly in the rural communities. As late as the panic of 1907 a representative of the house of J. P. Morgan & Co. gave as one of the causes of the money stringency and panic that of money being hoarded away in private places and kept out of circulation. As the intelligence of our people has advanced, this practice no doubt decreased, although it is yet to be reckoned with. In the 1920-21 depression the average citizen liked to carry a "bankroll" of much larger proportion than formerly. In the flush times of the war people became used to it and this practice has taken the place of the pot of coin hidden under the floor or the stocking stuffed full of money and hid in the bureau. The worst feature of hoarding is that it is more likely to be practiced in times of stress or depression when it is most harmful. The use of money as a store of value diminishes its efficiency for the purpose for which it is intended. It therefore increases the demand for money since an ineffi-

cient instrument does less work. Conversely, whatever increases the efficiency of money lessens the demand for it.
Whatever increases the rapidity with which money circu-
lates therefore diminishes the demand. It is one of the advantages of the introduction of banking habits that men
carry less money in their pockets and thus money acquires a
greater rapidity of circulation.

At the time of the Mississippi Bubble, 1720, under a paper
currency regime specie money was hoarded to such an extent that France was practically bare. Yeats' description
of this period was: "Under the belief that coin was being
hoarded, people were forbidden to keep at home a sum in
coin exceeding 500 livres, or to use any medium of payment
for amounts over 100 livres except bank notes. Still money
disappeared. The resources of charitable institutions, or-
phan schools, hospitals and almshouses were demanded by
the state and exchanged for paper. Finally, the penalty of
confiscation was proclaimed against all who should, from
the date of the proclamation, keep gold or silver in their
houses, whether coined or uncoined, instead of exchanging
it for paper money. With nothing left to confiscate, even
arbitrary power was at a loss. The precious metals appeared to have left the country. Foreign merchants could
not be compelled to take paper instead of gold, nor could
they be prevented from paying in French notes for the
goods they bought. Discontent and fear led to hoarding,
in spite of proclamations. The medium of exchange was
at length reduced entirely to paper. Trade, both foreign and
domestic, became paralysed."

Preceding and during the panic of 1893 large sums of
money were withdrawn from the banks and hidden away.
This was because the treasury had an over abundance of silver certificates and treasury notes and fear spread that the
treasury would never be able to redeem them in gold if it
were called upon. In this case confidence not only in the
banks but in the Treasury itself was shaken.

War.—The United States has been particularly fortunate

as regards serious foreign wars which often threaten the foundations of a nation's economical system. Only once have we been invaded—in the war of 1812—and that was by a surprise and entirely a fluke. In no other instance have we even been threatened by invasion by a foreign country. Our wars, on the other hand have been beneficial to our economic interests in the long run. In our Mexican War we gained great territory, including vast gold fields. In the Civil War we preserved the Union perpetually, preventing two nations instead of one. After the Spanish-American war, trade again followed the flag.

It stands to reason that business distress accompanies the outbreak of a first rate war and brings depression in countries who have trade relations with those at war. It may even cause suspension of gold payments. The aftermath of war has peculiar effect on economic conditions. After 1870 France, the defeated, with big indemnities was more prosperous than Germany, the victor. This situation was reversed following the World War when Germany, the defeated, was more prosperous than France, the victor.

While wars have caused many depressions, yet on the other hand quite a number of wars have been caused by commercial selfishness. In the Middle Ages when commerce began to take hold of the people as an economic science one country would suffer a period of depression while, perhaps, its neighbor prospered either because of discriminating tariffs or favorable natural conditions. This led to quarrels and war.

War, while it always stimulates business, really makes the rich richer and the poor poorer. Nations are coming to find that war no longer pays and it is admitted now that had Germany continued her peace-time course she would have conquered the commercial world, whereas she failed to conquer the political world. Eventually the fiddler must be paid by both victor and vanquished and many times their economic difficulties as an aftermath spread to involve the neutrals. While France staged her revolution amid streams of blood and flame, England silently and peacefully underwent her industrial revolution, increasing her wealth tenfold and putting her a half century ahead of her commercial competitor.

To prosecute a war naturally calls out the resources of a nation. Currency is inflated. Great quantities of money are put into use. This money is still out at the end of the war and overlaps for the period of two or three years, keeping conditions good during that time, as was the case following the Revolutionary War, the Civil War, the War of 1812, the Spanish-American War and the World War. Offsetting this is the overproduction in some lines. This material including food-stuffs having been put in warehouses in anticipation of war uses is held back for a while before being thrown on the market. Returning soldiers are paid off, thus putting money into circulation, helping the times immediately following war, but when this money is spent and the men have to get back into production and the surplus material begins to be sold, then follows trouble. The worst effects of after-war depressions could be avoided if the same skill, energy and resourcefulness was used in that direction as was used to prosecute the war. The depression of 1920 could have been prevented in a large measure had administrative ingenuity been properly used for a longer period after the war. When the armistice was declared and war industries stopped, throwing great numbers of men out of employment, the government of necessity got back of the situation and the weight of our financial structure was thrown back of peace industries that were languishing. The men were put back to work in these industries and the returning soldiers absorbed as fast as they returned. In fact, there was such a demand for labor that the Government was urged to speed up the return of the men. Great prosperity ensued until April, 1920, when the depression set in and gradually spread over the country, growing worse as the months went by. The presidential campaign was coming on, the President had been afflicted with paralysis, the Secretary of the Treasury, Mr. McAdoo, had resigned and there was no head to the Government. When various local crises sprang up as a result of after-war readjustment, there was no head to the government to help straighten things out. Cabinet members refused to take any step, fearing the consequences that happened to Mr. Lansing. Had there been an active executive at the head of the Government who was ambitious and willing to help solve the problems arising, the depression could have been averted or at least largely mitigated.

We bemoan war, as we should. We raise a great outcry against economic loss from it, as we should. But it is a little known fact that the loss sustained by securities and stocks of raw materials and merchandise during years of depression and forced liquidation is greater than the cost of carrying on the greatest military campaign in history. A recent speaker at a bankers' convention said that our national wealth had increased 30 per cent during the war, during which time we grew to be by far the wealthiest nation in the world, but that our entire gain had been wiped out during the depression of 1920-21. His statement is obviously only partly true but is of sufficient import to set us thinking.

CHAPTER XXIX.

SPECULATION, THE OUTSTANDING CAUSE OF DEPRESSIONS

The word "speculation" comes from the Latin "speculor," meaning to do or to contemplate. Defenders of the speculator call him a business look-out or economic forecaster. There are those who claim that speculation is necessary, as there were those of the old school who claimed gambling on the grain exchanges in imaginary transactions was a real benefit to the farmer. Modern forms of speculation grew up with the Stock Exchange. The first reported stock exchange was in Antwerp in the Fifteenth Century. A pamphlet published as early as 1542 described the "monstrous thing that the Antwerp merchants had devised; they bet with each other on the course of foreign exchange, one saying it would be 2 per cent, one 3 per cent, etc., and afterwards they settled by paying the differences." This is substantially the same operation as that which is carried on regularly today. In the Sixteenth Century speculators on the stock exchanges used the same methods still in vogue. They would set rumors afloat to depress the price of securities and then buy in. Day tells in his "History of Commerce" that "One day during the reign of Anne in England a well-dressed man rode furiously through the street proclaiming the death of the Queen. The news spread and the funds fell; the Jew interests on the exchange bought eagerly, and were suspected later of being responsible for the hoax, though it was not proved against them."

We have speculated ever since we have known what money was. In the year 1697 Professor MacLeod declared that "The frightful convulsions and collapses of public credit which have taken place during the last three-quarters of a century are chiefly due to this great wrong." In 1719 the word "stock jobbing" originated in a pamphlet put out by an Englishman named Child.

In another chapter I have described the relation of money to depressions, taking the stand that confidence really enters into the question more than money or forms of money. History indisputably proves that we have prosperity when we have confidence, and depression when we lack confidence. What brings about this lack of confidence? The speculator who buys cheap to sell dear, who gains control of certain commodities and pushes them so high that suddenly there springs up a lack of confidence in such values, resulting in a crash. If we could, by sane and lawful process, eliminate the worst of speculation we could retain normal confidence so as to eliminate the worst of depression.

This does not mean that there should be a curtailment of the credit system, but that credit should be more properly used so that our prosperity, while it might not reach such great heights, would be more lasting and permanent. Jay Gould said to the United States Senate Committee: "People will deal in chance. Your minister, doctor and barber have all the same interest in speculation." Gould, while partially right, was judging his neighbors by himself. Figures do not lie and the blackboards in the stock exchange tell an interesting tale. They amply show the difference between speculator and investor. Let us take the figures of the New York Stock Exchange, during the year 1906, which was a normal year, and note the fluctuations in a single day:

	1906		*1907*	
	High	*Low*	*High*	*Low*
American Smelting Company	174	138½	155	56¼
Atlantic Coast Line	167¾	131⅛	133⅜	58
Chicago, Milwaukee & St. Paul Common	198⅞	135¼	157½	93½
Chicago & Northwestern	240	192	205	126
Consolidated Gas	181¾	130⅝	140¼	74
Great Northern Preferred	348	275	189¾	107½
Illinois Central	184½	164	172	116
Missouri Pacific	136¼	106¾	92¾	44½
Pennsylvania Railroad	147½	122½	141⅝	103½
Reading	164	112	139⅛	70½

Can any one look at these figures, knowing the history of these corporations and their long record of regular dividend payments without default, and say that this is any other than gambling? Is it possible that legitimate investors would consider Pennsylvania railroad stock worth 147½ at one hour in the day and 122½ at another hour at a time when its solvency was unquestionable and had been unquestioned over several decades?

Members of the New York Stock Exchange explain that the actual value of the stock, as based on dividend payments, does not enter into these fluctuations, but they are caused by the necessities of the buyer or seller. The buyer having certain uses for more stock, such as for control of the directorate, would pay a heavy price for voting stock. On the other hand, the seller, pressed urgently by the need of money because of some tight situation he is in, will sacrifice. Certain conditions, it is explained, sometimes cause a group of men to have the same object at the same time, thus these wide fluctuations. It was a group of important financiers which became involved at one and the same time that caused the selling orgy and brought about such panics as 1903.

Henry Clews describes speculation as follows: "Speculation is a method for adjusting differences of opinion as to future values, whether of products or of stocks. It regulates production by instantly advancing prices when there is a scarcity, thereby stimulating production, and by depressing prices when there is an over-production."

If the speculator alone suffered from his own misdoings there would be very little objection to the practice, but the entire public is buffeted about on the winds and waves of the depressions which are of his making. As we gain experience in government the general public will become awakened to the havoc wrought by the professional speculator who usually leaves his victims to pay his losses.

Another evil of speculation is the large amount of capital that is tied up that would otherwise go into legitimate channels of production. As an example of the evil influences of speculations on borrowed capital, let us go back to the days preceding the 1907 panic. In August, 1907, an offer by the city of Boston of $4,000,000 in 4 per cent bonds brought bids for only $200,000. Three days later an offer by the city of New York of $15,000,000 4 per cent's brought bids of only $2,713,815 at par. Think of such a situation when at that time individual deposits in national banks alone were $4,322,880,141. Remember this does not include the money in state banks, trust companies and savings banks. Imagine then, if one's mind is capable, of the enormous sums of money that must have been tied up in speculative enterprises that were neither liquid nor dividend paying. This situation was brought about by just such methods as were described by a writer in Van Norden's Magazine, December, 1907: "Mr. Morse first, and then the Thomases and the Heinzes, had, after securing one bank, hypothecated the stock of that bank in various financial institutions, not only here but all over the country; had taken the money obtained by a loan on the stock of one bank to buy stock in another, had mortgaged that and bought into still another, and so on and on. . . . Furthermore, after securing control of banks, they had made loans to themselves for the flotation of promotion schemes and for the conduct of operations in the stock market."

Though our currency may contract or expand to take care of our needs without shaking the structure as a whole, and while we now have the best and strongest financial system we ever had, yet we still have with us the root of most of our troubles, and that is the all powerful desire on the part of our people to speculate, to get rich quick. If we can stop speculation with other people's money we can absolutely stop business depressions, outside of world catastrophe, or defeat in war. I do not go so far as to say that we will ever stop speculation entirely, admitting that the difficult feat of legally defining speculation could be overcome. The speculator is a person of evil and unworthy intent. He is nothing more than a dignified crap-shooter or race-horse tout. He wants to play for big game at the other man's expense. He has a burning desire to obtain the world's goods without work, either mentally or physically, and, incidentally, is usually an individual endowed with shrewdness and cunning. In his transactions he uses the people's bank balances in order, in turn, to rob the people. Taking a homely example: He borrows money to buy real estate which he sells, many times at an enormous profit, and at an ever increasing figure, until prices soar beyond reason. He sells the property, taking a small payment and carries it by borrowing the people's money from a banking institution, one of whose depositors he robbed in the transaction. Even at that, so long as man is created with shortcomings evil is bound to exist in the world, and it might be necessary to permit speculation, with its attending profiteering, if the speculator's own money is used in the transaction. A remedy might be found through a Federal law requiring that no national bank be permitted to loan money to any individual or corporation without an accompanying affidavit that the money was to be used for the strict promotion of legitimate production and not for speculative purposes. While there will be criticism directed against this plan on the grounds of our inability to define speculation, yet it is undoubtedly feasible and practicable. To be effective, this would have to be followed by state laws, but when once put into operation, one state would follow another as they have in the case of "blue sky" laws.

We all know the arguments in favor of the speculator. Speculation is supposed to prevent sharp fluctuations and soften their intensity by anticipating events. Speculation is supposed to enforce present economy in the face of probable future want and so is claimed to prevent famine; it is supposed to even up supply and demand; it is supposed to create a market and reflect the present and the future. It is doubtful if it is necessary to any of these, but if it is, let it be carried on by men who use their own money and keep the credit of the nation in production channels. When men

borrow other people's money through public banking institutions, the public has a right to demand that it be used to
make legitimate profits on production, giving employment to
people, and allowing the public as a whole to satisfy their
wants through the use of their own money. The credit system is wrongfully used when it is tied up in channels where
it is used, not to make a legitimate profit by production, but
to make a profit by raising prices. It is obvious that the
speculator can profit in no other way except by a continual
increase in price. Yet billions of dollars of capital and
credit are used for this purpose. Then when prices have
been driven up until the public rebels, depression must necessarily follow.

When we consider speculation in its broadest sense, we
do not refer simply to the activities of the stock exchange
operators, but to a general class who buy in order to make
a profit on an increase in price. If he does it with his own
money and loses no one is affected as a rule but himself, but
when he does it on other people's money he undermines the
very foundations of our financial system. What remarkable laws we have when a poor man is forced to give sixty
days' notice to draw his savings at a time when the wealth
of the country is tied up in the hands of speculators who are
robbing that very depositor!

The stock and grain exchanges are beneficial if properly
conducted, because they act as an instantaneous reflector of
future as well as present conditions. They act as a preven-
tion of serious overproduction. Furthermore, if we did not
have exchanges in this country, such as cotton, sugar, grain,
stock, etc., we would be left to the mercy of exchanges in
foreign countries. Our own exchanges many times have
been found to act as a balance against wild and unfavorable
fluctuations in the exchanges abroad.

"In an ordinary market there are millions of securities
purchased and held on speculation," says a financial writer.
"While these securities are regarded as belonging to the
speculator who has bought them, they are in reality in pos-

session of the banks which hold them as collateral for loans they have made upon them. The money lenders and bankers, therefore, have the largest amount of money invested in speculative securities, and the greater proportion of this money, it must be remembered, is the surplus funds of the country banks." If a portion of this money was taken out of speculative channels and tied up in legitimate production and merchandising channels there would be more general prosperity, a greater distribution of wealth and less liability of destructive depressions.

Such crises as those of 1903 and 1907 were brought on from absolutely no other reason than that an unreasonable amount of the country's capital was tied up in speculative channels. When we have stringency investigate speculation and there you will find the cause. In 1903, particularly, Mr. Frank Vanderlip, then Vice-President of the National City Bank of New York, predicted the trouble a year ahead and warned against ever-increasing speculation. In speculative periods there is often not an actual increase in values to justify extreme prices, but only imagination buoyed up by false ideas of prosperity which later burst and we are brought to earth facing stern realities. "Its excesses, when inspired by reckless men of great wealth," says another writer, "often are the source of national damage. Thousands of men, ignorant of the pitfalls of speculation and unaware of the gigantic odds against them, are annually ruined. Fascinated by the stories of great fortunes made by speculators, they blindly 'plunge' in markets where only the wisest, shrewdest and best-informed of the professionals stand a chance of winning a profit."

Speculation in government securities in England is illegal. In the United States we have a weak law prohibiting contracts made with a view to obtaining a "corner" on the market. England also has a splendid law, only partially enforced, but which acts as a deterrent, prohibiting the enhancement of stocks to the damage of the purchasing public. In France there is little speculation; the people are thrifty, and they have had fewer disastrous panics and depressions than any other commercial nation. Public sentiment in France severely condemns a man who acquires the name of bankrupt for any reason, and it is known that a French family will submit to the most excruciating poverty to keep this stain from the family name.

Through the pages of history we find minor depressions caused by bad harvests, uncertain conditions of currency, political uncertainty and other causes, but practically every major panic and depression which marks a distressing epoch in the commercial and industrial history of the world has been a direct result of speculation. It is high time that we curbed this monster. How long will we stand by and witness our banks fail, business men in bankruptcy, investors ruined, workmen in despair, all for the profit of a handful of speculators? The speculators runs prices up until he reasons they have reached the limit that people are going to pay. Then he gets out from under and waits for the crash to come. When things start down it frightens people. They begin to curtail. Money becomes tight. Commercial failures start and the depression is on. It is the break in values, pushed up beyond reason by speculation, that startles the business world. When prices are down again and "liquidation" is complete the speculator again starts buying to sell later at enhanced prices.

Various remedies have been proposed to curb speculation —one by requiring that "when a bank shall permit its money reserve to fall below 20 per cent it shall not increase its liabilities by making new loans other than by discounting or purchasing bills of exchange payable at sight, and would also during such a period forbid the payment of dividends." Another would forbid a national bank from "incurring deposit obligations in excess of ten times its capital and surplus, also limiting speculative loans to the amount of a bank's capital and surplus." In rare cases, however, are bank deposits against capital and surplus shown to be so excessive.

Every sane business man knows that there is a well defined demarcation between legitimate buying and speculative buying, and that line can soon be established through a practical trial of the system. Legitimate business men and home builders will thus be able to obtain reasonable sums for their needs when the need comes, instead of finding it loaned out to speculators.

The Blue Sky Laws of the various states have helped to curb flotation of the schemes of irresponsible promoters, and yet these stock jobbers know that they use the United States mails to sell stock that the individual states would prohibit. To show what little progress we have made in a century of time, let us quote Henry English, a writer who had a full grasp of the boom of 1824 and 1825, and who indulged in some criticism at the time which it is interesting to recall as being applicable to the present day. He pointed out that prior to that period of inflation the companies formed were "of such description that individual capital could not be supposed to be adequate for the completion of the object for which the company was formed. A majority of these, formed during 1824-1825, were of a nature adapted only to individual enterprise. The deceptive practices resorted to, to obtain a price far exceeding the real value of the property (in various Mining Companies), can only be explained by the guilty participation of the parties in the spoils. To acts of a similar nature is to be attributed the sacrifice of character which, in too many instances of late, has been the result of the proceedings of joint stock companies; when, by the connection of honorable men with a class of designing projectors, the innocent have been implicated with the guilty. It is, however, to be hoped that the lesson thus taught the public, and more particularly men holding high stations in life, will be the means of preventing a recurrence of the events of 1824 and 1825." After a century of time how little progress we have made! Is there a single sentence in this man's story that would not be applicable to the present day?

It is well known that the spirit of the Federal Reserve Act has been violated to aid and encourage speculation. "It was not intended that the paper presented for rediscount should have been drawn to carry stocks, bonds, etc., or goods in warehouses held for higher prices; nor to aid in securing capital for fixed investment in irrigation, water-power, street-railway, manufacturing plant, or similar purposes. On the other hand, it was intended to encourage loans based directly or indirectly on the movement of goods from the producer to the consumer." But many instances have been shown where money secured through the Federal Reserve has been used for speculative purposes and to obtain higher prices. There are so many ways to get around the letter of the law that the only preventive is a closer supervision by the Board over the member banks and by the member banks over their correspondent banks.

Almost every theory advanced as a direct cause of depression is proven untenable except that of speculation. Those who have advocated bimetalism and paper legal tender as a cause are forced to admit that depressions occur in countries on a strictly gold standard basis. They occur alike in high tariff or free trade countries, in nations of stable and unstable political governments, in times of stable and unstable foreign exchange. When we have had depressions that could not be attributed to speculation, they have resulted from known and obvious natural or political causes.

CHAPTER XXX

THE LABOR QUESTION IN DEPRESSIONS

As a whole organized labor has now reached a high pinnacle. It has helped the struggle of the masses upward to better living conditions. Whether from now on it will be of real service to the working man and to the world, or whether it will be self-seeking, short-sighted and destructive, depends upon its leadership. Certainly its influence is going to be felt in commerce and industry more than ever before. Now that we have strengthened our financial system, labor is going to be the big problem entering into the causes of future depressions. It will be principally up to labor to make or unmake industrial peace and prosperity.

Work is elevating, and it is neither socialistic nor idealistic to assume that if man wants to work he has the right to a chance to work. To fill one's time with profitable production is to take part in the world's onward march of achievement. The backward races are adverse to work. In the early history of our own race work was considered degrading, so that we should feel that we have reached an exalted state in our civilization when men universally have the will to work.

Let us go back and review the past. Ptolemy Philadelphus, a successor of Alexander, boasted that in his reign "No citizen was idle in Alexandria. Even the blind and lame were taught to labour." Labor certainly had not reached a high plane in the year 1526 when an ordinance by the king provided, "That the scullions in the royal kitchen should be furnished with proper clothing, and should not 'go naked, or in garments of such vileness as they now do.' " Women did the hard work, and it sometimes happened that if a man lost a horse or an ox he married a wife as the cheapest plan to recoup himself.

Previous to thirty years ago writers almost invariably

ascribed as one of the causes of depression the use of machines, thus causing over-production and creating unemployment.

Lord Playfair, writing on this subject in 1888, says: "It matters not whether the countries were devastated by war or remained in the enjoyment of peace; whether they were isolated by barriers of Protection or conducted these industries under Free Trade; whether they abounded in the raw materials of industry or had to import them from other lands; under all these varying conditions the machine-using countries of the world have felt the fifteen years of depression in the same way, though with varying degree of intensity."

Labor has at various times been temporarily depressed by inventions of modern machinery. In times past the guilds and unions have fought the introduction of various machines, but time proved that they were really a boon to labor and unions now take a different course.

In the Seventeenth Century working men protested vigorously when the large coaches were made, which carried as many as eighteen passengers, making the distance from London to York in four or five days. The workers pointed out "the vast amount of employment those eighteen persons would give to grooms, farriers, innkeepers, hostlers, saddlers, etc., if each were to ride his own horse instead of adopting the revolutionary practice of clubbing for a common conveyance."

Depressions have always been a serious setback to the organized labor movement. The first attempt to organize working men in this country was met by a counter organization of New York employers in 1836, and while twenty striking tailors were convicted of conspiracy, yet the movement was growing in force until the panic of 1837 gave it the final blow. The crisis of that year put a complete stop to the work of internal improvements and left thousands of men out of employment. In those early stages labor organizations could make no headway against unemployment.

As the decades went by labor was able to form again in battle array, but time and again it was hurled back by the depressions that periodically swept the country.

At the outbreak of the panic of 1857 labor had four national unions, together with a considerable number of scattered local unions. These practically were wiped out of existence during the depression of that year. The demand for labor during the Civil War which followed, and the rising cost of living with which wages had not kept pace, gave the labor organization new impetus.

Labor severely felt the panic of 1873 because of the large influx of laborers who came from foreign shores. During the period of business prosperity preceding the panic there was a great demand for labor and thousands were brought over. Aliens to the number of 460,000 came in the year previous, under a system whereby their wages were pledged to repay their transportation. This great surplus was thrown on the labor market, and in the panic of that year caused untold suffering and gave the young labor organizations a sharp setback. The unions were not strong anyhow, because of the strike of 1872, brought about by an organization known as the "Grand Eight Hour League." These strikes, with the exception of the building trades of New York City, were unsuccessful, and the unions went into the panic of 1873 already in a weakened condition, suffering at that time further reduction in wages to offset the decline in business which brought increased dissatisfaction. Two important strikes occurred, namely, on the Baltimore and Ohio and the Pennsylvania Railroads, in which violence was used and property destroyed, and armed conflicts took place between troops and strikers. Some European newspapers printed that there were "three million tramps in America out of a population of forty million."

After this depression labor again made headway, secured increased wages, and reached a higher point than ever before. In that period wages steadily advanced, with the exception of a short period during the depression of 1884. The presidential campaign was on during the depression of this year and the expression, "pauper labor," was heard on every hand, the unemployment situation being a paramount issue of the campaign. During this year a million men were reported idle, but the depression passed without serious consequences to labor, and further upward strides were made during the years that followed.

The depression of 1893 was marked by the great Debs Strike and Coxey's Army. Less prominent leaders followed Coxey in raising armies of unemployed, among them Randall, Browne and Kelley. Returns made to Bradstreet's, the results of which were published December 23, 1893, show that in 119 cities 801,055 men, with about 1,956,110 persons dependent upon them, were out of employment. In the mining industry labor had made headway, built up a strong organization, and had favorable contracts with the operators prior to the depression of 1893. Then all the agreements were broken because of the viciousness of the times and the workers received a severe setback.

The crisis retarded the steady progress labor was making during the rather dull times preceding. Idle farm hands tramped the country in search of work. Unemployed operatives crowded the streets of factory towns demanding work or food, and laborers abandoned the mining districts and flocked to the cities. Unskilled labor was prostrated and the ranks of skilled labor were badly shattered. Special committees were organized in nearly all of the large cities to provide food, and in many places relief work by public bodies was instituted. In the Spring of 1894 general want and distress led to labor strikes and riots, as in Chicago, and even to more abnormal outbreaks.

In 1907 wages of the cotton mill operatives in New England were reduced 10 per cent. Many mills closed down, others ran part time. The railroad companies proposed either to reduce wages or increase the freight rates, promising to give employment to thousands more men if the increase was granted. Wages were not generally reduced among the skilled operatives, but thousands were laid off. Later, the increase in rates was granted despite the strong protests of business men, but the promised return of prosperity was slow in coming.

During the depression of 1914, when the nations of Europe were tearing at each other's throat, business stagnation in this country resulted from the shock of closed stock exchanges and stringent money. The United States Steel Corporation failed to pay dividends for the first time in its history, although wages were not cut. Thousands of men, however, were laid off until war orders began to come from the other side.

In the depression of 1920 organized labor was hard hit. Officials admitted that they had faced the worst crisis in their history. The American Federation of Labor, which had gloried in a position of supremacy in the labor movement of the world, suffered enormous losses of members. It was reported that between one million and one and a half million members dropped from their rolls after the depression set in. At the peak of its strength the organization had approximately four million members. Financial stringency became so acute with the organization that it was necessary to furlough most of the paid organizers. Officials, however, made the prediction that labor would emerge from the storm stronger than ever.

In these periods of economic distress, when misery reaches its limit and forbearance is no longer a virtue, mutterings of discontent grow into clamor and tumult. They have changed the course of the economic world, often the political world, and their echoes reverberate through the chapters of history. Labor's greatest antagonist is business depression. Organized labor has overcome all obstacles, it has fought and, it may be truthfully said, has won against the lock-out, open shop and other deterrents, but it is absolutely at the mercy of industrial depressions. No accusing finger has ever been pointed at labor as guilty of bringing about depressions and their resultant afflictions until the depression of 1920. But labor's post-war greed was almost as great as that of capital. Since the previous depression labor had adopted new tactics. Their business agents delved into the records of the various industries. These records were becoming more and more open to the public as regulation of business came on. The labor representatives were able to ascertain just what industries were earning big profits and proceeded, through the strike, to gain for themselves all the traffic would stand. As a whole, labor acted very fairly during the war. While excessive demands were made in many cases, labor, under the patriotic leadership of Samuel Gompers, loyally supported the war, and arbitration was in most cases easy to obtain. During the inflation period brought on by the war labor profiteered probably to an equal extent with all other profiteers in every line of endeavor. Probably this statement would not be in order but for the inexcusable lowered efficiency, which was as bad as the utter lack of service on the part of capital. Business men, as a rule, were willing to pay the high wages demanded at the time had they been given efficient labor in return. This is the first depression in our history that labor must rightfully bear its part of the blame for bringing on.

We shall have to wait until a decade or two have passed before American business interests will realize what they escaped in the post-war period. With radical leadership we would undoubtedly have experienced the same troubles as happened in Germany, Austria, Italy and England. It may be a long time before labor again has the same able leadership as it has had under the trying times of the Gompers' regime. Long after he is gone business will turn to pay him honor and point to his regime as an example of sanity in leadership.

Labor will save itself from many setbacks by following its more conservative leaders. In 1921, at the height of the depression, the marine engineers who, as a result of war conditions, had built a powerful organization, were receiving an extremely high wage scale. They struck, against the advice of their president, William S. Brown, one of the ablest labor leaders in the country, and a member of the President's Unemployment Conference. They lost, of course.

During the depression of 1920-21 the unemployed were placed on the auction block in Boston and their services sold to the highest bidder. The plan was attempted in other cities, but prohibited on the grounds that it accomplished nothing in the way of a permanent solution of the problem.

The International Machinists Union, under President William H. Johnston, sought to bring a revival in business by securing orders through their Union from foreign countries. The Mexican Government placed large orders for machinery in this country under the supervision of the International Machinists Union.   President Johnston also attempted to go to Russia on the same mission, but was prevented by radicals who had gone from America to the Bolshevik country.

In October, 1921, the International Labor Board gave figures of the estimated unemployment as follows:

United States_____More than 3,000,000.
Canada _____Sixteen per cent. of organized labor.
Japan _____232,000, including 3,000 sailors in Kobe alone.
Britain _____The European country hardest hit—nearly 2,000,000 officially inscribed.
Switzerland _____22,000 wholly and 90,000 partially unemployed.
Denmark_____Sixty-five thousand.
Norway_____Seventeen per cent. of organized labor.
Sweden _____35,000 wholly and 42,000 partially unemployed.
Holland_____Sixteen per cent. of organized labor.
Belgium _____153,000.
France_____(Which was one of the countries least affected), 120,000 wholly unemployed.
Italy _____110,000 wholly and 300,000 partially unemployed.
Czechoslovakia ___37,000.
Germany_____The climax of unemployment was in September, 1920; in 1921 only 3 per cent. of the workers were wholly unemployed.

These figures are admitted to be low.   They do not include unorganized workers. Some statisticians claim double the number given here were out of employment.

The Idaho Legislature passed an act establishing the right of every person who has resided in the State for six months to ninety days' public work a year at 90 per cent of the usual wage if married or having dependents, otherwise at 75 per cent of the usual wage.

Duluth, Minn., adopted the policy of building sewers throughout the winter in order to equalize the amount of unemployment. Detroit found the digging of sewers in frozen ground no more expensive than under the blazing summer sun.

Business circles will respond more quickly to the disruption caused by labor troubles than anything else. There may be a nation-wide strike, such as a railroad or miners' strike, and business will immediately feel the effects. Local strikes, of course, will not cause general depression nor will a general strike cause prolonged business distress, because neither side can afford to hold out long.

If financial and natural conditions were sound, the effects would be over in a short time and business resume its normal course, so that labor troubles cannot be ascribed as an underlying cause of business depressions, but an important contributing factor. It is the general exorbitant demands and inefficiency of labor that frightens capital and cause buyers' strikes.

The average laboring man is, of course, not educated to the point where he can reason for himself from a scientific, economic standpoint. He feels many times that he has been crushed and that his employer has profited too greatly from his labor. That leads him to go to extremes when he gets the opportunity, which is not the right way to correct the evil of profiteering on the part of capital. He should not assume a right to profiteer just because another man does. "Two wrongs do not make a right."

A case at point is found in English history beginning in

the year 1824, after the law passed by Parliament a quarter of a century previous which forbade combinations of labor:

"Upon the repeal of the law against combinations the hopes of the workers soared. They had come to believe that by combination they might achieve everything for which they longed. A workman's paradise was to be instituted at once by the activities of unions, which were now at liberty to work in the open with no threatening shadow of imprisonment hanging over their leaders. Trade-unions sprang up like mushrooms overnight. On all sides there were strikes for higher wages. Unfortunately for the hopes of the workers a business panic occurred in England which forced the manufacturers to close their mills. All the strikes failed of their purpose, and many of the workmen could find nothing to do and were saved from starvation only by charity. Many of the unions broke up and workmen lost faith in their organizations."

As the years go by labor becomes more specialized. The modern workman when employment is scarce in his trade waits for it to pick up. When most of us were boys a workman was more or less a "Jack of all trades." When he could not work at his own trade he was supposed to work at anything he could get. Outside of common labor that is not the rule these days.

At a meeting of women workers held in New York during the depression of 1893 an appeal was being drawn up for their aid, and included in it was a request to the women of the wealthy class not to cut off their luxuries. There is a certain class of people who have an assured income which is affected only slightly in periods of depression. These people could do a patriotic service by buying liberally so as to give employment to those who are not so fortunately situated. They should keep in mind that they have incomes only because others work and produce, so they themselves are dependent on the well-being of others. The labor leader of the future, however, must prepare to advise his followers along more correct lines. Labor is developing some splendid and able leaders, men who are paid salaries as high as the earnings of the average business man. President Stone, of the

Railroad Engineers Union, was recently voted $25,000 a year salary. It is these men the country must look to for proper guidance of the labor movement, so that the public will not have occasion to react against the abuses of labor, as well as the abuses of capital. My experience as an employer is that the average business man does not object to paying a good wage. His experience teaches him that a good wage means money to spend beyond bare necessities, a portion of which will come back to him. Employers, too, have a right to demand an honest day's work for an honest day's pay. They have a right to expect willingness and personal interest and co-operation on the part of the workmen, and if this is unstintingly given public sentiment will stand solidly behind labor for a round and healthy wage and reasonable hours.

Labor today is a big element in considering risks. The manufacturer who is advantageously situated as to low power and transportation costs, together with a lower wage scale or greater efficiency, has a distinct advantage over another manufacturer where the opposite conditions prevail. Where labor costs are high and efficiency relatively lower, the manufacturer will not take the risk of making up stocks in dull times, but will shut down awaiting definite orders, so that the buyer absorbs costs and lessens the risk. More co-operation on the part of labor in this direction would help to keep the factory going on part time even in the most serious depression. The manufacturer with high labor costs is first to suffer loss when the market for his article weakens, so that he cannot be expected to keep his employees at work making stock for the future when depression, either local or general, sets in. The American laborer should by all scientific standards be more proficient than those of other countries. He is the best off materially, has more of the comforts of life which should create an incentive, and with the saloon gone, taking away the constant temptation to drink, he is physically and mentally in better condition.

Contrary to the general belief, labor has been growing more efficient. In the textile trade statistics show that the average production per man in 1880 was $1600 per annum, and in 1900 was $1700 per annum. The average of recent years would hardly be fair, because during the war period large numbers of new and inexperienced hands entered the factories.

Some business men condemn labor as a whole, but they should not overlook the fact that the unions of skilled workmen under the American Federation of Labor kept the country from a state that might have bordered on anarchy during the war period and immediately following, when labor had the upper hand and was very hard to control. Some thought the unions demanded excessive wages, and yet statistics show that they did not ask for anything like the increase that was demanded and given to the unskilled, itinerant workers of the Bolshevist type. For instance, the wages of unorganized labor more than doubled, while the organized unions estimated it at 40 per cent increase. The organized unions were far more reasonable in their demands and were always a restraining influence, without which we would undoubtedly have had more or less of the anarchy which swept over all the European countries.

When prosperity is general labor begins to fight for a share. In most cases business men must give in because they cannot afford to fight while there is a chance to make money. Labor wins. And then another group makes demands with the same results. This continues until the disputes become vicious. Then capital gets cautious, no new enterprises are undertaken, and if it happens that other adverse conditions come about at the same time the signal is automatically given and another depression sets in.

Business depressions throw out of employment an average of one out of every five wage-earners, which is a great national calamity. It is a loss to the nation in spending power of over four billion dollars per annum. What we lose in depressions could easily pay our national debt.

As early as 1856 Carroll D. Wright, special commissioner on American Trade Depression, reported that "if the employers in any industry would combine under an organization that should have positive coherence, there would be no difficulty, so far as that industry is concerned, in regulating the volume of production in accordance with the demand."

One of the early excuses given by those who formed trusts in America was that they would help regulate the law of supply and demand and avoid industrial depressions in the future. It may have helped some, but they have fallen far short of the promised goal.

In the early days of trade unionism the unions took the stand that wages should be regulated by the price of the product, and they were willing to accept wages based on that principle.

The coal miners of England went into an agreement of that kind with the employers, who formed an organization known as the "Coal Sales Association," but after the agreement went into effect, the Coal Sales Association for some reason went out of existence and the employers abandoned the idea.

This plan was also tried in 1865 by a trade union of puddlers, known as the United Sons of Vulcan, in the steel works around Pittsburg, who made an agreement with their employers to base their wages on a sliding scale, according to the price of the product. They had a commission which had access to the prices made. With the change in the method of making iron this union later amalgamated with other organizations who discontinued that method of dealing with employers.

As before stated the history of organized labor shows that they get their hardest knocks in periods of depression. It is, therefore, to their interest to help devise means of avoiding depressions. A simple and easy way would be to take up again the old sliding scale principle so that they can avoid violent reductions in wages, and at the same time reap the profit to which they are entitled in prosperous times.

It seems that this would be a good method, both to halt strikes and to avoid the connection that trade unions have in bringing about depressions because of necessary readjustment.

Under present conditions, when both prices and wages get too high, finance and employers get together to curtail production in order to force a lower wage. This is done with a very violent shock to business and the depression often times gets out of hand. There is no reason why it cannot be automatically done. There are, of course, objections to the plan. On the employers' side they claim that a certain part of the output is sold on contract at prices below the prevailing market, but certainly there can be an average arrived at by the simple process of mathematics. Along with that they should put in their agreements an understanding of uniform employment, so that the employer may not turn off large numbers of men, creating a great army of unemployed, but may reduce the hours per week when curtailment of production is necessary. In this manner everybody would have some kind of a job and it would simply be a case of adjusting his living conditions to the fluctuation of his pay and the hours per week that he can work.

We can solve our problems best by recognizing that labor has a right to improve its condition. As Machiavelli said: "A free government, in order to maintain itself free, hath need, every day, of some new provision in favour of liberty."

Ideas have also been advanced along the lines of unemployment insurance. If this plan is put into effect employees must directly or indirectly pay for it, and experience is that they will not do it. What they demand is a certain amount of money to spend. What is put away for them is not appreciated. The average working man feels that he will take a chance on the future. The trouble is that when he gets a job he thinks there will never come a time again when he will not have one. People who do not think and study cannot be made to see that another depression is ahead. We have never gone through one but what nine people out of ten are sure that we will never have another, and some who so think may refuse to prepare for it.

Labor suffers so terribly from unemployment due to industrial depression that it should be the first to take steps to avoid those conditions in the future. Mr. Halbert, General Superintendent of the Board of Public Welfare, Kansas City, in "Persistent Public Problems," sets forth a good idea:

"Perhaps, compulsory unemployment insurance for casual laborers is impossible, but if the opportunity for unemployment insurance was universal to casual laborers, it would create a rather strong moral presumption against the man who refused to take advantage of it, and a certain stigma, such as belongs to vagrants, would tend to attach to him, and people who did not carry cards which indicated their standing in this regard would be at a disadvantage in getting employment."

The labor leader of the future must not be of the type who creates hatred among employers by organizing men only to get wages, hours and conditions, but the duty of the labor organizer and business agent must also be to "sell" the union to the employer. He must not take an arrogant stand, but must be an emissary of conciliation to get the employer's good will and to show him how he can selfishly profit, himself, by employing union labor at such terms and conditions as the unions think they should have. The employer cannot be blamed for dreading conditions that existed immediately previous to the depression of 1920. In those inflated years of great demand and scarce labor the employer many times had to submit to being cursed and abused by his employees. He saw their efficiency lowered, and their arrogance became such that it was no pleasure to do business. It is safe to say that thousands of business men, before they would go through such an experience again, would lock the door of their factory and go fishing. True, the employer many times was equally as guilty. He mistreated and abused the public. He profiteered and gave no service. Such conditions are not good for anybody. Why is it that we lose our heads when we have prosperity? Why cannot we deserve prosperity? All of this backs up the argument of some that unemployment, depressions and hard times are a necessary evil connected with a larger good.

If labor cannot profit by recent history it can go back to the Tudor period in England, when the guilds made such restrictions as to apprentices and other conditions that they began to cramp the rising manufacturing industries which chafed under the vexations and began moving into the smaller and remote towns. The unemployed in the Sixteenth Century were indeed unfortunate, because a law was passed at that time in England providing that if an able bodied man was found "begging a second time he was to be mutilated by the loss of the whole or a part of his right ear."

The question with us should not be what to do with the unemployed individual, but rather, why is he unemployed?" This will lead to wide study by the public of periodic industrial depressions.

We must face the fact in the future that labor is going to demand the right to work, and they are likely to be in position to enforce it. Wise employers will begin to devise a system through which he can keep all of his employees under almost any condition. He must work out a plan of shorter hours and correspondingly shorter pay, or short layoffs by rotation. Unemployment affects not only the unemployed, but our whole economic structure, and we are drawing to a point in our civilization where we must find an orderly way outside of the precepts of socialism to give every family head the right and opportunity of steady work. If we neglect this, forgetting it during our prosperity, as we are wont to do, we are sure to invite further depressions, resulting in far greater costs than an equitable solution would entail. The dole system in vogue in England at the present time will never prevail in America. Our people do not believe in supporting non-workers. There is plenty of work to do entirely

outside of production which might at the time be all sufficient. How much better it would be if England would spend
her millions by providing and requiring a reasonable amount
of work. Certainly idle men can be used to beautify and
improve public property so that their time is not wasted in
idleness and they can be paid for making the world a better
and prettier place in which to live.

The old-fashioned employer liked to discipline labor by
creating a condition of unemployment, but we have all come
to realize that unemployment is a disease that undermines
the health of the economic body. It stops demand and affects
not only those who are thrown out of employment, but
frightens others, causing the curtailment in demand of every
kind.

The Wisconsin Legislature has had before it an employment liability law. Professor Commons, of the University of
Wisconsin, in an article published in the Survey, says: "The
theory of this proposal is that expansion of credit is a main
cause of unemployment, and that an insurance liability
should be placed on the manufacturer against the day when
he lays off the workmen. It is assumed that a banker will
not extend credit and a business man will not enlarge his
force without taking into account this liability."

There will be opposition to this plan, of course, but certainly it is more nearly an American plan than the European
system of accepting unemployment as inevitable and depression as necessary, endeavoring to arrive at a solution
through philanthropy. The states of Pennsylvania and California are now making a provision for the control of public
works to the end that this construction might be done during periods of depression as a safeguard against unemployment.

Business and labor, both of which suffer from depression,
should find a common interest. On the one hand is the laborer without employment, hopeless, with his last crust,
willing to work and seeking not charity, perhaps with a
family, and on his mind the dreadful knowledge of their

want; yet with the same status as the hobo, the tramp, or the bum. He vainly seeks employment, goaded to desperation by the thought of those who need his wages, until he feels that there is no spark of justice left in the world.

Take then the business man. What stories many could tell, those self-made men who struggled for years through repeated discouraging periods, building up the institutions which give employment to men, assuming the burdens of all the economic world. To these men all of our millions look to provide the pay-roll. Little do we consider them, a comparatively small part of every community, who furnish the money for all the rest of us to spend. The sanitariums that dot the country attest the mental strain which they undergo, doubly so in times of depression when additional troubles are heaped upon them and their fortune and their life's work threatened to be wiped out. These two, the workman and the business man, have felt the same dismay, the same tension of uncertainty. They ought to find a common ground where they can get together to eliminate these periods of distress.

" 'These are my jewels,' said the mother of the Gracchi, and she embraced her two sons."

Why cannot capital and labor join in brotherhood? They are the jewels of humanity.

CHAPTER XXXI.

AGRICULTURE AND DEPRESSIONS

The economic history of American agriculture has been a record of great forward strides and increasing prosperity, excepting in those periods when the hand of depression was laid upon her fair fields. The outstanding feature of economic history is that depression and prosperity have succeeded each other, just as civilization and anarchy have followed each other for thousands of years. America is probably the one nation in the world that has never had a famine. Our farmers have always produced in one commodity or another, or in one section or another. In taking the crop statistics of the country as a whole over a period of years, it is surprising how evenly they run from year to year and how steady has been their growth. A certain school of economists claim that the constantly recurring trade depressions follow the so-called cycle of agricultural prosperity. They argue that following a period of depression the output of agriculture is not at first sufficient to keep pace with consumption. The crops grown bring high prices because of scarcity. The farmer starts spending, marking an upturn in business. For a few years planting increases and greater prosperity results in a greater consumption until, finally, the agricultural output increases beyond the demand of consumers. As soon as this point has been reached, and a year of large carry-over is faced, prices decline sharply, bringing its blight to the farmer, who gets low prices for his overproduction so that he is usually in debt and unable to buy when depression comes.

"*Ceres,*" remarks a writer, "is triumphant democracy in the prime divinity of the Republic." We are by far the greatest agricultural nation in the world. The last census showed that 48 per cent of our population derived its living from the farm, so that agriculture is naturally important in the cause and effect of the trade cycles that revolve through the years of our history.

The history of the Roman Empire records periods when agriculture ascended the hills of prosperity and then went down again through the valleys of depression. It is not known just how much American money a Roman sesterce was worth, but it is recorded that an ass sold for 60,000 sesterces. Whether they had profiteers in those days or depreciated money is not recorded.

There could not have been a depression, but rather an inflation of agriculture when Marcus Terentius Farro, a Roman farmer wrote: "So men buy cows with black horns rather than with white, large goats rather than with small ones, and pigs with long bodies, provided they have small heads. The third point is the question of the strain to be desired. In this connection Arcadian asses are celebrated in Greece and those from Reate in Italy, so much so, indeed, that in my memory an ass went for 60,000 sesterces and a team-of-four at Rome were valued at four hundred thousand."

Depressions in the early centuries were largely agricultural depressions caused mostly from over-production, while in other years there would be crop failures and famines. The lot of the agriculturist in the manorial period was at times very bad. The tenants were ill-treated and often convicted on slight cause. The year 1381 records a general movement of the tenants toward greater economic and social freedom. The hard feelings engendered took violent form in the Peasants' Revolt, known as Wat Tyler's Rebellion.

In the early history of modern times in England agriculture particularly went through regular periods of distress. These depressions were a serious problem and later brought on regulatory measures, and were subject to numerous investigations to determine the causes. Francis Austin Channing, a member of Parliament, wrote a book in the Eighteenth Century called, "The Truth About Agricultural Depressions."

Regarding the first period following the war of the Revolution, Roosevelt in his "Winning of the West" tell of agricultural conditions: "The prices of the agricultural products of the West were absurdly low, a cow and a calf being given in exchange for a bushel of salt."

Johnson, in his "History of Domestic and Foreign Commerce," describes the agricultural conditions of that period: "The farmers of the grain-belt still found themselves in distressing circumstances. The fertile soil of the great Ohio Valley was yielding a product far in excess of the demand that existed for it, and each year found an increasing amount of unthreshed or unmarketable grain left in the fields and granaries. Foreign nations that profited by exporting their manufactured products to America refused admittance to American grain and flour, and though the grain-producing capacity of the United States had increased six-fold since 1790, the annual exports of flour, beef, pork, and grain were but little more than the average for the five years from 1790 to 1795. Of that which was exported but very little went to Europe, the chief foreign provision market being, as in colonial days, the islands of the West Indies. The plantations of the South were drawing much of their subsistence from the northern farms, but they were unable to absorb more than a small fraction of the tremendous surplus of meat and flour that was seeking a market. In 1824 corn could be bought at Cincinnati in any quantity for 8 cents a bushel. Wheat yielded the farmer 25 cents a bushel; flour sold as low as $1.25 per barrel. After the advent of low prices the high costs of transportation fell more heavily upon the farmer than before, a larger proportion of the value of agricultural products being sunk in the expense of carriage to market than of the value of any other commodities."

Drawing a picture of agricultural conditions in the depression of 1819, Congressman Martindale in a speech delievered in the House said:

"While this process of waste and devastation was going on the provision-market was depressed also. There was little demand for the farmer's provisions, for his beef, pork, and wheat. The price was greatly reduced. But the habits of the farmer and his family were formed, and suited to better times. The customs, tastes, and fashions of the country, and his immediate neighbors, imposed a kind of moral necessity upon him to measure his expenses by theirs, not by his means. His expenses were greater than his income. The consequences were inevitable: his cash was first exhausted, and next the produce of his farm; his credit next, and (by a mortgage) next the farm itself. The expenses which produced the mortgage prevented the redemption. The farm is sold to pay for foreign goods, and the merchant becomes the purchaser. This is no unreal picture, which has no original in nature."

In 1815 public land sales reached a million acres a year. During the period from 1816 to 1819 the income to the government from the sales amounted to nearly $30,000,000. Then during the depression, starting with that year, sales for the following three years hardly exceeded $4,000,000. The rise in the price of cotton from 26 to 34 cents per pound induced larger purchases of land; exceeding two million acres in 1817. By the decline of nearly half in the price of cotton in 1820, combined with other causes, land-purchasers were left in debt to the government more than twenty-two million dollars, and with a change from the credit to the cash system sales were reduced to much less than a million acres annually. In 1821 purchasers were so troubled to discharge their obligations that Congress provided that instead of paying the balances due, they might acquire, if they desired, an absolute title to a portion of the land purchased, which should be determined by the price paid and the amount paid thereon, on condition of relinquishing their ownership to the remainder.

In our early history the West Indies were our best customers for agricultural products. The worst depressions our agricultural export trade has experienced were during the Revolutionary War and Civil War periods. In times of European wars and various European crop failures there has been unusual demand for our food-stuffs and cotton, only to be followed by slumps of more or less severity on the return of peace or normal crop conditions. Agricultural exports rose to a high level in the years 1815 to 1818. The surplus cotton, flour, wheat, tobacco, rice, corn and provisions that had accumulated during the war of 1812 were released and flowed out of the country. In 1818 farm commodity exports were valued at over $62,800,000.

In the first few decades of our national history the price and demand for flour was considered the barometer of business. If flour was high business was good, because it depended almost entirely upon agriculture. If there were large exports of flour this meant the people could buy luxuries in return from Europe.

The effect of inflation on values is shown by the following estimate of the values of certain lands in Pennsylvania on three different dates:

```
1809_____$ 39 per acre—approximately normal conditions
1815_____ 150 per acre—bank expansion, great prosperity
1819_____  35 per acre—after the panic of that year
```

In 1820, when the depression starting in 1819 was at its worst, wheat sold at 20 cents a bushel in Ohio and Kentucky. The United States Gazette of that period said: "Whiskey is dull at fifteen cents a gallon."

The first speculative mania for agricultural lands west of the Alleghanies was after the war of 1812 and previous to the crisis of 1819, when people were swarming into that section. Over 20,000 people settled in Kentucky in one year and 12,000 in Tennessee, together with large numbers in other central western states. When the crash came on this new country was desperately hit. Thousands of mortgages were foreclosed and their would-be purchasers left homeless. Still greater suffering would have ensued had it not been that in some states relief laws were passed staying the proceedings against foreclosure. The State of Kentucky attempted to establish a state bank to help the new settlers tide over on their land purchase, but the plan proved unsuccessful.

The period from 1818 to 1830 was an era of general trade recession in agricultural commodities, because of peace in Europe, which lessened the demand, and through readjustment of general conditions in America, following the panic of 1819. From 1830 to 1836 there was general improvement in agricultural conditions. The opening of the Middle West increased the surplus in flour, grain and provisions, and the ever expanding cotton section of the South furnished its share, exports rising in 1836 to over $90,000,000, and being 80 per cent of our total export business. The panic of 1837 followed, bringing irregular fluctuations in agricultural products. During this period cotton was the only farm crop that increased in export shipments, although falling prices decreased the value to the farmers by millions of dollars.

A total of 17,600,000 acres of government land had been sold in 1836, a territory equal to Belgium and Holland combined, bringing into the national treasury $24,877,000.

Then came the depression of 1837, and the sales fell to 5,601,103 acres. It was the large surplus which accumulated in the Treasury from the sale of these lands and deposited in the state banks that brought on the over-expansion and speculation resulting in the panic of 1837.

In the speculative times previous to the panic of 1837 "the farmers extended their acreage, pawned their growing crops for the money to increase their acreage and put up grist mills, cotton gins, etc. The Mississippi Valley north and south was heavily mortgaged to eastern bankers. Many of the "wild cat" banks were loaning irredeemable currency to land speculators, who attempted to use it in buying government land in defiance of the law. An attempt was made to stop this practice and require payments for land to be made in gold and silver. It was halted by President Jackson, who directed his Secretary of the Treasury to require gold or silver from speculators, but in case of bonafide settlers bank bills should still be received."

Another important contributory factor leading to trouble

was the failure of the American crops in the years 1835 and 1837, unfortunately continuing in 1838. This lessened the purchosing power of the farmers and crippled the merchants. The value of flour and grain imported into the United States as a rule was insignificant, while that exported after 1830 was on the average about six million dollars annually; in 1837, however, the exports of grain fell off nearly a million dollars, while the imports of grain were increased more than four and a half million dollars.

Previous to the depression of 1837 agriculture on the Atlantic seaboard had begun to decline. The New England farmers lamented the spirit of speculation which caused the migration of young men to the "back country," as it was called. Southern states also poured their surplus population westward, their sons going to the unexploited gulf states and into Alabama, Mississippi, Arkansas and Missouri. Large tracts were to be had of the land offices at wholesale prices, and these were bought up by men of means or influence and retailed to would-be farmers at sufficient advance to realize a considerable profit. The sales were made on credit, but the land was usually mortgaged to the full amount of the deferred obligation so that ultimate returns were guaranteed, provided the tract was so situated as to be readily salable. The barren hill farms of Massachusetts, Vermont, and New York afforded but a meager reward to labor by comparison with the government lands still available in the Mississippi Valley, and in consequence the young men of energy and ambition were drawn to the West, "to the fertile prairies of Illinois and Indiana and the alluvions of Ohio."

In the short depression of 1848 agriculture suffered little because the English Corn Laws had been repealed in 1846, opening up a new market in that country. With the Mexican War stimulant agriculture took on new life, and for ten years experienced unprecedented prosperity. The foreign exports rose to a hitherto unknown level and domestic demand was stimulated by the rapid settlement of the

Mississippi Valley, railroad construction and the gold discovery in California. At the same time came the potato famine in Ireland, bringing great demand for American agricultural products.

Then came the panic of 1857 and its resulting depression, lasting until the outbreak of the Civil War. During the ten years preceding 1857 the value of all farm property increased over 100 per cent, a growth that has never been achieved in any country or in any age.

In the beginning of 1857, when prosperity reigned supreme, the Governor of the Territory of Nebraska said: "We can boast of flourishing towns and prosperous cities, with their handsome church edifices, well regulated schools and busy streets. . . . The appreciation of property has far exceeded the expectation of the most sanguine. Business lots upon streets where the wild grass still flourishes are readily commanding from $500 to $3,000 each; lands adjacent to our most prosperous towns sell readily at from $50 to $400 per acre. Credit is almost unknown in our business circles; no citizen oppressed for debt nor crippled in his energies by the hand of penury and want; but all, encouraged by the success of the past, look forward to the future with eager hopes and bright anticipations."

But this picture of prosperity was entirely changed by the succeeding depression and another Governor in a message to the Legislature in 1859 had this to say: "It is a matter of bitter experience that the people of the Territory have been made to pass through the delusive days of high times and paper prices, and the consequent gloomy night of low times and no prices."

The depression of 1857 was augmented by the finest harvest ever known in the United States, which happened to fall with one of the best harvests in Europe, making wheat almost unsalable.

Cotton exports increased from 1,667,000 bales in 1846 to 3,774,000 in 1860 and from a value of $42,767,000 to $191,-806,000. Western grain, which had gradually entered the foreign trade during earlier years, now for the first time became an item of real importance and caused a rapid rise in food exports. The maximum point in food shipments was reached in 1857, when 14,500,000 bushels of wheat, 10,250,000 bushels of corn and 3,712,000 barrels of flour, and breadstuffs of all kinds valued at $55,500,000 were shipped abroad. The panic and depression occurring at the end of the year, together with the bounteous crops in Europe, then halted the great export movement for a time.

Some years ago an English visitor, apparently with an ample imagination, wrote home the following description of an Illinois corn field:

"Nothing but corn was in sight over the great level plain. I wandered among the immense stalks, some at least fourteen feet high; a heavy dew had been falling during the night, and the morning sun was now well up in the heavens. Crack after crack resounded like pistol shots. It was the corn bursting its coverings."

Emigration received a setback during the depression of 1873, doubtless for the reason that prices were low and money to get a start in the West was not available. Land values had also declined seriously and speculative spirit was not in the minds of those going west. But in 1878-79 the western movement was resumed. Depressed times of that period in the East seemed to stimulate the western movement. The fall in prices of farm products had preceded the panic of 1873.

Farming had its difficulties in the depression of 1873. The pioneers had borrowed heavily from eastern mortgage companies to improve their farms, and if they made the mistake of borrowing a small amount their farm was usually foreclosed, for payment was utterly impossible. Those who borrowed large amounts were better off because the mortgage companies allowed them to stay and cultivate the land, hoping to get their interest, at least, until conditions improved. But in either event thousands of mortgages were foreclosed. Money was so scarce that farm products could not be moved to market.

Agriculture of the East has felt panics less than the West and South, obviously because that section was older and there were fewer mortgages carried, and the section was nearer the consuming markets. Eastern agriculture suffered worse in the depression of 1873 than in any other period. This for the reason that thousands of farmers went west on the prosperous tide previous to this year to open up new lands. This left the eastern lands with lesser demand, with the result of a greater falling off in their value.

In the depression of 1878 agriculture was favored because of an abundance of cheap labor and cheap lands which enabled the farmers to produce large crops at small cost. The demand in Europe happened to be good at the same time and great quantities of exports poured out of the country. While industry was suffering agriculture was in fairly good shape, although prices were low. Our exports in 1878 were more than three times as great as in 1876. They amounted to over $257,000,000 more than the total imports, the exports being almost entirely agricultural products. The good crops and large exports repeated again in 1879, thus pulling the country out of the depression.

In the depression of the '80's farm mortgages were so tremendous that they were alarming. These mortgages were held by eastern and European capitalists and carried interest from 1 to 3 per cent per month. An idea of the situation of that time is given by Henry M. McDonald, president of the Traders' Bank, Pierre, South Dakota, and printed in the New York Times, in which he estimated that "the volume of western-mortgage business, confined chiefly to Kansas, Nebraska, Minnesota, and Dakota, has reached the sum of $150,000,000 yearly. It may exceed these figures. That it is of great magnitude is evident from the fact that in all eastern cities (and in most of the towns and villages) are located numbers of agents who make a living from the commissions paid them for securing loans. Boston numbers more than fifty agencies of farm-mortgage companies. It is computed that Philadelphia alone negotiates yearly more than $15,000,000 on western loans. Kansas and Nebraska have 134 incorporated mortgage companies. The companies organized under the laws of other states, but operating in these two states, increase the number at least 200. In this reckoning no account is taken of firms and individuals, although a large amount of money is directly invested by lenders of this class. One feature of importance to be observed in this mortgage business, is the fact that the chief part of the power to put in bonds the lands of America comes not from the country, but from the city; while the country is gaining no equivalent power over the city interests of any kind."

As to the oppressive nature of the western farm mortgages of that period the Chicago Times said: "The syndicates that loan money at from 1 to 3 per cent per month are mainly made up of Scotch, English and New England capitalists, who have their agents throughout the South and West. These mortgages are falling due, and soon an immense number of southern and western farms will be in the hands of foreign mortgagors. The territories are covered with mortgages on new farms not yet patented. In many districts half the settlers borrow money at high interest to pay the small price required by the government in proving up. This is leading to wide-spread disaster. The object of the pre-emption law is perverted. Eastern and foreign capitalists get the land with such improvements as the settler has put upon it. The settler loses all by reason of the exorbitant interest he is compelled to pay."

The wheat crop of 1884 was the largest that had ever been harvested, and the price fell to 64 cents a bushel, half that obtained three years before. This price did not cover the cost of production, and many farmers were ruined. The inability of the agriculturalists to meet their obligations to eastern mills and workshops extended and prolonged the industrial depression, and the glut of the market became general.

With the preceding land boom and over-development during the big years of emigration a collapse was bound to ensue, and the progress of agriculture was greatly retarded because of the heavy burden of mortgages and the instability of farm prices.

After the first of August, 1891, a fortunate turn in the international grain situation brought about a radical change in the depressed conditions which had prevailed in the United States during the preceding eighteen months. The wheat crop of 1891 in the United States was the largest up to that time which had ever been grown. The returns showed a yield of 611,780,000 bushels in 1891 against 399,-262,000 bushels in 1890. The same remarkable increase was also true of the corn and coats crop. Moreover, the cotton crop in 1891 was unprecedented. The most significant feature in the situation, however, lay in the fact that this extraordinary increase in the production of cotton and cereals in the United States was coincident with a shortage in European harvests. The Russian wheat crop, which, next to that of the United States, was most largely depended upon by European consumers, was almost a total failure. The grain shortage in France was one of the most serious in the history of the country. The Russian Government issued a ukase against the export of rye on August 10th, and another against the export of wheat on November 21st. A decree removing the import duty on wheat was also promulgated in France. The market for American grain therefore was broad and eager. On account of the small crops of the two years 1889 and 1890, the European demand for American cereals quickly developed, and the pressue of export grain from the United States during the autumn of 1891 was very great. The export of breadstuffs almost equaled the enormous outward trade during the year 1879, following the resumption of specie payments.

Many writers insist that our 1893 panic would have come in 1891 had it not been for the inflated currency which postponed it until another day. Gold was going out of the country in great sums during the three years, but in 1891 scarcity of crops in Europe brought about large exports of American agricultural products and this had a tendency to bring the gold back and even the balance of trade for that year. The next year, however, our agricultural exports fell and we had a balance of trade against us of $68,800,000.

A widespread and far-reaching disaster for agriculture was that of 1893 and 1894, when the combination of crop failure and low prices ruined thousands of farmers. Riding through fertile sections of the states west of the Mississippi one could see farmhouse after farmhouse deserted, occupants having scraped together what money they could and returned east, where they could find refuge among friends and relatives. Others remained, eking out a bare existence, enduring privation and hardships described as almost beyond hope. Defaults were the rule, but the settlers who managed to survive the adverse times undoubtedly in later years were better off than the ones who returned east. The year 1894 was worse than 1893. This year witnessed the greatest crop failure of any single season. As figures clearly show, a small increase or decrease in crops does not affect business, excepting sentimentally; but "a great failure, such as was witnessed in 1894, gives the country a shock from which it may take several years to recover."

In 1893 considerable agitation swept over the East against western farm loans. Eastern people felt the panic of that year and resulting depression as much as the western people. With the prevalent stringency the eastern people began to look into their affairs, and it was thought that too much money had been sent west at high interest rates and sunk in farm loans of doubtful value. It is indisputable that western loans were over-done and were particularly of a reckless nature. In previous years many of these loans made in selected fertile sections of the West had brought splendid returns which led to the general impulse to purchase this class of securities. Eastern money poured west in such abundance that the nature of the lands was not properly investigated, which brought loss to the investors. The mania was finally restrained with the panic. Today, however, a western farm mortgage is considered the best kind of security, and eastern investors are not able to secure enough of them.

Agricultural products were scarcely affected in the depression of 1903, as this depression was confined largely to stock issues, many of which found a lower level and the companies remained solvent. Agriculture, on the other hand, had its own years of depression entirely aside from depressions in the stock market. In such years as 1903 the money stringency affected farm commodities only by preventing loans and retarding somewhat the movement of the crop.

The farming interests were less affected than any other in the short panic of 1907. Farmers in the West and South boasted that they were laughing at the discomfiture of the larger cities, and at New York in particular. It is quite true that the local banks which were known to be strong had little trouble in meeting the needs of their depositors, and country districts went along feeling the affects to some extent, of course, but in no degree panicky. The healthy condition of agriculture helped largely in speeding up business after the depression of 1907. The previous year agricultural products yielded $7,400,000,000 against a combined yield of mining and manufacturing of $3,000,000,000.

If figures count for anything, agriculture did not feel the depression of 1907 in the least. Starting with the year 1900, the total value of farm products was a little over five billion dollars. It gained steadily each year, reaching six billion in 1904 and in 1906, $6,755,000,000; in 1907, $7,488,000,000; and in 1908 in which the worst of the depression was felt, it was $7,848,000,000; jumping next year, in 1909, to $8,622,000,000.

Against those figures, production of pig-iron, a recognized barometer, starting at 13,789,000 tons in 1900, rose steadily to 25,307,000 tons in 1906; 25,781,000 tons in 1907; and dropping to 15,936,000 tons in 1908.

Again, take also the total bank clearings which rose to $157,000,000,000 in 1906; $154,000,000,000 in 1907, the year of the panic; dropping to $126,000,000,000 in the year of depression following.

Agriculture was affected peculiarly and in spots at the outbreak of the European War in 1914. For instance, cotton went to six cents, 50 per cent below normal for the period, caused by a sudden halt in the demand from Europe. The "Buy-a-Bale" movement swept the South. Corn was stationary, perishable products depressed. Wheat and live stock went up because of an apparently increasing demand from the warring countries.

Agriculture always profits from war, because food is a prime necessity, ranking equal with ammunition. Governments make frantic efforts to get large supplies of food stuffs because a nation at war knows that famine is even more to be feared than the enemy. They eagerly buy great quantities of food stuffs at high prices. This stimulates production in strictly neutral countries. When the conflict suddenly ends agriculture naturally is demoralized because of the large production, many times competing with governments that have laid by great storehouses of food.

The depression of 1920-21 was peculiar in many respects. Abundant crops usually spell good times. In former years the announcement that bumper crops were harvested meant an era of prosperity ahead, but at this time we found severe depression and great suffering in the midst of abundance. It was purely a reflection from war conditions.

Describing the adverse conditions of agriculture which prolonged the depression, Dr. Henry C. Taylor, Chief of the Bureau of Markets, United States Department of Agriculture, said: "In the city there is unemployment, in the country there are products without any market—both amount to the same thing. On the contrary, they simply can't help themselves. The ground there, it had to be planted, but the market had fallen off tremendously. The reason is that there is no fair price exchange between farm products and city products. To put it simply, the farmer has to buy on the basis of a 20-cent-an-hour wage, whereas the city man buys on the basis of a $1-an-hour wage. This condition causes depression all the way down the line. I understand that many farm machinery factories have closed down entirely, and the remainder are doing very little business."

He pointed out that althought there was an abundance of farm production, that fact was no indication of prosperity for the farmer.

In the 1920 depression the movement was started to ship the surplus farm products to Europe, taking in exchange bonds of those countries, particularly Germany, which country was badly in need of supplies. It was pointed out that we had better have German bonds than rotten products. On the other hand the movement was opposed particularly by financiers, because they thought it best to let Europe work out its own affairs rather than lean too much on us.

In some quarters over-production was given as the cause of the depression, but that was hardly true because, while we did produce more than our own needs, we always do so. It was not over-production so much as lack of proper international finances. What we over-produced could easily have been used in Europe, half of which was starving, and in China, where another great famine prevailed.

The farmers suffered during the inflation period previous to the depression from constant strikes of railroad men. In many instances their produce was lying at the side of the railroad track instead of being in market while the railroad men were striking. This caused great loss in many cases to the farmers, who grew bitter against the labor unions, and this accounts to a large extent for the poor showing made by a group of radical labor men who attempted to form an alliance with the farmers under the name of the Farmer-Labor Party and put a ticket in the field for the presidential election of 1920.

In 1920 America received its first agricultural setback on account of the importation of foodstuffs. The farmers made a stronger demand than ever in history for protective duties on products of the farm. Importations of Canadian and Argentine wheat helped in the decline from $2.50 to around

$1.10. When the first Congress under the Harding administration enacted the Emergency Tariff Law, placing a duty of 35 cents a bushel on wheat, the market responded and wheat went up about 20 cents a bushel. For the first time, also, the cotton planters demanded a protective tariff, reversing their years of tradition. The lowered price of cotton, which of itself was largely instrumental in bringing the general depression, caused the planters to look carefully into the underlying conditions. They soon discovered that the country was flooded with imported vegetable oils and awoke to the fact that cotton-seed had become a very important factor in the cotton industry. During the war they had received $55 a ton for cottonseed, which years ago had been thrown away. The price declined to $12 a ton because of large importations of soy bean oil, cocoanut oil, peanut oil, etc., from the Orient, which went directly into competition with cottonseed oil. They figured that had they received as much as $30 a ton, which they felt would have been a fair price, it would have meant about $400,000,000 to the cotton planters of the South. Hides were another commodity terribly depressed. Farmers claimed it would not pay to skin a cow, because often they were offered a mere pittance of 50 cents for a calf skin and up to $1.50 for a cow hide. The story went the rounds of the press that an Iowa farmer spent a year raising a calf which brought him, including the hide and meat, the sum of $3.00. He then went into a store and had to put $9 more on top of that in order to buy a single pair of shoes. Live lambs on the hoof brought an average of $1 in Texas. The farmers demanded duties to keep the cheap hides out, which came in from Mexico and Argentine, and to keep the cheap wool out from Australia and South Africa. It was pointed out that we have natural facilities for growing all the wool we use. Great expanses of land were still to be had in our western states for wool growing so that we could give employment to men and keep our wealth at home, and yet, through the low tariff, we imported 60 per cent of all the wool we used.

In 1920 the nation lost five billion dollars by the decreased value of its farm production, and six billion dollars in 1921. These figures are not arrived at by deducting the loss from the unduly inflated prices of the war, but from reasonable prices as against costs at the time.

In recent years American farmers to a large extent joined the capitalistic class by payment of their mortgages, and what financing they have to do can easily be taken care of by the country banks, which can rediscount with the Federal Reserve Bank. Until 1913 the national banks were prohibiting from loaning on real estate or accepting farmers' commercial paper for over ninety days. These provisions kept the national banks from being a great aid to agriculture. By the Federal Reserve Act of that year national banks not situated in Federal Reserve cities were permitted to make loans based on improved and unencumbered farms situated within their respective districts to amounts not exceeding 50 per cent of the farm's value, nor for a longer period than five years. It also permits Reserve banks to rediscount paper issued for farm purposes or for certain farm products. This system has no doubt helped to stabilize agriculture through depressed times. Farm Loan Banks have also been a help, but not up to expectations; in fact, at the time of the enactment of the act authorizing these banks, the sponsors boasted that it would be the means of forever ending depressed conditions in agriculture. In the recent depression farmers complained that the farm loan banks did little to alleviate conditions and that in a large measure it had failed in its purpose. These opinions proved premature, as the Farm Loan Board did, late in 1921, after a favorable court decision, render valuable aid to the farmers.

One of the principal aims of the Farm Loan System was to relieve pressure in time of depression. In former times mortgages coming due in bad years would find the farmer unprepared. His local bank, itself affected by the stringency, could be of little help, and after one or two extensions, perhaps, the mortgage would be foreclosed. Farmers may now secure long-time loans at low interest rates. A loan bank must have a paid-in capital of $750,000. In the event of the entire capital not being subscribed by individuals, corporations or state governments, the Secretary of the Treasury is authorized to subscribe the balance. Only stockholders can be accepted as depositors in the Farm Loan Banks and the banks are prohibited from doing a general banking business. Loans shall be for not less than $100 nor more than $10,000. A desirable feature of the Farm Loan measure is an arrangement by which the principal is paid by installments in not less than five or more than forty years. After a mortgage has run for five years payments of $25 or multiples of $25 must be accepted on the mortgage.

The farmers have always contended that speculation on the grain exchanges had a tendency to affect prices adversely, and have repeatedly sought laws to curb these practices, many of which have been enacted. No doubt the farmers are right, particularly in their opposition to the practice of selling imaginary commodities or transactions in which no actual commodity is involved. Legitimate grain exchanges are probably necessary in order to create an organized market. Otherwise, we would probably place ourselves in the position of following foreign grain exchange quotations and be at their mercy. If the present grain exchanges were put out of business, it is only a question of time until Winnepeg or Montreal would take the place of Chicago. In each depression this agitation has been renewed, and each time certain progress is made in eliminating evils that have been practiced to the detriment of the farmers.

The farmers began organizing during the depression of the late sixties, and each period of distress marked further organization among them. "The Patrons of Husbandry" was the first great farmers' organization, which later became known as the "Grange." In 1880 the "Farmers' Alliance" was formed. "The Farmers' Mutual Benefit Association" was also organized in the eighties and claimed a membership of 150,000. During this period the farmers first began to affiliate with the labor organizations. Later the "Farmers' Union" was organized and became strong. The depression of 1920 found the "American Farm Bureau Federation," claiming a million and a quarter members, to be the strongest farmers' organization. Some of the other farm groups have a working amalgamation known as the "National Board of Farm Organizations." The organized farmers were able to secure a great deal of advantageous legislation in 1921, which helped greatly to relieve the distress in agriculture in the late depression.

CHAPTER XXXII

THE TARIFF AND DEPRESSIONS

The tariff question has entered into every depression the country has had, without exception. It is a fact of history that we have invariably turned to the tariff as a means of relief in time of stress. Lowered tariff rates preceded almost every depression, obviously because the country became flooded with foreign goods, which eventually forced our factories to curtail and throw men out of employment. It is quite true, on the other hand, that we have enjoyed prosperity under low tariff laws. Several periods may be cited to justify this statement, and yet it must be admitted that those periods led up to the time of distress when we finally paid the fiddler. It is true, also, that high tariff cannot be claimed to be a panacea for the evils of depression, but it has always helped us out of depressions. In depressions we have great armies of unemployed, and it is only natural that the argument arises that we can put these unemployed to work if we make what we buy ourselves, where possible, instead of buying the product of foreign workmen. We are prone to forget the benefits of protection in our years of prosperity, the same as we forget to save for a rainy day. The argument against protection is that if we do not buy from foreign countries we cannot sell to foreign countries. That is going against the natural flow of commerce. What we can produce and manufacture in this country within a reasonable cost of production we should so do, and we will still have ample commerce to carry on with foreign nations in such commodities as we cannot produce here. For instance, we will always be importers of such widely used commodities as coffee, rubber, burlap, tea, cocoa, spices, hemp, tropical fruits, and a long list of other articles which cannot be produced in America. If we take the natural course we will protect and produce what nature has given to us and trade with those countries who cannot produce what we have to sell and who do produce what we must buy. It is quite true that our international bankers made loans to foreign countries that they are "sweating blood" to get back, and would like for us to let the barriers down and buy the products of their creditors so that they can collect their money. We may be influenced to let down the barriers for the benefit of the international banker and foreign trader, whose citizenship is often under foreign registry, but if we do we will bring about depression of American industries just as sure as night follows day. We have reached a certain plane of living in this country and we cannot go back. We can never produce as cheaply here as abroad, because we have reached a high standard of living, and as long as that fact exists we must have a reasonable protective tariff. But all that is an old argument and has no place here outside of the point that when we are smitten and in trouble economically we turn to the tariff for help, the same as we appeal to the doctor in sickness and to the Lord in grief.

During our first depression in 1785 American manufacturers, who had built up their industries during the Revolutionary War, found their trade both at home and abroad greatly diminished; they soon realized that their foreign trade was subject to greater restrictions than had prevailed prior to and during the war, and they found as well that it was impossible to hold the domestic markets for the manufactured goods that competed with imported products. At the close of the war the duties were made, at first for revenue only, but later for the twofold purpose of providing protection to home industries and trade, and raising much needed public funds. No federal government had as yet been established, and conditions had developed in the United States that caused the New England and most of the Middle States to adopt the principle of moderate protection to their own industries, and to make tariff laws accordingly. The

Southern States, not having manufacturing industries that suffered from foreign competition, and being large purchasers of foreign goods, did not, with the possible exception of Virginia, change their tariffs along protective lines.

A group of citizens presented a petition to the General Assembly of the State of Pennsylvania November 30, 1785, calling their attention to the adverse effect of importations on the iron industry of that State, and asked that duties be levied on such iron, claiming that the local industry was entitled to public protection and encouragement. These tariff laws were enacted by individual states, the State of Pennsylvania acting first by passing an act "to encourage and protect the manufacturers of this State by laying additional duties on certain manufactures which interfere with them."

Following peace in Europe in 1815 prosperity continued for a while because of an abundance of money, but manufacturers began almost immediately to feel the pinch. Many were embarassed and others entirely abandoned their properties. Those that were left petitioned Congress for assistance, and the tariff of 1816 was granted. Forty memorials from as many infant industries sent petitions to Congress. The tariff of 1816 did not provide for high duties and was passed more as an emergency measure, anyhow, because it provided for gradual reduction in the duties, but the crisis of 1819 brought about a stronger public feeling in favor of more protection for the struggling industries. In 1818 the iron interests were suffering so severely that a duty of 75 cents per hundred pounds, or $15.00 per ton, was imposed. With this advance, many of the iron-works in the country revived.

During this depression the farmers first turned strongly to the tariff. There was no foreign market for their surplus, so they resolved to create a domestic market. By building up extensive manufacturing industries at home it would give rise to a non-agricultural population that would consume their products. The English Corn Laws were still in force, enacted as a prohibition against American imports in years of normal production there.

The distress that followed the crisis of 1819 "brought out a plentiful promotion of domestic industry, of petitions and memorials to Congress for higher duties." The movement undoubtedly had deep root in the feelings and convictions of the people, and the powerful hold which protective ideas then obtained influenced the policy of the nation long after the immediate effects of the crisis had ceased to be felt. The notorious "auctions," or dumping of foreign goods, which caused the depression of 1819 caused the demand to go up for higher protective duties. Great quantities of imported goods were taken on credit and disposed of at auction.

Henry Clay at that time was a protectionist. He pointed out that the foreign manufacturers after crushing the domestic manufacturers had immediately raised the prices. Clay and other friends of protection, as described by Bolles, had advocated the doctrine that, "while the imposition of a higher duty for a time might enhance prices to the consumer, competition at home would reduce them; so that, in they end, they would be lower than if our dependence were wholly or chiefly on a foreign market."

It was the protection given by the tariff of 1824 that no doubt kept us from having a serious depression in 1825 and 1826, during the years of the great European depression. As it was, we experienced a minor depression in that year and manufacturers were affected even then by the great quantity of goods pushed into this country by the force of the depression in Europe.

Again, during the short depression in 1828 manufacturers and farmers urged protective duties which had gradually sagged off in order to help domestic industries and relieve the business stringency that existed. A national conference was held in Harrisburg, Pa., which urged the protection of all industries in order to give aid to American business.

The compromise tariff of 1833 provided a gradual reduction for ten years and Moore says, "While these changes were taking place a great many manufacturers were crowded out. Some, of course, were not progessive, and since they were not up to the times they could not compete with those who were. By far the greater part of the failures up to 1837, however, were due to the fact that lessening rates under the compromise tariff allowed many European goods to come in at a price that drove out American capital."

It was during the tariff agitation following the depression of 1837 that the argument was first advanced that American labor should be protected from competition of less highly paid foreign labor.

A description of conditions during the depression of 1837 is vividly drawn by a contemporary:

"The price of wool fell in the domestic market, the surplus wool clip was sent to England, and many of the costly merino sheep were killed for mutton and tallow. The iron manufacturers of the seaboard put out their fires. All but five of the forty plants of Morris County, New Jersey, were prostrated, the works were sold at auction, and the employees scattered. Some furnaces and forges were kept running by isolated farmers, but the eastern industry as a whole was ruined. The iron foundries of Pittsburg were adequately protected by the expense of transporting these bulky goods across the mountains, where fifty miles of land carriage cost as much as the ocean freight from Sweden; but the bagging industry of Lexington, Ky., was unable to cope with English competition, for imported cotton bagging flooded the country at prices far below the normal cost of production."

Another report says: "The cotton manufacturers of Massachusetts, Connecticut and Pennsylvania petitioned for protection against the low-priced goods from England and India; the paper manufacturers and printers protested against the competition of Holland and France; the sugar planters of Louisana, the cordage manufacturers of Massachusetts, the hat makers of New York, the gun-smiths of Lancaster, Pa., and the proprietors of the hemp factories of Lexington, Ky., were no less insistent on protection."

Some writers describe the depression of 1848 as resulting from the decreased duties under the bill of 1846. Also, according to Von Holst, "it was argued at the time of the panic of 1857, and has been maintained since, that the crash was caused by the low tariff of 1846, which led to large exports of specie to make payments for foreign goods and drained the country of metallic money." Rhodes and other writers take the oposite view: "In this reasoning cause and effect are confused, and in part, at least, inverted. It was the export of specie which increased the importations of merchandise and not the importations of merchandise which increased the export of specie."

Dewey says: "The reason for the crisis of 1857 is still the subject of controversy; one alleged cause is the lowering of tariff duties in 1857; and some protectionists trace the collapse to the slow but poisonous workings of the tariff of 1846, the argument being that the reduction of duties stimulated importations, which had to be paid for in specie, and that this drain of specie inevitably caused the panic."

It was hardly true, however, that we were drained of specie at that time. Gold from California furnished an abundance; but too much of it was sent outside instead of building up our own industries.

Some of the leading statesmen of the time believed the low tariff was the principal cause leading to the panic as shown by remarks of Governor Pollock of Pennsylvania in his message to the Legislature the following year, in which he charged the troubles of the time principally to the tariff then in force.

During the Civil War high tariff duties were laid on imports, the prime object being to raise money. Of course, this necessarily protected the manufacturers who, seeing opportunities for safer profits, invested in their business and built bigger factories, and for many years, when these tariff rates were left alone, our industries made great strides. Protection became a national policy, the Democrats lining up against it, and the Republicans taking the opposite view. The high protective tariff that had been enacted during the Civil War was one of the main reasons why we did not have an industrial collapse immediately following the war. The tariff kept foreign goods from being dumped into this country with the coming of peace and helped to maintain a price level more in keeping with war conditions, so that deflation was gradual.

In 1872 the tariff was revised downward, and while it cannot be said to be the direct cause of the crisis of 1873, it had a bearing on that catastrophe. That must be admitted, because in 1875 Congress put the duties back to where they had been before 1872 as a relief measure, which met with little opposition. The act of 1872 repealed the duties on tea and coffee, halved the duties on wool, and reduced the duties on imports generally. Friends of protection insisted upon the restoration of the tariff and the rates which were restored brought material prosperity to industry.

The revision of 1882 was intended to produce greater revenue, but brought no benefit to the agricultural sections, which favored it, because it disorganized the domestic market. Some attribute the short depression of 1884 to the attempt of the Democratic administration to enact the Morrison bill providing for an average reduction of 20 per cent in the import duties with important additions to the free list.

Britain was at this time in the throes of a tariff argument. "The opinion expressed by the Royal Commission," says Curtiss, "in its report to Parliament in 1886, that the depression in trade and industries was due to no exceptional or temporary causes has been confirmed by the experience of recent years which have followed. That system of free trade, or free imports, which in 1885 was sapping the vitals of British industries, was the essential cause of the loss of profits, reduced wages, lack of employment and universal stagnation in business."

Following the enactment of the McKinley bill in 1890 the business of the country was stimulated and the years 1891 and 1892 were fairly prosperous. Previous to the act of

1890, in Harrison's administration, importations of foreign goods exceeded in value that of any previous year. The outflow of gold, necessitated by the large trade balance thus created, caused severe money stringency and a panic among the banks of New York, Philadelphia and Boston which issued clearing house certificates. When the high tariff law went into effect the situation was almost immediately relieved.

The Wilson Bill, enacted in 1894, did not please the people nor aid the Government in collecting revenues. The tariff was blamed for the prolonged depression during the Cleveland administration. The election of 1896 returned the Republicans to power and a new protective measure was passed, which again started the hum of industry.

The duty on sugar had always been a source of large revenue for the Treasury, and when all these were lowered and taken off of sugar entirely the Treasury was practically empty following the 1893-94 depression. So depressing was the Wilson tariff on business that many Democrats favored higher duties.

The panic of 1907 so disturbed business conditions that a new adjustment was desirable, and the Payne-Aldrich Bill was enacted, revising the tariff to needs existing at that time.

The results of the tariff enactment of 1913 were just beginning to be felt when the European War broke out. Both sides made counter-claims; protectionists that business would have been ruined, and the free traders that time would have proven the benefits of the measure. However, after the war our markets were left exposed to the great surplus caused by stimulated production in all the non-warring countries.

We well know how the silk industry of MacClesfield, England, decayed and pulled that once flourishing city down with it when silk manufactures were admitted to England free. We also know how Patterson, N. J., sprung from nothing to a great industrial center under protection of silk manufactures. Again, we know that Liverpool once had a flourishing watch-making industry, which was ruined by free importation of watches into England, and the workmen who had spent a life-time in their trade clung on with constantly lowering wages until they died in poverty. And, on the other hand, we see in America a great and flourishing industry making American watches because they are protected from the cheap workmanship of Switzerland and Germany.

A great many economists fail to see the connection between protective tariff and prosperity. They claim that tariff benefits monopoly only and holds up the price to the consumer, but the practical business man knows that the opposite is the case. The trusts and monopolies invariably want low tariff. That is proven by the activities for low duties on the part of such so-called monopolies as the Sugar Trust, the Leather Trust, the Woolen Trust, etc. These corporations have found out in their business experience that the consumer will pay only to a certain amount for a commodity, and above that consumption falls off. Therefore, in order to make huge profits, the trust must devise means of buying cheaper and they, therefore, favor a low tariff so that they can be in a position to tell the American farmer that if he does not accept their price for his product they will import the product. It is well known that these so-called trusts have banking facilities, shipping connections, etc., to control 90 per cent of all the imports in their particular line. How could the ordinary independent business man import these commodities with his obvious lack of facilities to do so? Political agitators have given the unposted American public a wrong idea of this question. When it is admitted that we need higher tariff both for revenue, which must be raised by some kind of taxation, and for protection of our labor—as long as our people have a higher living standard than most foreign countries— then the only argument against the protective policy is that it increases the cost of living, and that is true only in a very

slight degree, if at all. The cost of living is secondary, anyhow, to steady work and good wages and prosperous business conditions. What do we gain by trying to cut the cost
of living a little and destroy or cripple our industries? We
are driving along the wrong line. If we want to cut the
cost of living, we cannot do it by opening our markets to
cheap labor and undermining our prosperity, but we can
do it by enacting laws against the profiteer, by keeping too
many middle men from handling our necessities of life, and
by prohibiting speculation in such necessities.

Every wise importer should realize that there is nothing
to be gained by low duties on articles that can be produced
here. He soon finds that he cannot do business if the buying power of the American public is destroyed. How can he
import if there is no demand and if our people are out of
employment and our business depressed? It stands to
reason that the importer will suffer along with the rest of
us. He should realize that in most cases high duties are no
insurmountable drawback if conditions are favorable
through good times and a resulting demand. As has been
said before, figures do not lie, and statistics indisputably
show that there have been more failures among importers
during periods of low tariff than of high tariff. Admittedly,
we cannot sell to foreign countries unless we buy from
them, but where nature has given us the material and conditions to build an industry we should protect that industry, and we can still buy from foreign countries unnum-
bered commodities that nature has so ordained cannot be
produced in this country. We can always sell to the foreigner our food products, iron and steel, cotton, implements,
automobiles, etc., and in return buy such articles as are already enumerated. That is letting things take their natural
course; it is going along the lines of least resistance. We
cannot think of any policy other than a protective tariff
as long as our American labor must compete with Hindu or
Chinese labor, for instance, which works for seven or eight
cents a day. People have an idea that distance itself is a

protection against foreign competition, but the rate across the Pacific Ocean is less than the freight rate from San Francisco to Denver. The rate on potatoes from Hastings, Fla., to New York is 85 cents per hundred, while from Denmark to New York it is 35 cents per hundred.

Whatever may be said pro and con on the tariff question by advocates of protection and free trade, it is admitted on all sides that the constant tinkering has been the cause of unsettled business conditions during many periods. Whoever may not be willing to agree that the different tariff laws have been the direct cause of depressions will have to admit that the lack of a definite and settled policy has many times retarded the progress of business. The act of 1897, which lasted for twelve year, until 1909, is the longest period in our history that we have let the tariff alone. The next rival to this period was that of 1846, when the tariff remained undisturbed for eleven years.

Tom Reed said about these word: "Some day will come the brotherhood of man and we will all speak the same language; workmen around the world will be paid the same wage with the same money; when there are no nations, but we are all one people. Then free trade will be both practical and glorious, but not before."

We need nothing more than to look back to our periods of depression under low tariffs and find armies of poor and dependent workmen who became transformed into industrious and enterprising citizens under the stimulous of protection to our domestic industries.

CHAPTER XXXIII

DEPRESSIONS AND FOREIGN TRADE

Business revivals following depression have often been prompted by a keen foreign demand for our goods. Such was notably the case in 1848, in 1879, in 1885, in 1891, in 1897, and 1915. We now have a larger foreign trade than ever, most of which we are going to hold. That is shown by the fact that the Baldwin Locomotive Company recently received orders to the amount of $16,000,000 from the Argentine National Railroads in competition with large foreign concerns. We could export a great deal more if the finances of foreign countries were stable and the exchange rate more favorable. However, economists rightly point out that we are capable of being prosperous by trading among ourselves. Foreign trade is not absolutely necessary to our national welfare. It averages only 5 per cent of our total business.

In colonial days the exports consisted mainly of furs, cereals, provisions, lumber, whale oil, tobacco, indigo, and naval stores. The imports were manufactured goods and the necessities of life.

At the close of the Seventeenth Century Great Britain had gained the commercial leadership of the world and her colonies in America achieved a commercial and maritime success even more notable than the triumphs of the mother country.

Foreign trade of the original colonies was carried on by chartered companies that operated the ships to carry both colonists and commerce. The progress or decline of our foreign trade was largely affected by regulations promulgated in the old country, such as bounties, preferential duties, drawbacks, etc. The most drastic of these was the Molasses Act of 1733, which depressed the important trade that had started with the French, Dutch, Spanish and Danish colonies in the West Indies. At that time foreign trade was done entirely on the mercantile theory, the principles of which were that, "Trade must be so conducted that the money value of the commodities exported from the country exceeds the money cost of the goods imported, so that there is a 'favorable balance of trade,' with a steady flow of coin or bullion into the country."

Immediately following the Revolution our foreign trade had to be reorganized. The greatest chaos and disaster existed after the war which made it doubly hard to make headway in the shipping industry. Great Britain had put into force the Navigation Act. British subjects were forbidden to purchase American built ships, and as the ceceding territory was treated as thirteen separate and distinct states, American vessels were excluded from British ports unless their cargo consisted of the products of the particular state where her owners resided. Under these regulations American merchants forfeited a trade worth $3,500,000 a year. America had a big trade with Jamaica and with the Bahamas which was now ruined. Separation from England brought serious depression in such products as indigo, naval stores and hemp, most of which were exported. Moreover, the prohibitory duties of the Corn Law were imposed upon all agricultural products, bringing like depression to all agricultural industries. Attempts to negotiate more favorable commercial treaties with Europe so as to relieve the shipping depression failed because, as Washington said, "We are one nation today, thirteen tomorrow; who will treat with us on these terms?"

For twenty years following the Revolution American traders had to take the risk of being captured by privateers from the Barbary States or by warships from fighting European countries, but in spite of severe depressions coming at intervals during this period by the year 1815 the United States held the position in the world's trade second only to Great Britain.

When the European wars were raging American shipping was prosperous. In 1802 and 1803, during a brief period of peace, it suffered an immediate decline; when the wars were renewed prosperity returned for a time, until after 1807, when Napoleon Bonaparte, refusing to recognize that there were any neutrals, inflicted his "continental policy" upon the commercial world, and England enforced her Orders in Council with men-of-war. Had the peace proved permanent there would have been, without doubt, a further decline in American commerce, as the European countries resumed their former commercial relations. With the reopening of war, however, the Americans enjoyed the advantages of their previous position; the exports of 1806 and 1807 exceeded a hundred millions in value, and marked a height which exports did not again reach for nearly twenty years.

TOTAL FOREIGN TRADE OF THE UNITED STATES

Year	Domestic Exports	Total Imports
1790	$19,666,000	$ 23,000,000
1791	18,500,000	29,200,000
1792	19,000,000	31,500,000
1793	24,000,000	31,100,000
1794	26,500,000	34,600,000
1795	39,500,000	69,756,000
1796	40,764,000	81,436,000
1797	29,850,000	75,379,000
1798	28,527,000	68,552,000
1799	33,142,000	79,069,000
1800	31,841,000	91,253,000
1801	47,473,000	111,364,000
1802	36,708,000	76,333,000
1803	42,206,000	64,666,000
1804	41,467,000	85,000,000
1805	42,387,000	120,600,000
1806	41,253,000	129,410,000
1807	48,700,000	138,500,000
1808	9,433,000	56,990,000
1809	31,406,000	59,400,000
1810	42,366,000	85,400,000
1811	45,294,000	53,400,000
1812	30,032,000	77,030,000
1813	25,008,000	22,005,000
1814	6,782,000	12,965,000
1815	45,974,000	113,041,000
1816	64,782,000	147,103.000
1817	68,313,000	99,250,000

Imports dropped from a value of $121,750,000 in 1818 to $87,125,000 in the following year, and exports of domestic products fell from $73,854,000 to $50,977,000 during the trade year.

VALUE OF EXPORTS AND IMPORTS OF THE UNITED
STATES, 1819 TO 1830

Year	Exports, domestic products	Imports
1819	$50,977,000	$87,125,000
1822	49,874,000	83,242,000
1825	66,945,000	96,340,000
1827	58,922,000	88,509,000
1830	59,462,000	70,877,000

An idea of the effect of the depression of 1809 on foreign trade may be gained from the following story told by an English trader who visited New York during this ruinous regime:

"The port, indeed, was full of shipping; but they were dismantled and laid up. Their decks were cleared, their hatches fastened down, and scarcely a sailor was to be found on board. Not a box, bale, cask, barrel, or package was to be seen upon the wharves. Many of the counting houses were shut up, or advertised to be let; and the few solitary merchants, clerks, porters, and laborers that were to be seen were walking about with their hands in their pockets. Instead of sixty or a hundred carts that used to stand in the street for hire, scarcely a dozen appeared, and they were unemployed; a few coasting sloops, and schooners, which were clearing out for some of the ports in the United States, were all that remained of that immense business which was carried on a few months before. . . . The streets near the waterside were almost deserted, the grass had begun to grow upon the wharves, and the minds of the people were tortured by the vague and idle rumors that were set afloat upon the arrival of every letter from England or from the seat of government."

When the embargo gave way our foreign trade quickly recovered, shippers taking advantage of their opportunity, and in one year we had recovered 91.5 per cent of our trade.

We surpassed in ship building in the early days because

of the abundance of oak and hard pine, and the best ship-
wrights in the world. We reached the height of our prestige
in 1810. Following that came a long period of normalcy
until 1846, when we passed the previous high water mark,
and the next fifteen years were very prosperous for American shipyards. At this time the construction of a schooner
of 500 tons cost $37,500 in the United States and $42,000
in England. Today the reverse obtains and probably with
a greater difference.

The advance which began in 1831 and ended in 1837 carried the foreign trade to a higher level than it had reached
during the abnormal rise of the years 1815 to 1818. The
exports of domestic merchandise rose from $59,462,000 in
1830 to nearly $107,000,000 in 1836, or to a point over
$33,000,000 in excess of the previous maximum of the year
1818.

VALUE OF EXPORTS AND IMPORTS OF THE UNITED
STATES, 1830 TO 1836

Year	Domestic Exports	Imports
1830	$ 59,462,000	$ 70,877,000
1831	61,277,000	103,191,000
1832	63,137,000	101,029,000
1833	70,317,000	108,118,000
1834	81,034,000	126,521,000
1835	101,189,000	149,896,000
1836	106,917,000	189,980,000

According to figures by Conant, in 1837, "the excessive
purchases of foreign goods, which did not have to be paid
for in either merchandise or bullion, is shown by the fact
that the imports from Europe increased from $62,893,883
for the year ending September 30, 1833, to $127,511,020 in
1836, and even the imports from other countries increased
from $38,154,060 to $49,068,134. This great increase in
consumption was offset only partially by the increase in
exports of American merchandise to Europe, which rose
from $56,556,837 in 1833 to $96,413,449 in 1836, while other
exports slightly fell off. The reaction was striking after the
breaking out of the crisis. Imports fell during the year ending September 30, 1838, to $62,017,575, while exports from
the United States to Europe fell only to $79,849,768."

The panic of 1837 was not the result of abnormal foreign trade, as the panic of 1818-19 to a large extent had been, but when the business reaction came a setback in imports and exports occurred. In one year the value of the imports shrank nearly $49,000,000 and that of the exports over $11,000,000.

VALUE OF EXPORTS AND IMPORTS OF THE UNITED STATES, 1836 TO 1846

Year	Domestic Exports	Imports
1836	$106,917,000	$189,980,000
1837	95,564,000	140,989,000
1840	113,896,000	107,142,000
1845	99,300,000	117,255,000
1846	102,142,000	121,692,000

The value of the exports of merchandise from the United States for the fiscal year 1847 was $156,741,598, an increase of more than 40 per cent over any preceding year; the excess of exports over imports was $34,317,249, a balance never again attained until 1876.

The depression of 1857 gave our shipping a serious setback. In 1845 it had become apparent that we would lose our foreign trade carried in American bottoms unless we quickly turned from the sailing craft to the new steam vessel. Congress came to the aid of shipping with a subsidy. The Pacific Mail plying around Cape Horn to California was subsidized for $250,000 a year and the Collins line from New York to Liverpool for $858,000. Other important lines received large subsidies. With the reaction of this year and sudden reduction of revenue, Congress proceeded to limit all subsidies to the amount of sea and land postage on the mails actually carried. Our shipping from that time gradually fell until in a few decades the American flag was practically off the seas. The decline of American shipping was marked by the depression of 1857.

Our foreign trade suffered severely during the Civil War. While the South did not win the war, she put the nation out of the shipping business until its revival in the recent world conflict. We came out of the Civil War with about a million tons of shipping less than we had at the beginning, and by 1900, over a period of forty years, we had not increased our tonnage.

The increase of our foreign trade helped to bridge over the short depression of 1878-79. Our large exports as a result of crop failure in Europe in 1891 quickly pulled us out of the depression of 1890. In the six months ending June 30, 1893, the balance of trade against the United States was $68,-800,000.

In the depression of 1893 on up to and including 1914 our own shipping was little affected because of our lack of tonnage. In previous years, from the time of the founding of the Republic until after the panic of 1873, our shipping had been an important factor in all depressions, because we were then one of the leading, and sometimes the leading, shippers and carriers of the world.

Our foreign trade expanded rapidly from the good times that started with the McKinley administration up to the depression of 1907. Exports of merchandise in the fiscal year 1896 amounted to $882,606,938, and rose by 1906 to $1,743,864,500. Imports of merchandise in 1896 were $779,724,674, and in 1906 they rose to $1,226,562,466.

In 1907 came the willingness on the part of American business to sacrifice goods for money, and in a few months our exports exceeded our imports two to one. The accompanying table will show how the quick expansion of exports brought gold into the United States:

*FOREIGN TRADE MOVEMENT, AUGUST 1 TO DECEMBER 31, 1907

Month	Imports of Merchandise	Exports of Merchandise	Excess of Exports
August	$125,806,043	$127,270,447	$ 1,464,404
September	106,365,180	135,318,342	28,953,162
October	111,912,621	180,256,085	68,343,464
November	110,942,916	204,474,217	93,531,301
December	92,288,771	207,179,436	114,890,665

*Table by Conant.

In Europe there is a great deal of agitation at this time urging the cancellation of debts among nations. Some claim it will help our foreign trade if we cancel the foreign obligations owing us. One British writer claims that Great Britain will not demand cancellation of the debt, but that America will be forced to take the step voluntarily in order to retain her foreign trade. It is a certainty that no American administration that even proposed such procedure could survive and it is a peculiarity that as long as two-thirds of the world was in debt to Great Britain no proposal of that kind came from her. Yet the instant she became a debtor nation she starts a cry for cancellation. The world in time will pay its debts. This is not the first time we have heard the cry of repudiation. At different periods since the beginning of modern times word has gone out that the world was bankrupt, and yet, with few exceptions, in the case of smaller states, every nation has paid its debts.

During the distress in Great Britain in 1816 Lord Brougham said in urging exports to this country that, "Ultimately the Americans will pay, which the exhausted state of the continent renders very unlikely." Yet the continent paid.

In 1920 we again had a merchant marine, rating probably third, and the shipping situation was an important factor in the depression. Two-thirds of our steel ships and all the wooden ships we had built during the emergency were laid up and thousands of seamen that had been trained to operate them were out of employment. While world shipping was adversely affected, yet there was considerable cargo, but foreign shipping took it away from us because of lower operating costs and consequently lower rates. It was early foreseen that if we could carry American products in American ships event at a loss, it would, in the final analysis, be a gain, because it would give employment to our seamen and operators and help us out of the depression.

The balance of trade between nations is sometimes misunderstood. In the long run the exports of merchandise from any country must equal its imports. Any difference

or so-called balance in any year must be offset by invisible
items, such as securities and credit extensions between
banks. We like to boast of greater exports than imports,
showing the balance of trade in our favor. An influx of
gold must naturally follow to meet these trade balances. We
were very proud when, in the eighties, we began exporting
more than we imported for the first time in our history, and
again during the war period when we passed from debtor to
creditor nation. Yet, in the early days, when we imported
far more than we exported, we prospered tremendously because of the fact that the money made by European nations
from their exports to us was handled by their agents, deposited on this side and loaned out to us for the development
of our new country. It was this capital, that we did not
have ourselves, that largely helped to develop America. Up
until the world war great shipments of American securities were held in Europe, most of which drifted back to our
hands through the stress of war necessities. Taking the
second phase of it—the imports of gold necessary to pay the
trade balance in our favor—we cannot help but reflect on
the Biblical quotation, "What profiteth it a man if he gain
the whole world and lose his own soul?" The trade balance
during the war period was so enormously in our favor and
the influx of gold so tremendous that it was a severe handi-
cap to us. It was one of the primary causes of the depression. We had so much gold that the exchange rate worked
decidedly against us. Dollars became so high that other
nations could not afford to buy them in order to pay us in
our own money, which we required. In 1920 had we been
good gamblers, and luck proved to be with us, we could have
made much money by selling our surplus to European countries that needed it, taking their money, backed by bonds,
and waiting for it to rise to normal value. Some advocated
this procedure on the grounds that we had better have
European money than rotten products. In one case this was
done very advantageously—in the case of the rice crop. In
1920 we had produced the largest crop ever grown. The

price was badly depressed and the producers suffered great loss. The Louisiana State Rice Milling Company, under the direction of Mr. Frank Godchaux, arranged to export large quantities to Europe, his company taking their securities in payment. Thus the surplus rice was exported and the balance left on hand brought very satisfactory prices, so that in a few months the trade was again in favorable condition. Thus it can be seen that there are many phases to trade balances between nations, and it is a fact that one nation cannot permanently profit at the expense of another. Temporary advantage may be gained, but a depression is bound to follow until the other nation catches up. It was thought by traders in the old days that when we bought from foreign countries we sent just so much money out of the country, and that when we exported we enriched ourselves and pauperized the purchasing country. That has proven to be a fallacy because, although we might export a great deal to one certain country from whom we buy but little in return, yet that same country may, in turn, have large exports to another country in a different part of the world from whom she also in turn buys but little, and so goes the cycle of trade until it evens itself up, as it is necessary to do.

Another phase affecting America's trade balances is the money spent by our tourists. For a period before the war our trade balance in exports as against imports showed largely in our favor, yet an important item was ordinarily overlooked, and that was the money taken abroad and spent by our tourists. For a period of years our tourists spent abroad sufficient to make up the difference shown by the trade balance in our favor, so that after all the influx of wealth was negligible. In fact, during the depression of 1907 terrific cries went up that the money stringency was largely due to the enormous amounts of American money being spent in Europe by wealthy tourists. Since our prosperity, starting in 1897, this complaint has been made in every period of financial crisis or stringency. A further offset in previous years against our favorable trade balance, and which was not shown in the figures was the payments to foreign nations for carrying our products. Had these payments entered into the figures in many cases a different tale would have been told. We never had a real trade balance in every way until the last years of the war and the prosperity immediately following the war, when we carried cargo in our own bottoms, paying ourselves for the services, when we sent little or no money abroad in interest payments on investments, and when the tourists' trade was stopped and little money went for that purpose. Then, really for the first time in history, did we have an actual trade balance, and that was offset by the loans we made to Europe which she still owes us, including the interest.

International traders set up the argument in every period of depression that we must increase our foreign trade in order to relieve the stringent conditions. They also are becoming more insistent that we must import in order to export. In the years of depressions our imports have invariably fallen because of our lack of buying power; for instance, in 1858 following the panic of the year previous, our exports for the first time exceeded the imports, unquestionably on account of our lack of buying power. This happened again in 1874, following the year of the panic preceding, and in 1893 caused by the panic of that year. In giving these figures it will be remembered that during the entire period we were a debtor nation. In other words, we normally imported more than we exported. In recent years, however, we have become a creditor nation, exporting to a larger extent than importing. No depressions have been brought about by the falling off of our foreign trade in recent years, although it was a contributing factor to the depression of 1820. Japan's panic of 1920 was brought about principally by the stoppage of foreign demand for her commodities. That panic which smashed prices of Oriental goods caused many failures and great distress among American importers on the Pacific Coast and in New

York, and was the forerunner of our industrial depression which followed.

In the depression of 1857 imports fell off $85,087,688 in twelve months. In 1861 they fell off $100,000,000, although this was an abnormal condition because of the outbreak of the Civil War. In the 1873 depression they declined $75,-000,000 in twelve months; the 1884 depression recorded a $90,000,000 decline; in the 1893 depression, when our commerce began to assume larger proportions, imports declined $212,000,000 in one year. In the 1907 depression they fell off $240,000,000 in the following year, 1908. In 1915, the year following the outbreak of the World War, they dropped $219,000,000, and in 1921, while full statistics are not yet available, it is common knowledge that there was a tremendous falling off. All of this goes to show that in times when there is a lack of buying power in this country the lot of the importer is hard, so there is nothing to gain for him, in the long run, by a desire to import foreign goods to such an extent that the prosperity of our people is undermined.

CHAPTER XXXIV

THE RAILROADS IN TIMES OF DEPRESSION

The history of American railroads has been closely entwined with the history of depressions. The panic of 1837 was helped in the making by building railroads beyond the needs of the country and taking capital away from enterprises which were necessary to support railroad development. The modern industrial corporation came into existence about the time railroad building started in the year 1830. As we saw our ocean shipping decline for various reasons, the money was taken from that industry and put into the development of the West, in which the railroads were the most important factors.

The London Financial Times some years ago said that were it not for the railroads "many of the richest agricultural states in the Union might still have been in the possession of the buffalo and the red Indian."

We have now had one hundred years of railroad history, which is divided into three periods; the first, the pioneer or experimental stage, the years from 1820 to 1850; the second period marked the development of the trunk lines, in the years from 1850 to 1890, and the third a period of consolidation into vast systems, from 1890 to the present time. Railroad building started as a means of solving transportation problems, and in the early years they were given State aid to a large extent. The year 1837, however, with the panic that came at the time, brought an end to state aid, and the works that had been created with such anticipation on the part of the states were sold by them to private corporations.

By that year the different states had appropriated $6,618,-868 for helping to build railroads, although at the same time $42,871,084 had been granted for building canals.

These public improvements to an excessive extent, so it was judged, helped to bring along the panic of that year. Thereafter the states withdrew more and more from active participation in railroad construction and it became in this country a distinctly private enterprise, unlike most of the European countries where there are still many state-owned railroads. After that year both state and national governments confined their encouragement of railroad construction to land-grants and bonuses in the form of bond issues. In these subsidies to the railways Congress made in all seventy-nine grants, amounting to nearly 200,000,000 acres of public domain. This aggregate was subsequently reduced to 158,286,627 acres, of which more than 108,000,000 were actually patented.

The intention was to occupy and possess the new lands in advance of settlement and secure the strategic places that would mean control and power over shipments and markets later on. The effect of this premature and, in many instances, needless construction was shown in 1873, as was also the case in 1893, by the wrecking of many lines and the plunging of others into receiverships.

Such speculation had resulted as a consequence of the land subsidies and of the promotion that went on that each community wanted a railroad at any price. "The railway mileage built in the United States in 1856 was 3,642 miles, and the construction for the nine years ending with 1857 was 21,000 miles. This construction, forming seven-ninths of the entire mileage of the country, had absorbed $700,000,-000, largely in foreign capital."

Commodore Vanderbilt, who founded the great Vanderbilt fortune, made much money out of railroads, and was mixed up in several of our early panics. As wise and far-seeing a man as he was it is a peculiar coincidence that about the time of the 1837 depression, when the few railstocks could be bought for almost nothing, the Commodore remarked: "I'm a steamboat man, a competitor of these steam contrivances that you tell us will run on dry land. Go ahead.

I wish you well, but I never shall have anything to do with 'em.''

In 1857 important railroads reaching into undeveloped sections of the West went into bankruptcy, among them the Illinois Central, the New York and Erie, and the Michigan Central. The railroad statistics for the period preceding 1857 are interesting:

		English Miles	Cost in Dollars	Cost per Mile
*United States	(1856)	24,195	846,825,000	$ 35,000
Great Britain	(1855)	8,297	1,487,916,420	179,000
France	(1856)	4,038	616,118,995	152,000
Germany	(1855)	3,213	228,000,000	71,000
Prussia	(1855)	1,290	145,000,000	63,000
Belgium	(1855)	1,005	98,500,000	30,000

Can we believe our eyes today? It is little wonder that our people went wild. What man could have withstood temptation under such alluring conditions? Nearly three-fourths of the railroads defaulted in their interest and other payments and went into the hands of receivers. Some of the best railroad stocks declined to three to five dollars a share, including Michigan Southern and Harlem.

A thousand shares of the Illinois Central stock, sold to wind up an estate, appraised at $800,000 before the panic, went at auction for $50,000. The New York Herald that year blamed the banks for locking up $15,000,000 in railroad securities which were not worth forty cents on the dollar.

In 1860 only three of our present great systems were in existence and prominent, namely, New York Central, Illinois Central, and Delaware, Lackawanna & Western.

In times of money stringency, crop failures, and business depressions, rail bonds became a terrible burden to the people. In the late sixties the question of transportation rates, elevator charges, etc., began to be agitated and out of this came an organization known as the "Patrons of Hus-

---
*Figures by Hyndman.

bandry," which in those early days undertook to build and control elevators and other commercial enterprises where it was claimed abuses had crept in from the operation of the railroads. The railroads were run recklessly, with a short-sighted point of view, and a great many favors were given to shippers as compared with the farmers and producers.

Jay Gould testified in 1872 that "the Erie Railroad had four states to look after, and it switched its politics to circumstances. In 1868 more than one million dollars was spent by the Erie Railroad for 'extra and legal services,' to control elections and to influence legislation."

In 1873 railroads were again involved and the principal causes of the panic was over-speculation in railroad securities. New York banks previous to that time had made unwarrantable advances to the railroads and were forced to close their doors. The New Haven and Willimantic Railroad pulled down the Brooklyn Trust Company; the Missouri, Kansas & Texas took with it the Mercantile Security Company. The Canada Southern bankrupted Kenyon, Cox & Co. The Vanderbilt roads involved the firm of Fisk & Hatch, and the Northern Pacific bankrupted Jay Cooke & Co., the failure of the latter being the general signal for collapse. By the close of 1872 it had dawned upon investors that railway construction was being overdone. Lowering prices threatened a curtailment of agricultural production and diminished the prospect of freight receipts. The high cost of operation, at prices and wages then prevailing, combined with unsettled conditions in Europe, checked the flow of capital westward. Funds could not be obtained for the fulfillment of contracts, and construction was brought to an abrupt stop.

By 1873 a fairly complete network of railroads had been built from the Atlantic Seaboard to the Missouri River, with some extensions beyond, one of which reached the Pacific Ocean, all built by capital drawn from Europe or the Eastern States, by the offer of exceptional rates of interest. In some cases the promoters had invested nothing themselves beyond the incidental expenses of organizing a company. All these roads were mortgaged for their full cost. In this depression the new roads were affected by a panic that swept Europe and were unable to market their securities in those financial centers. There was universal suspension of work on new roads. It threw tens of thousands of men out of work. During the three years following the crisis of 1873 railroads defaulted bonds in the amount of $789,367,655.

In 1872 a series of widespread strikes occurred among the railroads, but the strikers were finally beaten by the depression which came on and their union was disorganized and broken up.

Even the better established roads in the most populous sections of the country suffered reverses in this depression, particularly because of competition. For instance, at that time five trunk line railroads were competing for the trade from Chicago to New York. These were the Grand Trunk, New York Central, Erie, Pennsylvania and the Baltimore and Ohio. These roads had not received the large land grants that had been given to new roads to the Pacific Coast, and it was up to them to finance themselves from their actual carrying trade. This was the cause of too much competition for the traffic in those times so that some of these roads naturally could not weather the financial crisis.

The crisis of 1884 was brought about by the too rapid and speculative railroad building in the years immediately preceding. Railroads were forced to curtail construction and practice the most rigid economy in management. Coman attributes the crisis of 1884 to over-investment in railroads. "The mileage built in 1882 and 1883 (18,314) exceeded the construction of 1870 and 1871 by 5,000 miles. In 1884 and 1885 eighty-one railway corporations, holding 19,000 miles of track, were placed under receivership, and thirty-seven smaller railroad properties were sold under foreclosure. Owing to the waging of rate wars between competing railroad lines during the two years, 1884-85, and the diminution in the volume of traffic because of the depression in

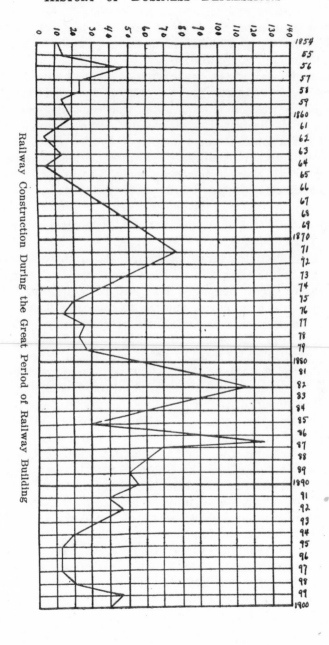

Railway Construction During the Great Period of Railway Building

interior trade after the crisis of 1884, dividends on railroad stocks were reduced and in many cases passed."

The period of consolidation into great systems had gotten fairly underway in the early nineties when the depressions of 1890 and 1893 came along. Most of the roads survived the short depression of 1890, but at that time they were face to face with the fact that serious difficulties awaited them. Public agitation had taken deep root against stock-jobbing and downright crookedness in railroad promotion schemes and finances. State legislatures began to assume an antagonistic attitude.

In the year 1891 twenty-one railroads, totaling more than 3,000 miles, with a capitalization of $186,000,000, were sold under the hammer.

Railroad building was not so marked a feature of the years preceding the panic of 1893 as of earlier panics, but there was a great demand for capital for equipping street railways with new power, and the railways, as usual, were among the first to feel the effects of slackening industry. The New York Sun printed an article in 1895 reading: "A list of dividends paid in 1893 which had ceased to be paid in 1895 showed a total of $61,710,000 per year.   Capitalizing this at 5 per cent and making an addition for smaller concerns not included in the list, 'the bad investments of the public, within three years, came fully up to $1,500,000,000, and are likely to exceed it.' "   In 1893 the Erie, the Philadelphia and Reading, the Northern Pacific, the Atchison, Topeka and Santa Fe, and the Union Pacific were among the great railway systems, representing hundreds of millions of obligations, which passed into the hands of receivers. The total capitalization in the hands of receivers was about $2,500,000,000 or one-fourth of the railway capital of the country. The earnings of railroads and the dividends paid to stockholders were seriously affected; securities fell to one-half and even one-quarter their former value.

In the difficulties of 1893 railroad stocks fluctuated wildly as shown by the following table:

RANGE OF LEADING STOCKS IN 1893

Railroads	Opening	Lowest		Closing
Baltimore and Ohio	94	54	July 27	67
New York Central and Hudson	109	92	July 26	98
Pennsylvania	54	46	Dec. 18	48
Atchison, Topeka & Sante Fe	34	9	Dec. 30	10
Chicago, Mil. & St. Paul	77	46	July 26	56
Illinois Central	99	86	July 18	89
Northern Pacific (pref.)	47	15	Aug. 16	18
Union Pacific	39	15	Aug. 26	18
Chesapeake and Ohio	22	12	July 26	16
Louisville and Nashville	72	39	Dec. 28	44

The year 1894 was a bad year for the railroads, with only 1,899 miles of new construction. Railroad earnings fell to $1,803 per mile, net, the lowest figure on record. During the period between January 1st and October 31st $1,200,-000,000 of railroad property was placed in the hands of receivers, representing one-third of the railroads in the country. Both freight and passenger traffic fell off, earnings declined, and some of the more speculative enterprises were unable to cover operating expenses and meet interest payments on their bonded debt. Creditors brought suit, and the roads, one after another, were given over to receivers. More than two hundred railway companies, representing fifty-six thousand miles of track and one-fourth of the railway capital of the country, went into the hands of receivers between 1892 and 1896.

The total foreclosures for sixteen years showed five hundred companies, with more than 50,000 miles and $3,000,-000,000 of capital, a result that came about largely through excessive building and industrial depression. The movement of consolidation was retarded by the depression of 1893 because so many roads were in the hands of receivers, but after they were reorganized the movement started again, resulting in the great railroad systems of today.

In the depression of 1903 Pennsylvania stock dropped from 127 5/8 to 110 3/4, New York Central fell from 156 to 112 5/8, Chicago and Northwestern declined from

*Table by Lauck.

224 1/2 to 153, Union Pacific from 103 5/8 to 65 3/4. The depression was almost entirely a railroad depression. The Hill and Harriman factions had been fighting desperately. The publicity given the controversy threatened to undermine the structure of railroad credits. In this depression, as in all others since 1893, the question of dividends did not enter. Stocks were affected purely from the speculative standpoint.

Preceding the 1907 difficulties railroads had been sued by several states and the bad condition of their inside affairs had been given detrimental publicity by such fights as the Harriman-Fish contest and others.

The March, 1907, flurry was a forerunner of the crash that came later. An account of the railroad fight which caused a short panic in that month is interesting. E. H. Harriman had ousted Stuyvesant Fish, who was head of the Illinois Central, and Fish had sworn revenge, aligning with him the Steel Trust group, Morgan and Carnegie. He also had Hill and James, the copper king. Harriman had with him the Rockefellers and the Standard Oil group and James Stillman, of the National City Bank. Plans were laid ahead to embarrass the Rockefeller banks in New York so they could not back Harriman when they got the latter in a "jam" with money at their disposal. "Suddenly, checks running into millions were presented to the Standard Oil banks to be certified. This tied up the money, causing it to be held in cash reserve, though still custodian of it. This had the desired result of running money up to 10, 20, or even 30 per cent. They were compelled to call loans to restore cash balances while holding millions of idle money, but the Rockefeller resources were thrown behind it. Their friends were warned not to buy stock or borrow money in anticipation of the squeeze. When the show-down came the Morgan crowd had bought over 600,000 shares of Harriman stocks, but Harriman seemed to have as much left as when they started." The panic of October followed, due largely to the evils of railroad stock speculation.

Previous to the 1907 depression the public was beginning to hold off from railroad investments because of the hostility of courts, state legislatures, and public agitation against them. But the panic gave new opportunity for the acquisition of railway properties, and Mr. Harriman utilized it by the purchase of a controlling interest in the Illinois Central and the Erie Railroad and secured sufficient stock in the New York Central, the Baltimore and Ohio and the Missouri Pacific to entitle him to representation in their management.

In 1907 railroad stocks suffered severely. The Atlantic Coast Line went from 133 3/8 to 58, Baltimore and Ohio from 122 to 75 3/8, The Chicago, Milwaukee and St. Paul Common from 157 1/2 to 93 1/2, Illinois Central from 172 to 116, Missouri Pacific 92 3/4 to 44 1/2, Pennsylvania from 141 3/8 to 103 1/2, Reading 139 1/8 to 70 1/2. By this period railroad expansion had largely run its course. Unlike the earlier depressions the earnings were not seriously affected and no important lines failed.

*The accompanying table will show the fluctuations of the principal railroad stocks during the panic of 1907, which will indicate losses of millions of dollars in these securities:

PANIC OF 1907

	High 1905-06	Low 1907	Fall from High
Atchison, Top. & Sante Fe Gen. 4s_	104½	89½	15
Baltimore & Ohio 1st 4s_____	105½	88	17½
Baltimore & Southwestern 3½s____	93	80	13
Central of Georgia Consol. 5s_____	114½	85	29½
Central of New Jersey General 5s__	132	113	19
Chesapeake & Ohio Consol. 5s_____	119½	101	18½
Chesapeake & Ohio General 4½s___	109	87	22
Chicago & Alton Ref'd. 3s_____	82½	58	24½
Chi. Burl. & Quincy, Ill. Div. 3½s__	95¼	82½	12¾
Chi. Rock Island & Pacific Gen. 4s_	103¼	88	15¼
Chi. Rock Island & Pacific Ref'd 4s_	97	80	17
Chi. Rock Isl. & Pac. R. R. 4s 2002	81½	49¾	31¾
Colorado & Southern 1st 4s_____	96½	75	21½
Delaware & Hudson Conv. 4s_____	112⅞	88	24⅞
Erie 1st Consol. Prior 4s_____	102	84½	17½
Illinois Central Gold 3½s_____	100	91¼	8¾

*Table by Babson.

	High 1905-06	Low 1907	Fall from High
Kan. City, Ft. Scott & Mem. Rf'd 4s	87⅞	61	26⅞
Lake Shore Deb. 4s 1931_____	100	83	17
Louisville & Nashville Unified 4s__	104¼	92	12¼
Mo., Kan. & Tex. 1st 4s_____	103	89½	13½
Mo. Pacific Coll. 5s_____	108½	89½	19
New York Central 3½s_____	99¾	85	14¾
Norfolk & Western Div. & Gen. 4s__	99½	81½	18
Northern Pacific 1st 4s_____	106¼	93⅝	12⅝
Pennsylvania Conv. 3½s 1915_____	101	83½	17½
Reading Co. General 4s_____	102⅝	86½	16⅛
Rio Grande Western 1st 4s_____	100	81	19
St. Louis & San Francisco Ref'd 4s_	88	66½	21½
Southern Pacific Ref'd 4s_____	97⅝	82	15⅝
Southern Railway Consol. 1st 5s___	119⅛	90	29⅛
Union Pacific 1st 4s_____	106¾	92½	14¼
Wabash 1st 5s_____	119	99⅝	19⅜
Wabash, Pittsburgh Term. 1st 4s__	90½	58	32½
Western Maryland 1st 4s_____	88⅝	59⅞	28¾
West Shore 1st 4s_____	109	94	15

The principal railroad difficulties in the depression of 1920 was the reorganization of the Missouri, Kansas and Texas and the Denver and Rio Grande. These were the only important lines which experienced financial difficulties up to December, 1921. Just as railroad speculation entered into our early panics, the railroad stiuation also entered the depression of 1920. When increased freight and passenger rates were authorized the public immediately showed its resentment. People hurried to make their trips and return before the higher rates went into effect. Those who were already away hastened home. Business men resolved to cut their purchases to the bone on account of the exorbitant freight rates. Orders were cancelled by the thousand. There was no loud protest nor agitation, but firm and silent resolve on the part of the people. The rates were unjust. In a very few months the railroad managers themselves admitted that high rates certainly did not stimulate traffic. The Bourbons among them insisted that rates be maintained because the resentment would soon pass and the public would finally accept them in good grace. This did not come to pass, however, because resentment grew with unabated force and prolonged the depression.

The railroad situation received a great deal of blame for the troubles of 1920-21. The roads reduced pay of their employees, cancelled many trains, cut down their overhead, but maintained exorbitant freight and passenger rates. The cry was constantly heard among all classes of business that delayed railroad rate liquidation was the cause of prolonged distress. The railroads countered with the claim that if they were prosperous and making money they would buy material and supplies and revive industries depending upon them. They also claimed that they were entitled to the high rates because their properties were commandeered during the war and they were not allowed to make the big profits other industries made; but they failed to mention the point that the Government guaranteed and paid them interest on millions of dollars worth of watered stock, establishing that stock at a definite figure after years of argument and dispute. The Government's final stamp of approval on that watered stock meant fortunes to the railroads.

Hobson says: "Excessive production of transport-machinery, especially of railways, has played an important part as an immediate cause of modern trade depression. The depression beginning in 1873, and culminating in 1878 is described as having its origin 'in the excessive lock-up of capital in the construction of railways, especially in America and Germany, many of which, when built, had neither population to use them nor traffic to carry.' "

Mr. Bowley points out that "after each of the great railway booms of the century, for instance in England about 1847, in America before 1857 and 1873, in India in 1878, and on the Continent in 1873, the collapse has been very violent; for the materials are bought at exaggerated prices; the weekly wage during construction is enormous; no return is obtainable till the whole scheme, whose carrying out probably lasts many years, is complete."

Again, Hobson says: "A great deal of this railway enterprise meant over-production of forms of transport-capital and a corresponding withholding of current consumption. In other words, a large part of the 'savings' of England, Germany, America, etc., invested in these new railways, were sterilized; they were not economically needed to assist in the work of transport, and many of them remain almost useless, as the quoted value of the shares testifies. It is not true, as is sometimes suggested, that after a great effort in setting on foot such gigantic enterprises, a collapse is economically necessary. If the large incomes and high wages earned in the period prior to 1873, when capital and labour found full employment in these great enterprises, had been fully applied in increased demand for commodities and an elevated standard of consumption, much of the new machinery of transport, which long stood useless, would have been required to assist in forwarding goods to maintain the raised standard of consumption. This argument, of course, assumes that ignorance or fraud have not caused a misdirection of investment."

No one would accuse old Henry Clews of being a radical or a demagogue, and yet Clews in no uncertain language accuses railroad manipulation as being the primary cause of practically all of our business depressions from 1837 to and including 1903. He said, "They rest upon an intrinsically rotten and dishonest foundation." Had it not been for the actual wealth created by opening up the new countries through which they passed results would have been worse. Clews says regarding their value, "They are essentially deceptive and unjust and involve an oppressive taxation upon the public at large for the benefit of a few individuals." Periods of depression caused great loss to railroad stockholders when at different times most all the American railroads failed, but those on the inside bought up the fragments, consolidated them with other lines, and in the end reaped still larger profits.

The statement is often heard that the railroad balance sheet is the best reflector of business conditions. It is true that the history of railroads has been closely aligned with the history of depressions, and scandals of high financing, with the result of loss of millions of stockholders' money is still fresh in the minds of those living today who can look back over various periods of depression. It is claimed that the bursting of the Credit Mobilier, followed by the illegal finance methods exposed in the Erie Railroad scandal, brought on the panic of 1873. Some railroad men got the credit for bringing on a few of our panics. No doubt Jay Gould deserves considerable of the blame for the crisis of 1873 and Hill and Harriman that of 1903 and 1907. There is also no doubt but that a lot of dishonest financiering during the latter part of the Nineteenth Century in railroad circles helped to bring about most of the disastrous depressions which swept the industrial world.

In the latter part of the Nineteenth Century the public was wild over railroad investments. They saw a few men, such as Gould, Vanderbilt, Cooke and others, make great fortunes in the railroad business. True, it later proved these fortunes were made more by manipulations than from profit, but this led to great speculation in railroad stocks which periodically went through the storm and their values were swept away. However, it may safely be predicted that our railroad panics like our money panics are a thing of the past. The railroads of the country are so all-important that they affect materially every interest. If they do not earn we can expect hard times; on the other hand, if the rates are as high as the railroads claim they must be in order to earn, industry is adversely affected so that the railroad problem is going to be one that more and more affects the prosperity and progress of the country in the future.

Our economical life is so interwoven with the railroads that they are a part and parcel of every line of industrial endeavor. We can get an idea of how important they are when we think of their nominal capitalization, stocks and bonds, amounting to more than eighteen billion dollars, and on these securities over $600,000,000 must be paid annually in interest and dividends. American railroads are the largest single vested industry in the world.

CHAPTER XXXV

THE MONEY QUESTION AS A FACTOR IN DEPRESSIONS

So great was the influx of silver from the new mines in Mexico and Peru during the Seventeenth Century that a revolution in prices ensued. Silver became so plentiful in Europe that a given weight of it would only purchase 25 to 50 per cent of what it would have brought before the discovery of the American mines. The serious result of this price revolution can be left to the imagination of the reader.

With the recurrence of trade depressions, the money question has been debated from every angle. Many writers point to the above and similar examples to prove that business depressions are governed by the rise and fall in the production of precious metals.

Some people wonder why gold producing countries, such as the United States, Australia, South Africa, are not enormously wealthy. But if all their gold were retained they would soon be gold poor. When a person gets beyond the point of earning just enough to secure the necessities of life, he becomes an investor; wants to live from the work of others. Therefore he must lend his money out on interest and an abundance of gold in a given country naturally brings small interest rates. So that the gold is sent out of the gold producing countries to those countries where it will bring the largest interest returns. Gold flows to countries where there is a strong demand for money and high rates of interest.

Some believe today we are on a gold basis, having heard so much of the gold standard, but "if a lender of money wishes to secure repayment in gold, he must, today, as well as before this act was passed, expressly stipulate for gold in the contract."

From 1850 to 1875 there had been produced as much gold as was produced from the discovery of America in 1492 to the year 1850—357 years. In forty years we had produced about $5,300,000,000 of gold as against the previous production of about $3,000,000,000. What has become of this gold? We know we have more gold than ever before, yet most of it is hidden from sight. We know how much is in the National Treasury and the bank gold reserves of the world, yet where is the production outside of this amount? The only answer is that it is hidden in countries afflicted with unstable finances, or used in the arts.

In the United States, France and other countries we have what is called the "limping standard" of silver coins, the amount of which is strictly limited. For instance, in this country we have a certain amount of silver dollars with silver certificates issued against them. The value of the silver dollar fluctuates, sometimes being one-half its face value, yet they are accepted without question in trade because of the limit placed on their issue. If this limit were taken off it is easy to see that there would be immediate financial difficulty and consequent trade depression. Again, we issue paper money redeemable in gold, which is readily accepted at its face value. Suppose, however, there should be an over-issue of this money. In case of catastrophe of some sort confidence would be undermined and the holder of these notes would immediately present them for redemption. They would be redeemed and yet the fact that the Treasury was being drained of its gold would of itself create a lack of confidence and trade depression would result. Gold itself is not always of the same value and many times the over-production of gold has led to serious economic consequences. For these reasons many believe that confidence in the economic and governmental structure is a stronger foundation than metallic money, because it has been proven by experience that money itself, of whatever kind, loses its value to a considerable extent when there is lack of confidence.

Most of our panics have been money panics, and the depressions that followed were caused by scarcity of circulating medium, due to banks, of necessity, restricting loans and credit. Hoarding of circulating medium, particularly gold and silver, is also an important factor.

"During the depression of 1837 the ratio between gold and silver coinage was set at 16 to 1. Gold had hitherto been undivided and the weight of the gold dollar was reduced from 27 grains to 25.8 grains, nine-tenths fine. Following this, gold rapidly came back into circulation. In the years that followed, all kinds of circulating medium in the form of paper was used, which resulted in great confusion on account of the lack of uniformity of note issues. It is recorded that as many as 5,400 different kinds of spurious or counterfeit notes were in circulation from 1837 until the establishment of the national banking system in 1863."

Our smaller circulating medium is issued purely on a confidence basis. For instance, silver coins smaller than the dollar are legal tender up to ten dollars only, while copper and nickel coins may be legally tendered for only 25 cents.

In every depression the cry arises for more circulating medium and we heard the cry even in the depression of 1920-21. Some proposals have been made for various stable governments of the world to pay their debts to each other through an issue of fiat money which would be exchanged from one to another and put into circulation. The proponents of this scheme claim this money would be as good as treasury notes issued by the various countries, or Federal Reserve notes issued in this country, because a mortgage on taxes and individual property could be placed back of them as security. Admittedly that is true, so far, but the difficulty of such a large issue of fiat money is that confidence would not hold. Some day such notes issued in the form of paper money would have to be retired and there would be a question in the minds of the public whether the various governments could raise taxes sufficient to pay their ordinary running expenses and retire these notes at a given time. Furthermore, revolution in any one country could cause repudiation, as in the case of Russia, thus upsetting the whole scheme. Any number of additional reasons could be given why public confidence in such an issue would be shaken. The final analysis is that such money is but a promise to pay and its value would depend upon public opinion as to the ability of the various governments to so pay.

As periods of depression have brought about a clamor on the part of the public for more money, the politicians often accede to the persistent demands and open the way for inflation through laws permitting the issue of paper money authorized as legal tender. Eventually these issues, which may have started to relieve depression, were of themselves the eventual cause of another depression through speculation, extravagance and finally panic. From the adoption of the Constitution down to the time of the Civil War the United States Government had never issued paper money. Gold and silver alone had been legal tender.

The 1857 crisis was known as the gold crisis. The situation in the United States was complicated, as it was in France, by the changes in the metallic circulation caused by the great production of gold. "Gold took the place of silver as the overvalued metal at the coinage ratio, was invariably chosen by debtors for payments, and silver having become the dearer metal, disappeared from circulation, in spite of bimetallic enactment under the relentless operation of Gresham's law."

It was following the crisis of 1837 in this country and 1839 in England that financiers and economists in both countries took up the doctrine that "Bank-notes are a form of currency entirely distinct from other commercial paper and forms of credit; that an expansion of banknote issues, even when redeemable in coin on demand, is a potent cause of commercial crises; that the way to prevent crises is to place fixed limits upon bank-note issues." This plan was later adopted in practically all countries where, particularly in crises, the clamor arose for an unlimited issue of paper money.

We no longer have the question of unsound currency in America, France or Britain, and yet we have depressions, so the recurrence proves the fallacy of the money question being at the root of the evil. The depression of 1857 came on with an abuandance of gold. There was no lack of specie, so the money question could not be blamed. But one of the surprising features of the panic of 1857 was the disappearance of gold from circulation in spite of the enormous production of the preceding years.

Quite an array of authorities attribute the depression of 1857 to an over-supply of gold. The theories as to the gold output and its relation to depressions are inconsistent.

From 1800 to 1848 prices gradually fell while the gold output rose steadily from the new mines in Russia and Siberia, more than tripling. Immediately following the discovery of gold in California and Australia in 1848, the world's output increased more than six times in three years. Prices rose 40 per cent. It is probable that from this and a few other instances in history so many writers connect the increase of gold with high prices.

Following this brief period the figures show fairly even production up to the crisis of 1873, just preceding which prices went slightly higher and gold production slightly lower. From then on the world's gold output steadily increased, while prices increased only gradually up to the outbreak of the World War. But the violent rise of prices during the war, it is conceded, is entirely foreign to any connection with the gold output. It is apparent then, that the time-worn theory of the gold output and prosperity or depression is almost entirely without basis in fact. Gold sells at about the same price per ounce, regardless of the cost of material, supplies and labor. As these costs mount during the period of inflation the mines are likely to curtail, and when depression sets in and costs are reduced the mines will be opened or reopened so that production of gold must naturally be larger in times of low prices than of high prices.

In the period of fifty to one hundred years ago there used to be an entirely different reason given for these years of financial failing followed by industrial reorganization. It was commonly set forth that lack of uniformity in laws, conflict of systems, lack of a strong central government and the fluctuating value of fiat money were the underlying

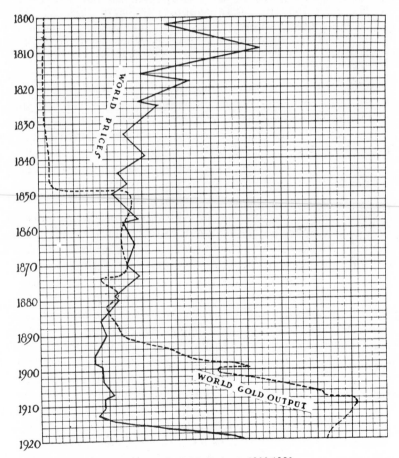

Prices and Gold Output 1900-1920

causes. True, in those days there was no strong central government. This developed with the Civil War period. There was no closely interwoven banking system. There was no sound basis for paper currency.

Conant says: "The fact that the problem remains essentially one of capital and credit rather than of the stock of gold was demonstrated, however, by the conditions of the crisis of 1907. In spite of the outpour of gold from the mines at a rate never equaled or approached in the history of the race, demand outran supply, the new gold did not offset the maladjustments of capital, and the money market found gold an unsatisfying element when what was re-- quired was more saved capital in forms adapted to the continuance of production."

After our various crises had passed, the blame was ordinarily laid to money when, in reaity, it was the abuse of what money we had that was the real cause. It is true that a new country, poor in specie and with large demands for loanable capital for development, may be forced by the necessities of her situation to adopt monetary devices which would not be tolerated under better conditions. But many of these systems were perfectly harmless if they had not been abused. This fact was shown by the great development of the United States under what were really very unstable money systems. It was not until the Civil War that we had our present National Banking System, and yet, previous to that time, we had developed a wonderful system of railroads, canals, commerce and trade, and built up large cities and thriving communities. The whole West and the South were built up largely on money that later proved of no value and passed out of existence. It has only been in more recent years that we have adopted the gold standard. How we did it, with all the violent panics, crises and depressions as recorded in this book, is the commercial marvel of all time.

Leslie M. Shaw, known as a conservative of conservatives, while Secretary of the Treasury under President Roosevelt, proposed the following: "I would add an amendment permitting national banks, with the consent of the Comptroller of the Currency, to issue a volume of circulating notes equal to 50 per cent of the bond-secured circulation, at a tax of 6 per cent, the same to be returned at will (by the banks) or by the direction of the Comptroller, by the deposit of an equal amount of lawful money, with any sub-treasury." This proposal was a modified form of the present Federal Reserve notes and would do very well in normal times, but in a crisis under a national strain it is doubtful if this would have served any better purpose than the old greenbacks, proving that most any kind of money will do when confidence is right, but when confidence is shaken there might be another tale to tell. Comptroller Ridgley, after the panic of 1907 said: "It is not a lack of confidence of the people in the banks, but more, it is a lack of confidence of the banks in each other."

Cleveland in his book, "The Bank and the Treasury," (1908) says: "Those who have expressed opinion concerning the cause of the recent panic used the same fatalistic philosophy as was employed centuries ago in accounting for ravages of 'black death' and the scourges of smallpox and cholera. From time immemorial the same conclusions have been reached. After learned discussion, those in position to command respect for knowledge of financial situations have each time announced that sudden collapses of bank-credit have been due to an undefined, intangible, uncontrollable something called 'lack of confidence.' " He goes on to ask: "With such a diagnosis of the malady by those who are looked to professionally for prescription of remedies, question may be raised as to whether we may ever hope to find relief from financial ills. May we hope to correct a financial disease that is diagnosed as the result of a mental attitude of persons who may not be located and specifically treated?   Congress is asked to pass remedial laws. What legislation will make business safe as against 'what some people may think'? How many bankers may be required to conduct their business to prevent 'some people' from losing confidence? Does not such an analysis suggest that the philsophy of banking is still surrounded by the ignorance and mysticism of the dark ages, and that public inquiry is still lacking in methods of scientific research?"

Some will agree and others disagree with this writer.
Some will claim that depressions do not come from lack of
confidence and that we are going to remedy the causes and
avoid them in the future. It is going to require something
more than a changed state of mind. We are going to have
to change our system by law and curtail the practice of
gambling with other peoples' money. On the other hand, it
is true that there have been panics and depressions caused
by lack of confidence, particularly in the old days of money
panics and depressions. This is proven by the fact that
after our hysteria we went right ahead with the same identical money issued on the same basis. We attributed certain
panics to our currency system, and yet before we changed
the system we went ahead for periods of years prospering
beyond precedent. One trouble is that we are over-confident
when we should be cautious. Those watching the economic
situation have invariably been able to foretell trouble ahead
and yet who will not admit that the public absolutely refuses
to take heed. And then, on the other hand, when in the
middle of a period of depression, with conditions much
sounder, credits well deflated, reserves higher, we witness
the phenomenon of entire lack of confidence at the time
when, for our own good and for sound reasons, we should
have confidence. If this is not a study in psychology, what
is it?

It is plain to students of the question that in time of
stringency it is not a question of lack of currency so much
as the need of a proper system of deposit accounts, similar to the Baltimore plan which has been suggested, whereby
a borrower whose paper may not be approved by the Federal
Reserve Banks can get what he must have above all things,
a loan. Once given the loan he has no difficulty in finding
a medium of exchange by which he can transform this loan,
in the form of a deposit credit in a way to meet his obligations and save himself from hasty ruinous liquidation.
This is simply a system whereby business men exchange
what might be termed certificates of credit in the same way

that banks have always done among themselves through their clearing houses in times of stress.

"If we analyze the habits of the gold-using countries, who are infinitely the richest countries of the world," writes a contemporary, "we see that their medium of exchange consists of gold, a note issue and various instruments of credit. Now the note issue is based on gold and the instruments of credit are based on both the other two. That implies that any diminution in one will effect a proportionate diminution in both the others. It is also true that in a financial crisis all credit is naturally contracted, which results in the natural consequence, that there is a lower proportion of instruments of credit based on gold and notes in hard times than in good times. Let us suppose for the sake of example, that such a ratio of credit to actual currency is about 7 to 1 in a normal state of trade, sinking as low as only 5 to 1 in times of stringency. The fall might possibly be much greater. However, on that hypothesis and in order to see the immense effect of the drain of a small amount of gold, we may assume a sudden withdrawal from general use for temporary purposes of $250,000,000 in gold out of a supposed world stock of $10,000,000,000. Out of these $10,000,000,000 not more than $5,000,000,000 will presumably be near enough to the source of the initial disturbance to be susceptible to the first sudden shock. The remaining $5,000,000,000 are therefore by hypothesis considered to be far enough away to be quiescent; because no shock is great enough at one moment to actually effect the whole world, even though the ultimate effects of the shock will spread everywhere. Let us also assume a ratio of 2 to 1 for notes based on gold. The whole stock of money before the shock, say in October, within the affected area is then supposed to consist of $5,-000,000,000 of gold, of $10,000,000,000 of notes and of $105,000,000,000 of credit embodied in paper, such as bills, cheques and drafts. This last figure is estimated at the favorable ratio of 7 to 1, based on the combined currency of gold and notes together. Now the sudden and unannounced withdrawal of $200,000,000 of gold in November, if it caused, as it certainly would, a temporary stringency and a panic, would compel the immediate hoarding and retention of at least an equivalent amount of gold and of a proportionate amount of notes by bankers and financial houses, resulting in abstraction from use of at least $500,000,000 of gold and $1,000,000,000 of notes. At the same time the proportion of private paper credit would shrink rapidly to the panic ratio of 5 to 1 on the reduced currency. The total available medium of exchange, using the term in its widest sense, at the end of November would have fallen to $4,500,000,000 of gold, $9,000,000,000 of notes, provided there had been no fresh issue by the states involved, and $67,500,000,000 of paper credit. In other words, the total available money within the area of disturbance would have been $120,000,000,000 in October and $81,000,000,-000 in November, a shrinkage in the real medium of exchange in current use over that area of $39,000,000,000, due to the sudden abstraction of only $200,000,000 of gold."

As before stated business depressions are more or less interwoven with the financial situation. In times of speculation, over-production and expanded credits, business must suffer until the financial situation relieves itself. With crop failures, strikes, political uncertainties and lack of demand, business must again adjust itself, but more easily because at such times the financial system can use its reserve to tide over the period. To avoid serious depression, then, it is necessary to keep the financial system healthy so that it can contract and expand with facility and ease. In times of prosperity credits must not be expanded to such an extent that there are not ample reserves to carry borrowers in case of sudden stress or even to loan them more if their collateral justifies it. This will keep any solvent institution from falling. On the other hand, in times of unfavorable conditions such as crop failures, etc., credit should not be extended on too liberal a basis, but sparingly, so that when the tide turns the debtor does not have to exhaust himself in liquidating his debts, but can more quickly return to his normal buying power. Every business man and investor should study carefully the Federal Reserve Act and watch the reports of the Board, which are valuable in many ways, particularly when it can be plainly seen that the limit of credit is reached.

On this one question the business man can agree with the theorist: That money is valuable to the extent that it reflects confidence. Legal tender notes are not dollars. It is

clear that this money that we carry in our pockets is a
promise to pay. A promise to pay a dollar cannot of itself
be a dollar. Money, then, is valuable only to the extent of
the knowledge or confidence that it can be exchanged for
a gold dollar. But even after we get the gold it will also
fluctuate and the metal in it buys more goods or less goods
under different conditions.

The most valuable thing, therefore, in the business world,
is not money, not gold, but confidence. Gold is valuable because of the universal confidence in that metal. Outside of
.its scarcity, it has little practical value. In fact, gold is like
everything else, even the commonest thing, in that in times
of great production it has become cheap and its buying
power lessened.

As we examine the pages of history we find that prosperity and depression have come during every kind of money
condition. In spite of all that has been said and written
on the money question as affecting panics and depressions,
we are coming to realize that we have been chasing false
causes. The indisputable fact is that we have had prosperity
when we have had confidence, and we have had depression
when there developed lack of confidence. Today all great
countries of the world, excepting China, are on a gold basis,
yet civilization does not use gold currency in its trade between individuals, and we do not care for gold. If it is
tendered we almost invariably pass it back, preferring
paper. Why? Confidence in the paper. And while the paper
is mostly redeemable in gold we know that there is not anywhere near sufficient gold to redeem all the issues.

The advance of civilization is getting us past the stage
of considering gold the one single thing of value. We have
reached a point where we can capitalize our accumulated
wealth in other forms, such as farms, real estate, public
utilities and certain industries.

Advocates of the gold standard used to point out the disastrous results of the issue of both silver dollars and legal
tender paper money. It is true that both of these forms of

currency have at various times depreciated in value, but that was because the eventual over-issue was foreseen and sharp traders immediately began to discount their face value. In 1890 the Government accumulated a large quantity of gold and offered to redeem all outstanding paper money at par, yet very little of it was ever sent to the treasury for redemption. Why? Because confidence in it had been restored. It would have been interesting to see what would have happened if all the greenbacks issued at that time, totaling around $400,000,000, had been sent in for redemption. They could not have been redeemed without serious embarrassment of far-reaching consequence. Yet every individual had confidence, because he knew his neighbor had confidence. No bank could pay its depositors at any one time, that is universally known and yet its notes are accepted without question.

All economists are familiar with Gresham's law i. e. that bad money drives out good money. This applies to paper money as well as to metallic money. When competition works freely there is an effort to do all work at the least expense and with the largest returns. On that basis a fiat paper money ought to circulate and do the money work, but the difficulty with such a suggestion is that the holders of the paper money want finally, something that can be converted into value. Hence there must be a value basis for money of any kind. We have come to a point where that basis does not have to be gold, provided we have confidence in the commodity that takes the place of gold, with possibly a comparatively small reserve of gold mostly for use in settling international balances. "Gold's utility does not lie in the substance of which it is composed but in the service which it renders. It is a common impression in the case of standard gold money, that the money is valuable because it is gold, whereas it would be more accurate to say that gold is valuable because it is money. We all know that a silver dollar and a paper dollar are each worth a dollar, not because of the substance of which they are made but because they do the work of a dollar. Nor is the case of a gold dollar essentially different. It may be admitted that gold as a substance has utilities apart from its use as a monetary medium, but these are of second rank. Apart from its use for adornment, its employment in the arts is extremely limited. On the other hand, a very large portion of the gold stock of the world is performing the function of money, and there can be no doubt that were gold deprived of its money function it would greatly depreciate in value as compared with other commodities. The use of gold as money heightens the value of gold, and the value thus given to gold is imparted to the other forms of money which do a similar service in the affairs of the world."

So fluctuation in the value of precious metals is the strongest argument in favor of the point that confidence or lack of confidence enters strongly in the economic question. As before stated, the purchasing power of gold has varied over a wide range, sometimes because of increased or decreased production, but more generally according to strength of confidence on the part of the people in governmental policy and business conditions. History easily proves that the value of money, from gold on through to paper, rises and falls like the value of any other commodity, proving that psychological confidence supercedes materialistic forms of money.

A Summary of United States Finances

BANK CLEARINGS.*			Year.	Total money in circulation.	Circulation per capita.
Year.	New York.	Total United States.			
	Dollars.	Dollars.		Dollars.	Dollars.
1855......	5,632,912,098	....	1800...............	26,500,000	4.99
1860......	7,231,143,057	....	1810...............	55,000,000	7.60
1865......	26,032,384,342	....	1820...............	67,100,000	6.96
1870......	27,804,539,406	....	1830...............	87,344,295	6.78
1871......	29,300,986,682	....	1840...............	186,305,488	10.91
1872......	33,844,369,568	....	1850...............	278,761,982	12.02
1873......	35,461,052,826	....	1855...............	418,020,247	15.34
1874......	22,855,927,636	....	1860...............	435,407,252	13.85
1875......	25,061,237,902	....	1865...............	714,971,860	20.58
1876......	21,597,274,247	....	1870...............	676,284,427	17.51
1877......	23,289,243,701	....	1871...............	718,616,114	18.17

BANK CLEARINGS.*

Year.	New York. Dollars.	Total United States. Dollars.
1878	22,508,438,442	
1879	25,178,770,691	
1880	37,182,128,621	
1881	48,565,818,212	
1882	46,552,846,161	
1883	40,293,165,258	
1884	34,092,037,338	
1885	25,250,791,440	
1886	33,374,682,216	
1887	34,872,848,786	52,126,704,488
1888	30,863,686,609	48,750,886,813
1889	34,796,465,529	53,501,411,510
1890	37,660,686,572	58,845,279,505
1891	34,053,698,770	57,298,737,938
1892	36,279,905,236	60,883,572,438
1893	34,421,379,870	58,880,682,455
1894	24,230,145,368	45,028,496,746
1895	28,264,379,126	50,975,155,046
1896	29,350,894,884	51,935,651,733
1897	31,337,760,948	54,179,545,030
1898	39,853,413,948	65,924,820,769
1899	57,368,230,771	88,828,672,533
1900	51,964,588,564	84,582,450,081
1901	77,020,672,494	114,819,792,086
1902	74,753,189,436	116,021,618,003
1903	70,833,655,940	113,963,298,973
1904	59,672,796,804	102,356,435,047
1905	91,879,318,369	140,592,087,616
1906	103,754,100,091	157,681,259,999
1907	95,315,421,238	154,476,830,537
1908	73,630,971,913	126,238,694,398
1909	99,257,662,400	158,877,192,100
1910	102,553,959,069	168,986,664,000
1911	92,420,120,000	159,539,539,000
1912	96,672,301,000	168,685,953,000
1913	98,121,520,000	173,193,009,000
1914	89,760,344,971	163,849,811,000
1915	90,842,707,724	163,098,715,000
1916	147,180,709,461	242,235,794,000
1917	181,534,031,388	305,044,436,000
1918	174,524,179,029	320,988,542,000
1919	214,703,444,468	387,912,219,000
1920	252,338,249,466	463,769,613,000

Year.	Total money in circulation. Dollars.	Circulation per capita. Dollars.
1872	741,548,708	18.27
1873	753,799,412	18.09
1874	776,083,031	18.13
1875	754,101,947	17.16
1876	727,609,388	16.12
1877	722,314,883	15.58
1878	729,132,634	15.32
1879	818,631,793	16.75
1880	973,382,228	19.41
1881	1,114,238,119	21.71
1882	1,174,290,419	22.37
1883	1,231,047,925	22.93
1884	1,243,925,969	22.65
1885	1,293,061,836	23.03
1886	1,250,011,531	21.78
1887	1,317,539,143	22.45
1888	1,372,164,870	22.88
1889	1,380,361,649	22.52
1890	1,429,251,270	22.82
1891	1,497,440,307	23.45
1892	1,601,347,187	24.60
1893	1,596,701,065	24.06
1894	1,661,307,165	24.56
1895	1,601,968,473	23.24
1896	1,506,434,966	21.44
1897	1,640,983,171	22.92
1898	1,837,859,894	25.19
1899	1,904,071,881	25.62
1900	2,055,150,997	26.93
1901	2,175,307,961	27.98
1902	2,249,390,551	28.43
1903	2,367,692,169	29.42
1904	2,519,142,859	30.77
1905	2,587,882,653	31.08
1906	2,736,646,628	32.32
1907	2,772,956,455	32.22
1908	3,038,015,488	34.72
1909	3,106,240,657	34.93
1910	3,102,355,605	34.33
1911	3,214,002,596	34.20
1912	3,284,513,094	34.34
1913	3,363,738,449	34.56
1914	3,402,015,427	34.35
1915	3,569,219,574	35.44
1916	4,024,130,567	39.29
1917	4,763,575,632	45.74
1918	5,379,427,424	50.81
1919	5,766,029,973	54.33
1920	6,087,555,087	57.21

*United States Statistical Abstract.

CHAPTER XXXVI

PIG IRON AS A BAROMETER OF BUSINESS

Pig-iron is accepted in business circles as an accurate barometer of trade. It is indisputably a good barometer of immediate existing conditions, and this chapter contains some data bearing upon the subject. There are other barometers, however, that some think are better, particularly cotton, and a chapter in this book is devoted to cotton as a barometer, as well as another chapter comparing these two great commodities, and how they reflect the status of business.

The world has used iron almost since we have had a trace of history. It is said that semi-savage tribes discovered iron from forest fires which left the ores in a molten state. America made iron from the very beginning; a year after the Jamestown colony was settled iron was smelted from Virginia ore.

Extensive iron making is an industry of countries advanced in manufacturing. It requires excellent transportation facilities, many laborers, much capital to build and operate the enormous plants, and the large market which only a vast population can give. It very distinctly is not a frontier industry, and this is just as true in the new states of the United States as it is in Australia or South America. As a result, six countries dominate the iron making of the world, and three of these are of distinctly minor importance. The United States, Great Britain, and Germany make four-fifths of the world's supply; Belgium, France, and Russia are the next group, and after they have been named there is little left of the world's iron industry as at present developed.

In 1800 England was the leader in production of iron, producing at that time, with a population of 8,000,000, about

three to five pounds per capita. Let us compare that with
the production at the close of the World War when the output from America, Germany and Great Britain ranged from
500 to 1,000 pounds per capita. For the period of colonial
times in America no complete data is available, but during
the Revolution the output of the United Colonies must have
increased quite markedly, for the demand for iron products
was heavy and most of it had to be supplied by colonial
furnaces and forges.

The iron industry got away to a bad start following the
Revolution, when it had been stimulated by war demands
and non-importation.   At the close of the war, however,
iron came in great quantities from Great Britain and local
industry could not compete. A study of the iron industry
leads to the conclusion that the production of the latter half
of the Eighteenth Century in America was more important
as a factor in the world's output than during the first fifty
years of the Nineteenth Century. During the latter period
the United States lost ground steadily as compared with its
leading competitors. It was not until the Civil War that it
produced the same percentage of the world's iron output
that it had made at the time of the Revolution. While at
the close of the Revolution production in England and
America was about even, yet fifty years later England was
making six times as much pig-iron as the States.   It was not
until 1890, over a hundred years after the Revolution, that
the two countries again reached equality for a moment.

Pig-iron acted as a good barometer in the 1837 depression.
Early in 1836 iron advanced in Philadelphia from $32 to
$50.25 per ton, but with this advance consumption apparent-
ly fell off and material commenced to accumulate. By the
end of the year the accumulation of iron became alarming.
Iron began falling in price also before the financial panic
broke.

In 1847 iron prices again advanced and yet there came a
check in demand, but this depression lasted a very short

time on account of the gold discoveries and the outbreak of the Mexican War.

In the four years previous to 1857 iron was more or less depressed, while all other industries flourished immensely. It was also true that iron showed less the effect of the panic of 1857 than any other industry. In this instance it could not be taken as a correct barometer of actual conditions. It was at the time of the 1857 derpression that iron first was characterized as being "either prince or pauper" of industry.

Our great advance in iron during the last half of the Nineteenth Centruy is owed to the protective tariff policy. Iron and steel making was then regarded as an infant industry and protection placed on foreign imports stimulated production and manufacture of products in this country.

Iron reflected the English panic in 1890, precipitated by the Baring failure, to the extent of 35 per cent within five months. Iron consumption fell from a rate per annum of 9,200,000 tons in November, 1890, to a rate per annum of 5,900,000 tons in April, 1891. In a five-month period during the 1893 depression iron consumption fell from a 9,400,000 ton per annum rate to a 3,800,000 ton per annum rate. This was a far greater falling off than the average industry recorded, even during the panicky months when the depression was at its lowest. The output of pig-iron, which had been about 9,157,000 tons in 1892, fell to 6,657,000 tons in 1894.

During the depression of 1893, lasting to 1896, new economies were introduced into our industrial establishment. Even with an abundance of water in our inflated capitalization we found we could sell pig-iron at a profit at $10 to $12 per ton; steel rails were sold with a liberal return to capital at $17.50 per ton, and bar iron entered a profitable market at 95 cents per hundred.

Cotter's "History of the United States Steel Corporation" gives the uncertainty in the trade as one of the primary reasons for the formation of the giant trust, setting forth that the control of the industry in a few hands would stabilize it against the sharp rise and fall of previous times.

"It was inevitable that there should be a dark side to the picture and that it should be particularly black in obedience to the natural law that provides that the severity of the fall shall be proportioned to the height of the climb. The boom times of the steel trade were succeeded with disheartening regularity by periods of dearth. One year steel manufacturers were building themselves palaces and purchasing steam yachts, the next they were mortgaging all they had to pay wages. One year the steel worker was a man favored above all others of his class, the next he was getting his meals on charity from the 'soup houses'. To this day steel veterans speak of the dull times of the trade as 'soup-house days.'"

At these times competition, always fierce, became more ruthless than ever. The old adage regarding love and war was stretched to include the steel industry, and everything was considered fair that might help to keep the mills running full. Prices were cut—and wages with them; steel was "dumped" on foreign markets at less than manufacturing cost, and steel makers resorted to every means that offered to divert orders from competitors to themselves. It was a case of 'dog eat dog', and failures, with their unavoidable accompaniment of unemployed labor, were all too frequent. The frequent and prolonged periods of depression had forced upon steel makers the conviction that some way of combining to prevent their recurrence was desirable, even ncessary, if the United States was to keep and increase its lead in the manufacture of the metal most needed by the age.

In the 1903 disturbance iron dropped from a 20,200,00 ton per annum rate in June of that year to a 10,100,000 ton per annum rate within six months. There was no widespread financial panic, but a general deflation and slowing up. In May, 1907, consumption was at the rate of 27,000,000 tons per annum and prices were the highest on record. It held this rate until October, when the panic broke, and within three months had fallen to a rate of 12,500,000 tons per annum. The unfilled orders of the United States Steel Corporation, however, at that time were indicative of a slowing up. On January 1, 1907, the unfilled order of that corporation amounted to 8,489,718 tons, while on September 30th, a few days before the panic, they had decreased to 6,425,000 tons, a falling off of 24 per cent.

Let us note from this table the advance of iron during the prosperity immediately preceding the depressions of the periods given:

```
*From $38.00 in 1823 to $75.00 in 1825
 From   35.00 in 1833 to   70.00 in 1837
 From   23.00 in 1843 to   52.50 in 1845
 From   19.00 in 1852 to   50.25 in 1856
 From   20.00 in 1861 to   80.00 in 1864
 From   30.00 in 1871 to   61.00 in 1872
 From   19.00 in 1879 to   41.00 in 1880
 From    9.00 in 1897 to   22.25 in 1899
 From   13.15 in 1900 to   23.84 in 1902
 From   12.33 in 1904 to   24.50 in 1907
 From   15.26 in 1915 to   44.39 in 1920
```

The table below will show the decline in the price of iron following the periods of depression:

```
*From $70.00 in 1837 to $22.00 in 1843
 From   52.50 in 1847 to   19.00 in 1852
 From   50.25 in 1856 to   20.00 in 1861
 From   80.00 in 1864 to   30.00 in 1871
 From   61.00 in 1872 to   19.00 in 1879
 From   41.00 in 1880 to   17.75 in 1885
 From   21.00 in 1887 to    9.00 in 1897
 From   22.25 to 1899 to   13.15 in 1900
 From   23.84 in 1902 to   12.33 in 1904
 From   24.50 in 1907 to   17.75 in 1909
 From   16.57 in 1913 to   15.26 in 1915
 From   44.39 in 1920 to   18.75 in 1922
```

---

* Figures by Hull.

Right after the shock of 1907, the steel corporation having absorbed its principal competittor—the Tennessee Iron and Steel Company—got independents together with them at the famous Gary dinners and artificially regulated conditions through an agreement as to prices. How can an industry be an accurate barometer of trade where supply and demand can be controlled through other than natural courses?

The table below shows the cycles of trade as indicated by pig-iron prices. It will be noted that with few exceptions they follow the general trend of business and finance as a whole through the periods of depression and prosperity:*

DOWN CYCLE	UP CYCLE
1819____$39.75 per ton January	
1820____ 35.00 per ton Average	
1821____ 35.00 per ton Average	
1822____ 35.00 per ton Average	
1823____ 35.00 per ton Average	
	1824____$37.25 per ton January
	1825____ 46.75 per ton Average
	1826____ 46.50 per ton Average
	1827____ 46.50 per ton March
1828____$35.00 per ton January	
1829____ 35.00 per ton Average	
1830____ 35.00 per ton Average	
1831____ 35.00 per ton Average	
1832____ 35.00 per ton Average	
1833____ 38.50 per ton Average	
1834____ 28.50 per ton December	
	1835____$29.25 per ton January
	1836____ 45.50 per ton Average
	1837____ 47.00 per ton June
1838____$35.00 per ton January	
1839____ 30.00 per ton January	
1840____ 32.75 per ton January	
1841____ 28.50 per ton January	
1842____ 27.75 per ton January	
1843____ 25.00 per ton August	
	1844____$27.00 per ton January
	1845____ 32.00 per ton August

* Compiled to 1911 by Joseph H. Lynch.
From 1911 from figures of U. S. Department of Commerce.

DOWN CYCLE   UP CYCLE

1846____$28.00 per ton January
1847____ 30.25 per ton Average
1848____ 26.50 per ton Average
1849____ 22.75 per ton Average
1850____ 20.00 per ton July

                                    1851____$21.50 per ton January
                                    1852____ 22.62 per ton Average
                                    1853____ 36.12 per ton Average
                                    1854____ 38.00 per ton August

1855____$35.12 per ton January
1856____ 27.12 per ton January
1857____ 26.75 per ton January
1858____ 22.25 per ton January
1859____ 23.37 per ton January
1860____ 22.75 per ton January
1861____ 18.67 per ton October

                                    1862____$20.00 per ton January
                                    1863____ 32.25 per ton January
                                    1864____ 75.25 per ton Sept.

1865____$58.12 per ton January
1866____ 46.87 per ton Average
1867____ 44.12 per ton Average
1868____ 39.25 per ton Average
1869____ 40.67 per ton Average
1870____ 31.25 per ton December

                                    1871____$34.25 per ton March
                                    1872____ 53.87 per ton Sept.

1873____$45.17 per ton January
1874____ 30.25 per ton Average
1875____ 25.50 per ton Average
1876____ 22.25 per ton Average
1877____ 18.00 per ton December

                                    1878____$18.50 per ton January
                                    1879____ 21.75 per ton Average
                                    1880____ 28.50 per ton Average
                                    1881____ 26.25 per ton Average

1882____$25.75 per ton March
1883____ 22.42 per ton March
1884____ 19.81 per ton March
1885____ 17.99 per ton March
1886____ 18.71 per ton March
1887____ 20.93 per ton March
1888____ 18.00 per ton March

                                    1889____$18.50 per ton Nov.
                                    1890____ 19.90 per ton Nov.
                                    1891____ 17.75 per ton Nov.

DOWN CYCLE   UP CYCLE

1892____ 17.50 per ton January
1893____ 14.52 per ton January
1894____ 12.66 per ton January
1895____ 13.10 per ton January
1896____ 12.95 per ton January
1897____ 11.75 per ton January

                                   1898____$12.00 per ton January
                                   1899____ 25.00 per ton Dec.

1900____$20.00 per ton June
1901____ 15.87 per ton June
1902____ 22.19 per ton June
1903____ 19.92 per ton June
1904____ 14.94 per ton June

                                   1905____$17.75 per ton January
                                   1906____ 20.91 per ton Average
                                   1907____ 23.14 per ton Average

1908____ 18.75 per ton February
1909____$17.75 per ton January
1910____ 16.86 per ton Average
1911____ 15.75 per ton Average

                                   1912____$16.06 per ton Average
                                   1913____ 16.57 per ton Average

1914____$15.74 per ton Average
1915____ 15.26 per ton Average

                                   1916____$21.18 per ton Average
                                   1917____ 43.61 per ton Average
                                   1918____ 36.66 per ton Average
                                   1919____ 31.09 per ton Average
                                   1920____ 44.39 per ton Average

1921____$21.34 per ton November
1922____ 18.75 per ton February

CHAPTER XXXVII

COTTON AS A BAROMETER OF BUSINESS

To those who may have a tendency not to appreciate the importance of the fleecy staple, let them read the history of cotton and they will find interwoven in it the history of the progress of the republic. No other industry compares with it in importance. The idea that it is sectional is a mistaken one, because when it is carried abroad from the southern ports through the lanes of commerce, gold flows back in return through the ports of the North. And the money that we ourselves spend for it in domestic use finds its way into every factory and every bank in the northern industrial centers. It is truly a national commodity. Alexander Hamilton, himself born on a cotton plantation in the West Indies, saw great future possibilities for it, and Thomas Jefferson, then Secretary of State, purchased one of Whitney's first gins.

We are all familiar with the fable of the vegetable lamb, which came from the stories of Herodotus, who took it from the mouths of Nomads, who traded by caravan between India and Europe and told the western world that in India there grew "plants bearing fruit within which there is a lamb having fleece of surpassing beauty and excellence."

Cotton first made its appearance in England in the year 1298, and in the Sixteenth Century had begun to be of such general use that a clamor arose among the British wool growers and manufacturers gainst its use, claiming it was so much cheaper that it would ruin the whole industry. They demanded high duties in order to keep the cotton out of the country. Opposition arose to this measure, and the wool interests were given relief by an act providing that every dead person should be buried in a woolen shroud, in default of which persons directing funerals should be fined, as Blackstone says in his "Commentaries on the Laws of England": "Thus encouraging the staple trade on which in great measure depends the universal good of the nation." It is credited with being the controlling influence in that remarkable period known as the Industrial Revolution in England in the Eighteenth Century.

The story is told that a large cotton buyer in England became wealthy and powerful by establishing an underground system whereby he was able to obtain information from the spot markets in America two or three days ahead of his rivals. Then came the telegraph. The rival installed a private wire. The first cotton buyer, although known as keen and shrewd, did not believe that such information could be sent with any degree of accuracy over a wire running into his office. He ridiculed the idea, but at an opportune time the rival got news ten days ahead of the first factor, which information caused the latter great loss and sent him to an inglorious oblivion. That was the time of the inventions of Arkwright, Cartwright, Crompton, Watt and Hargreaves, which greatly stimulated cotton manufacturing and cheapened the product.

A little cotton had been grown in the Southern States for domestic use before the War of Independence, but the quantity was insignificant. Previous to the year 1790 we had not shipped a single pound abroad. In 1791 cotton was exported for the first time, only 189,000 pounds being shipped that year. Suddenly the export of the staple assumed enormous proportions and by 1794 we were shipping over one million pounds abroad, the next year over five million pounds and so it continued with still greater strides.

In our earlier history cotton was much higher, on an average, than in later years because of the higher cost of transportation and ginning. In the business depression which started in 1808 middling cotton sold on the market at only about 19 cents. A year later it had dropped to 16 cents. It was not at that time considered the important commodity that it began to assume following the European wars of that period. The export price of our great "money crop" fell from 32 cents in the depression of 1818 to 17.5 cents in 1820. The first great "bull movement" in the cotton market was inaugurated in 1824-25 in Liverpool, when prices advanced from 7d. to 16¾d. per pound. While the advance was simply speculative, it is said to have originated in the attempt of a Liverpool house to prove that cotton production had reached its limit, and that the demand was greater than the supply. It was currently reported that one hundred millions sterling had been raised by capitalists to buy up all cotton in sight. But no doubt one cause of the attempt to "bull" the market was the very small surplus stocks at Liverpool. This extraordinary rise in prices was reflected in our own markets, the New York market advancing from 12 to 30 cents a pound.

Following this, the panic of 1825 broke in England. The reaction reached America in September, 1825, and the fall in price created a short depression in the South and embarrassed a number of banks in the North. It was not widespread nor of sufficient magnitude to be called a general crises.

Three years later came the depression of 1828, which brought about a remarkable fall in the price of cotton and all the people of the South were in distress.

It was during this depression that the matter of improving the general grade of cotton was brought forcibly to the southern people, and planting was revolutionized by the study of better seed and cultivation. From these experiments came Sea Island cotton, with its long and strong fibre. In 1830 cotton sold for 6 cents a pound and gradually rose until 1835 when it sold a 20 cents. It broke in 1836 and its break hastened the crisis of the following year. While the country has always realized the importance of cotton in our commercial life, it was at this time that it began to be taken as a barometer of business conditions, present and prospective.

Both Callander and DeBow, writing of the period previous

to the depression of 1837, describe the situation in similar
words: "Cotton brought in $1,000,000,000 in twenty years,
but this vast revenue was not expended at home. It was
distributed to the cotton factors and shipmasters of the
North and Great Britain, to the farmers of the western
country, to the ironmongers of Pittsburg, to the manufacturers of New England. The cotton crop enriched every
section of the country except the cotton belt. It set in motion a system of internal commerce which promoted the
prosperity of the United States more than any other single
cause." No wonder southern children sing of the "bell-
shaped, changing-hued cotton blossom thusly:

> "First day white, next day red,
> Third day from my birth I'm dead;
> Though I am of short duration,
> Yet withal I clothe the nation."

President Biddle, of the Second National Bank, had ma-
neuvered things so as to make a lot of money out of cotton
previous to the panic of 1837. He bought the cotton from
the southern planters, placing it in warehouses at Havre and
Liverpool, paying the planters in National Bank notes and
getting hard money from Europe. These bank notes were
issued without security and for unlimited amounts, and
when the crisis came the notes depreciated as much as 30
per cent, causing great loss to the Southern planters who
held them. When the market became glutted in Europe and
the price fell panic followed in those countries. On March
15, 1837, news reached New York that the great cotton
house of Herman Briggs & Co., of New Orleans, had failed
for $8,000,000. The whole Southwest collapsed. In New
Orleans every important house went down, one concern
owing over $15,000,000. Cotton fell in a few days from 17
to 10 cents, and the effect in New York was immediate.
J. L. & S. Joseph & Co., with connections in New Orleans,
failed for several millions, and a general crash followed.

In 1835 cotton commanded 20 cents in New York and was
equally as high in England, due to the speculation of the

times, but the crop of 1838, following the depression of the previous year, brought a very low price. In 1839 the first convention of cotton planters was held at Macon, Ga., where various plans were proposed to improve conditions and secure better prices.

Until 1836, with few exceptions, the crops had yielded very profitable returns. Then, with the financial panic of 1837, the cotton mills curtailed consumption, while the planters increased the crops. The inevitable result was an accumulation of stocks and a fall in prices. That year cotton was the first commodity that pointed the way to the coming crash. In a few days during the early part of April it fell nearly 50 per cent. A month later New York banks began suspending specie payment.

In 1837 speculation was not confined to western lands; there was equal recklessness over cotton plantations in the Southwest, particularly in Mississippi and Louisiana, and in the real estate of the cities which controlled the cotton trade; "the demand for the raw staple was greatly increased by the growth of manufactures of cotton goods in this country and by favorable conditions in England. The result was a rapid advance in the price of cotton, and also in the cotton crop which in Tennessee, Alabama, Mississippi, Arkansas, Louisiana and Florida increased from 536,000 bales in 1833 to 916,000 bales in 1837. Southern cities looked forward to a continuance of the great prosperity. At Mobile, for example, the assessed valuation of real estate increased from $4,000,000 in 1834 to $27,000,000 in 1837, although the number of polls assessed in the latter year was less than in the former."

In 1846 cotton reached a very high point, causing speculation in that commodity in England, resulting in a panic. In the depression of 1847, which followed, so great was the difficulty in realizing money, even on cotton, that extensive shipments were made on very limited advancements. In a review of the situation in 1847-48 the New Orleans Price Current said: "Seldom, if ever, within the period of its history, as the leading commercial interest of our country, has the cotton trade been subjected to so trying an ordeal as that through which it has just passed. The early prices obtained were satisfactory, until October, when the commercial revolution which prostrated credit in Great Britain, and which spread to the Continent and to the Indies, put a sudden check to our prosperous course and produced a more rapid depreciation of prices than we remember ever to have witnessed."

Before the panic of 1857 cotton went to nearly 14 cents, making a steady advance during the prosperous years preceding and then falling precipitately with the crash.

Of the economic disturbances occasioned by the Civil War none was more trying than that caused by the prostration of cotton cultivation and the disruption of the foreign and domestic cotton trade. Our Civil War created the famous cotton famine in Europe, causing severe depression among her manufacturers. The rebellious southern states thought the business stagnation in England and France would be so bad that they would intervene in the Civil War. It was the opinion of some that it was entirely improbable that the Confederate States would ever have seceded had they not felt that Europe's dependence on American cotton would bring intervention in their behalf.

The South had high ideas of its importance, as shown by a speech by Senator Hammond in 1858. "Without firing a gun, without drawing a sword, should they make war on us, we could bring the whole world to our feet. What would happen if no cotton was furnished for three years? I will not stop to depict what every one can imagine, but this is certain, England would topple headlong, and carry the whole civilized world with her. No, you dare not make war on cotton. No Power on the earth dares to make war on it— cotton is king."

Charles Francis Adams, whose father was minister to England during the Civil War, says: "The European cotton famine of 1861-63, at the time a very momentous affair, is now forgotten; yet upon it hung the fate of the American Union." The story of that Lancashire Cotton Famine of 1861 to 1864 has never been adequately told in connection with our Civil War.

Mrs. Jefferson Davis wrote in her biography: "The President and his advisers looked to the stringency of the English cotton market, and the suspension of the manufactories, to send up a ground swell from the English operatives that would compel recognition."

The famine caused the price to be quoted at $1.80 per pound on the New York market, but after the war planting was resumed and good prices were had. But the trade again felt the decline and depression in the year 1869.

Cotton was fortunate in the depression of 1873 because of small stocks at the close of 1872 and decreased production in 1873, but along with other commodities, it was depressed in 1879.

During the eighties prices on raw cotton were maintained with remarkable uniformity, although during the short business depression of 1884 there was an accumulation of manufactured goods, the supply being temporarily in excess of the demand. In 1893 cotton proved to be a splendid barometer of conditions. There was a short crop both in 1892 and 1893, and under the law of supply and demand there should have been much higher prices, but, instead, prices advanced only slightly in this country as well as in Europe. The business depression among the New England manufacturers caused such a reduction in consumption that we sent at least 300,000 to 400,000 bales more to Liverpool than would otherwise have been received, and thereby kept that market constantly overstocked. After the panic, however, the price went up and reached as high as 17.25 cents in 1904.

During the depression of 1914, incident to the outbreak of the war, cotton led the way through it all. It was first to lead the way down and first to lead the way up. At the outbreak of the war cotton was greatly depressed and proposals for relief were outlined by Festus J. Wade, of St. Louis, which helped to take a large amount of surplus cotton off the market. A full account of the cotton loan plan of that time was published in the first annual report of the Federal Reserve Board January 15, 1915.

In the Fall of 1921, when it was apparent that curtailed acreage and bad weather conditions would reduce the year's crop probably 50 per cent, cotton markets of Liverpool, New York and New Orleans were scenes of wild buying, raising the price from around 12 cents to around 20 cents a pound, an increase of 80 per cent in three weeks. This was hailed everywhere in America as a sign of improving business, and business did improve in most sections because of liquidation of loans to the banks of the South and in turn to the banks of the North. Then again came evidence of the influence of cotton on the delicate mechanism of business. Some predicted the staple would go to 25 or even 30 cents, carrying other commodities with it to a higher plane, and were preparing for a quick return to prosperity. But cotton went no higher, rather it lost considerable of its gain and likewise business faltered and remained only slightly improved, but stationary.

Never in the world's history have producers enjoyed such an exalted position as that held by the cotton planters of the South previous to the last few decades. People of Europe and other continents had built great cotton textile factories and had become used to this material, and it seemed at one time as though the people of half the civilized world would go unclad were it not for cotton. A cotton famine haunted the minds of the foreign manufacturers for years, and it was so important to America that it furnished over half our total exports until the time of the Civil War. In periods of depression which have affected the South along with the rest of the country, many times even more seriously, movements have been undertaken to curtail the acreage of cotton. When times were hard and the demand dropped off overproduction was always claimed, and the economists pointed out that the South would fare much better if they grew less cotton and more of other crops.

Another astonishing fact is that the world's cotton crop, of which just about three-fourths is produced in the United States, exceeds the value of the world's output of precious metals by 50 per cent. The value of eleven years' cotton crop from 1901 to 1911, inclusive, was over $8,000,000,000, against a total production of gold and silver for the same period of $6,000,000,000. It is cotton that gained for us a favorable trade balance three decades ago and has maintained it ever since.

Such eminent authorities as Theodore H. Price, W. A. Law and others agree with the writer that cotton is the most accurate barometer of American business conditions.

For over a century we had largely a monopoly of the cotton trade of the world and only in recent years have we had competition. During the last decade Egyptian cotton has been imported into this country to a considerable extent, so much so that the cotton planters of Salt River Valley in Arizona and the Imperial Valley in California have petitioned Congress for a high duty on Egyptian cotton which competes with them. The striking and unexplained fact is that while Egypt, in close proximity to Persia and India, where the plant originated, and with ideal growing conditions, has developed a commercial cotton industry only in the last fifty years.

The late William B. Dana, formerly editor of the "Commercial and Financial Chronicle," once said that cotton, "being practically imperishable and always convertible, possessed more of the attributes of a legal tender than anything produced by human labor except gold. It is the world's Golden Fleece; the nations are bound together in its globe-encircling web; so that when a modern economist concerns himself with the interdependence of nations he naturally looks to cotton for his most effective illustration, as witness the following: 'A manufacturer in Manchester strikes a bargain with a merchant in Louisiana in order to keep a bargain with a dyer in Germany, and three or a much larger number of parties enter into virtual, or perhaps actual, contract, and form a mutually dependent economic community (numbering, it may be, with the work people in the group of industries involved, some millions of individuals)—an economic entity so far as one can exist which does not include all organized society.' "

The foregoing figures will make clear the following important facts not generally understood:

*1. That during the past five years a total foreign trade of over nineteen billions of dollars has been "cleared" by the shipment back and forth of only $220,577,952 worth of gold and silver; which means that hardly more than one per cent of the balances arising from this enormous commerce have been settled in cash or bullion.

2. That during the same five years the trade balance in favor of the United States (including gold and silver) aggregates $2,573,011,666, and that during the same period the total value of raw cotton exported was $2,759,447,880.

3. That for the past five years the average annual balance of trade in favor of the United States (including gold and silver) has been $514,602,333, and that the average value of the raw cotton exported has been $551,889,576.

The sequence of these statements will make it plain that our annual payments in merchandise, gold, and silver to foreign countries exceed their payments to us in kind by $514,-602,333, and that since the value of our cotton exports exceeds this sum it is accurate to say that "our debts are paid in cotton."

Those who have studied the subject closely estimate that this annual balance in our favor of, say $500,000,000, is applied to the liquidation of the following debits:

Interest at five per cent in a principal of $4,000,000,000, being the normal value of American stocks, bonds, and other evidences of American debt held abroad____$200,000,000

*Theodore H. Price in the Outlook: New York, Sept. 9, 1914.

Spent in Europe annually by Americans
    resident or traveling abroad_____ 100,000,000
Remitted out of their earnings by Europeans
    resident in America_____ 100,000,000
Insurance and freights_____ 100,000,000
                                          ————————
                                        $500,000,000

These figures are, of course, conjectural, but it is evident that, if any of the items are underestimated, American indebtedness abroad unpaid must be increased by the amount of such underestimate, for our payments cannot exceed the net balance of trade in our favor, known and ascertained to be about $500,000,000 a year.

COTTON AND THE BALANCE OF TRADE

By means of the following table and calculations, Mr. Theodore Price attempts an arithmetical demonstration of the claim that cotton maintains a balance of trade in favor of the United States in its annual dealings with Europe.

UNITED STATES EXPORTS AND IMPORTS

Fiscal year ending June 30	Merchandise Imported	Merchandise Exported	Balance in favor U.S.	Value Gold and Silver Imported	Net Gold and Silver Exported	Total net balance in favor U.S.
1914	$1,893,925,657	$2,364,579,148	$ 470,653,491		$ 70,138,289	$ 540,791,780
1913	1,813,008,234	2,465,884,149	652,875,915		38,914,392	691,790,307
1912	1,653,264,934	2,204,322,409	551,057,475		26,232,294	577,289,769
1911	1,527,226,105	2,049,320,199	522,094,094	32,284,651		489,809,443
1910	1,556,947,430	1,744,984,720	188,037,290		85,292,977	273,330,367
Total	$8,444,372,360	$10,829,090,625	$2,384,718.265		$ 188,293,301	$2,573,011,666
Average	1,688,874,472	2,165,818,125	476,943,653	$ 32,284,651	37,658,660	514,602,333
Total value raw cotton exported						2,759,447,880
Average value raw cotton exported						551,889,576

*During the fiscal year ending June 30, 1911, total exports included the following classes of materials, the value of which was in excess of $50,000,000:

Cotton (Including manufactured cotton goods valued at $28,844,627)	$ 639,319,928
Wheat and wheat flour	142,407,631
Cattle, meat, and dairy products	132,926,979
Iron and steel—manufactures of	106,559,621
Copper—manufactures of	144,895,519
Oils	144,708,447
Tobacco and manufactures of	60,445,440
Wood manufactures—timber and lumber	66,953,878
Coal	59,921,013
TOTAL	$1,498,138,456

* Read Scherer's "Cotton as a World Power".

CHAPTER XXXVIII

WHY COTTON IS A BETTER BAROMETER THAN PIG-IRON

A college professor and a business man were recently talking about business cycles. The professor was purely theoretical and he was asking the business man why business could not foretell the coming of a depression by watching the pig-iron barometer. The business man replied that the machinery of statistics worked very slowly, and before they could be gathered and published they would be tardy. That is one of the reasons why cotton is a better barometer. It is reflected on the ticker from three important centers every minute of the day, and not only can the fingers be kept on the pulse of the present, but the future is always reliably predicted by such agencies as the futures market and the usually reliable forecasts promulgated by the Department of Agriculture. In cotton we have before us in dependable figures the past, present and future, but in pig-iron we have nothing to go by except the past, and then it is always too late.

Cotton has three pulse centers, one checking another—Liverpool, New York and New Orleans. It is on these great exchanges that cotton buyers and sellers concentrate their judgment on the future supply and demand, one in the center of the foreign markets, another in the world's financial center, and the third in the heart of the producing section. When the speculative markets are affected abnormally by manipultation or other reasons, the spot prices in the growing market may become the real gauge of cotton values.

Our production of iron during the first fifty years of the Nineteenth Century was comparatively an unimportant factor in the world's output, yet during all this time cotton was one of our principal products of domestic consumption and had become established as a recognized barometer of our trade conditions.

It is indisputable that natural conditions, such as crop failures or large surplus, affect business conditions. Therefore a commodity that will reflect natural conditions, as well as speculative conditions, is the best to watch. How can pig-iron production foretell crop conditions? It may reflect it, but it cannot foretell it. What the business man wants is a barometer that will guide him before events happen rather than after they have happened.

Cotton stands today in about the same relative importance that it did previous to the Civil War. At that time the Report on Commerce and Navigation for the year ending June 30, 1859, showed that of all products of the forest and of agriculture the North exported goods to the value of $45,305,541, as against $193,399,618 from the South, of which $161,434,923 must be set to the credit of cotton. Tested from the standpoint of national manufactures, regardless of exportation, cotton shows a similar striking importance. Its value as a manufactured product in 1860 was $115,681,774, as against $73,454,000 for wool, and an almost equal amount for forged, rolled, wrought, and cast iron taken together.

Cotton reflects both speculative and legitimate trade, and as long as speculation affects business, as it admittedly does, cotton will be the best barometer to go by for all purposes. There is no futures market in pig-iron, so that commodity cannot possibly foretell what is expected to happen, with any degree of accuracy. Cotton reflects agricultural conditions as well as manufacturing conditions. Adverse conditions at the cotton-goods mill will affect the price on the farm in a single day. Cotton was the first to indicate an approaching crash before the crises of 1819, 1825, 1837, 1847, 1857, 1873, 1893, 1907, 1914 and 1920. In each period, with the exception of 1837 and 1857, pig-iron trailed after the depression had well set in. The price of pig-iron is controlled artificially to a large extent.

Any commodity whose price and output can be largely controlled by a group of financiers sitting around a table cannot be a reliable barometer. Does it not stand to reason that those men will follow existing conditions rather than precede expected conditions? We did not hear much about iron output as a barometer of business until the organization of the United States Steel Corporation, and the propaganda then set in motion that it was the best barometer of business conditions has been a mighty good advertisement for Steel Corporation stock.

A chart of cotton fluctuations show how delicately cotton is affected by general conditions. In the good times preceding the New York financial panic of 1903 cotton was carried to a 17 cent basis, only to drop precipitately with the financial difficulties. What other general commodity could have been so quickly affected by a disturbance in the financial center? Take the situation in 1907, quoting Henry Clews: "The partial recovery in the stock market and the gradual return of confidence were coincident with and in the face of a rising market for cotton. There was an advance in middling cotton to 13½ cents a pound, the highest price on record for thirty-two years. Yet there was no dearth in the supply of cotton, and no sign of a corner, or the possibility of one, and we carried over into the new crop year, which began on the 1st of September, a visible supply of 1,200,000 bales of American cotton, making a world's supply of 2,300,000 bales, or nearly 540,000 more than at the same time last year."

According to the reports in the United States Department of Commerce, July, 1913: "The value of cotton exported during the fiscal year 1912 amounted to $565,849,271, or 26.1 per cent of the total value of all articles of domestic merchandise exported during the year. It exceeded the amounts for iron and steel manufactures, meat and dairy products, and breadstuffs combined, these three groups ranking next in importance among articles exported. These large exports, combined with the more than five million bales consumed in domestic manufacture, strikingly indicate the importance of cotton in the economic affairs of the nation."

The first signs of the depression of 1920 came with the closing of the cotton textile mills in New England. Following this came a severe slump in the raw cotton market. Cotton led the way in the downward movement all through the depression, and thousands of business men who followed the course of pig-iron will attest that had they followed cotton they could have saved great sums of money.

The production of pig-iron carried far over into the depression of 1920 because of previous contracts for domestic and export demand. It is true that when construction gets under way, using the product of the furnaces, it involves the purchase of other supplies and equipment, but by that time prosperity is already upon us and everybody knows it. What business men require is an industry that will indicate ahead the trend of conditions so they can prepare for them and take advantage of that knowledge. A great many of the best business men refused to believe that a depression of serious proportions was ahead because pig-iron was keeping up both in price and in output. When it was thought that the depression had run its course and clamor had started to get things on an upward turn an agitation against the high steel prices swept the country. Business men and economists everywhere pointed out that everything else had declined, many commodities had gone to normal, but steel prices, remaining high, was holding business back. Cotton had come to be a pre-war basis before the first cut in steel prices, although pig-iron had begun to decline slightly in both prices and output. Again in 1921 cotton led the way up, followed by other commodities.

Another point of importance is the large proportion of exports of cotton, an average of over 60 per cent, which is of itself a reflector. Our iron and steel exports are so insignificant in proportion that they can not possibly reflect foreign conditions and therefore we must find a barometer that will reflect all conditions—present, future, natural and foreign. What will do it better than cotton?

Those who are earnest in believing that pig-iron production is the best barometer point out that practically all production depends upon iron, and that it is used in almost everything we do, in the machinery that makes our food and our clothing, in the construction of houses and shelters, in our transportation, and in every element of human endeavor. Although all this is true, yet we must realize that iron and its products will keep; it does not wear out daily like clothing or be soon consumed like food. The business of making it can halt for a period, but the products of cotton absolutely must be replaced. Iron and steel are not bought from day to day as an ordinary commodity of business. It is well known that by far the larger portion of the output goes into construction, and it is also well known that big construction enterprises are organized, planned, and financed at the end of the depression when prices are low. Contracts are then made for the delivery of iron or steel to be used in this construction at the prevailing low prices. Then, as soon as construction starts, labor is given employment, money is spent, and we think we are having prosperity. These enormous orders given by large contractors and institutions enable the mills to run on fair capacity. Then when the smaller buyers come into the market, thinking they see prosperity ahead, they are forced to pay the prices that prevail on a rising market. Steel companies may be turning out orders the same day which range in price as much as 50 per cent.

CHAPTER XXXIX

INDICATIONS OF APPROACHING DEPRESSION

Anyone who would attempt to give a formula to foretell the exact arrival of a trade depression would be foolish indeed. However, experience is a great teacher, and we can gain a fair idea of what to expect in the future from the lessons of the past. The average depression runs in more or less disastrous form for three years, followed by three years on the up-grade, then three years of over-expansion and speculation. This theory is not original. It is the sum total of the deductions arrived at by all economists. Whoever would bank on it might win, and again he might have occasion to curse the professional economists. The records of agriculture show that it also follows along this line. For a few years planting increases and greater prosperity results in a greater consumption, until finally the agricultural output increases beyond the demand of the consumers. As soon as this point has been reached, and a year of large carry-over is faced, prices decline sharply, bringing its blight to the farmer who get low prices for his over-production. He is usually in debt and unable to buy when depressions come. If there are any two features that coincide through the history of depressions it is that the cycle of agricultural depression coincides in point of time with the period of business depression and vice versa. In this country agriculture is dependent upon business and business upon agriculture. It is almost impossible that during severe reaction one could be at all prosperous without the other.

The peculiarity is that business has been known to blame agriculture for its vicissitudes, and agriculture invariably decries business for its difficulties. The fact is they are both friends in need and should be friends indeed. Agriculture blames business for sudden declines in price and a ruinous market, and business blames agriculture for its greed, for over-production and for demand for high prices.

If our "foresight was as good as our hindsight" there would be no such thing as depressions. But even so, careful perusal of existing facts, together with fair judgment, can go a long way toward keeping the individual from being enmeshed in the crises and setbacks that come from time to time.

High interest rates are always an indication of trouble ahead, because it means scarcity of money. As bank reserves are depleted the banks are necessarily less able to make loans, and for what loans they do make they exact high rates. It is also a certainty that the man who borrows money on high interest rates is either doing so on flimsy securities or is forced to do so by exigencies. In either case there is underlying unsoundness. At this point the business man or investor should begin to delve carefully into statistics, particularly obtaining such newspapers and periodicals as will give him dependable information regarding bank reserves, discount rates, trend of stocks, and crop and marketing conditions pertaining to such commodities as cotton, wheat, etc.

That 1873 would bring a serious depression, if not a financial crisis, should easily have been foretold. In October, 1872, there was a deficiency of more than $1,000,000 in the bank reserve of New York city. This alone spelled trouble ahead, unless prompt and sound measures were taken to remedy the situation. It is true the bank reserves in a particular locality may sometimes be low without underlying conditions being bad generally, but with low bank reserves in the leading financial centers, coupled with speculation, crop failures or numerous other conditions, the situation is ominous.

Previous to the panic of 1907 financial reports indicated unsound conditions. Interest on time loans had risen from 6 to 7 per cent, and banks and trust companies had extended their loans until their reserves were depleted below the legal minimum required. By watching such a barometer closely the average investor would have an opportunity to exercise caution, because it was apparent that the normal limits of safety were being ignored. However, this crisis was unlike most previous crises because of its suddenness, and it would be a most extreme pessimist who would lose faith in the country as a whole when things were going along smoothly and general conditions looked as rosy as they did in 1907. In fact, there is little question but what this panic was criminally induced. It was brought on by financial transactions that year not entirely within the law. The solvency of banks in general could not be questioned, because the average dividends paid by national banks had increased in seven years from 3.94 per cent to 11.8 per cent in 1907. The crash came in October with the exposure of personal speculation on the part of officers of several financial institutions and industrial corporations. It was at the time of great crop movement, when a surplus of money is sent to the interior, and at this particular time New York banks were in no position to meet demand payments in cash. Had these speculations been unearthed at a different time probably the panic would have been averted, but the special strain upon reserve cities at that time was more than they could stand. The banks of England and Germany raised their discount rate, and the extraordinary demand for money forced the rate of interest on call loans 40 or 50 per cent, and in some instances 125 per cent was paid for money in order to save the borrower from entire ruin.

Professor Johnson, writing in the *Political Science Quarterly*, says: "Crises are doubtless inevitable, for the conditions leading up to them could be prevented only by a more than human combination of sagacity and discretion. Panics, however, are unnecessary; they are almost invariably the products of remediable defects of the credit system."

During periods of prosperity the prices of stocks and

commodities tend to rise higher and higher, "so that if an investor buys at the beginning of such a period the chances are that the market value of his principal will increase as well as the rate of return upon his invested capital. On the other hand, if he buys near the end of such a period he is doomed to disappointment. For these periods of prosperity, owing to the delicate nature of our credit system, terminate with startling suddenness by a precipitous decline in the market value of securities, by a shrinkage in the volume of industry and business, and by a curtailment of profits and dividends."

In late years crop reports of the United States Department of Agriculture have exerted a widening influence on financial matters. Close study is made as to crop conditions as a barometer of those conditions. It is well known that poor crops in a given section affect the amount of railroad traffic. Rich crops mean heavy freight traffic with large earnings for the railroads.

It may be taken as a certainty that contraction of credit and depression will sooner or later follow an exorbitant rise in the price of commodities and property, extremely high wages, extravagance, and wild speculation. It stands to reason that a halt must come in this direction.

Babson gives twelve subjects as barometers which indicate the tendency of business:

"1. Building and Real Estate: Including all New Building and Fire Losses.

2. Business Failure: Failures, by number, amount and percentage.

3. Bank Clearings: Total Bank Clearings; Bank Clearings excluding New York.

4. Labor Conditions: Immigration and Emigration Figures.

5. Money Conditions: Money in Circulation; Comptroller's Reports; Loans of the Banks; Cash Held by the Banks; Deposits of the Banks; Surplus Reserve of Banks.

6. Foreign Trade: Imports; Exports, Balance of Trade.

7. Gold Movements: Gold Exports and Imports; Domestic and Foreign Exchange and Money Rates.

8. Commodity Prices: Foreign and Domestic Commodity Prices; Production of Gold.

9. Investment Market: Stock Exchange Transactions and Security Prices; New Securities; New Corporations Formed.

10. Condition of Crops: Crop Conditions and Other Commodity Production.

11. Railroad Earnings: Gross and Net Earnings; Idle Car Figures.

12. Social Conditions: Labor Troubles and Political Factors."

During the years 1897 to 1907 the deposits in national banks increased from $1,669,000,000 to $5,256,000,000, while the cash reserve increased from $420,281,000 to $701,000,-000, indicating that the ratio of cash holding to loans in 1897 amounted to 22 per cent, whereas in 1907 the ratio had fallen to 16 per cent. These figures were convincing evidence of a slump immediately ahead.

Watch the aggregate percentage of bank capitalization, capital and surplus, to the amount of customers' accounts sold. While liquidation is going on the ratio will be brought up, but when expansion starts in the ratio will be carried down, and when down too low it is an absolute certainty that contraction is ahead, which in highly speculative periods is sure to mean depression. Of course, these periods are sometimes tided over or postponed by artificial means, but when that is in evidence it is all the more reason to be certain that a day of reckoning must come.

CHAPTER XL

INDICATIONS POINTING TO THE END OF
DEPRESSIONS

Statistics will begin to point out returning good times after the depression has run its course, but caution must be exercised, because it is a peculiarity of all depressions that there have been flurries of improvement which some took for a permanent upturn only to be followed by a setback. This has been noted in each depression and these false starts are often misleading. In 1921, September and October showed quite a spurt in cotton, followed by pig-iron production, the two best barometers. Then cotton declined, and iron production likewise. Foreign trade also fell off after the upward movement.

After the depression has run its course for a while, bright spots are found here and there where conditions look good, and sometimes business men decieve themselves by thinking the country in general is coming back to prosperity at once, only to find that it was premature. Real prosperity must be general. Whoever fails to look beyond his immediate locality may find himself facing losses. By watching the reports of the Federal Reserve Board and statistics in the financial papers and periodicals, noting carefully to what extent bank loans have shrunk, reserve ratios have arisen, and discount rates declined, one may get a fair idea of coming events. If these conditions are favorable more than likely it is only a question of time until an upward trend is sure to start.

Investors and business men should not go ahead until liquidation has been completed. It is almost a certainty that a depression will run two years at least, and most likely three, with a gradual improvement setting in at the end of the second year. The average depressions of the past bear out this statement.   Indications of improvement are shown in increased bank clearings, decreased failures, decreased unemployment, increased bank loans, higher commodity prices, steadying foreign exchange, reduction in idle freight cars, increased railroad earnings, increased building activity, etc.   Not any one of these may be taken as a sure indication, but the group as a whole is certain to indicate an upward movement.   A great many shrewd business men go almost entirely on increased bank loans and discounts.   During the depressions reserves accumulate, and when conditions become stabilized bankers begin to want to let that money out so as to earn.   Then credit expansion starts. These business men often disregard all other conditions on the theory that if tremendous sums of money are being loaned by the banks, it is going to get into circulation, and then is the time to start preparations to get their part of it. In the manufacture of commodities, particularly, that is a pretty good barometer to follow.

Certainly no two business cycles run exactly the same courses.   We cannot benefit from an analysis of previous revivals as much as from previous depressions.   If anything, it is harder to foretell the exact coming of the revival than the depression.   We know that certain conditions are bound to bring depression.   Just how soon it is going to break is the only thing we have to guess at.   But with revivals, unforeseen events and conditions blind us to the future.   Where we have artificially stimulated prosperity it has been shortlived, as in the case of 1890, when an inflated currency helped for a while, but resulted in a worse panic and depression in 1893.   Stimulated revivals have been cut short because they were unsound.   The leaders of business and finance were unwilling to underwrite prosperity founded on such a basis.

When better conditions start a feeling of confidence spreads rapidly.   Salesmen come in from the road with increased orders, instead of cancellations.   Manufacturers and transportation companies employ more men.   Sometimes it starts slow and there is a gradual upward movement, and again it comes with a rush. A long series of failures come with depression and stringent money. These failures not only cause loss to their owners and stockholders, but to their creditors, and must be written off and forgotten. In the meantime, the bankers' policy of contracting credits and liquidating loans has built up a higher reserve ratio, enabling them under more favorable conditions to provide credit at favorable rates of interest.

A bank's deposits cannot by any means be taken as a criterion of their conditions or of affairs in general. Of course, healthy deposits are a sign of activity, but many times deposits are in excess of what a bank should carry for its surplus and also a large amount of so-called deposits are credit accounts sold by the banks to their customers. These are mere book credits and not actual credits.

Very often investors and business men figure out that the harvesting of fall crops, the turn of the year, the coming of spring, the enactment of certain laws, or various foreign conditions would mean the return of prosperity and put out their money accordingly, only to suffer loss because their guess was wrong. If they had looked more into statistical facts they would probably have found that underlying conditions were not right for a permanent upward tendency, because business was not entirely readjusted and there had not been sufficient liquidation.

In times of depression banks scrutinize their loans carefully, many times making only such as they can rediscount with the Federal Reserve Banks and then squeezing them all possible. They are also liquidating their old loans, and as a revival of business depends upon easier credit, it is necessary to examine closely the loan and discount figures of financial institutions of the country. When the old loans have been well liquidated then the banks are more willing to extend further credit. In other words, when the business man pays one loan under difficulties the banker has confidence and is willing to make further loans.

Expansion of credit increases deposits. For instance, a manufacturer may go to his bank to borrow $100,000; even though he might have the best kind of collateral, he could not get the loan unless he carried sufficient balance to justify it. Commercial loans are based on balances at a ratio of 20 per cent; therefore a banker loaning $100,000 only puts out $80,000, because he already has $20,000 of the borrower's money on deposit and usually the loan is not all used at one time, more or less of it being left on deposit, checks against it sometimes being days and weeks before being debited on the books of the banks. Some banks admit that as much as 30 per cent of the amount of their loans is left on deposit to be reloaned. Borrowers who do not carry sufficient bank balances are forced to go to investment companies who charge commissions for making the loan. The point is, the deposits item in a bank statement carries little meaning.

It is not wise to watch the reserves of an individual ban¹ or an individual locality. Of course, no individual bank can reflect general conditions any more than could any individual locality. Further, reserves are always low during crop moving season because of the drain on the banks for money to take care of the harvest needs, particularly in the west and south.

Statistics tend to show that depressions average one about every nine years, but the crisis does not last more than one year, as a rule, and business seldom remains below normal for more than two years, although good times may not set in for three years. But to say that there is any certainty to cyclical periods would be ridiculous on the face of it. They all come about under different conditions, they last for different periods and are different in their degrees of severity.

Rising prices, although not always infallible, are a good barometer of returning good times. When prices start upward on account of less production or increased demand, merchants and manufacturers have a tendency to place future orders or larger ones. Prices then stiffen under the influence of recuperating demand, making what is called a firm market. Manufacturers will make stock ahead on a strong market, bankers will loan more liberally, buyers will place orders, feeling that goods are going higher, thus confidence increases among all classes. Investors are more liberal in buying stocks, which in turn strengthens these stocks, construction of all kinds starts up and a general revival is on.

Our modern system of corporations, with large amounts of fixed capital, will automatically act to check the seriousness of depressions in the future. The time was when business was conducted by individuals or firms, and the individual himself, was mostly affected by industrial depressions. It was then a comparatively easy matter for a firm or individual to withdraw its capital or such portion as it could, and liquidate. Business unorganized was helpless, but under present methods of fixed capital liquidation is both ruinous and undesirable. Therefore business, as a whole, by force of necessity, must get back of the situation. A modern corporation usually remains in business indefinitely and must pay dividends. They must then use every resource of their management and board of directors to keep the wheels of industry going, reducing costs if necessary, creating demand by advertising, and generally helping to pull trade out of depression.

The Department of Commerce at present is very progressive and efficient in gathering statistics of the greatest value as a guide to business conditions. A great many private corporations now have statistical departments through which they gather all the data pertaining to their own and allied industries. They have at their finger tips the entire history of their trade so that they can foretell fairly well in advance what to expect. Our governmental departments should devise a plan of issuing brief and concise bulletins for the average business man who may, through them, keep posted in advance regarding the different barometers that indicate the business future. In the past this information has been too largely placed in the hands of "financial insiders" who have been able to use it for their own profit.

The biggest single factor in the return of prosperity is the return of confidence. During every depression there is a contraction of credit and mounting reserves which, in itself, is the very basis of confidence. Then with natural and political conditions right—good crops, peace and sound administration—prosperity is soon upon us.

CHAPTER XLI

SUPPLY AND DEMAND

The archaic law of supply and demand does not have as full bearing on cycles of depression as is generally supposed. There is no scientific reason why over-production should cause depression, nor that under-production or moderate crop failure should cause depression. In referring to what is known as crop failure, let us not forget that we have never had a complete crop failure in the United States.* Time and again we have over-produced and carried our surplus in orderly fashion. This pertains to both manufactured and agricultural products. Following over-production agriculture curtails and should be able to do so without disturbing the economic fabric. Manufacturing should and does ease off, not by throwing great numbers of men out of employment, but by decreased hours or shorter working weeks. We do this constantly in normal times in various industries. If the buying power keeps up curtailment for a short time regulates the production. Over-production has been wrongly accused by theorists of cutting capers in financial deviltry, but the word "over-production" has been much misused, because statistics repeatedly prove that we have over-produced many times without resulting depression. Furthermore, it is a rare occurrence when industries and agriculture over-produce at the same time. It is apparent, then, to any student of economics that over-production can be curtailed in such lines as it affects without undermining the financial structure. The word "over-expansion" is more descriptive, the extravagant use of the wealth at hand being the basis of the evil. So much for supply, whether long or short.

---

*See Tables on page 416.

Supply and demand, like salt and pepper, are old affinities, and like man and wife they sometimes do not get along. Of the twain demand is the most troublesome. In creating supply it is only natural that business take into consideration the demand, but supply is many cases, such as with crop failure, is in the hand of God. Over-production is, ordinarily, in control of man. In production, therefore, business has in sight certain demand. When eventualities arise to lessen that demand then comes trouble. It is surprising almost beyond belief, when one takes the statistics of production both in agriculture and manufacture, to find how evenly the figures run. Many times in years of depression we blame over-production when we have not over-produced but have slackened our demand; a decreased buying power brought about through contraction or lack of circulating medium or through a deliberate refusal to buy on the part of the public.

The disaster that sweeps the country in periodic cycles is a punishment for our misdoings and a reminder that prosperity when abused must bring reaction.

The central buffer which receives the ultimate shocks and adjusts the balances is finance, and it depends upon the soundness of finance when the strain comes whether the law of supply and demand can go its natural course or become entangled in the meshes of speculation, war, inflated currency and other direct causes of depression. At best, supply and demand cannot be more than a slight contributing cause to depression.

Business men may also be misled in assuming that demand means consumption. There is a vast difference in the two. We saw a very forceful instance of that recently, preceding the depression of 1920. The stereotyped talk of every salesman was "under-production, lack of goods, high prices." Buyers were led to believe that a shortage existed in every line, and because of that prices would go higher. Counting orders on file as demand, it is true that the demand existed, but that was very different than if the goods had passed into consumption.   When we woke up with the depression upon us we found that rather than short stocks and under-production we had really over-stocked.   Our splendid army of salesmen had presumably without knowledge aforehand, created a fictitious demand.   That was only natural.   It is the old story of boom times.   It is easy to stretch our imagination when things look rosy.   We must not be placed in a class of "easy marks" when we believe the under-production propaganda that appears in boom times.

So-called gluts do not necessarily mean over-production, but may mean faulty distribution.   Gluts do not frighten manufacturers or merchants.   These are ordinary occurrences affecting one commodity and then another, which again proves that over-supply is not necessarily a cause for depressions of any consequence.   We need some new words in the English language, and they should be terms specifically describing degrees of stringency or shortage, as well as degrees of glut or plethora.   Either descriptive word may mean a lot, on one hand or the other.   That is to say, there may be a slight shortage or a great shortage, or a medium shortage; likewise a small glut, a medium glut or a large glut.

George Binney Dibblee, of Oxford, writing in 1912, described such a thing as a depression being brought about as the result of a deadlock between buyer and seller.   Through search of records up to Dibblee's time I have not found an example of the case in question, nor does Dibblee mention one, because he was writing theoretically.   However, our depression of 1920 gives us as near an example of this condition as we shall probably ever have.   Here in America we found the seller stubbornly holding out for a certain level of prices, and the buyer equally as stubborn in his determination to buy for less, this situation eventuating into a complete general depression.   This does not mean that the recent depression may be attributable wholly to the buyers' strike, but it enters as a forceful factor and illustrates clearly that such a thing as Dibblee describes is possible.

AVERAGE YIELD OF CORN

America is the one important country in the history of the world that has never had a famine nor even a serious crop failure. Corn is a good example, being a universal crop, and produced in every state in the union. This table shows how even the figures run. In some instances as much as 25 per cent decrease in shown, but that denotes decreased acreage following over-production as often as decreased yield.

Year.	Acreage (000 omitted).	Average yield per acre.	Production (000 omitted).	Average farm price per bushel Dec. 1.	Farm value Dec. 1 (000 omitted).	Year.	Acreage (000 omitted).	Average yield per acre.	Production (000 omitted).	Average farm price per bushel Dec. 1.	Farm value Dec. 1 (000 omitted).
	Acres.	Bush	Bushels.	Cents.	Dollars.		Acres.	Bush	Bushels.	Cents.	Dollars.
1849	-------	----	**592,071**	-----	--------	1892	70,627	23.1	1,628,464	39.4	642,147
1859	-------	----	**838,793**	-----	--------	1893	72,036	22.5	1,619,496	36.5	591,626
1866	34,307	25.3	867,946	47.4	411,451	1894	62,582	19.4	1,212,770	45.7	554,719
1867	32,520	23.6	768,320	57.0	437,770	1895	82,076	26.2	2,151,139	25.3	544,986
1868	34,887	26.0	906,527	46.8	424,057	1896	81,027	28.2	2,283,875	21.5	491,007
1869	37,103	23.6	874,320	59.8	522,551	1897	80,095	23.8	1,902,968	26.3	501,073
1869	-------	----	**760,945**	-----	--------	1898	77,722	24.8	1,924,185	28.7	552,023
						1899	82,109	25.3	2,078,144	30.3	629,210
1870	38,647	28.3	1,094,255	49.4	540,520	**1899**	**94,914**	**28.1**	**2,666,324**	-----	--------
1871	34,091	29.1	991,898	43.4	430,356						
1872	35,527	30.8	1,092,719	35.3	385,736	1900	83,321	25.3	2,105,103	35.7	751,220
1873	39,197	23.8	932,274	44.2	411,961	1901	91,350	16.7	1,522,520	60.5	921,556
1874	41,037	20.7	850,148	58.4	496,271	1902	94,044	26.8	2,523,648	40.3	1,017,017
						1903	88,092	25.5	2,244,177	42.5	952,869
1875	44,841	29.5	1,321,069	36.7	484,675	1904	92,232	26.8	2,467,481	44.1	1,087,461
1876	49,033	26.2	1,283,828	34.0	436,109						
1877	50,369	26.7	1,342,558	34.8	467,635	1905	94,011	28.8	2,707,994	41.2	1,116,697
1878	51,585	26.9	1,388,219	31.7	440,281	1906	96,738	30.3	2,927,416	39.9	1,166,626
1879	53,085	29.2	1,547,902	37.5	580,486	1907	99,931	25.9	2,592,320	51.6	1,336,901
1879	**62,369**	**28.1**	**1,754,592**	-----	--------	1908	101,788	26.2	2,668,651	60.6	1,616,145
						1909	108,771	25.5	2,772,376	-----	--------
1880	62,318	27.6	1,717,435	39.6	679,714	**1909**	**98,383**	**25.9**	**2,552,190**	57.9	1,477,222
1881	64,262	18.6	1,194,916	63.6	759,482						
1882	65,660	24.6	1,617,025	48.5	783,867	1910	104,035	27.7	2,886,260	48.0	1,384,817
1883	68,302	22.7	1,551,067	42.4	658,051	1911	105,825	23.9	2,531,488	61.8	1,565,258
1884	69,684	25.8	1,795,528	35.7	640,736	1912	107,083	29.2	3,124,746	48.7	1,520,454
						1913	105,820	23.1	2,446,988	69.1	1,692,092
1885	73,130	26.5	1,936,176	32.8	635,675	1914	103,435	25.8	2,672,804	64.4	1,722,070
1886	75,694	22.0	1,665,441	36.6	610,311						
1887	72,393	20.1	1,456,161	44.4	646,107	1915	106,197	28.2	2,994,793	57.5	1,722,680
1888	75,673	26.3	1,987,790	34.1	677,562	1916	105,296	24.4	2,566,927	88.9	2,280,729
1889	78,320	27.0	2,112,892	28.3	597,919	1917	116,730	26.3	3,065,233	127.9	3,920,228
1889	**72,088**	**29.4**	**2,122,328**	-----	--------	1918	104,467	24.0	2,502,665	136.5	3,416,240
						1919	100,072	28.6	2,858,509	134.7	3,851,741
1890	71,971	20.7	1,489,970	50.6	754,433	1920	104,601	30.9	3,232,367	67.7	2,189,721
1891	76,205	27.0	2,060,154	40.6	836,439						

NOTE.—Figures in **bold** are census returns; figures in roman are estimates of the Department of Agriculture. Estimates of acres are obtained by applying estimated percentages of increase or decrease to the published acreage of the preceding year, except that a revised base is used for applying percentage estimates whenever new census data are available.

Let it be remembered that "trade crisis" and "financial crisis" are not the same. We sometimes have one without the other, although they both bring about business depressions.

Abundance of money, whether gold or unconvertible paper, means at any level of prices a greater demand for goods, regardless of supply. We witnessed this condition in 1919, when sugar reached as high as twenty-five cents a pound wholesale in the face of unprecedented production. It is true that strong propaganda was carried on preaching that a shortage existed, but large buyers knew there was an ample supply. They bought in the face of it, realizing the tremendous demand and anticipating it would go higher, or that they could work it off before the next crop. Many other commodities maintained high prices in the face of abundant supply because of ample money and inflated credits, but in direct controversy to the ancient and generally accepted law of supply and demand.

CHAPTER XLII

PROFITEERING

Probably for the first time in our history profiteering enters in as a primary cause of depression. In our early periods profiteering in western lands and real estate values was practiced, although the word "speculation" might be more descriptive.

During the late war a wholesale grocery concern had a case instituted against it by the Department of Justice for profiteering dismissed on the ground that there was no such word in the dictionary as "profiteering." Another case of technicality in the law. In their next issue, Mr. Webster's successors will probably define *profiteer* as "one who takes advantage to make excessive profits; one who sells at a price beyond reason."

In the early years of the First Century the people of Rome raised such a complaint against the high price of corn that Tiberius fixed the retail price. During a period of scarcity the mob attacked Claudius (41-54 A. D.) and threw bread at him. To avoid a recurrence of this indignity, Claudius adopted every means to insure the continuous importation of food throughout the winter months, and even agreed to indemnify corn merchants who suffered loss by storm.

In the Middle Ages, to the Jewish money lenders fell most of the scorn against profiteers. In those days money was bartered as a commodity because there were few, if any, banks and interest rates were sometimes extortionate. St. Louis of France published an ordinance relative to the Jews, the predecessors of the Lombards in his dominions, whereby "for the salvation of his own soul, and those of his ancestors, he releases to all Christians a third part of what was owing by them to the Jews." Louis at the same time took to himself a percentage of what he saved the people.

Another historical record of profiteering is found in the
Mediaeval Ages, when the Guild movement swept over
Europe. In those times the Guilds sought to regulate prices
on their output, each Guild member being a small manufacturer on his own account. Penalties of unbelievable severity
were placed upon any members who sold below a certain
price, and regulations were often made restricting the output. Most of these regulations were soon given up because
they defeated their own object. When the price was set too
high, as one historian puts it, "the people suffered less by
going without than by paying the high prices." Here probably was the first buyers' strike in retaliation for profiteering. And profiteering destroyed the Guilds; they raised
prices so high that in 1437 dissatisfaction became widespread, attracting the attention of Parliament, and an act
was passed prohibiting the making of rules and prices unless
submitted to the Justice of the Peace for record.

The preamble of an act of Henry VI's reign recites that:
"Masters, wardens and people of guilds, fraternities and
other companies corporate, dwelling in diverse parts of the
realm oft-times by color of rule and goverance and other
terms in general words to the granted and confirmed by
charters and letters patent, of diverse kings, made among
themselves many unlawful and unreasonable ordinances, as
well as in prices of wares and other things for their own
singular profit and to the common hurt and damage of the
people."

Even in our war of the Revolution, when Washington's
soldiers were bleeding at Valley Forge, the profiteer got in
his despicable work. After seeking to punish by fine and
imprisonment persons who should advance the price of commodities, the different colonies began to hold price conventions and to attempt to fix prices of labor and of commoi-
dities.

The first instance of a "buyers' strike" against profiteers
in our country outside of the "Boston Tea Party," if that
might be called one, was just preceding the depression of

1837, when popular meetings were held in New York for
the purpose of protesting against the high prices of provisions and the undue inflation of bank credits. One of these
meetings, on February 14th, became riotous, a flour ware-
house was gutted, and the military were called out to preserve order.

De Tocqueville, a foreigner visiting America in 1873, described us thusly: "An American clings to the world's
goods as if he were certain never to die, and he is so hasty
and grasping for all within his reach that one would suppose that he was constantly afraid of not living long enough
to enjoy them."

Those Americans who travel know that this is our reputation most everywhere today.   We are known as money-
worshippers, and that we get all we can, without limit.

There is no way by which prices can be raised without
its effect upon those who do it. One raise brings on another as the commodity and the money it brings goes through
the channels of trade, and as we exchange our money so
rapidly in this country it soon comes back to us in the form
of increased prices on what we spend our money for. Again,
an orgy of profiteering is bound to come back on us because
it requires more capital to do business on. It increases the
risk, less service is rendered, and a let-up must follow because the currency is strained to take care of the volume of
business transacted at high prices, whereas we could do the
same volume with a greater turnover and equal profits resulting from the same amount of capital involved. In some
respects corporations are made the "goats" in regard to
profiteering. The corporation which earns 15 or 20 per
cent on its capital is stigmatized and the public takes it for
granted that such a corporation has underpaid its working
men and charged exorbitant prices for its product. But
the public forgets that it is necessary to put by a surplus
fund to take care of its preferred stock in times of depression. And that at the same time laws are being constantly
passed, state and federal, holding them to be the legitimate

prey of the tax gatherer.   On the other hand, the individual
would not think of giving his investment and time to make
such a small profit.   The big earnings of a single business
man may be entirely due to the wisdom and efficiency of his
management, yet the corporation which may serve as well
and often cheaper is condemned.   It is not the object here
to defend the profiteering corporation.   The profiteer of
every class is to be proscribed.   His practices are against
public interests and should be condemned, because unless
he is checked reaction against him will always follow
through buyers' strikes.   But when we consider the profiteer, let us not always look for him in high places, because
more often he will be found among the small shop keepers
and the every day individual who is conducting a personal
business.

The profiteer plays havoc in easy times, but he will
eventually hang himself unless he has a monopoly.   Huge
profits on an individual sale do not necessarily mean eventual success, but rather in competitive lines more often spells
failure.   We Americans have a world-wide reputation of
lacking one quality in our national character, and that is
thrift.   As a rule, as smart as we think we are, very often
our resourcefulness is limited to the performance of raising
prices.   The country swarms with a motley outfit known as
"cost experts" who range over the nation preaching higher
prices, based on a cost system which they sell for a price,
and which invariably leads to price raising.   Of course,
their stock in trade, in order to sell their system, is more
profits for their customer.   But it is indisputably proved that
the man who makes the outstanding success in business is
the one who serves the public at less cost than others.   A
great many so-called cost systems lead to profiteering, which
the public resents, and thus the demand for the commodity
in question is lessened.   What a demand there would be for
cost experts who would show us how to profitably lower
prices rather than how to raise them!

The most phenomenal business successes of our day and

generation have been those men who got rich by selling cheaper than anybody else, making their money on the volume and not the individual sale, as in the instances of Henry Ford, F. W. Woolworth, the ten-cent store man, B. H. Kroger, owner of 2,500 grocery stores, and others. In recent years profiteers have used the labor unions in milching the public. For instance, the photo engravers entered into a contract with the Photo Engravers Union whereby a certain wage scale and working conditions were to be agreed upon, provided the union would refuse to work for any concern not charging a given scale of prices. The bait thrown to the union was a higher wage than they even demanded . In other words, exorbitant prices were charged the public and a small portion of the loot thrown to the union. The result was immediate decrease in use of engravings on the part of the publishers, advertisers and others, and the engravers felt the depression of 1920 before it began to be felt in most other lines of business. Thus profiteering cut off the use of their commodity except in absolute necessity.

We think we have advanced in our civilization and our ethics, but let us go back to 1632, where we will find the identical conditions and the same practices that exist today :*

"The kings most excellent Majestie, taking into Consideracion the manifold evil Practizes which for private gaine are too often put in use as well by Cornmasters and Hoorders of Corne as by Marchants and others to in (sic) Inhance the Prices of Corne and graine to the generall prejudice of all other his Majesties subjects, especially laboring men and those of the Poorer sorte which hath appeared not onely in the time of the late darth, but in the yere now past when, by the goodness of God, there was such plentie & abundance of Corne as seldome hath byn greater and yet the rates & prises of Corne in maine parts of this Kigdome, especially in the Cittie of London and the parts neere ad-

---

* Quoted by Gras—"Evolution of the English Corn Market."

joyning, wer kept up a farre higher prices then was fitt to
be in a time of so great and generall plentie. And that how-
soever by the Provident and Constant Care of his Majestie
parts of his Privie Councell transport (a) con of Corne was
restrained even in the plentiful yere yet in mainie parts
of the kindome false Rumors were and are spred and de-
vulged of great Transportacon of Corne lycensed and au-
throsed to the great dishonour of his Majestie and the State
and of a wicked purpose to keep Corne and garine at moderate Prices His Majestie with the advice of his Privie
Councell doth hereby publishe and declare That all said
Rumors were false . . ."

Similar practices are in vogue to this very day!

In Russia where the peasant's mind is not much given to
reason, when profiteering is practiced against him, "his
remedy is to kill the nearest Jew."

Various remedies have been proposed to curb the practice.
The best lawyers say there is no way under present
laws to prosecute profiteers, and that it is going to be extremely hard to enact laws that will be constitutional. However, a way is sure to be found, as a way has always been
found to regulate industry when it affects public interests.
The recent profiteering laws passed in the District of Columbia, New York and other states, have been upheld, and if
rent profiteers can be controlled it is a certainty that prices
of other necessities of life can be controlled. Unless it is
done profiteering is going to enter more and more into the
causes of future depressions. Buyers' strikes are a flareback
from profiteering and our experience has already taught us
all we need to know about the economic consequences of
them. When the manufacturer and merchant is reproached
for profiteering they immediately accuse labor of profiteering equally as much. But neither can afford to be accused of profiteering. Labor leaders have only to put their
ear to the ground to find out if the public is with them. The
labor movement cannot make headway against public opinion. Labor leaders may win conflicts occasionally without

it, but later they will lose all they have gained. While public opinion is with them they make permanent and substantial headway, and no cry is made of the labor profiteer.

The growing tendency to profiteer, unless curbed, is going to have the menace of depression ever hanging over us. Moderation in profits during prosperity will prolong those periods but wildly exhorbitant prices are bound to bring reaction.

CHAPTER XLIII

REPORT OF THE PRESIDENT'S UNEMPLOYMENT CONFERENCE

SEPTEMBER 26—OCTOBER 13, 1921, WASHINGTON, D. C.

. DIRECTORY OF MEMBERSHIP

John B. Andrews, Executive Secretary American Association for Labor Legislation, 131 East Twenty-third Street, New York City—Member Economic Advisory Committee and Executive Secretary Committee on Public Hearings.

Winslow B. Ayer, President Eastern & Western Lumber Company, Front and Twenty-first Streets, Portland, Ore.—Committee on Constructions.

Charles M. Babcock, Highway Commissioner of Minnesota, 920 Guardian Life Building, St. Paul, Minn.—Committee on Public Works.

Julius H. Barnes, President U. S. Food Administration Grain Corporation, 1917 to 1919; U. S. Wheat Director; Chairman Institute for Public Service, 42 Broadway, New York City—Committee on Organization, Room 713; Chairman Committee on Employment Agencies and Registration, Committee on Civic Emergency Measures, Committee on Foreign Trade.

George E. Barnett, Professor of Statistics, John Hopkins University, 827 Park Avenue, Baltimore—Economic Advisory Committee.

Ernest S. Bradford, Statistician, Argyll Avenue, New Rochelle, N. Y.—Economic Advisory Committee.

Wm. S. Brown, President National Marine Engineers Association, 313 Machinists Building, Washington—Committee on Shipping.

W. L. Burdick, North Dakota Agriculturist—Committee on Statistics, Committee on Agriculture.

Bailey B. Burritt, Executive Secretary Association for Improving the Condition of the Poor, 105 East Twenty-second Street, New York City—Economic Advisory Committee.

William M. Butler, President Butler Mills, New Bedford Cotton Mills, Hoosac Cotton Mills, 77 Franklin Street, Boston, Mass.—Committee on Manufacturers, Committee on Foreign Trade.

James A. Campbell, President of the Youngstown Sheet & Tube Company, Youngstown, Ohio—Committee on Statistics, Chairman Committee on Manufacturers.

W. S. Carterm, President of the Brotherhood of Locomotive Firemen and Enginemen, 901 Guardian Building, Cleveland, Ohio—Committee on Transportation.

Elizabeth Christian, Secretary International Glove Workers' Union; Secretary-Treasurer National Women's Trade Union League, 311 South Ashland Boulevard, Chicago, Ill.—Committee on Registration and Employment Agencies, Committee on Civic Emergency Measures.

Edgar E. Clark, Ex-President Order of Railway Conductors; member Roosevelt Anthracite Commission 1902; formerly chairman Interstate Commerce Commission, American Bank Building—Chairman Committee on Transportation, Washington, D. C.

Bird S. Coler, Commissioner of Public Welfare; Chairman of the Industrial Aid Bureau, New York City—Committee on Employment Agencies and Registration, Committee on Public Works, and Committee on Emergency Civic Measures.

Mrs. Sara A. Connery, Secretary of the United Textile Workers of America, Bible House, New York City—Committee on Manufacturers.

John T. Connery, President Miami Coal Co., 332 Michigan Avenue, Chicago, Ill.—Committee on Mining.

Mayor James Couzens, President of the Detroit Board of Commerce; former Vice-President Ford Motor Car Co.; Mayor since 1919. Address, Dime Bank Building, Detroit, Mich.—Committee on Organization, Committee on Statistics, Committee on Civic Emergency Measures, Committee on Public Works.

Joseph H. Defrees, President Chamber of Commerce of the United States, Mills Building—Committee on Organization, Committee on Employment Agencies and Registration, chairman Committee on Foreign Trade, Washington, D. C.

Henry S. Dennison, President Dennison Manufacturing Co., Framingham, Mass.—Economic Advisory Committee, Committee on Manufacturers.

Davis R. Dewey, Professor of Economics and Statistics, Massachusetts Institute of Technology, 2 Berkeley Street, Cambridge, Mass.—Economic Advisory Committee.

Major Roy Dickinson, Editor Printers Ink, East Orange, N. J.; formerly Chief Industrial Morale Section, Office Chief of Staff, U. S. A.—Committee on Manufacturers.

John Donlin, President Building Trade Department American Federation of Labor, Washington, D. C.—Committee on Constructions.

Carroll W. Doten, Professor of Economics, Massachusetts Institute of Technology, 222 Charles River Road, Cambridge, Mass.— Economic Advisory Committee.

John E. Edgerton, President Lebanon Woolen Mills; Fuel Administration of Tennessee; Chairman War Resources Committee for Tennessee and United War Work Campaign; President National Manufacturers' Association, 50 Church Street, New York City—Committee on Manufacturers.

John H. Fahey, 40 Court Street, Boston, Mass., former President U. S. Chamber of Commerce—Committee on Foreign Trade.

W. F. Field, President Pittsburg Coal Company, Oliver Building, Pittsburg, Pa.—Committee on Mining.

Mortime Fleishhacker, Chairman of the Labor Mediation Board of the Pacific Coast during the war; President Anglo-California Trust Co., Sansome and Market Streets, San Francisco, Calif.—Committee on Employment Agencies and Registration.

P. A. S. Franklin, President International Mercantile Marine, 9 Broadway, New York City—Committee on Shipping.

Edwin F. Gay, President New York Evening Post, New York City, formerly Dean Graduate School of Business Administration, Harvard University—Economic Advisory Committee.

James S. Gibson, President Waterfront Employers' Union, 1220 Post Street, Seattle, Wash.—Committee on Shipping.

Samuel Gompers, President American Federation of Labor, Washington, D. C.—Committee on Manufacturers.

E. S. Greff, Chief of the Transportation Division, Department of Commerce, Alternative Executive Secretary with R. A. Lunquist on Committee on Shipping.

John M. Gries, Chief of the Division of Building and Housing, Department of Commerce—Executive Secretary Committee on Construction.

A. F. Haines, Vice-President Pacific Steamship Co., 112 Market Street, San Francisco, Calif.; Waldorf-Astoria, New York City—Committee on Shipping.

Salmon P. Halle, President National Council of Retail Associations. Address, Halle Bros. Co., 1226 Euclid Avenue, Cleveland Ohio—Committee Civic Emergency Measures.

George Edmond Haynes, Member Commission on Race Relations of the Federal Council of the Churches of Christ; formerly Director of Division of Negro Economics, U. S. Department of Labor, 1716 T. Street, N. W.—Member Committee on Civic Emergency Measures.

Clarence J. Hicks, Executive Assistant to President of the Colorado Fuel & Iron Co.; Executive Assistant to President of the Standard Oil Company, 26 Broadway, New York City—Committee on Employment Agencies and Registration, Committee on Manufacturers.

Dr. Thomas P. Hinman, President Hand Trading Company, Pelham, Ga.; President Farmers Bank, Pelham, Ga.; President Pelham Phosphate Co.; President Pelham Oil & Trust Company—Committee on Manufacturers.

A. L. Humphrey, President and Director of Westinghouse Air Brake Co., Pittsburg, Pa.; Industrial Inspector of Ordnance Department during War; Member Fuel Commission, State of Pennsylvania; Vice-President National Council for Defense; Director National Chamber of Commerce—Committee on Manufacturers.

Edward Eyre Hunt, engineer, New York City, Secretary of the Conference on Unemployment and Executive Secretary Committee on Organization.

Jackson Johnson, Chairman of the International Shoe Co.; President of St. Louis Chamber of Commerce, Fifteenth Street and Washington Avenue, St. Louis, Mo.—Committee on Employment Agencies and Registration, Committee on Manufacturers.

Clyde L. King, Professor of Political Science, University of Pennsylvania, Philadelphia; R. F. D. 3, Media, Pa.—Economic Advisory Committee, Executive Secretary Committee on Agriculture.

Gordan Lee, Chief of the Automotive Division, Department of Commerce—Executive Secretary Committee on Manufacturers.

John H. Kirby, President of the Kirby Lumber Company, Houston, Tex.—Committee on Construction.

William M. Leiserson, Impartial Chairman Men's and Boys' Clothing Industry, Rochester and New York City—Executive Secretary Committee on Employment Agencies and Registration, Committee on Civic Emergency Measures, Committee on Publications.

John L. Lewis, President United Mine Workers of America, Merchants Bank Building, Indianapolis, Ind.—Committee on Mining.

Samuel A. Lewisohn, of Samuel A. Lewisohn & Sons, 61 Broadway, New York City—Economic Advisory Committee and Committee on Mining.

Samuel McCune Lindsay, Professor of School Legislation, Columbia University, New York City—Economic Advisory Committee and Chairman Committee on Public Hearings; Committee on Organization, Committee on Publications.

Bascom Little, 7711 Euclid Avenue, Cincinnati, Ohio—Committee on Construction, Committee on Civic Measures, and Committee on Public Works.

Otto T. Mallery, Member Pennsylvania State Industrial Board, Philadelphia, Pa.—Economic Advisory Committee and Executive Secretary Committee on Public Works.

C. E. Markham, President of the Illinois Central Railroad Co., Chicago, Ill.—Committee on Organization, Committee on Statistics, and Committee on Transportation.

Gen. R. C. Marshall, Jr., formerly Chief of the Construction Division of the Army; General Manager Society of the General Contractors of America, 1039 Munsey Building, Washington, D. C.—Committee on Public Works, Chairman Committee on Construction.

George H. McFadden, 121 Chestnut Street, Philadelphia, Pa.—Committee on Foreign Trade.

T. W. Mitchell, Engineer, Philadelphia—Statistician to the Economic Advisory Committee and Executive Secretary Committee on Statistics.

Wesley C. Mitchell, Professor of Economics, New School for Social Research, 465 West Twenty-third Street, New York City—Member Economic Advisory Committee, Committee on Statistics.

Charles P. Neill, former U. S. Commissioner of Labor Statistics; Umpire Anthracite Conciliation Board; Manager Bureau of Information of Southeastern Railways, Woodward Building, Washington, D. C. —Executive Secretary Committee on Transportation, Committee on Civic Emergency Measures.

Thomas V. O'Connor, President Longshoremen's Union; Member of U. S. Shipping Board—Committee on Organization, Chairman Committee on Shipping.

Paul A. Palmerton, Chief of the Rubber Division, Department of Commerce—Executive Secretary Committee on Foreign Trade.

Raymond A. Pearson, President Iowa State College of Agriculture, Ames, Iowa; Ex-Assistant Secretary of Agriculture—Committee on Transportation, and Chairman Committee on Agriculture.

John A. Penton, Publisher Iron Trade Review, 1136 Chestnut Avenue, Cleveland, Ohio—Committee on Manufacturers.

Andrew J. Peters, former Member of Congress; former Assistant Secretary of the Treasury; former Mayor, Boston, Mass.—Committee on Civic Emergency Measures, Chairman Committee on Public Works.

E. M. Poston, President of the New York Coal Co., 8 East Broad Street, Columbus, Ohio—Committee on Mining.

W. C. Proctor, President Proctor & Gamble, Cincinnati, O.—Committee on Manufacturers.

Capt. John H. Pruett, President National Organization of Masters, Mates and Pilots of America, 423 Forty-ninth Street, Brooklyn, N. Y. City—Committee on Shipping.

H. H. Raymond, President American Steamship Owners Associations, Pier 36, North River, New York City—Committee on Shipping.

William M. Ritter, Wm. M. Ritter Lumber Co., Columbus, Ohio—Committee on Construction.

Henry M. Robinson, Member Second Industrial Conference; Chairman of the Bituminous Coal Commission 1920; President Los Angeles Trust Company, Los Angeles, Calif.—Chairman Committee on Organization and Chairman Committee on Statistics.

R. H. M. Robinson, Vice-President United American Lines, 39 Broad, New York City—Committee on Shipping.

William S. Rossiter, formerly Chief U. S. Census; President of the Rumford Press, Concord, N. H.—Chairman of Economic Advisory Committee.

John D. Ryan, Director Aircraft Production 1918; President of the United Metals Selling Company—Chairman Committee on Mining.

Charles M. Schwab, Chairman Bethlehem Steel Corporation; Director General of Shipbuilding, United States Shipping Board Emergency Fleet Corporation 1918, 111 Broadway, New York City—Committee on Organization, Committee on Manufacturers and Committee on Shipping.

Henry R. Seager, Professor of Economics, Columbia University, New York, N. Y.—Economic Advisory Committee.

Edwin R. A. Seligman, Professor of Economics, Columbia University, New York City—Economic Advisory Committee.

W. H. Stackhouse, President National Implement & Vehicle Association, Springfield, Ohio—Chairman Committee on Manufacturers.

Benjamin Strong, Governor of Federal Reserve Bank of New York, 15 Nassau Street, New York City—Committee on Foreign Trade.

Ida M. Tarbell, 132 East Nineteenth Street, New York City—Committee on Organization, Committee on Public Works, Committee on Civic Emergency Measures, Committee on Publications.

M. F. Tighe, President of the Amalgamated Association of Iron, Steel and Tin Works, House Building, Pittsburg, Pa.—Committee on Constructions, Committee on Manufacturers.

Ernest T. Trigg, Member First Industrial Conference, Vice-President and General Manager of John Lucas & Co., Drexel Bldg., Philadelphia, Pa.—Committee on Construction, Committee on Public Works, Committee on Organization.

Miss Mary Van Kleeck, Director Women in Industry Service, U. S. Department of Labor, 1918-1919; Director of Industrial Studies Russell Sage Foundation, 130 East Twenty-second Street, New York City—Committee on Mining, Committee on Statistics, Committee on Civic Emergency Measures, Chairman Committee on Publications.

John P. White, United Mine Workers of America, 1102 Merchants Bank Building, Indianapolis, Ind.—Committee on Mining.

Walter F. Willcox, Professor of Economics and Statistics, Cornell University, Ithaca, N. Y.—Economic Advisory Committee, Committee on Statistics.

John B. Williams, General Manager First National Pictures Corporation, New York City.

Matthew Woll, President International Photo Engravers Union of North American Federation of Labor, 6111 South Bishop Street, Chicago, Ill.—Committee on Organization, Committee on Statistics, Committee on Public Works, and Committee on Civic Emergency Measures.

Leo Wolman, New School for Social Research—Economic Advisory Committee.

Col. Arthur Woods, former Police Commissioner of New York, Assistant to Secretary of War in Charge of Re-establishment of Service Men in Civil Life, 1919, 32 East Thirty-second Street, New York City—Committee on Public Works, Room 705, and Chairman Committee on Civic Emergency Measures.

Evans Wollen, Member Economic Policy Committee of the American Bankers' Association; President of the Fletcher Joint Stock Land Bank, Indianapolis, Ind.—Committee on Public Works.

Allyn A. Young, Harvard University, Cambridge, Mass., Chief of the Division of Economics and Statistics, American Commission to Negotiate Peace, 1918-1919; Member Economic Advisory Committee—Committee on Statistics.

Clarence Mott Wooley, President of American Radiator Co., appointed representative of Secretary of Commerce on War Trade, Washington, D. C., 1917, 104 West Forty-second Street, New York City—Committee on Organization, Committee on Statistics, Committee on Civic Emergency Measures.

Thos. C. Atkison, Washington Representative of the National Grange, Washington, D. C.—Committee on Agriculture.

Edwin H. Brown, Hewitt & Brown, Architects, Minneapolis, Minn.; Chairman Small House College Service Bureau—Committee on Construction.

Alexander E. Cance, Professor of Agricultural Economics, Massachusetts Agricultural College, Amherst, Mass.—Executive Secretary, Committee on Agriculture.

Gray Silver, Washington Representative of the American Farm Bureau Federation, Munsey Building, Washington, D. C.—Committee on Agriculture.

REPORTS OF CONFERENCES

The first tasks of the President's Unemployment Conference were to canvass the available figures concerning the numbers of men now out of work in various parts of the United States, and to consider the best means of mitigating the suffering threatened by the existing emergency. While the proportion of wage and salary earners now out of work is probably somewhat larger than at any previous time in our history, the present emergency is not without precedent. A similar situation prevailed in the winter of 1914-15, in 1908, and in 1894, to go no further back. Four times in a single generation the numbers of the unemployed in the United States have been counted by millions, and the idle capital of the country has been counted by billions of dollars.

The conference reports were detailed and lengthy and only brief excerpts of importance can be given here as a matter of record on the subject:

"The world-wide scope and the long successions of business crises do not prove that the problem of controlling the business cycle is a hopeless one. On the contrary, history, when examined in detail, proves that the problem can be solved at least in part, for the leading business nations have made incontestable progress toward diminishing the violence of business crises. Each step in this direction has resulted from a wise use of lessons drawn from past experience. The creation of the Federal Reserve System is a notable example of American achievement in this field. That measure prevented the crisis of 1920 from degenerating into a panic. Having devised a method of mitigating the severity of crises, we can with good prospects of success, turn out constructive efforts to the further problem of mitigating the severity of depression. The ebb and flow in the demand for consumable goods may not be subject to direct control; but, on the other hand, it should be possible in some measure to control the expansion of the national plant and equipment. If all branches of our public works and the construction work of our public utilities—the railways, the telephones, etc—could systematically put aside financial reserves to be provided in times of prosperity for the deliberate purpose of improvement and expansion in times of depressions, we would not only greatly decrease the depth of depressions, but we would at the same time diminish the height of booms. We would, in fact, abolish acute unemployment and wasteful extravagance. For a rough calculation indicates that if we maintained a reserve of but 10 per cent of our average annual construction for this purpose we could almost iron out the fluctuations in employment."

The conference presented a summary of its recommendations for an emergency program for immediate action, concisely as follows:

The problem of meeting the emergency of unemployment is primarily a community problem. The responsibility for leadership is with the mayor and should be immediately assumed by him.

The basis of organization should be an emergency committee representing the various elements in the community. This committee should develop and carry through a community plan for meeting the emergency, using existing agencies and local groups as far as practicable. One immediate step should be to coordinate and establish efficient public employment agencies and to register all those desiring work. It should coordinate the work of the various charitable institutions.

The Emergency Committee should regularly publish the numbers dependent upon them for employment and relief, that the community may be appraised of its responsibility. Begging and uncoordinated solicitation of funds should be prevented.

Private houses, hotels, offices, etc., can contribute to the situation by doing their repairs, cleaning and alterations during the winter instead of waiting until spring, when employment will be more plentiful.

Public construction is better than relief. The municipalities should expand their school, street, sewage, repair work and public buildings to the fullest possible volume compatible with the existing circumstances. That existing circumstances are favorable is indicated by the fact that over $700,-000,000 of municipal bonds, the largest amount in history, have been sold in 1921. Of these $106,000,000 were sold by 333 municipalities in August, 1921. Municipalities should give short time employment the same as other employers.

The Governor should unite all State agencies for support of the mayors and, as the superior officer, should insist upon the responsibility of city officials, should do everything compatible with circumstances in expedition of construction of roads, State buildings, etc.

The Federal authorities, including the Federal Reserve Banks, should expedite the construction of public buildings and public work covered by existing appropriations.

The greatest area for immediate relief of unemployment is in the construction industry, which has been artificially restricted during and since the war. We are short more than a million homes, all kinds of building and construction are far behind national necessity. The Senate Committee on Reconstruction and Production, in March of this year, estimated the total construction shortage in the country at between ten and twenty billion dollars. Considering all branches of the construction industries, more than two million people could have been employed if construction were resumed. Undue cost and malignant combinations have made proper expansion impossible and contributed largely to this unemployment situation. In some places these matters have been cleaned up. In other places they have not, and are an affront to public decency. In some places these things have not existed. In others costs have been adjusted. Some materials have been reduced in prices as much as can be expected. Where conditions have been righted construction should proceed, but there is still a need of community action in providing capital on terms that will encourage home building. Where the costs are still above the other economic levels of the community there should be searching inquiry and action in the situation. We recommend that the Governors summon representative committees, with the cooperation of the mayors, or otherwise as they may determine, to (a) determine facts; (b) to organize community action in securing adjustments in cost, including combinations, restrictions of effort, and unsound practices where they exist, to the end that building may be fully resumed.

Manufacturers can contribute to relieve the present acute unemployment situation by—

(a) Part time work, through reduced time or rotation of jobs.

(b) As far as possible manufacturing for stock.

(c) Taking advantage of the present opportunity to do as much plant construction, repairs, and cleaning up as is possible, with the consequent transfer of many employees to other than their regular work.

(d) Reduction of the number of hours of labor per day.

(e) The reduction of the work week to a lower number of days during the present period of industrial depression.

(f) That employees and employers cooperate in putting these recommendations into effect.

During the period of drastic economic readjustment, through which we are now passing, the continued efforts of anyone to profit beyond the requirements of safe business practice or economic consistency should be condemned. One of the important obstacles to a resumption of normal business activity will be removed as prices reach replacement values in terms of efficient producing and distributing cost, plus reasonable profit.

The conference presented a summary of matters that required constructive and immediate settlement as an aid to the recovery of business:

Readjustment of railway rates to a fairer basis of the relative value of commodities, with special consideration of the rates upon primary commodities, at the same time safeguarding the financial stability of the railways.

Definite settlement of tariff legislation in order that business may determine its future conduct and policies.

Limitations of world armament and consequent increase of tranquility and further decrease of the tax burden not only of the United States but other countries.

Steps looking to the minimizing of fluctuations in exchange, because recovery from the great slump in exports (due to the economic situation in Europe) can not make substantial progress so long as extravagant daily fluctuations continue in foreign exchange, for no merchant can determine the delivery cost of any international shipment.

The committee on agriculture reported as follows:

There is no acute problem of unemployment in the agricultural industry. On the contrary, this industry is absorbing or at least providing a haven for great numbers of unemployed from the industrial centers. In the face of falling prices and vanishing profits farmers have maintained their production of food and other raw material even when they had no assurance or reasonable hope of receiving for their products an amount equal to their production costs.

In instances they have done this on mere subsistence wages. Cotton farmers, for example, have willingly accepted from banks advances of $10 per month with which to pay their laborers with nothing advanced for the living of their own families. Railroad freight rates on commodities transported to and from the farm must be substantially reduced without delay. The prices of materials, farm implements, and supplies must be adjusted to the price level of farm products. Manufacturers and dealers must realize that farmers can not, at present price levels, resume normal buying and thereby restore normal employment.

Better credit facilities must be provided for agriculture which will furnish funds for production, and orderly marketing for long periods suited to the requirements of the industry, at reasonable rates of interest and without opportunity for the unscrupulous to charge unreasonable commissions, premiums, or brokers charges. A recent nation-wide referendum showed that tens of thousands of farmers have been paying 6 to 10 per cent interest, plus 2 to 10 per cent brokerage, on money borrowed. Exports of agricultural products should be stimulated with the aid of our merchant marine, foreign credits, and by such other proper means and encouragements as will aid foreign commerce.

History is repeating itself. Previous wars have been followed by periods of depression which have in turn been followed by prosperity. Prosperity has come with the revival of agriculture which has provided an expanding domestic market for manufactured products, thus restoring industrial activity with the employment of all classes of labor. This course of events is inevitable. We can only hasten or retard its progress.

CHAPTER XLIV

CONCLUSION

Ferrero in his book, "Ancient Rome and Modern America," tells of the decline of the great empire. He describes conditions very similar to those existing today. The demand of the people was for wealth and luxury. The cities built great temples and amphitheaters and held carnivals and festivals. This drew the population from the agricultural districts to invade the cities in search of pleasure. These centers of population eventually swarmed with the unemployed, and instead of placing them in industries that would produce wealth, the empire gave them employment in construction of more public buildings, finally draining the agrarian taxpayers until they were unable to bear the burden. We have only to read the history of the decline of Rome to learn that we cannot solve the problem of depression and unemployment simply by the much agitated plan of public work. Our population must be put to production. Otherwise our producing classes are bound to be burdened with greater taxes in order to keep up these public works. That procedure is all right as a temporary expedient, but our attention must be directed to helping our producing industries where men can be given useful employment. Ferrero says: "If not destroyed, modern civilization might be profoundly shaken and weakened in the event of its imitating the policy of Rome and seeking to favor the cities overmuch at the expense of the country. There is a further lesson to be learned by us moderns from the history of the Decadence of the Roman Empire, and that it, not to mistake the glamour of the external manifestations of wealth and power for signs of real wealth and power. A civlization is not always in reality richer and stronger in times when it bears the most visible marks of so being; we are rather apt to find that, when it is most dazzling in outward seeming, its decadence has already begun.   We often halt in stupefaction and admiration before the great ruins of ancient Rome, especially those offered by the European provinces of the empire.   We think how great, powerful and rich must have been the empire which could rear monuments so massive that all the centuries have not been able to sweep them entirely from the face of the earth.   And yet, if we are to look at these relics in their right light, we must remember that practically all the great Roman monuments, whose remains survive to our day on a large scale, belong to the Third, Fourth and Fifth Centuries of the Christian era—to the centuries of decadence and dissolution."

Public construction work and private repair work, giving employment to the idle, is the method generally adopted in all countries to help get business back to normal.   The idea is held that every dollar paid out in this way in hard times creates demand for goods.

Proposed remedies along the lines of the Huber Unemployment Bill, recently introduced in the Wisconsin Legislature, will be watched with interest.   That plan provides for a system of unemployment insurance.   Employers would be required to pay an annual assessment into the fund to be used to guarantee a given number of days employment each week to workers who have been residents of the State for not less than six months.   Supporters of the plan claim that employers will then, of their own accord, so adjust their business that their employees will be taken care of voluntarily to the extent of the provisions of the law.   In the meantime certain corporations are initiating plans of insuring their employees against unemployment through various methods, mostly by setting aside a certain total of the payroll with the consent of the employees, as an insurance fund, the employers providing an equal amount and guaranteeing a certain minimum employment through the year regardless of conditions.   But all this assumes that de-

pressions will continue to come about.   What is needed
is measures to avoid the need of such schemes.   Heretofore
we have bent our energies to finding a cure, but henceforth
we must work along the lines of finding a preventive.   We
hear a great deal about a guarantee of bank deposits and a
few states have enacted laws that guarantee state bank deposits, some of which have worked out very well.   The law
has   probably protected the depositor against loss.   But
whether it would be practicable to apply on a nation-wide
scale is a serious question.   However, a law for deposit insurance would be needless if we had laws to protect against
dangerous expansions of bank credits; in other words, reach
the cause.   If the cause is reached, it is needless to legislate regarding ill-effects.   Such laws would answer a two-
fold purpose, the first one being practically a deposit guarantee and secondly, insurance against crises and depressions.

The Federal Reserve Act, while admittedly not perfect,
has been a bulwark of strength to the nation's finances.
Where is the man who doubts but that we would have had
a crisis and panic in 1920, had it not been for the Federal
Reserve System?   We are bound to witness more or less
credit fluctuation constantly, entirely outside of crises, to
help which the Federal Reserve has its place.   In the agricultural sections the amount of funds needed immediately
after the crop is harvested is greater than at other times.
An elastic currency is thus provided to move the crops so
that finance in the rest of the country keeps its equilibrium.
In case, also, of local crop failures the Federal Reserve is
used to tide over a bad season, to carry the producers until
they can recuperate their losses in a good season.   Again
in case of catastrophe, such as the Baltimore or San Francisco fire, the shock on finances attended with such enormous losses can be lessened through help extended by the
Federal Reserve.

Local disasters are now being dealt with by skilled financiers, through well organized systems of transferring resources where needed from one party or locality to another,

using in the operation the maximum of credit and the minimum of gold.

Legislative acts cannot prevent human optimism, but they can control the money of the people and prevent to a large extent undue acts of over-optimism. We all agree that we must have better control of credit expansion and in order to do so we must control those who cannot control themselves.

Our great difficulty is that in good times our people are quick to forget the periods of distress. We are sure there will never again be such low prices, never will there be such unemployment, never such depressed conditions. We are certain that economic troubles are a thing of the past.

The writer planned and organized the Southern Tariff Association in 1919, at the peak of the boom, and I shall never forget that some of the leading business men of the South looked at me in amazement and told me that they were very sure that we would never have need for a protective tariff in this country again.   Inside of twelve months cotton had fallen from 35 cents to 12 cents a pound; foreign agricultural products were flooding the country, depressing prices and ruining thousands of southern planters and business men, and they were holding mass meetings all over that section demanding relief.

Depressions thrive on uncertainty. They could be shortened and the upward movement accelerated by a uniform, collective action on the part of business to remove uncertainty.   The individual firm or corporation may have liquidated its output; it may be willing to add additional employees, place contracts for supplies and generally push things up to normal; but they are held back by the constant fear that liquidation has not run its course. There is a lack of concerted action on the part of all business to resume. The individual company often makes a mistake and suffers loss in its patriotic willingness to take a reasonable chance and push ahead, but before long it finds itself alone in the effort. Others are not ready or willing. Likewise, after liquidation has run its course, banks become overstocked with money. They are unable to make loans at more than normal interest. The banker likes commercial loans, if the collateral is good, at 6, 7, or 8 per cent, together with the feature that the deposits may amount to 25 per cent of the loan. This is preferable to bond issues at 4 or 5 per cent, which often send the money out of the community and are neither as liquid nor as profitable. But the individual banker who may be ready wants to wait until the general upward swing is underway so he is reasonably certain to have his loans paid when they become due. He has gone through a spell of slowly liquidating frozen credits and wants to avoid getting into the same rut again. Therefore it is apparent that more concerted action by business and finance would lead us more quickly out of the valleys of depression.

The banker often times is blind to the public welfare. Many times his own safety is uppermost in his mind to such an extent that he will abandon the interests of the community, allowing business to collapse, to his resultant loss in the long run. But as the progressive banker assumes more and more the modern attitude that he is the servant and not the master of his constituency, he will be more apt to follow business and not to lead. Even today most of the bigger corporations that have large payrolls and commodity drafts to meet control their own banks. They are not dependent upon the independent bankers who may or may not be able to loan their requirements. Even smaller business men and investors are often in position to dictate to their banker, instead of their banker to them. Bankers are human; they want business, and business consists of deposits. They cannot get good fat deposits without interest unless they extend accomodations. It is not often these days that a business man crawls into a bank on his hands and knees and begs for a loan of a few dollars. If his collateral is ample and he is willing to pay the prevailing rate on commercial paper, he is smart enough to know that he is doing the banker a favor. All of this leads up to the point I wish to make, namely, that the banker who is in the best position to watch the course of events and the recognized barometers of business is going to be so dependent upon the business men that these eager borrowers, mad for money making, will press him into over-expansion against his will and against his better knowledge. For that reason the public, the business man and investor must themselves study the question of business depressions. It is inevitable, it is beyond any power we have or will likely obtain, to prevent depression or contraction following over-stimulation, specu- lation and over-expansion. The principal way to prevent depression is through education, because through education we should learn moderation.

Depressions are prolonged by the instinct and practice of the trained buyer to withhold purchase until a rising mar- ket sets in. That process may be long and painful. It is, however, something beyond the control of the individual buyer. Often times prices on their downward trend during a depression have reached the point where the buyer is willing to go into the market to supply his needs for present and future, but he will not do so as long as the trend con- tinues downward. If things could start upward as soon as the buyer is willing, depressions could be brought to shorter duration. A remedy for such a situation could be found through trade associations. In a great many commodity lines trade associations already exist which are sufficiently strong and able to hold their product at a reasonable level. But associations will never properly function for the best economic purposes until they also realize that they must voluntarily set a maximum as well as a minimum. During the high tide of 1919 the wheat growers were offered $2.00 per bushel for their product. They held out for higher prices, then the depression set in and later they were forced to sell for slightly over $1.00 per bushel. In that same year the cotton growers were offered 30 cents. They held out for 40 cents, and a great many were finally forced to sell for 10 to 12 cents. Had they been sufficiently organized so as to set a reasonable minimum above cost of production allowing as much more up to a reasonable maximum, it would have been a great benefit both to their members and to the public. The same conditions existed with some branches of the lumber industry that had an understanding among the members (some claim unlawful) that certain prices were to be asked. These prices were so unreasonable that the public revolted, causing the most severe depression in the lumber industry that it has known for years. Had these interests not been unreasonable the buyers' strike in their commodity could have been largely averted, because great sums of money were ready to be invested in the building industry. When trade associations take into consideration the interests of the people as well as their own, they will have it in their power to help largely in avoiding depressions.

What deceives the average business man is orders booked. Manufacturers and contractors report unfilled orders carrying them far into the future, and these go out in statistical reports. They forget, as they painfully did in 1920, that those orders may be cancelled over night.

We not only need greater vigilance on the part of the business man, but the authorized departments of the government should watch for special conditions affecting future trade. After they have the facts, they should boldly place those conditions before the public, regardless of who they may immediately affect. When the Department of Agriculture first began gathering statistics so as to make prognostications of coming crops they met with every hindrance. Many attempts were made to stop it. Various interests were obviously affected by whatever reports might be sent broadcast, and those whose interests were adversely affected naturally made bitter complaint. For years we have heard that the department's figures could not be taken as authoritative, but while some mistakes were made at first, the organization was soon improved, and today we hear little complaint against the practice of sending out reports or against the correctness of the reports.

There should be a special corps of experts under a special bureau whose duties it would be to keep the country posted as to exact conditions. The experts in charge of this bureau should come jointly from the Departments of Commerce, Labor, Agriculture, and the Treasury. They should have their fingers on the pulse of business, manufacturing, agriculture, employment and finances.

Because we have always had depressions is no reason why we always shall have. We used to think we should always have panics, but now the most advanced countries are practically secure against them. Even when the German army threw shells into Paris there was no financial panic. We can control the situation both against our own mistakes and extravagances as well as against natural causes, but to say that we can avoid depressions entirely would be beyond reason. We shall most likely always have wars, natural disasters, crop failures and labor difficulties, but provision can be made against them so that the sharp edges are taken off and their effects largely mitigated.

It is necessary that we establish a school of thought on economic history in order that the rising business generation may profit more from our past experience. Our business men must be intelligent observers of events at large and sagacious interpreters of symptoms.

Sir A. Conan Doyle may be said to be an authority on mysteries. He says the reason many mysteries remain unsolved so long is that men reason forward instead of reasoning backward. If we are going to reach a solution that will help us in problems of depression we cannot do it by theorizing, but we can make some headway by making use of the lessons of the past and studying the history of those which have gone before.

Even though we may work out a system that will prove effective against these evil days, we have to consider that we may still be affected by what transpires economically in

other countries. It is true that our foreign trade amounts
to less than 5 per cent of our total, and it is possible for us
to prosper without regard to it, yet it stands to reason
that our foreign trade will grow in proportion in the future
and conditions abroad are going to have an increasing
psychological effect. It therefore behooves us not only to
put our own house in order but, for our own selfish interests,
we must get our heads together around the table with the
representatives of other nations and help them solve their
problems. Whether we do this through the instrument of
the League of Nations or some other body of similar nature
does not matter, but it must be done. No one knows better
than the business man how dependent we are upon other
countries and how we are affected by their economic conditions. When we can sit on Long Island or in Washington
and talk to Berlin, Moscow, Japan, or South America by
wireless, we must know that the world has grown so small
that what affects one materially is bound to affect another.
The war went around the world; the influenza went around
the world, and the depression of 1920 went around the
world.

In 1920 the nation lost $5,000,000,000 in decreased values
of farm products, $5,000,000,000 more in the loss of earning
power among labor, and untold wealth in depreciated values of property and business stocks, while the financial system lost millions in failures. What we lost
in this one single depression would pay the national debt.

Business men who have made a study of the question have
become thoroughly imbued with the idea that these depressions run in cycles and will always come. Instead of joining in efforts to prevent them they adjust themselves to
anticipate them. As the question is studied more and more
the idea of the cycle comes just that much more to prevail
and the rising generation is taught the idea of the cycle. We
are never going to get anywhere along these lines. We
must stop propagating the cycle idea and work along more
constructive lines. In other words, we must endeavor to

eliminate depressions instead of giving up to the idea that they are a fixed evil in our economic life. They have led to a great deal of economic suffering in the past and will do so in the future, unless they are curbed. Some day one of them will get away from us. In 1921 we were threatened with a gigantic railroad strike. The public thought it was outrageous that a million men should quit their jobs when there were four million others out of employment. Railroad managers took the stand that they did not care if the men did strike, as that would give them the opportunity to put the wage scale still lower. But secretly, the wiser railroad heads dreaded a strike and so did the wiser Government officials, because underneath the surface there were ominous possiblities. Leaders of other labor unions advised against the strike and notified the railroad workers that they would not support them, but suppose there had been more radical men at the head of the labor organizations, as there might be at some future time, and a great strike was on; at the start of the first riot there would have been a portentous army of four million unemployed, as large as we put under training in the World War. Augmented by general dissatisfaction on the part of the people as a whole, who could tell what might have happened? Some day we are going to sit by and allow one of these depressions to run its course, so we think, and in such a time when the people are dissatisfied, when they have suflered loss and inconvenience, when millions are out of employment and other thousands facing ruin and in such state of mind that men become resolved, a lighted match in some spot will cause a blaze that might envelope the nation. This will come when we least expect it, when we sit in false security, when we think it cannot happen. And when that time comes—if it should come—we will see our mistake in accepting the principle that these periods are unavoidable. Before this happens is the time to adopt such means as are necessary to avoid the speculative and profiteering debauches which cause them.

We can avoid these difficulties by looking more to the spiritual side, keeping constantly in mind that the continuance of good times and reasonable prosperity depends upon true aims, fair profits, conscientious service, and moderation in our desires. We must get past that false philosophy made possible by "David Harum" and "Get-Rich-Quick Wallingford" which lionized the trickster and applauded the shrewd individual who "put something over" on the other fellow and got away with it.

The established order shows the way. The sun ascends and sets, the tides rise and fall, the winds come and go, the seasons follow one another, all smoothly and in order, as the poet might express it—in perfect unison with the music of the sphere. So when we have reached the higher state of perfection to which we constantly aspire, we may learn to regulate our economic life so that even with the vacillations which must take place it will follow the smooth undulations of nature herself.

Depression is a punishment for economic immorality. We can avoid it then by tuning our business life to restraint and unselfishness. Cleanse it of greed and injustice, and when we do this we will have good times, because we deserve them. Then will the sun of prosperity shine on our beautiful America through the clouds of distress, and these dread intervals of darkness will come no more.

BIBLIOGRAPHY

Albert Aftalion—*Les Crises Periodique de Surproduction*. 1913.

Allard—*Le Crise Agricole & Manufacturiere Devant la Conference Monetaire de Bruxelles*. 1893.

Albert—"Roosevelt and The Money Power; Responsibility of Dishonest High Finance for the Panic of 1907." 1907.

Andrew—"Substitutes for Cash in Panic of 1907." 1908.

Andrews—"The United States Treasury and the Money Market. The Partial Responsibility of Secretaries Gage and Shaw for the Crisis of 1907." 1907.

Abbott—"A History of Greece", G. P. Putnam's Sons. 1895.

Ashley—"Surveys, Historic and Economic", Longmans, Green & Co. 1900.

Andreades—"History of the Bank of England", P. S. King & Son. 1909.

Atwood—"The Exchanges and Speculation", Alexander Hamilton Institute. 1918.

Ashley—"The Adjustment of Wages", Longmans, Green & Co. 1903.

Alexander Hamilton Institute—"Modern Business—Exchange and Distribution." 1918.

Armsden, J.—"Trade Depression"; or "The Cause of 'Cutting' and its Remedy", Reeves, London. 1892.

Adams, E. D.—"The Control of the Purse in the United States". 1894.

Adams—"Taxation in the United States, 1789-1816." 1884.

Avery, E. M.—"A History of the United States and Its People", Vols. I-VII, Cleveland. 1904-1910.

Babson—"Business Barometers", Babson's Statistical Organization. 1915.

Babson—"Factors Affecting Commodity Prices".

Beveridge—"Unemployment, A Problem of Industry", Longmans, Green & Co. 1908.

Benton—"Thirty Years' View", Appleton. 1879.

Bowker, R. R.—"State Publications: A Provisional List of the Official Publications of the Several States"; 4 parts. 1899-1908.

Bishop, J. L.—"History of American Manufacturers from 1608 to 1860" (3 vols.). 1868.

Bigelow—"Tariff Policy of England and the United States Contrasted". 1877.

Bronson—"A Historical Account of Connecticut Currency, Continental Money, and the Finances of the American Revolution." In papers of New Haven Historical Society. Vol. I.

Burton—"Financial Crises", D. Appleton & Co. 1902.

Burton—"John Sherman". 1906.

Baley, Rafael—"History of the National Loans of the United States", Tenth Census. Vol. VII. 1884.

Baden-Powell, G.—"Protection and Bad Times with Special Reference to the Political Economy of English Colonization", Trubner, London. 1879.

Bouniatian—*Wirtschaftskrisen und Uberkapitalisation.* 1908.

Bennison, W.—"Causes of the Present Money Crisis Explained, in Answer to the Pamphlet of J. H. Palmer and a Remedy Pointed Out"; Wilson, London. 1837.

Blood, F.—"Inquiry into the Causes of the Depression of Trade and Agriculture". Correspondence between F. Blood and J. Bright. Guest, Birmingham. 1879.

Bogart—"Economic History of the United States"; Longmans, Green & Co. 1920.

Bishop & Keller—"Industry and Trade"; Ginn & Co. 1918.

Brown—"Principals of Commerce"; MacMillian Company. 1916.

Bolles—"The Financial History of the United States"; D. Appleton & Co. 1883.

Bilgram—"The Cause of Business Depressions"; J. P. Lippincott Co. 1914.

Bianco, Jose—*La Crisis, Nacionalizacion del Capital Extrajero.* 1916.

\ **Brown**—"The Financial Conspiracy of 1907". 1913.

Callender, J. S.—"Selections from the Economic History of the United States, 1765-1860".

F. A. Cleveland, F. W. Powell—"Railroad Promotion and Capitalization in the United States"; Longmans, Green & Co., New York. 1909.

Chapman—"History of Trade Between the United Kingdom and the United States". 1899.

Copeland—"Report of the Tariff Board on Cotton Manufacturers". 1912.

Culbertson—"The Tariff Board and Wool Legislation". 1913.

Curtiss—"The Industrial Development of Nations"; Geo. B. Curtiss. 1912.

Chapin—"An Historical Introduction to Social Economy"; The Century Co. 1917.

Chadwick—"The Heroic Age"; Cambridge University Press. 1912.

Conant—"History of Modern Bank Issues"; G. P. Putnam's Sons. 1909.

Catteral—"The Decennial Publications of the University of Chicago"; University of Chicago Press. 1903.

Clews—"Fifty Years in Wall Street"; Irving Pub. Co. 1908.

Conant—"A History of Modern Banks"; G. P. Putnam's Sons. 1909.

Cotter—"Authentic History of the United States Steel Corporation".

Coman—"Industrial History of the United States"; MacMillian Co. 1905.

Clere—"The A, B, C of Foreign Exchange".

Cleveland—"The Bank and Treasury"; Longmans, Green Co. 1908.

Cornwallis—"History of the Crisis (1873)"; Lippincott's Magazine.

Courtois, Alphonse, fils—*Histoire des Banques en France;* Paris. 1881.

Cunningham—"Western Civilization in its Economic Aspects"; J. & C. F. Clay at University Press, Cambridge. 1898.

DeBows—"Statistical View of the United States".

Dewey—"Financial History of the United States"; Longmans, Green Co. 1912.

Daly—"Radical Pioneers of the Eighteenth Century"; Swan Sonnenschein, Le Bas & Lowry. 1886.

Davis—"The Influence of Wealth in Imperial Rome"; MacMillian Co. 1910.

Dill—"Roman Society in the Last Century of the Western Empire". 1899.

Drage—"The Unemployed"; MacMillian Co. 1894.

Day—"A History of Commerce"; Longmans, Green & Co. 1908.

Dibble—"Laws of Supply and Demand"; Constable & Co. 1912.

Dunbar—"Theory and History of Banking"; G. P. Putnam's Sons. 1901.

Depew, C. M.—"One Hundred Years of American Commerce"; 2 Vols. 1895.

Duguid—"The Story of the Stock Exchange"; Grant Richards. 1901.

Evans—"The Commercial Crisis of 1847-48". 1848.

Evans—"History of the Commercial Crisis of 1857-58 (in England)". 1859.

Escher—"Elements of Foreign Exchange"; Bankers Publishing Co. 1918.

Evans—"Domestic Exports from the United States to All Countries, 1789-1883". 1884.

Elliott—"Debates in the State Conventions on the Adoption of the Federal Constitution, Together with the Journal of the Federal Convention". 1854.

Eckel—"Coal, Iron and War"; Henry Holt & Co. 1920.

Fitz Simon—"Historical Epochs, with System of Economics"; Taintor Brothers, Merrill & Company. 1882.

Faculty of Political Science of Columbia University—"Studies in History Economics and Public Law"; Columbia University. 1914.

Felch, Alpheus—"Early Banks and Banking in Michigan"; Ex. Doc. 38, 52d Cong. 2d Sess.

Fiske, John—"The Critical Period of American History". 1892.

Ferrero—"Greatness and Decline of Rome, Empire Builders". 1909.

Ferrero—"Ancient Rome and Modern America"; G. P. Putnam's Sons. 1914.

Fowler—"The Crisis (in England) of 1866". 1867.

Gallatin, Albert—"The Writings of Albert Gallatin". 1892.

Gouge, W. E.—"A Short History of Paper Money and Banking in the United States". 1840.

George—"Progress and Poverty"; John W. Lowell & Co. 1883.

Gibbins—"Industry of England"; Chas. Scribner's Sons. 1903.

Gras—"The Evolution of the English Corn Market"; Harvard University Press. 1915.

Gibbins—"Economic and Industrial Progress of the Century". 1903.

Garvey—"The Silent Revolution"; Wm. & Frederic Cash.

Goschen, Geo. J.—"The Theory of the Foreign Exchanges"; London. 1895.

Greene, E. B.—"Provincial America, 1690-1740"; Amer. Nation Series VI, New York. 1747.

Gibson—"The Cycles of Speculation"; Moody Corp. 1907.

Hammond—"The Cotton Industry"; MacMillian Co. 1897.

Hecker—"The Epidemics of the Middle Ages"; Geo. Woodfall & Son. 1844.

Hepburn, A. Barton—"History of Coinage and Currency in the United States and the Perennial Contest for Sound Money"; New York and London. 1903.

Hinsdale—"The American Government"; Werner School Book Co.

Hobson—"The Evolution of Modern Capitalism"; Scribner's.

Hasse, Adelaide, R.—"Index of Economic Material in Documents of the States of the United States"; Carnegie Institute, Washington Pub. Co. 1907-1915.

Hallam—"View of the States of Europe During the Middle Ages"; W. J. Widdleton. 1874.

Hatch—"A Reproach to Civilization; A Treatise on the Problem of the Unemployed". 1906.

Hobson—"The Problem of the Unemployed"; Methuen. 1906.

Huebner—"Agricultural Commerce"; D. Appleton & Co. 1915.

Herrick—"A History of Commerce and Industry"; MacMillian Co. 1917.

Hull—"Industrial Depressions"; Frederic A. Stokes Co. 1911.

Heeren—"Historical Researches", Vols. 1-2; Henry G. Bohn.

Haney, L. H.—"Congressional History of Railways Down to 1850"; Madison, Wis. 1908.

Hallam—"Europe During the Middle Ages"; Alex. Murray & Son. 1869.

Hewins—"English Trade and Finance in the 17th Century".

Ingalls—"Business Crises" (Pamphlet). 1878.

Ingram—"A History of Political Economy". 1893.

James—"Dark Scenes of History"; Harper & Brother. 1850.

Juglar, Clement—"*Les Crises Commerciales et de Leur Retour Periodique en France, en Angleterre et aux Etals-Unis*", Paris. 1903.

Johnson—"Crisis and Panic of 1907".

Johnson—"History of Domestic and Foreign Commerce of the United States", Vols. 1 and 2; Carnegie Institute of Washington. 1915.

Jevons—"Investigations in Currency and Finance". 1909.

Kelley—"The Financial Problem and Business Situation Discussed from a Practical Standpoint".

Knox—"History of Banking in the United States"; Bradford Rhodes & Co. 1900.

Kemmerer—"Seasonal Variations in the Relative Demand for Money and Capital in the United States"; National Monetary Commission. 1910.

Kinley—"The History, Organization and Influence of the Independent Treasury System of the United States". 1910.

Kyle—"The Farm Bureau Movement"; The MacMillian Co. 1921.

Lauck—"The Causes of the Panic of 1893"; Houghton, Mifflin & Company. 1907.

Levi, Leon—"The History of British Commerce and of the Economic Progress of the British Nation, 1763-1878"; London. 1880.

Lalor—"Cyclopedia of Political Science and Political Economy"; Maynard, Merrill.

Lonsdale—"The English Poor Law". 1899.

Lindsay—"History of Merchant Shipping and Ancient Commerce". 1883.

Laughlin—"Banking Progress"; Chas. Scribner's. 1920.

Livingston, John—"The Erie Railway; Its History and Management from 1832 to 1875"; New York. 1875.

Laughlin—"Gold and Crises".

MacPherson—"Annals of Commerce". 1805.

Morey—"Outlines of Greek History"; American Book Co. 1903.

McCulloch—"Men and Measures of Half Century". 1889.

McCulloch—"The Works of David Ricardo"; John Murray. 1876.

Meyer, B. H.—"A History of the Northern Securities Case", Madison, Wis. 1906.

Mill—"Principals of Political Economy"; D. Appleton Co. 1884.

MacVeagh—"Financial Panic of 1893" (paper). 1911.

Moore—"Industrial History of the American People"; MacMillian Co. 1913.

Marvin—"The American Merchant Marine"; Chas. Scribner's Sons. 1916.

McMaster—"History of the People of the United States".

McVey—"Railroad Transportation"; Cree Publishing Co. 1910.

Mitchell—"History of Greenbacks".

Meyer—"New York Stock Exchange in the Crisis of 1907".

Noyes, A. D.—"The Banks and the Panic of 1893"; Political Science Quarterly.

Nasse—"On the Agricultural Community of the Middle Ages". 1872.

Nourse—"Agricultural Economics"; University of Chicago Press. 1916.

Noyes—"Thirty Years of American Finance, 1865-1896". 1898.

Osgood—"A History of Industry"; Ginn & Company. 1921.

Oberholtzer—"Jay Cooke Financier of the Civil War"; Geo. W. Jacobs & Co. 1907.

Oman—"The Dark Ages"; Rivington's. 1914.

Osgood—"American Colonies in the 17th Century".

Pitkin, Timothy—"A Statistical View of the Commerce of the United States of America", 2nd edition. 1835.

Postlethwayt, Malachy—"Britain's Commercial Interest Explained and Improved. In a Series of Observations on the Several Branches of our Trade and Policy" (2 Vols., London). 1747.

Parmelee—"Poverty and Social Progress". 1916.

Purdy—"The City Life, the Trade and Finances". 1876.

Philbrick—"The Mercantile Conditions of the Crisis of 1893". 1902.

Ripley—"Financial History of Virginia".

Rabbene—"The American Commercial Policy" 1895.

Ryner—"The Crises of 1837, 1847 and 1857 in England, France and United States". 1905.

Ringwalt, J. L.—"Development of Transportation Systems in the United States", Philadelphia. 1888.

Scott—"The Repudiation of State Debts"; Thos. Y. Crowell & Co. 1893.

Shaw, W. A.—"The History of Currency, 1852 to 1894", New York and London. 1895.

Smith, Adam—"An Inquiry into the Nature and Causes of the Wealth of Nations"; Edited by James E. Thorold Rogers, 2 Vols, Oxford. 1880.

Stevens—"Analysis of the Phenomena of the Panic in the United States in 1893"; Quarterly Journal of Economics.

Smith—"The Story of Iron and Steel"; D. Appleton & Co. 1908.

Swank—"History of the Manufacture of Iron in all Ages"; The American Iron and Steel Association. 1892.

Stopel—*Die Handelskrisis in Deutschland.* 1875.

Schuckers—"Finances; Panics and Specie Payments". 1874.

Salisbury—"The Speculative Craze of '36" (paper).

Sayous—*La Crise allemande de 1900-1902; le charbon, le fer & l'acier Luivi d'un indes des principaux cartels miniers et sideiurgiques d'Allemange.* 1903.

Seybert—"Statistical Annals". 1818.

Scherer—"Cotton as a World Power"; F. A. Stokes Co. 1916.

Smith—"Commerce and Industry"; Henry Holt & Co. 1916.

Sakolski—"The American Railroad Economics".

Selfridge—"The Romance of Commerce"; John Lane Co.

Tipper—"The New Business"; Doubleday, Page & Co. 1916.

Taine—"The Ancient Regime"; Henry Holt & Co. 1891.

Toynbee—"The Industrial Revolution of the 18th Century". 1915.

Terry—*La Crisis*, 1885-1892, *Sistema Bancario*. 1893.

Tooke, Thos.—"Thoughts and Details of the High and Low Prices of the Thirty Years from 1793 to 1822", London. 1824.

Thurston—"Economics and Industrial History"; Scott, Foresman & Co. 1900.

Turner—"Bulletin of the University of Wisconsin—Economics. Political Science, and History", Series B, Vol. 1; University of Wisconsin. 1897.

Taylor—"Persistent Public Problems"; Vail-Ballou Co. 1916.

Taussig—"The Tariff History of the United States"; G. P. Putnam's Sons. 1914.

Upton—"Money in Politics". 1884.

Von Bergmaun—*"Die Wirtschaftskrisen"*. 1895.

Wright—"Industrial Depressions".

Winsor Justin—"Narrative and Critical History of America".

Watkins—"King Cotton"; Jas. L. Watkins & Sons. 1908.

Willis—"Federal Reserve"; Doubleday, Page & Co. 1850.

Wildman—"Money Inflation in the United States"; G. P. Putnam's Sons. 1905.

White—"The Barometers of Business"; Bert L. White Co. 1918.

White, Horace—"Money and Banking"; Ginn & Co. 1914.

Willis, Henry, Parker—"A History of the Latin Monetary Union". 1901.

Walley—"The Financial Revulsion of 1857" (Address). 1858.

Wright—"Industrial Evolution of the United States"; Flood & Vincent.

Yeats—"Growth and Vicissitudes of Commerce in all Ages"; Geo. Phillip & Son. 1887.

Among publications containing information used in this work are: Commercial and Financial Chronicle, New York; New York Post; New York Times; Washington Herald; Philadelphia Public Ledger; London Economist, Bankers Magazine, London; Wall Street Journal; Nile's Register (Publication files 1811-1849); Report of Boston Board of Trade Committee 1858 to make Investigation of Financial and Mercantile Embarrassments; Commercial Year Book; Seybert's Statistical Annals; Pitkin's Statistical View; Speeches in Congress from Annals of Congress and Reports of Committees, (Select Committee on Depressions in Labor and Business, 1879;) Reports of the Secretary of the Treasury of the United States, 1789-1849; Charts Illustrating the Statistics of Trade, Employment, and Conditions of Labor, St. Louis Exhibition, 1904 (Published by Bureau of Statistics, Dept. of Commerce); American Economic Review (Published by American Economic Association) 1911.

The publications of the mercantile agencies, Dun and Bradstreet, furnish authoritative statistics on commercial and bank failures. Consular reports issued by the State Department furnish information regarding industrial conditions in foreign countries. Bulletins and reports of the Department of Labor contain concise information on unemployment. The records of the Treasury Department contain valuable documents on coinage, currency, production of precious metals, and tariff statistics. The Bureau of Statistics under the Department of Commerce issues the Statistical Abstract which contains a valuable collection of material on the important industries, such as cotton, iron and steel and general manufacturers. The Department of Agriculture issues reliable statistical information on crop production and consumption. The Library of Congress at Washington where most of the material was gathered contains countless files of newspapers, periodicals, reports, pamphlets, etc., and is a mine of information on the subject.